From Béla Kun to János Kádár

Miklós Molnár

From Béla Kun to János Kádár

Seventy Years of Hungarian Communism

Translated by
Arnold J. Pomerans

WITHDRAWN
UTSA LIBRARIES

BERG

New York / Oxford / Munich

Distributed exclusively in the US and Canada by
St Martin's Press, New York

English edition
first published in 1990 by
Berg Publishers Limited
Editorial offices:
165 Taber Avenue, Providence, RI 02906, USA
150 Cowley Road, Oxford OX4 1JJ, UK
Westermühlstraße 26, 8000 München 5, FRG

English edition © Berg Publishers Ltd 1990

Originally published as *De Béla Kun à János Kádár:
Soixante-dix ans de communisme hongrois.*
Translated from the French by permission of the publishers.
© Presses de la Fondation nationale des sciences politiques, Paris/
Institut universitaire de hautes études internationales, Geneva 1987

British Library Cataloguing in Publication Data
Molnar, Miklos
From Bela Kun to Janos Kadar : seventy years of Hungarian communism.
1. Hungary.   Political parties. Magyar Kommunista Part
I. Title   II. De Bela Kun a Janos Kadar English
324.2439′075

ISBN 0–85496–599–8

Library of Congress Cataloging-in-Publication Data
Molnár, Miklós, 1918–
    [De Béla Kun à János Kádár. English]
    From Béla Kun to János Kádár : seventy years of Hungarian
communism / Miklós Molnár : translated by Arnold J. Pomerans.
        p.   cm.
    Translation of: De Béla Kun à János Kádár.
    Includes bibliographical references.
    ISBN 0–85496–599–8
    1. Communism—Hungary—History.   I. Title.
HX260.5.A6M6513   1990
324.2439′075—oc20   89–28943
                                                              CIP

Printed in Great Britain by
Billing & Sons Ltd, Worcester

Contents

Contents

Foreword

The history of the Hungarian Communist Party (HCP), from Béla Kun to János Kádár, covers a span of over seventy years. Born out of the revolutionary turmoil following the First World War, its first act became Communist legend in 1919 when the party, in league with the Social Democrats, proclaimed the one and only Soviet republic outside the USSR that was to have any staying power. One of its most recent achievements, under János Kádár's leadership, was equally the stuff of legend: the creation of the 'Hungarian model', which aroused so much envy and admiration, criticism and scepticism. Between these landmarks, the HCP knew few successes and many reverses.

Its ranks were devastated, its cadres persecuted – virtually destroyed – during a quarter-century of clandestine activity under the Horthy régime. Then, as soon as Hungary was liberated from German occupation, the Communist Party championed an alliance in the spirit of the defunct Popular Front, now resurrected as the National Independence Front. There followed many years of unrelenting Stalinism, during which the Hungarian Communists excelled in anti-Titoist and persecutory enthusiasm under the leadership of Mátyás Rákosi. Trials, persecutions and a deranged economic policy punctuated this period, which nevertheless culminated in a brief reformist phase under Imre Nagy and eventually in the revolution of 1956. The result was a deeply split party that veered between Nagy's innovative tendencies and the entrenched authoritarian reflexes of his opponents. The reformist experiments of János Kádár were born in the wake of the events of 1956, and those experiments continued into the 1980s.

The HCP, by turn revolutionary, sectarian, torn apart by a revolution, then once again innovative and reforming, has experienced a stormy, indeed a unique, history. Yet despite its undeniably original approach, it has also been a party like the other Communist parties: a party obsessed with the utopian objective of a dictatorship of the proletariat considered as the midwife of a no less utopian society; a generous party, too, and one open to change; a party equally capable of producing martyrs and torturers, as well as great intellectuals such as György (Georg) Lukács, visionaries such as Imre Nagy, pragmatists such as János Kádár. It has been a party like all the others, yet also a party unlike all the others.

Within the confines of this relatively short study, I shall attempt to highlight its double nature and also, as far as possible, the phases of a development exceptionally rich in varied, even contradictory, experiences.

This development, covering three generations, took place in external circumstances so multifarious that it would be rash to try to proffer a comprehensive view of all the propositions and hypotheses that have been advanced in analyses of its various periods. Times have changed and the party has changed with them. Despite the precarious position of any Communist leader, the influence of the most prominent Hungarian Communists remains an undeniable fact. A Béla Kun, a Rákosi, an Imre Nagy, a János Kádár have all left their marks on the history of the party no less than have external circumstances, if perhaps less deeply so than the – equally changeable – masters in the Kremlin and the Communist International. For, when all is said and done, it was always the latter who dictated to the party what line to follow, what decisions to take, what arguments to advance. The HCP, despite its pinch of originality, was until the late 1980s closely tied to Moscow: an integral part of the international communist system.

The three decades of the Kádár era did nothing to modify this conclusion. However, the party's more recent experience did differ in some degree from that of the Soviet model, and the difference was not purely economic. The present-day Hungarian Communist has a sense of pursuing a particular path and building a specifically Hungarian society. In other words, the portrait of the present-day Hungarian Communist is not identical with a portrait from 1930 or 1940, tinged as that would be with a sectarian spirit, utopian ideas and intolerance. We still lack a long enough perspective to flesh out the new portrait, or to take definitive stock of recent experiences. Attempts at an assessment have nevertheless been made in the final chapters.

A small but important part of the material in this book is based on the author's own experiences and also on many encounters with Hungarian compatriots and old comrades; with Communists who continue to work inside the party and with others who, like the author, have left it. Most of its data, however, come from archive, eyewitness and other sources: newspapers, journals, reviews and books. I owe a great deal to the work of Hungarian historians who, often under difficult circumstances, have during the past decades published extremely valuable contributions to the history of the party and who have so generously helped me in my work. My especial thanks go to Tibor Hajdu, Miklós Lackó, György Litván and to Ágnes Ságvári. I would also thank the Institute for Party History which, albeit grudgingly, granted me access to its library and to part of its collection. My thanks are also due to Annie Kriegel and to François Fejtö, Péter Gosztonyi and Pierre Kende for their kind advice and to Anna Kecskés for the contribution she has made in preparing the bibliography.

Preface to the English Edition: The End of the Story

Since I finished writing the French original of this book in 1986, János Kádár has died twice. On 22 May 1988, at the end of a stormy party conference, he lost his post of general secretary of the Communist Party and his place in the Politburo, but was allowed to save his face by being made honorary president. Less than a year later, in May 1989, he died a total political death. The old man was stripped of all his titles and offices, and on 16 June he was shown sitting before his television set meekly watching the national obsequies and reinterment of Imre Nagy, the man he had sent to his death thirty-one years earlier. Kádár lived on for another few weeks. However, well before his second, physical, death, the long chapter of 'Kadarism' had made way for another chapter of Hungarian history, one full of hope mixed with uncertainty but holding out the promise of freedom and democracy. The collapse of Kadarism thus marked, not only the failure of the 'Hungarian model' based on the reforms ushered in twenty years before, but also the bankruptcy of forty years of Communist rule.

In the middle of the 1980s, there was nothing to suggest the precipitate collapse of the Communist régime led by the 'grand old man' from the socialist camp. With the exception of Zhivkov in Bulgaria, Kádár was the oldest European Communist leader and also the most popular in his own country and the most respected in the West. True, Hungary's economic decline had already reached crisis point, but the repercussions were not yet obvious to the average person. Hungary, infinitely better provisioned than the USSR, Poland or even Czechoslovakia, still showed a prosperous face, beguiling most visitors, observers and journalists. Foreign relations, especially those with the World Bank, the International Monetary Fund, Austria and a number of other Western countries, had also taken a favourable turn. As for the political landscape, it remained, if not under a blue sky, at least without thunder-clouds. János Kádár's authority went unchallenged and the party continued its policy of tolerance of critical and even of oppositional trends, the more so as, being confined to a few *samizdat* groups, the opposition failed to attract the masses or the party rank and file.

No wonder, therefore, that the Thirteenth Party Congress held in 1985 confirmed Kádár's middle-of-the-road line: the reforms were not dropped, but they were not to be speeded up or given a more radical form. Stability, carried to the point of inflexibility, came to characterize the 'Hungarian model', until then admired and considered the acme of socialist achievement. In reality, however, things had been going from bad to worse ever since the beginning of the decade, not to mention the earlier setbacks caused by the vacillating attitude of the leadership to the reforms – reforms that were never properly implemented or even stifled under a smoke-screen of empty reformist rhetoric. I shall be returning to this point; here I wish merely to recall that this sleight of hand no longer worked. The government was forced to admit its failure to a nation increasingly dissatisfied with the deteriorating standard of living. Economists, Communists included, were quick to read the signs, and R. Nyers, the father of the 1968 reforms, put his finger on the problem when he said that the party had split in two: the party of reform and that of the anti-reformers.

It would seem that it was in 1987 that the first signs of the hidden crisis were brought into the open. In June of that year, under the pressure of public opinion, the party decided on a major reshuffle. At the highest level, twenty leading officials were dismissed and many more were shunted sideways. The promotions included those of Judit Csehák and János Berecz to the Politburo, of three young party officials, including Miklós Németh, to the Secretariat, and of seven others to the Central Committee. There were also changes in the Council of State and, most important of all, in the cabinet. Károly Grosz was made prime minister. As leader of the government and later of the party he was to play a crucial but difficult role during the next two years.

At the time it was not clear in which direction the changes were meant to lead, nor is it in retrospect. It seems likely, however, that János Kádár, who was their chief architect, was mainly concerned with consolidating his own, flagging, position by pleasing every-body: the reformists by superannuating or dismissing such incompetents as Pál Losonczi, the former head of state, and György Lázár, the former prime minister (who was subsequently fobbed off by being appointed assistant general secretary of the party); the conservatives by the appointments of Károly Grosz and of János Berecz; women by the promotion of Judit Csehák; the waverers by the elevation of relatively unknown party officials without a clear political profile. Yet basically there were no real changes at all. The new team continued as before with a policy of compromise between would-be reformism and the moderate conservatism characteristic of declining Kadarism. But the art of compromise and the piecemeal concessions that had helped Kádár in easier times could not save him from the looming threat of empty state coffers. The collapse of the régime had become inevitable for economic and political reasons no less than in the wake of developments abroad.

Thus, in 1987, *glasnost* spread very rapidly and the Soviet old guard was replaced with a younger team. True, on the purely economic level, Hungary was – and continues to be – better off than the Soviet Union, and the same was true in terms of political and civil liberties. Criticism of the official ideology, of the institutional system and also of abuses and mistakes of all sorts had been tolerated much more under the Kádár régime than in Gorbachev's Soviet Union. But *glasnost* nevertheless took Hungary by surprise, both by its suddenness and also by its momentum. This was the period, in 1987 and 1988, when such journals as *Ogoniok* and such newspapers as the *Moscow News* kept publishing staggering revelations of Stalin's crimes, of the gulags, the trials, and the disarray and corruption during the rule of Gorbachev's predecessors.

This avalanche of disclosures in the Soviet media, reported by the Hungarian press, and also the publication of several books on *glasnost*, made the Hungarian people feel that they were being left behind by the Soviet Union.[1] That impression was partly false, because Kádár's Hungary had already finished the job of exposing the crimes of the Stalin period, in Hungary's case those committed by Rákosi. For two decades, Hungarian political commentators and novelists as well as a number of film-makers had been making revelations of a kind that now took the Soviet public by surprise and were found to be all the more shocking for that. Thus Hungarians were not nearly as shattered by the latest Soviet revelations of Stalin's crimes as Soviet citizens were by the discovery of the (partial) truth about Trotsky, Bukharin, the trials, the gulags – a whole history of lies and fabrications.

In addition to the time-lag between the introduction of a relative measure of freedom of information in Hungary and the advent of *glasnost* in the Soviet Union, there was yet another gap. Mikhail Gorbachev did not have to worry about revealing the truth about his predecessors. Kádár, by contrast, was in some ways his own predecessor: he bore responsibility for the crimes and errors committed over three decades and even partial responsibility for the Rákosi regime whose minister of the interior he had been before becoming its victim. The Rajk trial, for instance, had never been fully exposed as the sham it had been, precisely because of the role Kádár had played in it. *A fortiori*, it was impossible to tell the truth about the persecution and trial of Imre Nagy under the reign of the future architect of the 'Hungarian model'.

This model itself dated back to 1968, which explains why it preceded *perestroika* but also why it looked so outdated. János Kádár never tired of stressing, without of course mentioning Gorbachev by name, that no one could teach Hungary any lessons when it came to reforms. And basically he was perfectly right, though it may not have looked like that on the surface. Thus, while *perestroika* produced no measurable effects in the economic sphere, it nevertheless appeared to be a dynamic and bold advance, something the Hungarian model did not seem to be. It was this fact which made the reputable Hungarian weekly *Heti Világgazdaság* (World Economic Weekly) write on 15 July 1989 in its János Kádár obituary that his legendary pragmatism and his common sense deserted him after 1985 when 'he failed to recognize in time the significance of the changes personified by Gorbachev or the new elbow-room' they gave him.

Today there is a tendency to exaggerate the economic mistakes of the Kádár régime to the point of forgetting the undeniable advances Kádár ushered in. By encouraging this line of attack, the current leaders are doing no more than Gorbachev did with Brezhnev: they blame every possible error on him. It remains a fact, however, that Kádár, like so many aged actors and politicians, had grown sclerotic – politically and probably physiologically as well. Rumour has it that he even lost his mind. In any case, Kádár did not look on Gorbachev or his reformist policies with a kindly eye. Far from it: people say that there was bad feeling between them. More importantly, in addition to not wanting to 'learn the new lesson', Kádár had reason to fear the contagion of *perestroika* in his own country, and the resulting destabilization. In fact, it was not so much Gorbachev's achievements as his image which destroyed the picture, so patiently constructed, of Kádár the reforming, paternalistic and pragmatic administrator.

As I put it on p. 226, 'sooner or later the party had to come up against new demands that had not so far been expressed except by a few intellectual groups. So can the leopard really change its spots?' New demands, because 'the Hungarian experience has produced too few convincing results. It has left too many fundamental demands unsatisfied to earn the unstinting support of public opinion. Only a much more radical reform programme can help to turn it –

even in the absence of political freedom, pluralism and independence – into something more than a slightly improved form of Soviet socialism. Any such radical programme is slow in coming precisely because of the system's structural sluggishness, not to mention the external restraints imposed by Moscow and by geopolitical circumstances' (p. 205).

Since the collapse of Kadarism, social and political expectations have grown apace. Hungarian public opinion is no longer satisfied with reforms that fall short of political freedom, pluralism and independence. I shall be returning to this point at the end of this preface, but even here I must point out that my prediction about the curbs Moscow was likely to impose has been proved wrong. Of course, no one can tell *how far* Moscow will go in tolerating changes in Hungary that have already put an end to the political monopoly of the Communist Party. But, having entered that caveat, I hasten to add that by all accounts the Soviet leaders did nothing to keep János Kádár in the saddle in 1988, nor did they prevent his final removal in 1989. More than that, Moscow seems to have given tacit or explicit approval to the rise to power of the most outspoken reformists, led by Imre Pozsgay, promoted to the Politburo on 22 May 1988 and considered as the head of the radical wing of the party and even, covertly, of an opposition party.[2] An even more encouraging sign is that the Soviet leadership, or at least a powerful section of it, has at long last permitted the rehabilitation of Imre Nagy and of the other victims of the post-1956 repression, together with the *de facto* introduction of political pluralism in 1989 and its enshrinement through new laws and the coming elections. This is much more than a simple change of politicians following the dismissal of a sclerotic and headstrong leader. Since Kádár's fall, the entire political landscape has been radically transformed. In October 1989 the rights of political parties and the electoral law were ratified, and on 23 October the Hungarian People's Republic became the Hungarian Republic.

But to return to the collapse of Kadarism, it cannot be stressed enough that the chief agent of the transformation was Hungarian public opinion. Without it, nothing of the kind would ever have happened. The East Germans, the Rumanians and the Czechs were equally familiar with the Gorbachev phenomenon, but took their time. What prepared the ground for the great transformation of Hungary was highly specific and not completely bound up with Gorbachev.

It all began with the accelerating economic crisis. All indicators of the health of the economy went into the red: GNP, inflation, the national debt, the balance of trade, the budget. Moreover, real salaries fell by close on 8 per cent in eight years (5 per cent of this in a single year). For a while, overtime (Hungarians are famous for working extra hours and for doing a thousand jobs on the side), made up for the losses, but in 1987 the net per capita income fell as well, and more so for the poor than it did for the better-off. Thus while state expenditure grew from year to year (increasing the budget deficit as well as the foreign debt), private individuals had less and less to spend. In 1988, consumption took a brutal dive (almost 5 per cent less than the year before) and this applied to provisions (meat, milk, sugar) as well as other products – something not seen in Hungary for thirty years.[3]

The increase in the budget deficit, in fact, was outstripped by the increase in the foreign debt. In Chapter 10 I mention that the foreign debt amounted to approximately 7,000 million dollars in 1986. By 1989 that debt had risen to more than 18,000 million. If, as seems likely, the last figure will have to be revised upwards, the foreign debt will have doubled within the space of three years. It is here that János Kádár's greatest mistake probably lay. Profiting from the country's sound financial reputation, he and his various governments accumulated an intolerable burden of debt. Today, Hungary has one of the largest per capita debts in the whole world, while its exports keep shrinking from year to year. The foreign loans, in fact, did little for the modernization of the country or of the productive machine. Despite warnings by the experts,[4] including many communist economists, most enterprises in the state sector remained in deficit and did little or nothing to modernize their equipment or their management. 'We are sliding inexorably towards Third World standards', the papers were saying with monotonous regularity.[5] The mountains of dollars wasted, incidentally, drove up private and public spending. The main reason why the standard of living could be maintained in the early 1980s, and why its fall could be slowed down until 1987, was that foreign loans were being used to prop up wages and salaries and to keep down prices. This situation proved untenable in the winter of 1987–8 under the joint pressure of foreign debtors, the alarm signals sent up by experts of all political hues and popular discontent. Needless to say, the nation at large was made to foot the bill; as in all heavily indebted countries, the state started to squeeze the taxpayers. There were sharp price rises and, on 1 January 1988, for the first time in any socialist country, the mass of wage earners was made to pay taxes on all additional incomes including annual bonuses and other special benefits. Needless to say, this new measure, which was probably fair, proved highly unpopular and often counter-productive: it led to the paralysis of a number of flourishing concerns, now over-taxed precisely because of their greater efficiency. Many craftsmen (31,000 in all) returned their licences.

The psychological effects of the new taxes were perhaps even more devastating than the economic consequences. They drove home the fact that the Hungarian nation at large was being made to foot the heavy bill for the government's waste and mistakes, and that the state was doing little if anything to overhaul the economy or the administration. The free market was confined to a very small sector, the infinitely vaster state sector remained in deficit, the unproductive staff of the hypertrophied administration continued to weigh heavily on the state coffers – against this background, the new tax was simply the last straw. The public had had enough. At the same time the whole idea of reform had lost its appeal. If *that* is what reform means, we would just as soon do without, I heard people say during my many visits to Hungary in recent years.

In this climate of general economic dissatisfaction, political opposition grew apace. The process began with a re-examination of the party leaders' responsibility. While Kádár was still in office, he and his closest collaborators were made to take the whole blame. In 1987, this man, so popular only a little while back, began to be openly criticized in the papers, over the radio and even – an unprecedented event – at party meetings, many of them televised. For the first time in the history of Communism, the downfall of a leader was not played out in the wings, but before millions of shattered television spectators. And, immediately after his removal in 1988, his successors, Károly Grosz and János Berecz in particular, became the focus of critical attention. In a very short time, both lost all of their authority and credibility. They were attacked for being inconsistent and for failing to come up with a credible plan to get the country out of its mess. To be credible, such a plan could no longer be confined to curing the *symptoms*, but had to tackle the *root* of the evil, in other words the system. Now, in 1988 and early in 1989 that system had already shed much ballast by renouncing the Communists' exclusive control of the youth training programme and other sensitive areas and, a more fundamental issue, of the government. At its session on 10 January 1989, Parliament began to debate a draft law – which was adopted – on free associations. These could henceforth be set up and run almost as freely as in the Western democracies. The right of free association, according to Kálmán Kulcsár, the minister of justice, who moved the plan in

Parliament, also applied to political parties.[6]

True, a special law on the rights of political parties, an electoral law and a new draft constitution had still to be ratified by Parliament, but the right of free association was a decisive step towards pluralism and democracy. When that law was passed, many newly formed associations had already made their appearance in public, amongst them such revived political organizations as the old Social Democratic Party and the newly formed Democratic Forum. Pluralism had become a fact. But public opinion now wanted this process carried to its logical conclusion: the complete dismantling of the Communist system. And they had their way: in the spring of 1989 that system ceased to dictate daily government business.

As I write these lines the outcome has been finally settled. The party, following the Polish example, has agreed to open round-table discussions. General elections were announced for the spring of 1990. The course of pluralist democracy has become unstoppable. Finally, the autumn congress of the Socialist Workers' Party of Hungary (MSzMP) resulted in the dissolution of the party as it was and the founding of the Hungarian Socialist Party (MSzP). To preserve unity within the framework of the newly founded MSzMP proved an illusion. Within a short time hardliners have reorganized the MSzMP. It has a political identity, will have nostalgic voters, but cannot have a real political future. The MSzP, on the other hand, has no political identity, but has a political future, although not more significantly than any of the other six to eight most important parties. It gave up some of its strength by dissolving the workers' militia, abolishing party cells at workplaces, forgoing most of the party assets. It cannot employ force or ask for Soviet intervention; it must obey the rules of the game. (It could, of course, cheat like cardplayers do.)

Before looking at some of the more specific topics exercising Hungarian public opinion, I shall first try to define what I mean by that term. There has, of course, always been such a thing as public opinion, buried deep down in the minds of the 'silent majority'. The Communist system was disliked, if not actually detested, by the majority of the population. But under the joint effect of fear and the lulling of minds with Kádár's so-called 'liberalization', most Hungarians preferred not to voice their opinion in public. Nine out of ten Western reporters apparently learned the truth about Hungary from taxi drivers taking them to their hotels or to the banks of the Danube or perhaps from some editor of a *samizdat* journal, usually one of the same dozen or so. But *nobody* really knew what a million peasants, or two million workers or another two million members of the active population, let alone retired people, were thinking. True, several scores of thousands of Communists left the ranks of the party in 1988–9. The collapse of the Young Communists was another established fact; an umbrella organization, the Council of Hungarian Youth Organizations, founded on 27 November 1988 (at a meeting in the Parliament buildings) had taken its place. It comprised twenty-seven affiliated societies, and thirty-three others sent regular observers. One of its founder members was the Association of Democratic Youth (FIDESz), the great rival of the Young Communists. I could quote many further instances of the spread of the opposition to increasingly broad strata of the population. The opinion polls also reflect the new political climate. Even so, the first public demonstration of popular abhorrence of the Communist régime was the funeral of Imre Nagy and of other victims of the repression. I shall be returning to this point.

Before then, the expression of so-called public opinion was confined, throughout all the crucial years of the disintegration of the Communist system, to the intelligentsia, that is, to publicists and other writers. Things are not all that different in other parts of the world and especially not in Communist countries from Moscow to Peking – Poland being the honourable exception. Hungary lacks an organization comparable to Solidarnost and its offshoots in factories and villages. It is because of this difference (which is not necessarily a handicap on Hungary's pluralist road) that Hungarian public opinion, as we have seen, is mainly expressed through the media. According to a tradition going back to 1956 and also having earlier historical roots, writers and journalists have for a long time been playing a leading role in sharpening the conflict between society and the state.[7]

In addition, three large-scale campaigns did much to whip up the anger of the average person: the protests against the plan to build two hydroelectric power stations on the Danube (the so-called Bos/Gabcikovo–Nagymaros plan); the plight of the Hungarian minority in Rumania and the influx of refugees from that country; and finally the revelations of what really happened in 1956.

This writer is not qualified to pronounce on all of the ecological, economic and technical aspects of the hydroelectric plan. It was first mooted in 1979. In addition to Hungary, it involves Czechoslovakia as the main partner and Austria as the financial backer (following opposition by the Austrian ecological movement and by large sections of the Austrian people to the plan to build a dam upriver, on Austrian soil).

Hungarian public opinion, first sporadically and then on a massive scale, was alerted to the problems involved after the collapse of the original Austrian project and its 'displacement' on to Hungarian soil. According to its critics, including many scientists, the construction would cause considerable ecological damage without providing any real benefits (Austria would have to be repaid with electricity supplies well into the next century).

Let me give a few concrete examples of this rise in public opposition. In February 1988, fifty people demonstrated against the plan following an appeal by an ecological group, the Danube Circle. On 28 May, 2,000 people went on a protest march past the Austrian embassy in Budapest. In July, the Academy of Science, which had been dubious about the project for a long time, came out against it. In September, two international congresses met at Budapest and voiced their opposition to the dams. On 30 September, there were fresh public demonstrations. On 4 October a human chain linked hands on the banks of the Danube and a mass demonstration was held in Debrecen. On 31 October, several thousand people held a torch procession on the embankment and on the bridges across the Danube. On 5 November, there followed a protest march by more than 10,000 people; there were 6,000 signatures to an appeal to stop the work. In December, 70,000 people signed a petition against the decision by Parliament to continue the project. As a result of all these protests and demonstrations, the plan was cut in half in 1989: the building of the first dam near the Austrian border would be continued, but the second dam near the town of Nagymaros would be scrapped.

The state also backed down on another 'front', that of the Hungarian minority in Rumania, and not for the first time either. Even earlier it had stood up to the Ceausescu régime on their behalf (if only to appease public opinion at home), but in 1988 it was faced with a more explosive situation. The Rumanian plan, condemned throughout the world, to destroy thousands of villages led to an accelerated exodus of Magyars (and incidentally also of Rumanians) from Transylvania. In the winter of 1988–9, some 30,000 refugees crossed the border illegally and asked for political asylum in Hungary. Reluctant at first, the Hungarian government ended up by providing them with shelter, food, work and identity papers.

The greatest triumph of public opinion, however, came in another area: the re-evaluation of the events of 1956. For more than thirty years the official view had always been that Imre Nagy was a counter-revolutionary traitor who deserved to be 'strung up'. That story had cemented the 'legitimacy' of the Kádár régime. Official speeches had trumpeted it forth and scholarly texts had proclaimed it. The dismissal of János Kádár in May 1988 had changed nothing in that. His successors, headed by the new general secretary of the party, Károly Grosz, kept up the legend: 'It was right to put Imre Nagy on trial', he told *Newsweek* in July 1988, and a few days later, still on an official visit to the United States, he repeated that claim: 'The Hungarian government does not intend to rehabilitate Imre Nagy.' At the very most, Károly Grosz added, Nagy's family would be allowed to reinter his ashes, which had been buried in 1958 in a common grave together with the bodies of the other victims and of animals from the Budapest Zoological Gardens. János Berecz, then the régime's second in command and one of the most unbending leaders, spoke the same kind of language. And when Imre Pozsgay, the leader of the reformists inside the party, declared that what had happened in 1956 was a 'popular insurrection' (not a counter-revolution), Károly Grosz, attending an international economic conference at Davos, was quick to contradict him.

The party leadership was therefore divided on this subject and, incidentally, on many others as well. Thus, while the general secretary of the party paraded his firm opposition to all forms of *political rehabilitation*, that is to all attempts to rewrite this important page of history, acts of *clemency* helped to blur the hard line, for instance the pardon of the victims of the repression on 1 October 1988. But a pardon is no rehabilitation, let alone a political and legal vindication. And it was a frank and complete rehabilitation that public opinion demanded in the name of historical truth. Now, in June 1988, a committee had been set up under the chairmanship of Miklós Vásárhelyi, Imre Nagy's press chief and companion, to ensure the establishment of historical truth in the name of justice. However, anyone out in the street demanding the same thing, for instance on 16 June 1988 during the thirtieth anniversary of the trial, was still beaten up by the police; the alleged 'ringleaders', such as the publisher Gábor Demszky and the former leader of the 1956 workers' council, Sándor Rácz, were taken to the police station. This familiar scenario had been enacted for years, both on 15 March, the anniversary of the national revolution of 1848, and on the anniversary of the revolution of 1956.

There was deadlock until the spring of 1989. Meanwhile the TIB – the Hungarian Committee for Historical Justice founded in June 1988 – continued to propagate its ideas in the press which, for its part, became freer and freer. There were discreet negotiations with various party and government representatives about the exhumation and reburial of the victims' remains. For a long time the authorities refused to budge. The decisive change came in the spring of 1989, a little before the final disappearance of János Kádár from the political scene. Between March and June the party renounced its political monopoly, thus opening the way for democratic pluralism and also for a reappraisal of the revolution of 1956 and the trial of Imre Nagy.

On 16 June 1989, thirty-one years after he was put to death, Imre Nagy and his comrades in misfortune were buried a second time, and not more or less in private by the families concerned, as the party had envisaged, but in public, before an entire nation in mourning. This extraordinary event is still fresh in every Hungarian's memory. Life came to a stop for a whole day. The national television network transmitted the ceremony from morning to night, until the last funeral wreaths had been placed on the graves of the five victims of the trial and of close on 400 others executed with them, and until the last funeral orations were over. According to reliable estimates, 250,000 people paid their last respects to their heroes by marching in procession to Heroes' Square, the usual venue of mass demonstrations.

The mountain of wreaths and flowers included a wreath laid by members of Parliament headed by the President of the Assembly, Mátyás Szürös; another, from the cabinet, was carried by Miklós Németh, the young prime minister, and by Imre Pozsgay, the minister of state. None of them, however, represented the Communist Party, which was absent from the ceremony, not by choice but at the express request of the TIB, which had organized the funerals.

On 16 June 1989, it was not merely the victims of Communism who were being buried, but also the entire Communist epoch. As the funerals started, round-table discussions were opened between the government and the opposition, and these talks were to culminate in the creation of a democratic state. During that summer of 1989 everything had not yet been settled. There were to be further conferences, discussions, parliamentary debates and elections. The Communist Party, though shaken, was still in power and in control of its many offshoots, and it still had its staunch adherents. Its hold and influence were probably stronger than those of the Polish Communist Party which suffered a humiliating defeat at the elections. A similar defeat is not ruled out in Hungary; on the other hand the party may receive enough votes at the elections to form a coalition government with one or several of the political organizations that sprang up in the wake of the political storms of 1989. Finally, it is quite on the cards that the present form of the Communist Party, the MSzMP, may split into two or three separate Communist parties. The leader of the reformist wing, Imre

Pozsgay, no doubt entertained that idea, and may well have been dissuaded by the Soviet Union. At the other extreme, the champions of the old post-Stalinist régime have not yet laid down their arms, metaphorically or actually. Their influence inside the armed forces, including the party's special militia, remains strong. They have, moreover, banded together in several associations, one of which bears the name of Ferenc Münnich, and any of which may well be thinking of turning itself into a political party. In any case, the Communist Party will never again be able to govern on its own. A page of history has definitely been turned over, though a military *putsch*, with or without Soviet participation, remains a theoretical possibility.

Faced with this rapid succession of events, the observer is bound to feel confused. Future historians will no doubt be able to clarify the course of events, if not tomorrow then the day after, but at present the visible manifestations of this political earthquake do not provide a sufficient explanation of it.

Despite widespread disaffection, popular pressure in Hungary – or, for that matter, in Poland – has never been strong enough to compel the party to make such a drastic climb-down. As for the revolt of the intellectuals, though it fed on itself and, strengthened by its successes, spread further afield month by month, it failed to spill over to workers, peasants or even to the vast middle stratum of office workers and the self-employed. The 'white revolution' of Hungary took place in great calm, without major incidents and without any obvious risk of explosion.

The régime simply disintegrated, by implosion rather than by explosion. Outdated ideological foundations, lack of combativeness and inability to renew its action programme – all these signs of decrepitude could have been detected over a long period. They also bear out Raymond Aron's perspicacious comment: 'A monopolistic party régime probably runs the risk of death once it is touched or corrupted by the democratic spirit of compromise'.[8]

Now, the Hungarian party, more than any other – with the sole exception of the Polish United Workers' Party during the 'Solidarnost summer' – ensured its survival and relative success in the heyday of the 'Hungarian model' by fairly substantial extensions of economic and political freedom. It allowed itself, to use Raymond Aron's words, to be 'touched and corrupted' by the spirit of compromise to the point of losing its cohesion. It had reached the extreme limit of 'liberalization', a limit that left it with two alternatives: a brutal leap backwards (but how far?) or a bold advance that threatened its identity.

Some Communist parties realize that history faces them with this pitiless choice. Thus the Italian Communist Party has chosen the second alternative, while trying to recover its breath and to overhaul its apparatus. The French Communist Party, by contrast, has opted for the first alternative, preserving its identity against all odds, but at the risk of falling by the wayside. Consciously or otherwise, Mikhail Gorbachev is trying to take the middle road (but, again, how far?).

We may take it that he advised the leaders of the Hungarian Communist Party to follow his example. But the Hungarians, having reached the end of the road, had no choice in the matter anyway. Some Hungarian intellectuals engaged in the political struggle still believe that it is possible to reverse the present course with the help of a restructured party, a 'party of order'. To others, including the present writer, the point of no return has been reached: the disintegration of the Communist Party is irreversible. If it is indeed, then we have to ask ourselves what precise role Moscow played in the developments in Hungary during the late 1980s, and particularly during the last few months of the crisis that culminated, in May, June and October 1989, in the beginnings of a pluralist system and the reburial of the remains of Imre Nagy. Decisions of such magnitude could not have been taken without the consent, tacit or otherwise, of the Soviet leaders. As I write these lines, I do not know what was said and by whom to whom during these supposed consultations. Sooner or later, it will all come out and we shall know much more about one of the most astounding events at the end of our century. One thing, however, is quite certain even now. Either by direct intervention or precisely by its non-intervention in a process that could only have been reversed by outside intervention, the Soviet Union surrendered part of the promised land of Communism.

But is there a promised land left anywhere in Europe? In the mythical and millennial sense there never was. The author of these lines had not even finished the Preface when the story reached its final stage far beyond the other East European cases. Not only the idea and the system, but also the empire, reached its last days. Forty-five years after the day when the Soviet shock-brigades raised the red banner on the Reichstag, the 'order of Yalta' is approaching its end. It has lasted a long time. But the account of the new order is beyond the scope of these pages.

Miklós Molnár

List of Abbreviations

AVO/AVH   State Protection Authority (political police)
CP   Communist Party
FIDESz   Association of Democratic Youth
GPU   State Political Administration (secret police of USSR)
HCP   Hungarian Communist Party
MDP   Hungarian Workers' Party (Communist Party united with Social Democratic Party)
MSzMP   Socialist Workers' Party of Hungary (= HCP)
NEKOSz   National League of People's Colleges
SzDP   Social Democratic Party
SzETA   Hungarian Foundation for Aid to the Poor
TIB   Hungarian Committee for Historical Justice

–1–

From Monarchy to Revolution

Born under the impetus of the Bolshevik revolution, like all of the other European Communist parties, the Hungarian Communist Party, founded in 1918, was not predestined for the role it was to play. Neither its emergence, in March 1919, as the guiding force of the first Hungarian Soviet Republic, nor the widespread repercussions of this sudden entry on to the political scene, could have been predicted from its antecedents, or from the modest position it occupied in Hungary at the end of 1918. A political conjunction, extraordinary from all points of view, must serve as our preliminary explanation.

In October 1918, a month before the party saw the light of day, the Austro-Hungarian monarchy was in its death-throes. The military defeat on the Italian front and the armistice signed at the Villa Giusti on 3 November merely put the finishing touches to the disintegration of an empire of 52,799,000 inhabitants, extending from Galicia to Austria and, in the south, as far as the Adriatic. Its territory, covering 676,615 square kilometres, was to be shared out among the 'successor states': Poland, Czechoslovakia, the Kingdom of the Serbs, Croats and Slovenes, Rumania (officially now Romania), the new Austrian Republic and Hungary. A big loser, the last-named ceded to its neighbours, by the Treaty of Trianon, two-thirds of its territory and a little above two-thirds of its population.

Count Károlyi's Republic

The military defeat, side by side with an economic upheaval, led to a grave political crisis. Three opposition parties – the Independence Party led by Count Michael Károlyi, the Bourgeois-Radical National Party, and the Social Democratic Party – decided on 25

October 1918 to set up a Hungarian National Council.[1] Three days later, the endemic troubles, which had been continuing for more than a month, assumed revolutionary proportions. There was a mass demonstration in Budapest on 28 October; the revolution broke out on the night of 30 October. The Soldiers' Council, formed the previous day, placed the general who was commanding the city under arrest – no unit would, in any case, have taken orders from him. The army was in disarray; its remaining forces placed themselves at the service of the National Council, and delivered the capital to it in one day.

Count Károlyi then formed a coalition government under the aegis of the National Council. On 13 November, King Charles of Habsburg signed his abdication; on 16 November, before a crowd estimated at 200,000 persons, Count Károlyi proclaimed the advent of the First Hungarian Republic.

The many radical measures taken during the five months of the various Károlyi governments (many times reshuffled, particularly following Károlyi's election as President of the Republic) tended to modernize and democratize the country, inadequately according to some, and too much so for the taste of others.

Right-wing historians have never ceased to accuse Károlyi and his ministers of defeatism, treason, complicity with Communism or, at the very least, unforgivable weakness in dealing with the Left. As for Communist historians, while they see some merit in the politics of the Republic, they condemn Károlyi for his lack of firmness when dealing with the Entente, for his lack of resolution on the social plane and for his anti-Communism in dealing with what they describe as a revolutionary mass movement.

Just five months of democratic rule is not, however, enough to determine whether the system introduced by the Károlyi government reflected the structures and aspirations of society. These aspirations, as we shall see, remained basically unchanged under the Károlyi régime, under the dictatorship of the proletariat and under Horthy, thus giving rise to a variety of interpretations. Though the debate between left-wing and right-wing historians may fail to answer the basic question, it nevertheless places the Károlyi government squarely where it probably belongs: in the centre. With its reformist vigour, its concern for the workers, its incipient land reforms, its vacillations and weaknesses, this democratic government did attempt to accommodate all of the tendencies and forces that had been brought into play; despite its uncertainties, it stood a very good chance of laying the foundations of a Western liberal system.

More than by its merits and demerits, however, its fate was determined by external circumstances. In 1918–19, Hungary, uprooted and in the throes of radical change, lacked the ability to satisfy the nation's social needs: it was at the mercy of historical developments imposed by military and political circumstances.

Let us return to the latter. The armistice of Padua, agreed on 3 November 1918 between General Diaz and the Austro-Hungarian general staff, was to be extended on the Balkan front by an armistice with the Serbian Army and with the Eastern Army of the Entente. From its inception, the Károlyi government was keen to enter into negotiations with General Franchet d'Esperey who, for his part, repaired to Belgrade to receive, on 7 November, the Hungarian delegation led by Count Károlyi himself. A persistent legend has it that this general was responsible for the harsh armistice conditions imposed on Hungary. In fact, Franchet d'Esperey, while adopting a brusque attitude towards the Hungarians, proved to be relatively sympathetic, going so far as to allow the Hungarian government to appeal directly to Clemenceau, with the request that Hungary's historic frontiers (with the exception of Croatia-Slavonia) be guaranteed until the Peace Conference. The provisional line of demarcation that was suggested proved acceptable to Budapest in the light of the troop movements and exaggerated territorial claims of Hungary's neighbours. That is why, on 13 November, the then representative of the Budapest government signed this second armistice (officially described as a military agreement) in Belgrade.

Nevertheless, the issue was far from settled. Paris considered the armistice conditions imposed on Hungary to be too mild and went so far as to disown General Franchet d'Esperey. Pichon, the French Foreign Minister, even reprimanded him drily for having exceeded his authority by signing an agreement with representatives of an 'alleged Hungarian state that has not been recognized by the Allies and has no international existence'.[2] Even more significant than this rebuke was the continuous and growing pressure Paris exerted on Budapest, through Franchet and General de Lobit, to make fresh concessions. In particular, during the months following the Belgrade armistice, the demarcation lines were pushed forward in favour of Hungary's Czechoslovak and Rumanian neighbours, and in Ruthenia in favour of the Western Ukrainian Republic.

Károlyi – who had meanwhile been elected President of the Republic – was unable to justify these setbacks indefinitely to a public that was psychologically unprepared for them and was just beginning to appreciate the disastrous effects of the defeat. Being liberal and favourably disposed towards the Entente, his government would have preferred occupation – even of Budapest itself – by French forces. Now, on 20 March 1919, Lieutenant-Colonel Fernand Vix, head of the Entente military mission, handed President Károlyi a note from General de Lobit demanding a further withdrawal of the Hungarian Army prior to the Peace Conference.[3] Hungary was to evacuate a further zone to a depth of approximately 100 km, almost as far as the Tisza River, the eastern part of that zone to be occupied by the Rumanian Army, and the western part to be proclaimed a neutral zone under a Hungarian civil administration subject to Allied military control. This demand was virtually an ultimatum.[4]

President Károlyi and the government, then led by Dénes Berinkey, felt they could not comply. The government resigned and the President of the Republic announced his intention of appointing a Social Democratic government. In fact, it turned out to be a Socialist–Communist government, that is to say a government set up by a quickly unified party. It opened a chapter in the history of Hungary that was fraught with dire consequences and offered the Communist Party – which split off again from the Social Democrats several months later – a unique historical opportunity.

Given the prevailing confusion and the contradictory documents describing the events, it is impossible to tell precisely what occurred in the presidential palace. From the memoirs of Count Károlyi to those of his widow and numerous other witnesses, as well as from documents, there runs a shaky line that stretches from the allegation that Károlyi held out his hand to the Communists to the claim that he did nothing of the kind.[5] It seems certain that the proclamation issued in his name and declaring that he had 'passed power into the hands of the proletariat' was a near-fabrication. The proclamation was drafted by the Radical Pál Kéri, and when Károlyi refused to sign it, it was printed without his knowledge in the official gazette. That is how Károlyi finally learned that he had 'resigned' when in fact, in his capacity of President of the Republic, he was preparing to appoint a new Socialist government. It is impossible to tell whether Károlyi intended to install a 'purely Social Democratic' government or a Socialist–Communist government, as Károlyi himself does not seem to have been too familiar with the relations then prevailing between the Communists and the Social Democrats.[6]

The Social Democrats, moreover, gave out that they were preparing to form their own government, when in fact they had gone cap in hand to the Communists to work out the terms of an agreement. For the rest, they themselves were divided. The representatives of the moderate wing, including Ernö Garami, the party secretary, categorically rejected any association with the Communists. Others envisaged various forms of political association; yet others advocated the complete fusion of the two parties. The last solution was to prevail, in circumstances that were as dramatic as they were astonishing.

The leading Communists at the time were in prison accused of having instigated an attack by a crowd of malcontents on the offices of the Social Democratic Party newspaper. It was in prison that the fusion of the two parties was accordingly negotiated. At the same time, a Hungarian Soviet Republic was proclaimed with immediate effect, a republic that was to be based on the dictatorship of the proletariat and to be run along Leninist lines.

Hungarian Society after the First World War

No Communist party has ever fulfilled the prediction made in the *Communist Manifesto* that a communist society would arise from the ashes of capitalism. The Hungarian Communist Party was no exception. It took power in 1919, not on the ashes of capitalism or of bourgeois society, but following the military collapse of Austria-Hungary and the consequent disarray of Hungarian society. Austria-Hungary, though not one of the most highly developed European countries, experienced a period of remarkable growth and prosperity at the end of the nineteenth and the beginning of the twentieth centuries, and the Hungarian party benefited greatly from these developments.[7]

Under the Dual Monarchy, Hungary's national revenue quadrupled: the mean annual growth rate of 3.7 per cent was greater than that of Great Britain (2.6 per cent), Germany (2.6 per cent) and Russia (2.5 per cent).[8] With an annual growth rate of 6 per cent, Hungarian industry experienced an even faster expansion. In short, Hungary was a rapidly developing country, albeit still 'semi-feudal' and hence far from having attained the general Western, and particularly the German or Austrian, level. In fact, the figures, reflecting rapid growth in the industrial, commercial and financial sectors and in the spread of the liberal professions and in cultural activities, do not reflect the true state of affairs in other sectors which had barely been touched by modernization, or in Hungary's political structures, social relations and collective expectations. More so than even its relative backwardness, it was the ultraconservatism of an archaic Hungary that earned it the title of semi-feudal country.

At the end of the First World War, Hungary suffered considerable losses; these dealt the 'grandeur' and the 'national spirit' a severe blow. The fact was that this grandeur and this spirit had, for better or worse, helped to shape Hungary's national identity. Not counting Croatia, the 'lands of the Holy Crown of Hungary' had covered, in round figures, more than 282,000 square kilometres within the confines of the Carpathians, with 19 million inhabitants. After the Treaty of Trianon, just one-third of that territory (about 93,000 square kilometres) and barely 8 million inhabitants remained. With the exception of the German minority and a few small ethnic groups, no non-Magyar nationalities were left in the country. By contrast, 3 million Hungarians now found themselves in territories annexed by the neighbouring states.

With 'Great Hungary' there also disappeared the idea of the Hungarian state as a collection of 'lands of the Holy Crown', and an entire doctrine – legal, political and ideological – whose function it was to legitimize the thousand-year Magyar domination of the countries and people of Hungary. All that remained was St Stephen's Crown, the golden symbol of the ancient glory and a throbbing nostalgia for the past. The psychological shock was all the greater in that Hungary, one of the oldest states of Central Europe, had, ever since the compromise of 1867, enjoyed a privileged position within the Dual Monarchy.

At the time of the revolution of 1918, the masses clamoured for independence, but this clamour, no doubt natural after four centuries under a foreign dynasty, could not make up for the advantages of the dual system or for the material losses suffered in 1918. Hungary had been reduced to the dimensions of a small country, had lost nearly all of its mineral resources, with the exception of coal, its hydroelectric potential, its timber, its access to the sea at Fiume (Rijeka) and, last but by no means least, its economic balance within the Carpathian bounds of the Hungarian kingdom and the vaster unity of the Austro-Hungarian Empire.

The Hungarian economy was henceforward compelled to develop within tighter confines. These confines nevertheless comprised the most highly developed sector of the old economy, particularly in respect of human and industrial resources, equipment, the urban infrastructure, roads, and so on. Within the new frontiers, approximately 30 per cent of Hungary's population was involved in the industrial, mining, commerce and transport sectors, as against 24 per cent in the old Hungary;[9] the new illiteracy rate was 19.7 per cent as against 33 per cent for the old.

And yet, at the end of the war, Hungary was described, perhaps somewhat crudely, as a 'country of 3 million rural beggars'. Now, this figure included about 2 million (a quarter of the total population) agricultural workers or persons dividing their time between wage labour and the exploitation of plots measuring an average of 1 *hold* (0.57 hectare), and the class of about 1 million poor peasants, owners of plots of from 1 to 5 *holds* (0.57 to 2.58 hectares). All of these categories combined owned approximately 10 per cent of the cultivated land.

At the other end of the scale, some 12,000 landowners held about half of the agricultural land. Their estates ranged from about 60 to about 600 hectares, and a few dozen of them (including the Crown, the Catholic Church and several magnates) even owned fabulous estates ranging from 8,000 to 80,000 hectares and more. In other words, a thousand landowners holding more than 600 hectares each, and representing 0.1 per cent of all landowners, controlled more than 2.7 million hectares (30 per cent) of arable land, forest and pasture.[10] This thousand and a few institutions constituted the so-called class of '1,000-*hold* proprietors'.

Hungary was thus a 'country of 3 million beggars' on the one hand and of a thousand magnates on the other; in between there was a rural middle class incapable of investing in or of improving its land, and a somewhat more prosperous stratum numerically too weak to constitute a separate rural class. The starkness of this polarization is best brought home by the fact that about 55 per cent of the country's total population still belonged to the primary, that is the agricultural, sector.

In 1920, 2 million persons, or a quarter of the population, were engaged in the industrial and transport sectors and some 400,000, 5 per cent of the population, in the commercial and financial sectors. The heading of 'various occupations' covered 1,128,200 persons, or 14.2 per cent of the population in 1920, including civil servants, clergymen and members of the liberal professions.

This distribution of the population into various sectors is not, however, reflected in the Hungarians' mentality or in Hungary's socio-political structures. In fact, despite a large middle class, Hungary had preserved its archaic character on the political, cultural and intellectual planes. What we have here is a form of 'uneven development': the growth of the modern sectors did not entail modernization of the 'deep country'. The countryside, the traditional centre of political decision-making and all the values that go into social behaviour, was bypassed by modernization. The explanation of this phenomenon, and also of Hungary's 'semi-feudal' character, involves factors too complex to be examined here. Its roots go back to the sixteenth century when, in the view of many specialists and of Marxists in particular, a 'second serfdom' helped to block the development of the country.[11] Among the political and administrative factors, the stability of the system of provincial self-government (that of the *comitats*) helped to maintain the supremacy of the nobility at the expense of the bourgeois element. It is true to say that debt, impoverishment, indeed the economic bankruptcy of the gentry, which made up 5 per cent of the population, were offset by the growing strength of the bourgeoisie – Budapest in particular becoming in the nineteenth century the modern metropolis of an industrial, commercial and cultural middle class. But that bourgeoisie was not very sure of itself, thanks largely to its foreign – German and Jewish – origins. The Jewish element expanded rapidly in the nineteenth and at the beginning of the twentieth centuries: from about 2 per cent to double that figure and reaching 5 per cent of the population (1 million in absolute figures) at the time of the First World War.

While this urban middle class, including the Jews, was able to enter certain fields without difficulty, other spheres, for instance the civil service, remained closed to it. The civil service continued to be, at all levels, the privileged domain of the gentry. Ruined and uprooted, the Hungarian gentry streamed into the civil service and into the army. Here it merged with other social groups to form what became known as the 'seigniorial and Christian' middle class, on which Hungary so prided itself until the Second World War.

The curious consequence of all these developments was a kind of cultural split: the adoption of influences from the liberal West went hand in hand with rigid adherence to conservative ideals. Budapest, in 1900, was partly comparable to Vienna, though much more profoundly marked by archaic conservatism than the Austrian capital. This conservatism was a form of mimicry – the new social classes imitated the life style of the gentry – and remained a marked trait of Hungarian society until recent times.

The picture drawn here so briefly will have made it clear that all of the Hungarian political parties vaunting Western ideologies, be they liberal, radical or socialist, and the Communists and bolshevist Marxists among them, were faced above all with a lack of solid social foundations on which to build. The historians of the HCP have none the less set Magyar Communism in a continuum that goes back to the beginnings of the workers' and socialist movements on the one hand and to radical theories on the other hand.[12]

Many Social Democrats and many radicals did, in fact, join the HCP in 1918, as their counterparts in other countries joined Communist parties all over Europe. The old Social Democratic Party in particular had been made up of several factions, including that of the followers of the anarcho-syndicalist Ervin Szabó, and several of these played an important role in the creation of the Communist Party. It is also certain that the young Communist Party attracted into its ranks a numerically important fraction of rank-and-file members of the SDP. The HCP was thus the offshoot of various antecedents and initiatives, all of which were part and parcel of the common 'prehistory' of the workers' movement, without, however, constituting a continuous process culminating in the birth of the HCP. It needs to be emphasized that, unlike what happened in Germany and later in France, Italy and elsewhere, the Hungarian Social Democrats at no time split up formally, allowing the Communist Party to build on their division. In the event, the organizing nucleus of the HCP came from quite a different quarter, namely from Russia.

However, before we even open that chapter, we must stress that the social plane on which the Communist Party took its stand in 1918 was to remain unaltered for the next two decades.

Hungary's collective outlook and institutions barely changed to cope with the changes unleashed by the defeat of 1918. Similarly, its social structures underwent few changes despite the new economic realities so harshly imposed by the loss of two-thirds of the country's former territory. During the quarter-century following the war, Hungary was admittedly to witness important economic and, to a lesser extent, social adjustments as well as a modest growth rate,[13] but, all in all, these developments were insufficient for a radical transformation of the structures present in 1918.

The Communist Party thus needed to surmount a double difficulty in the twenty-five years following its failure in 1919. A party with practically no roots, driven underground by the Horthy régime, it was also destined to battle in a fundamentally unfavourable social environment.

−2−

The Emergence of the Communist Party

The Beginnings[1]

Three steps led to the emergence of the HCP.[2] They were taken in turn by Socialist Revolutionaries, left-wing Socialists and Hungarian prisoners of war in Russia supporting the revolution and the Bolshevik Party. In October 1918, the first two planned the formation of a Communist circle (the Karl Marx or Ervin Szabó Circle) or of a Socialist Revolutionary Party distinct from the Social Democratic Party (SDP), to which end a meeting was called at a printing works in 12 József Square on 15 November.[3] However, as far as we can tell from various sources, the party was not set up on that occasion. The most likely date is 24 November; the venue was a private apartment in Városmajor Street, in a residential district of Buda, on the right bank of the Danube.

It was here, at all events, that Béla Kun and his associates, having returned from Moscow on 19 November, met their left-wing Socialist comrades and joined with them to found the Communist Party. It is no less possible, however, that this step may already have been taken by János Hirossik, a Socialist worker whose name appears on certain publications as 'founder of the party'.[4]

In either case, the Communists who had returned from Moscow played a crucial role in the effective establishment of the HCP, not least thanks to the prestige of the Russian Bolshevik Party, of its leader Lenin and of his principles of revolutionary organization, which the group from Russia had adopted.

The origins of this group, led by Béla Kun, went back to 1917. In several prisoner-of-war camps in the USSR, especially in Siberia, large numbers of Hungarian soldiers had gone over to the revolution. While still in Omsk, Ligeti had launched the Hungarian journal *Forradalom* (Revolution). At about the same time, several other Communist groups had sprung up, especially in Tomsk, Krasnoyarsk, Tver and Petrograd. In addition, a central organization in Moscow united Hungarian Communist prisoners of war in a group called the Hungarian Group of the Communist (Bolshevik) Party of Russia. Founded on 24 March 1918, this group published a journal, the *Szociális Forradalom* (Social Revolution), and also a number of propaganda pamphlets written notably by Béla Kun, Tibor Szamuely and Károly Vántus. In May it became part of the International Federation of Foreign Groups of the Communist (Bolshevik) Party of Russia under the presidency of Kun and with headquarters in the Hotel Dresden in Moscow. At the end of 1918, the group counted some 90 members in Moscow and from 150 to 170 members in various other Russian towns and Red Army units.[5]

It should be noted that the Federation, which comprised Hungarian, Rumanian, Yugoslav, Czechoslovak and German groups and which was joined soon afterwards by Finnish, French, Bulgarian and Anglo-American units, was directed by the Central Committee of the Bolshevik Party, through its Hungarian, Rumanian and other sections which were set up in 1918. The International Federation of Foreign Groups had the task of enrolling foreign members into the Communist Party and of 'uniting them in the Third International'.[6] It was, *inter alia*, responsible for propaganda and organization among prisoners of war and the brigades fighting the Czech Legion.[7] Finally, it controlled the German and Austro-Hungarian Prisoner-of-War Councils which were created in 1918 after the collapse of the German Reich and the Dual Monarchy. In other words, the Hungarian group was part of a large network with the following objectives:

1 the organization of fighting units for the Russian Revolution;
2 propaganda for, and organization of, revolutionary uprisings in Germany and former Austria-Hungary;
3 the organization of embryonic Communist parties to be incorporated into the nascent Third International.

All of this was to happen under the leadership of the Central Committee of the Bolshevik Party, in which Béla Kun enjoyed great prestige and played an exceptionally important role.

The Hungarian branch of the Russian Communist Party set up a school of 'agitators', twenty of whom apparently repaired to Hungary in October 1918, followed by more than eighty in November. Meanwhile several meetings were held to pave the way for the foundation of the HCP. On 25 October, Kun outlined the principles underlying the creation of a Hungarian Communist party of the Bolshevik type. Finally, on 4 November, the Austro-Hungarian Communist group of the Bolshevik Party, again meeting in the Dresden Hotel, Moscow, decided on the foundation of the Hungarian Communist Party, the Hungarian section of the Communist International. The meeting, specially convened for that purpose, declared its readiness to work under the leadership of the Central Committee of the Bolshevik Party, the Third International not yet being in existence. The new party urged its members to return to Hungary with the least possible delay. A provisional central committee made up of Károly Vántus, Béla Kun, Ernö Pór, Hariton Beszkarid, Emil Bozdogh, Mátyás Kovács, Mátyás Krisják, Iván Matuzovits and Ferenc Drobnik was elected.[8]

Next day, Kun and several others left for Hungary, where they arrived in the middle of November. Other 'agitators' dispatched from Moscow in October were already there.[9] Yet others arrived later, among them Tibor Szamuely, who had been sent on a mission to the Spartacus League in Berlin and remained there until January 1919. In the circumstances, it is difficult to give the precise number of Communists sent back home from Russia.

The relatively small number of Hungarian Communists in Kun's group at the end of 1918 and the beginning of 1919 suggests that the number of 'agitators' and emissaries sent to Hungary did not exceed 250–300 persons, as a rump was left in Russia to deal with the half a million or so former Hungarian prisoners of war, many of whom had joined the Red Army. That rump kept growing from the original 3,400–3,500 (6,600 according to another source) members of the seventy-six groups of Hungarian Communists in Russia who were registered with the Central Bureau. These persons, none of whom participated in the activities of the party during the life of the Hungarian Soviet Republic, were either sent on clandestine missions to Hungary during the second half of 1920 or in 1921, or else settled in Russia for good.

The original Moscow group included Béla Kun, Ferenc Jancsik, Ernö Pór and József Rabinovics. Ernö Seidler and Károly Vántus became members of the first Central Committee which was elected at constitutive meeting(s) of the HCP,[10] and so, after his return to Hungary, did Tibor Szamuely. The Central Committee thus included three of the nine members of the Provisional Central Committee set up in Moscow on 4 November, namely Kun, Pór and Vántus.

The two other groups to make common cause with the Communists were represented by Béla Vágó, Ede Chlepkó, Rezsö Fiedler, János Hirossik, Jenö László, László Rudas and Béla Szántó (left-wing Social Democrats who had broken with their old party); and Ottó Korvin and József Mikulin (Socialist Revolutionaries).

Other sources mention the presence in the leadership of Ferenc Münnich, Mátyás Rákosi, Sándor Kellner and Gyula Alpári. In addition, some of the left-wing leaders of the Hungarian Soviet Republic and several future Communists, such as Jenö Varga and Jenö Landler, were still members of the Social Democratic Party at the time.

Though the group from Moscow undoubtedly played a pivotal role in the organization of the new party, it needed the support of the other groups in imposing its Communist principles. Among these groups, the Socialist Revolutionaries were of particular importance; they were divided into two factions, one of which constituted the left wing of the Galilei Circle which had, in 1918, brought together members of the intelligentsia and radical students idolizing the poet Endre Ady. Their ranks included a number of future Communists, Ottó Korvin and Imre Sallai among them. A group very close to the Galilei Circle and influenced by Ervin Szabó was also linked to the Socialist Revolutionaries. Ervin Szabó and his followers were inspired by anarcho-syndicalist ideas, and it was from this position that, during the first years of the twentieth century, he attacked the German as well as the Hungarian Social Democrats.

As a political theorist and a sociologist, Szabó set his stamp, by his work and personality, not only on his own group but also on a large section of Hungary's left-wing intelligentsia. An anti-militarist, Szabó engaged in revolutionary anti-war propaganda, particularly from 1917 onwards. After his death, in September 1918, several of his followers turned to Communism, especially József Révai. Within the ranks of the left-wing Social Democrats who had rallied to the HCP at the very outset, János Hirossik seems to have played the most important political role. Close to Gyula Alpári, he became in 1910 one of the leaders of the left-wing opposition within his party, which expelled him in 1912.

While the personal itineraries of these men differ, all of them shared a deep dissatisfaction with the Social Democratic Party, which they considered revisionist, and with the Second International, whose leading subsidiaries had become paralysed through their support for the war. The October Revolution in Russia and the anti-militarist and internationalist revolutionary policies of the Bolsheviks could only widen the gulf between these left-wingers and the established parties.

The fact remains that all these groups constituted no more than a tiny minority of the socialist, not to mention the radical, leaders.[11] Apart from the Communists who returned from Moscow, this minority, if we are to take the word of Vilmos Böhm, the Social Democratic leader, consisted of a mere 'handful of people', all of them personal malcontents 'who had left the party or had been expelled from it'.[12]

No matter what their personal motives, however, account also needs to be taken of the profound political and ideological reasons favouring revolutionary action and also of four crucial and radicalizing factors: the war, the Russian Revolution, the rout of the Austro-Hungarian Army and the collapse of the monarchy. The combination of these factors forced the great and prestigious Social Democratic Party to merge, in March 1919, with a Communist Party that had been in existence for a mere four months.

It is against this background that the emergence of the Communist Party and its rapid rise to power has to be viewed. Here we shall not pass in review the events following the 'Chrysanthemum Revolution'[13] in October 1918 which carried Károlyi to power – for we have already, in the previous chapter, tried to retrace the main course of events prior to 21 March 1919, the date of the fall of the Democratic Republic and the advent of the Soviet Republic under the leadership of the now unified Socialist–Communist Party. All we shall attempt is to examine the relationship of forces between the two working-class parties before their fusion, and also their actions during the 133 days of the Hungarian Soviet Republic.

The Soviet Republic

Thanks to the revolution, to the proclamation of a republic, and to the ensuing crisis which radicalized the working and lower middle classes, the HCP undoubtedly gained ground during the first months of 1919. However, the material published by the Historical Institute of the Central Committee of the HCP does not specify the precise number of supporters in 1919. According to the then Secretariat of the party, there were 10,000 members in January, and from the indictment against the Communist leaders imprisoned by the Károlyi government, we gather that there were 30,000 to 40,000 members in March.

By comparison, the Social Democratic Party, whose membership was based on the trade unions, was a much more powerful force. Between 1913 and the eve of the revolution the number of trade unionists had doubled to more than 200,000. By December 1918, there were already 721,000 members, not including the recently founded farmworkers' unions. These numbers, however, embraced a mass of floating supporters borne in on the flood of the rising revolutionary tide. They included such tardy socialists as a squad of gendarmes and members of the Union of Timber and Coal Merchants.

According to Vilmos Böhm, the solid Social Democratic core never exceeded 50,000 to 60,000 workers. It is therefore no wonder that he attached such great importance to the part played by the much smaller Communist nucleus built around the party and not based on the trade unions.[14]

In critical times, the numbers of supporters are not everything. According to Böhm, the extravagant propaganda put out by the HCP was bound to catch the ears of 'the immense army of unemployed, the tens of thousands of invalids living in atrocious conditions, the hundreds of thousands of demobilized, homeless and demoralized soldiers . . . It was on these masses that Béla Kun based his entire policy. Against organized, class-conscious workers, he lined up unorganized masses to whom class-consciousness meant nothing'.[15]

Admittedly, today no less than at the time, different views have been expressed, though most observers agree that there was determined Communist infiltration of factories, trade unions and social-democratic organizations. But while there is no denying these wrecking tactics, there would have been a general slide of Social Democrats to the left in any case. In addition, the unorganized masses, the demobilized soldiers, the war wounded, the unemployed and even the *lumpenproletariat* undoubtedly provided the Communists with a wide hunting ground. In 1905, Lenin himself had advocated tactics aimed, beyond the urban proletariat, at all other disadvantaged strata of society: 'all without exception: artisans, the destitute, beggars, domestic servants, vagabonds, prostitutes'.[16]

As for the financial resources of the HCP, bourgeois and Social Democratic authors alike stress that funds from Moscow enabled the party to publish newspapers and pamphlets and to allocate money to a variety of organizations and activities. It was only in the 1960s that party historians ceased to make a mystery of the provenance of these funds:

The HCP maintained close links with the Bolshevik Party. There was a courier service between Budapest and Moscow, a dangerous job done by persons familiar with the roads, former prisoners of war from the two countries. They carried messages in both directions and kept Lenin informed about the maturing revolutionary situation in Hungary. Through couriers, the Bolshevik Party provided financial backing for the HCP thus facilitating the publication of newspapers, of propaganda sheets and pamphlets and also the purchase of arms.[17]

Thanks to all these circumstances, the CP was able to seize the leadership of the revolutionary movement – started even before the actual foundation of the HCP.[18] That movement aimed at the establishment of a Soviet Republic and at the dictatorship of the proletariat in a programme deemed premature by the SDP.

Numerous mass demonstrations accompanied this second revolution. Beside the Soldiers' Councils, the Workers' Councils gained greater and greater importance in Budapest and other centres, but also in the countryside where farm labourers and poor peasants called for an end to the feudal system of big estates. The SDP was nevertheless able to obtain the exclusion of Communists from the Budapest Workers' Council and from the trade unions a few days later. Of the great revolutionary mass organizations, only the Soldiers' Council remained linked to the CP, which also managed to retain a local foothold in various trade-union branches.

Held responsible for a shooting affray, the leaders of the CP and some 200 other militants, Béla Kun and several members of the Central Committee of the Communist Party and the Association of Youth Movements amongst them, were arrested in February 1919. A provisional Central Committee was set up to run a campaign for the release of the prisoners. In the end, far from being humiliated, the CP benefited from this affair. In the SDP, the left wing, led by several future Communists such as Landler and Varga, gained the upper hand over the centrist leadership. The prison in which the Communists were locked up became a kind of meeting place where prisoners and visiting Social Democrats could debate the chances of seizing power following the unification of the two parties.

After the resignation of Count Károlyi, the other Social Democratic leaders, with few exceptions, rallied to this Communist plan. On 21 March, an official delegation went to the prison to put the finishing touches to the agreement from which the united Socialist–Communist Party and the Hungarian Soviet Republic were born.

The new body called itself the Socialist Party of Hungary and adopted the provisional programme proposed by the Communists. This included joining the Third International, an alliance with Soviet Russia, the nationalization of the means of production, the seizure of power by the proletariat and the establishment of a Soviet Republic.

At a joint meeting of their leaders, the Hungarian Social Democratic Party and the Hungarian Communist Party have today agreed on the complete union of the two parties.

Until such time as the revolutionary International will have decided on the definitive name of the party, the name of the new united party shall be 'Socialist Party of Hungary'.

The union will be based on the equal participation of the HCP in the leadership of the party and in the government.

The party will immediately seize full power in the name of the proletariat. The dictatorship of the proletariat will be exercised by the Councils of Workers, Peasants and Soldiers. For this reason, the proposed elections to the National Assembly elections will obviously be shelved.

A proletarian army will have to be established without delay to disarm the bourgeoisie.

To ensure the power of the proletariat and also to oppose the imperialism of the Entente, the fullest and closest military and spiritual alliance must be concluded with Soviet Russian government.

Budapest, 21 March 1919

In the name of the Social Democratic Party of Hungary: Jenö Landler, Zsigmond Kunfi, Jakab Weltner, József Pogány, József Haubrich.

In the name of the Hungarian Communist Party: Béla Kun, Ferenc Jancsik, Béla Szántó, Béla Vágó, Károly Vántus, Ede Chlepko, Ernö Seidler, József Rabinovits.[19]

Following the unification, the leadership of the new party seems to have remained in the hands of the Social Democratic Party and its tried and tested political apparatus. The HCP was dissolved and the Communists joined the various organizations of the old SDP. By contrast, the Communists had a very strong hold on the Revolutionary Governing Council.[20] A Directorate of five members was charged with defining, before the next party congress, the policies of the dictatorship of the proletariat. The Revolutionary Governing Council and its subsidiary, the Directorate, thus played an executive role as well as functioning as the Central Party Committee, and so held the real reins of power.[21] Béla Kun's influence in it was decisive. The party congress, meeting on 12–13 June, strengthened the position of the Communists even further. Five of the thirteen members of the Central Committee came from the old CP and one or two others came from the Socialist Left.

Within the united party, power seemed to be divided between

the old Communists and the Social Democratic centrists, with the Socialist Left acting as arbitrator. This situation did not fail to vex Béla Kun and his comrades, just as they were displeased by the presence of moderate elements in government departments. The Communists and Béla Kun himself were, however, able to change the political course steered by the Republic, thanks largely to the support of the left-wing Socialists and probably also to the support of the USSR, and especially of Lenin, who followed daily developments in Hungary with close attention. [22]

Lenin urged Béla Kun and his comrades to copy the Bolshevik example: absolute mistrust of the old Social Democrats and recourse to terror. In effect, the police apparatus of the dictatorship of the proletariat, established and run by the Hungarian Communists independently of the official police force, was to prove an important instrument of power. One heavily armed detachment called itself 'Terror Squad of the Revolutionary Governing Council'; [23] it was also known as the 'Lenin boys'. Dissolved under Social Democratic pressure, this detachment was nevertheless partly incorporated into the services run by Ottó Korvin, head of the political section of the Ministry of the Interior.

The history of the CP thus coincided, during the 133 days of the dictatorship, with that of the united party (which at its June congress adopted the name of Hungarian Socialist–Communist Workers' Party). The extremely complex organization of political power, the frequent changes, the rapid political developments, and finally the war, make it impossible to retrace its history in full in these pages. [24]

A skilful allocation of posts enabled the Communists, as we have remarked earlier, to keep political – and especially executive – power in the hands of the party and its allies. The joint programme based on the agreement of 21 March enabled them moreover to implement revolutionary measures of a more Bolshevik than traditional socialist type.

The measures taken included the nationalization of all enterprises employing more than twenty persons, of all banks and financial institutions, of insurance companies, of apartment buildings and of the wholesale trade. All great fortunes deposited in banks were confiscated and medium-sized deposits were placed under government control, as were retail shops. The decrees adopted under the dictatorship of the proletariat thus affected not only the upper but also the middle classes. Nor were the liberal professions spared: lawyers, doctors and artists were all subjected to government control and often, especially in the case of lawyers, limited in their activities. It goes without saying that Béla Kun and his comrades could not have anticipated Soviet Russia by inventing a New Economic Policy (NEP), and they were given no time to draw lessons from their own experiments. In particular, excessive expropriations slowed down the country's economic life, already disrupted by the consequences of the war, so causing a scarcity of raw materials and food, forcing the introduction of rationing and accelerating inflation. The Hungarian crown, which had been on a par with the Swiss franc before the war, had lost two-thirds of its value – 30 francs to 100 crowns – by the end of 1918, and fell further to 18 francs in April and to 11 francs in August. This collapse was aggravated by the fact that the government, following the example of the Károlyi administration, kept replacing the 'blue' notes of the monarchy with 'white' banknotes, which further increased popular distrust of the currency. The issue of new money from June onwards, which coincided with the withdrawal of the old notes, was unable to restore confidence in or prevent the hoarding of, and speculation in, blue notes.[25]

In a predominantly agricultural country such as Hungary, the political treatment of the peasantry becomes of prime political importance. With a suitable land-reform programme, a dictatorship exercised in the name of the proletariat might well have gained the support of the poor peasants and farm labourers, those '3 million beggars', victims of the system of latifundia inherited from feudal times. However, instead of distributing the estates of the big landowners to the peasants, as the Bolsheviks had done in the USSR, the Hungarian Communists handed them over to agricultural co-operatives. This 'great leap forward' disappointed a very large political 'clientele' and gave rise to a sense of insecurity and hostility among the better-off peasants.

What with penury, insecurity, price rises, the depreciation of money, unemployment and so forth, the generous social provisions could not offset the economic troubles, even though numerous measures were taken in favour of the most disadvantaged wage earners, the poor, children, women and others.

The setbacks suffered by the régime during the four months of its existence did not affect its domestic policy. In fact, despite the dissatisfaction of vast strata of the population, the strength of the united party continued to grow apace: from 800,000 after unification the number of trade-union members, automatically included in the party, went up to 1.5 million in August. As for the balance of power in the leading committees, the Communists were able to maintain a slight preponderance thanks to the support of left-wing

Socialists. In fact, neither at the congress of the new party held on 12 and 13 June nor at the National Congress of Councils (Soviets), did centrist Social Democrats manage to carry the day.[26] The new Revolutionary Governing Council, the real holder of power, elected at the end of the Congress of Councils by the new Executive Committee, consisted of nine Communists and left-wing Socialists as against six centrists. The resignation from the government of Zsigmond Kunfi, the head of the centre group, left the field to Béla Kun, his main partner and adversary.

The Congress of Councils acting as the Constituent Assembly promulgated a new constitution. It, too, bore the stamp of the left-wing majority: in particular, it endorsed the principle of the dictatorship of the proletariat. The State took the name under which it was to be known for the five weeks it had left, namely *Magyarországi Szocialista Szövetséges Tanácsköztársaság* – Federal Socialist Republic of the Councils (Soviets) of Hungary ('Federal' because Burgenland and Sub-Carpathian Ruthenia were still part of Hungary; it is also quite possible that by using that term the Constituent Assembly may have wished to emphasize the self-governing aspect of Soviet power). The Republic, we read in Section 2, 'is the republic of workers', peasants' and soldiers' councils'.[27] In reality, the Constitution vested real power in the centre, leaving little authority to the local soviets, elected – like the delegates to the congress – by universal suffrage but on single lists.

Because the short-lived Hungarian Soviet Republic was the only one of its kind in Central Europe with a relatively durable dictatorship of the proletariat, its brief history has been the subject of a host of analyses. Despite their original enthusiasm, the Russian leaders, Lenin at their head, were quick to round on Béla Kun's team for the errors they committed during the 133 days of the Republic. The critics blamed Kun above all for having agreed to a union between the Communist and Social Democratic Parties, and ignored Kun's valid protest that, without the Socialists, the tiny Communist Party would never have been able to seize power and that its leaders would not have been let out of prison.[28]

In a proclamation to the Hungarian proletariat, Lenin even went so far as to exhort them to make short shrift of the Social Democrats and the vacillating and irresolute petty bourgeoisie.[29] Little by little Kun was forced, in his defence, to admit as an error what he had regarded as a dire necessity. In an article published in Moscow in 1924, he blamed the defeat of the dictatorship of the proletariat on four factors: (1) the impossibility of a strategic retreat in a territory as small as Hungary; (2) unfavourable international circumstances; (3) the absence of an effective Communist Party; (4) the unsuccessful land reforms.

Under point (3), returning to the question of the two parties, Kun admitted that it had proved impossible 'to correct the error of the unification' because 'the Communist Party had dissolved into the Social Democratic Party and the latter had melted into the workers' councils and the various institutions of these councils'. 'During the dictatorship there was no organized workers' party of any kind.' In the opinion of many Communists, he added, that was not even necessary. 'The councils – that's all.'[30]

According to the American historian Bennett Kovrig, Georg Lukács was among those who questioned the necessity of keeping the party alive once the proletariat had seized power.[31] Kun did not share this opinion. He nevertheless said in one of his speeches that, though the party was unquestionably the ideological guide, it was 'a grave error to believe that, as an institution, the party was above the workers' councils. No, it is not above them. The workers' councils represent the working class as a whole'.[32]

The problem of power was keenly debated throughout the 133 days of the proletarian dictatorship. Who ran that dictatorship? The Hungarian Communist Party as such was not, unlike the Russian Bolsheviks, strong enough to do so. This explains Lenin's qualms: qualms Béla Kun's reassuring telegrams were unable to dispel completely. As for the Socialist–Communist Party, unified since the proclamation of the Hungarian Soviet Republic, it too was unable to direct the dictatorship. The Social Democrats, who made up the large majority of the unified party, admittedly endorsed the *idea* of the dictatorship, but not the *practice* of dictatorial power. That was why, in the view of several leading members of the party, Béla Kun amongst them, it would have been best to 'separate the trade unions from party organizations', so that the party might become the unhampered arm of 'the vanguard, of the élite of the proletariat'.[33]

In fact, to all intents and purposes, the party delegated power to the Revolutionary Governing Council and the five-member Directorate.[34] As a result, it was the Revolutionary Governing Council rather than the party which emerged as the centre of revolutionary power in the 'Hungarian model' of the dictatorship of the proletariat, and *a fortiori* the Directorate – a kind of revolutionary junta wielding exceptionally wide control.

Perhaps we should round out this picture by recalling the role of the councils, and particularly of the Budapest Council of Workers and Soldiers, also known as the 'Council of the Five Hundred'.

This council, elected on 11 April 1919, appointed a municipal directorate of five members (Dezsö Bokányi, Jenö Barna, István Biermann, Ignác Bogár and Péter Ágoston). Beside its municipal functions, the Budapest Council – thanks to its privileged position, as the representative of the proletariat of the capital – played a particularly important political role. On many occasions, the Revolutionary Governing Council sought its advice on, or endorsement of, political, economic and military decisions.

As for the councils in the provincial towns and districts, we know very little about the way they were run. In many cases, they undoubtedly enjoyed great authority and autonomy, not least because of the weakness or vacillation of the central government, which saw itself more as an executive organ of proletarian power than as the source and incarnation of that power.

In his address to the National Assembly of Councils on 22 June, Zoltán Rónai, the People's Commissar, made the point perfectly clear:

> The provisional situation has filled many comrades with false ideas about the dictatorship of the proletariat. So far – this much is certain – we have been living in a transitional phase of the proletarian revolution. What we have had has not been the complete dictatorship of the proletariat [shouts of Hear! Hear!]. The dictatorship of the Revolutionary Governing Council is not the dictatorship of the proletariat [shouts of Hear! Hear! Bravo!].

And the People's Commissar went on to argue that the election, by the Assembly, of a Federal Central Executive Committee (of 150 members) would open the path for a true dictatorship of the proletariat exercised by the elected councils.[35]

Zoltán Rónai belonged to the moderate Socialist wing of the government. Others, such as Béla Kun and his comrades lately arrived from Moscow, had already witnessed the whittling away of the power of the Russian soviets in favour of the dictatorship of the party. It nevertheless remains a fact that the constitutional plan adopted by the Assembly stipulated the creation of a classless society in which 'the principal means of class domination, namely the power of the state, will be eradicated'.

The life of the Hungarian Soviet Republic was too short to allow us to judge the matter. We do know, however, that the Communists lacked the means – and some of them the intention – of turning the party or the central government into the sole custodians of proletarian power. Moreover, most of them were unfamiliar with the situation in the USSR or with the speeches and writings of the Bolshevik leaders. The only widely read work of Lenin, as the Hungarian historian Tibor Hajdu has pointed out, was *State and Revolution*, a short text that some considered an 'anarchist' tract because its author insisted that the 'withering away of the state' was the culmination of the revolutionary process.

All of these factors explain Béla Kun's hesitations over the errors with which he was reproached in Moscow after the collapse of the Hungarian Soviet Republic. More than a confession of his own errors, his self-criticisms appeared to be an admission of the congenital weakness of the Communist Party he himself had founded on the eve of 1919. To complete the list, Kun need merely have added another confession, made by his comrade Jenö Varga who, analysing the causes of the collapse, invoked its deepest cause: the absence of a revolution. The HCP did not seize power by force of arms: power was handed to it on a platter. It was a chain of special circumstances, not a proletarian revolution, that led to the creation of the Soviet Republic.

It was also a chain of circumstances rather than political errors by the Communists that led to the fall of this republic. Kun was not mistaken in blaming the military circumstances and the international atmosphere for the failure of his enterprise. He compared, albeit discreetly, the unfavourable climate in Hungary in 1919 to the favourable climate in Russia in 1917, which had been 'mentioned several times by Comrade Lenin as one of the factors in the success of the Russian Revolution'.[36]

This self-defence by Béla Kun calls for a brief return to the events of March–April 1919. During the 133 days of the Hungarian Soviet Republic, from 21 March to 1 August 1919, the international situation, though unstable and chaotic, was fairly favourable in some respects, and fairly unfavourable in others, to the Socialist–Communist government in Budapest. Until the signing of the Versailles Treaty, the Allies were often divided on what to do about Central and Eastern Europe and even about Russia. In late March, the American diplomat William C. Bullitt returned from his mission to Lenin with proposals for an agreement. Although that agreement had few chances of being implemented and was decisively turned down in the end,[37] it nevertheless had a favourable effect on the cause of the Magyar Soviet Republic.

Lloyd George, who had just declared his opposition to the suppression *manu militari* of the Hungarian revolution (the Foch plan) – a revolution he described as necessary in that backward country – suggested, after hearing what Bullitt had to say on 28 March, that General Smuts be sent to Budapest as a special emissary: what was needed was a *modus vivendi* with the Hungarian Soviet Republic, so that Hungary might possibly serve as an intermediary between Russia and the Entente. At about the same time, Wilson and Lansing received a report from Professor Brown, then in Budapest, which also favoured negotiations with the Hungarian Soviet Republic.

During the first week of April, Smuts spent two days in Budapest (he refused to leave his special train), trying to negotiate an agreement with Béla Kun on the basis of far more clement Allied proposals than those contained in the ultimatum of 20 March which had caused the resignation of Count Károlyi. A delegation from Budapest was to be invited to attend the Paris Peace Conference. The Revolutionary Governing Council, after long debates and deliberations, decided to turn down Smuts's proposals and, instead, called for a conference to be attended by the Allies and the various member states of the old monarchy. All these plans came to nothing, and historians continue to argue about the rights and wrongs of the Revolutionary Governing Council's rejection of the Smuts plan. In any case, the rejection of this unique chance was bound up with Béla Kun's and his comrades' perception of the international situation and of the revolutionary perspectives it entailed.

There was Austria, first of all. At the end of March, Kun still believed that an Austrian revolution, if not imminent, was at all events inevitable. According to the unpublished minutes of the Revolutionary Governing Council, Kun declared at a meeting held on 27 March that 'Renner realizes that the path of dictatorship is inevitable . . . Now, if there is a revolution in Austria, there will also be a revolution in Bohemia. And then we shall carry the revolution to the frontiers of France.' Following the failure of the uprising in Vienna, such developments were no longer on the cards, but on 4 and 5 April, during Smuts's visit, the hope had not as yet been extinguished. In particular, it was anticipated that the Hungarian government's military weakness was to be repaired with the connivance of the Austrian Social Democratic government. At the same session, on 27 March, Assistant People's Commissar Pogány declared that only Austria could supply the arms and that 'Julius Deutsch, Minister of War, very honestly [*sic*] allows gun-running to the Hungarian proletarian power'. A few days later, at the seventh session of the cabinet, on 2 April, he again declared that 'gun-running from Austria' was continuing and that 190,000 guns had already come in.[38]

Relations with Austria remained very important throughout the

133 days of the life of Soviet Hungary. In mid-June, emissaries from the Communist International, dispatched in fact from Hungary, organized an attempted insurrection in Vienna, to which we shall be returning.

On the day Smuts left Budapest, the Bavarian Soviet Republic had not yet been proclaimed. According to Leo Valiani, Kun made contact with comrades in Munich during the ensuing weeks and had high hopes of the creation of a revolutionary belt comprising Hungary, Austria and Bavaria.

Needless to say, there were also plans for union with Soviet Russia. The establishment of the Communist International in Moscow coincided almost to the day with the seizure of proletarian power in Budapest. But even more than the symbolic support of the Communist International, it was Soviet military power that was expected to come to the rescue of Soviet Hungary. Here, too, the Budapest government had a brief moment of hope, or at all events, of illusion. The Red Army took Kiev in February and continued to advance towards Bukovina and Galicia, as far as Kamenets-Podolsk, close to the old frontier of the monarchy, approximately 150 km from the Hungarian frontier in the Carpathians. In April, only Galicia and Bukovina still separated the sister Soviet republics of Russia and Hungary. Soviets from Moscow to Munich – there was a dream to conjure with for a week or two.

On 28 April, Lenin enjoined Rakovsky, President of the Soviet government in the Ukraine, to concentrate on the Bukovina front: a few days later he gave the same instructions to Vatsetis, commander-in-chief of the Red Army; the plan was to join forces with Soviet Hungary. All Lenin's hopes, however, were disappointed by the Kolchak offensive and also by the reversal of the military and political situation in the Ukraine where battles raged on several fronts over several thousand kilometres.

In March–April, when hopes of a Red Army breakthrough were still running high, Béla Kun opened ambitious diplomatic negotiations to establish a federation of three Soviet republics: Hungary, the Ukraine and Russia. To that end he drafted a federal plan which he telegraphed to Moscow.[39] However, the Soviet Ukraine and Hungary were separated by the western Ukraine and eastern Galicia, controlled by Petlyura's Ukrainian Directorate. It was in these circumstances that a curious deal was struck between Béla Kun and Vladimir Vinnichenko, the Ukrainian Social Democrat who was a member, and for a short time head, of the Ukrainian Directorate. Vinnichenko repaired to Hungary on 31 March 1919 with an offer to Kun: he would let the Red Army pass through the territory occupied by the Ukrainian Directorate in exchange for Moscow's recognition of the independence of the Ukrainian Republic under a coalition government composed of various local Socialist parties.[40]

The unpublished minutes of the Budapest Revolutionary Council confirm that such an offer was made. At its meeting on 27 March, Béla Kun informed the council that 'the head of the Ukrainian Legation, Kalagan, has asked us to act as mediators between the Ukraine and the Russian Soviet Republic so that the three republics might form a contiguous territory. Tomorrow, I shall be making radio contact, not only with Lenin, but also with Golubovich. Vinnichenko is expected here tomorrow and we shall be conducting the negotiations with him.'[41] The text of Kun's radio-telegram to Lenin is not included in *Budapest–Moszkva*, the published version of the relevant exchanges. It does, however, include a telegram dated 31 March by Chicherin acknowledging receipt of 'your communication concerning the Ukrainian poet [i.e. Vinnichenko]' and adding that he was unable to deal with that question in such haste.[42] According to the minutes of the Revolutionary Council meeting of 7 April, Kun made a further reference to the Ukrainian situation, but no details are given and we cannot tell whether or not Chicherin had replied by then. Nor is there any mention of a possible negative reply from Rakovsky, President of the Soviet Government in the Ukraine. Kun, for his part, seems to have persisted until the end of April. At a meeting of the council held on 26 April, he announced that Linder (a former officer who had rallied to the cause of the Soviet Republic) 'has just returned from western Galicia. They [the Galicians] are ready to attack the Rumanians from the rear.'[43]

Stefan, People's Commissar for Ruthenian Affairs, then warned Kun against the 'strongly nationalistic' Galician government, which was quite capable of swallowing up Sub-Carpathian Ruthenia (reoccupied by the Hungarian Red Army).[44]

Here we shall not be reconstructing the confused situation in the Ukraine and in Galicia, nor the precise attitude of Béla Kun's conversational partners. It is certain that such Social Democrats as Vinnichenko and such Socialist Revolutionaries as Vsevolod Alexandrovich Golubovich, the former president of the Ukrainian Rada (or Soviet) in Kiev, were both trying to gain recognition from the Allies as the representatives of an independent Ukraine and, in view of the advance of the Red Army, to reach a compromise with the Soviet authorities.

The French government put forward several plans for military incursions into the region from Poland. In mid-April, General

Haller's Army Corps tried to prevent a meeting between the Hungarian and Red Armies, in the second of which several thousand former Hungarian prisoners of war had enlisted. On the diplomatic front, France opposed the establishment of an independent Ukraine. One telegram mentions Vinnichenko's representations to the French and that, tired of waiting for a French reply about opening negotiations at Salonica, he 'had left for Budapest and Vienna'. The date of this telegram – 3 April 1919 – confirms what else is known about his journey.

The French documents also reflect Parisian disquiet about the plans for a union between the Soviet government in Kiev and the Ukrainian Directorate and also about the proposed agreement between Golubovich and Kun, announced on 22 April in the journal *Kurjer Poranny*.[45] On 6 May 1919, the Russian Affairs Section in the French Foreign Ministry prepared a long report on the situation in the Ukraine: 'Unable . . . to support the dismemberment of Russia, we cannot countenance recognition of an independent Ukraine.' As for the military situation, another report asserts that the plan for the link-up of the Russian and Hungarian Soviet armies was discovered on 'a captured [Hungarian] airman'. The same report also states that 'aeroplanes are providing permanent liaison between Hungary and the Bolshevik Red Army'.[46]

The list of all of these abortive plans is helpful inasmuch as it allows us to correct the many analyses of the situation in which Hungary found herself in 1919 – analyses that ignore the promise of the outset and dwell almost exclusively on the final failure.

A full account of the external factors, diplomatic and military, would go far beyond the framework of this study. In any case, the relevant facts are fairly well known, having been the subject of a host of studies, memoirs and papers on the Peace Conference and the discussions between President Wilson, Clemenceau, Lloyd George and Orlando or Sonnino. The members of the Council of Four followed the course of events in Soviet Hungary almost week by week.[47] The four Great Powers, moreover, were well informed on the subject, thanks to regular reports from such semi-official agents as Professor Philip Marshall Brown, President Wilson's adviser, and from diplomats on the spot or from persons on special missions, General Smuts among them.

As the reader will have gathered, all attempts at negotiation or mediation came to nothing, and this was for two connected reasons. The French Diplomatic Service and its head, Stephen Pichon, displayed unmitigated hostility towards Hungary, both as an enemy country and also as a communist state. It is difficult to tell which of these two factors weighed more heavily with him, but the French were in any case anxious to put the speediest possible end to the Hungarian Soviet Republic, not least with the help of the Rumanian and Czechoslovak armies. At the same time, the *cordon sanitaire* so beloved of Marshal Foch was to pass through Hungary; the plan also favoured providing Rumania and Czechoslovakia with the necessary military support.

The French idea of intervention by the Entente with the help of these two countries was rejected, but from the middle of April Soviet Hungary nevertheless found herself at war with her two neighbours. Rumanian troops occupied north-eastern Hungary, advancing as far as Debrecen and Szolnok, while Czechoslovak troops were stopped and then driven back by the Hungarian Red Army after its mobilization on 3 May. Between the middle of May and the middle of June, the Hungarian Army even launched a victorious counter-offensive in the north, advancing as far as Salgótarján, Miskolc, Kassa (Kosice) and the Polish border. Two notes by Clemençeau, dated 7 and 13 June respectively, persuaded the Revolutionary Governing Council to halt these operations and to order a retreat by the Northern Army. This decision was questioned, first of all by Béla Kun's own comrades and later by the detractors of his policies.[48] In any case, a 'Brest-Litovsk-type' solution, which would have allowed the Soviet régime to be saved at the price of territorial or even of political concessions, was not an option open to Kun. A study of the documents leaves no doubt that the French were determined to lance the Hungarian abscess. As in so many other situations, Clemenceau's firmness carried the day over the hesitations of his partners in the Council of Four, even though their resistance led to the shelving of official intervention plans. Such plans, moreover, proved unnecessary.

A Soviet régime in the heart of Central Europe, a vanquished and suspect enemy country forging hostile schemes against its neighbours, a country allied to, and a potential military support for, Soviet Russia, Soviet Hungary had no chance of evading its fate, the less so as some of the ambitions of the revolutionary government were bound to increase the hostility of the Allies, and that of France in particular. In fact, under the protection of the Hungarian Red Army commanded by Colonel Stromfeld, a Soviet Republic of Slovakia led by Antonin Janoušek was proclaimed on 16 June at Eperjes (Presov). At the same time, Communist emissaries from Budapest, led by Dr Ernö Bettelheim, were preparing a Communist *putsch* in Vienna, in concert with Austrian Communists. Vast sums of money to organize the seizure of power flowed in, yet the attempt failed, not only because of mass arrests on 14 June but also because the Viennese Council of Workers' Deputies refused to join it.[49]

Numerous attempts to overthrow the Hungarian régime from within added to the problems of the Revolutionary Government. There were revolts by peasants, by railwaymen, by the Danube river fleet, and by others. At the same time, at Szeged – and earlier at Arad – anti-Bolshevik resistance was being organized, notably by Count Gyula Andrássy. Admiral Horthy, the future regent of Hungary, placed himself at the head of a national army, consisting mainly of detachments of officers, and made ready to march on the capital. The military defeat of the Hungarian Red Army at the hands of the Rumanians on the Tisza front sealed the fate of the dictatorship of the proletariat. The Hungarian Soviet Republic fell on 1 August 1919. Its leaders and most prominent militants fled to Austria. For the next quarter of a century the history of the HCP would be reduced to activities by emigrants in Moscow, and in Hungary itself to the often courageous but insignificant acts of clandestine cells led by a handful of local militants and by emissaries sent out to Hungary by the Comintern.

–3–

The Clandestine Party from 1919 to 1930

A quarter-century of underground existence, persecuted by the police, the number of active members reduced to a few hundred – small wonder if the Communist Party was deeply scarred by its long and unequal struggle. Police informers and *agents provocateurs* rendered its situation even more precarious and necessitated strict rules of conspiratorial behaviour: clandestine operations, the organization of small, isolated cells, the fewest possible contacts, and a strict hierarchy of lines of communication. The 'outside' activities of the party were thus limited to propaganda and the infiltration of several legal organizations, while its 'internal' activities were beset with doubt and suspicion, each member suspecting the rest of treachery or deviationism. In fact, it was enough for one member of the illegal organization to betray one of his comrades or to break down under interrogation for a whole chain of arrests to be set off, and it happened time and again.

In these precarious circumstances, the Communist Party was nevertheless able to give proof of considerable moral force: a force maintained by loyalty and the conviction that the Communist cause was just. The courts trying Communist militants – for instance, the two prosecutions of Mátyás Rákosi and others in 1925–7 and in 1935 – were often turned into political platforms for the propagation of Communist ideas.[1] The party's martyrology is studded with memorable incidents including particularly the execution of Imre Sallai and Sándor Fürst in 1932, the heroic death of Zoltán Schönherz in 1942 and of young Endre Ságvári, killed gun in hand in July 1944 by the gendarmes who had come to arrest him.

Over and above being a real force in the political life of Hungary, the party was also the representative of a universal idea and the mouthpiece of Moscow, the centre of the international Communist movement. Its main function was to hang on – while waiting for better days. It formulated no real alternatives to the revolutions of 1917 and 1919; it was wholly devoted to what Annie Kriegel has called the 'global strategy of world revolution'.[2] In the eyes of the party, the old régime had been dealt a death-blow in 1919 (and was merely enjoying a short respite), whereas Hungarian public opinion was convinced that Communism had been dead and buried since the same date. And because the gap between the party and political reality was so great, the Communists found themselves consigned not only to illegal activity but also to stultification and vegetation on the fringes of political life.

After the Defeat

As the chief target of the repression that followed the fall of Soviet Hungary, the Communist Party was almost completely destroyed between 1919 and 1924. This was a period marked by two years of government instability followed by a measure of consolidation under the government of Count István Bethlen, formed in 1921. Inside the country, few Communist militants escaped the repressive measures of the established authorities, of the officers' squads led by Admiral Horthy, the future regent of Hungary, and of the various volunteer corps that were independent of his national army.

The number of victims claimed by White Terror in 1919–20 is uncertain, and so is the number of victims of the preceding Red Terror. Between 1,000 and 5,000 persons were killed and tens of thousands were taken prisoner, many having been cruelly tortured before they were sent to their death or to prison. How many Communists were included? It is still difficult to tell. Documents and books on the history of the Communist Party provide fragmentary data and do not add up to a proper assessment. Thus some of them deal with events in particular villages, factories or regions, or with atrocities committed against such well-known militants as Ottó Korvin or Jenö László or against the 'Lenin boys', who were executed after a summary trial. For the rest, the terror also turned on the Jews, regardless of political affiliation.[3]

It was thanks to various demonstrations of international solidarity with the victims of the repression, and above all thanks to the boycott of Hungary by the International Federation of Trade Unions during the second half of 1920, that numerous internees were freed. Their ranks included, in 1921, ten former people's commissars. Another 400 prisoners were exchanged against Hungarian officers in Russian prisoner-of-war camps. Yet others managed to emigrate. The Communist Party, or what remained of it after the collapse, was obliged to work from Vienna as it tried to reorganize its ranks and smuggle militants into Hungary.

In fact, of the old Central Committee, only Ottó Korvin and János Hirossik remained in Hungary where, after Korvin's arrest, Hirossik was left in sole charge until the summer of 1920. The other leaders, with the exception of Szamuely – who, having been turned back at the Austrian border, killed himself – ended up in Austria. Although interned for several months, Kun and his comrades were able to constitute themselves into a Provisional Central Committee.[4] Until its suspension by the Comintern in March 1922, this Provisional Committee in Vienna changed its composition four times, mainly because of internecine quarrels. As early as August 1921, the executive committee of the Comintern tried to settle these disputes by denouncing the main culprits, the so-called Kun and Landler wings, but in vain. Until the First Congress of the reorganized Communist Party, held in Vienna in 1925, the internecine struggle continued unabated. The differences between Kun and Landler bore more on tactical and organizational problems than on basic issues. Neither faction questioned the fundamental programme of the party: to struggle against the Horthy régime pending a new proletarian revolution and a second dictatorship of the proletariat. Nor did either faction, unlike the Czech communists, postulate that 'the organic growth of the workers' movement' was a prerequisite for revolution.[5] The only thing Hungarians argued about was the means of getting there. 'The Kun faction', we are told in the *History of the Hungarian Revolutionary Workers' Movement*, 'underestimated the activity of Communist groups inside Hungary and insisted on the urgent creation of an illegal [Communist] mass party'.[6] To that end, Hungarian Communists who had left their country, as well as former prisoners of war who had become Communists in Soviet Russia, were to be sent back home.

The Landler wing opposed this plan on two grounds: firstly, the returning militants would be an easy target for the police and, secondly, such a large-scale incursion was premature so soon after the 1919 débâcle. Landler preferred the infiltration of Hungarian trade unions and of the Social Democratic Party. The Comintern, itself divided, issued rather obscure instructions while trying to reconcile the two incompatible views. However, the resolution passed in August 1921 seemed to bring the balance down on Landler's side. The stress was now laid on the need to emerge from illegality on every possible occasion and to make maximum use of the available legal means for the propagation of Communist ideas. The infiltration of the trade unions was therefore to be continued, but so was the clandestine return of militants to Hungary.

All in all, therefore, Kun's influence remained preponderant. The Provisional Central Committee appointed by the Comintern included, apart from Kun himself, three members of his wing, with Landler, Lukács and Hirossik ranged against them on the other side.[7] On several occasions committees were set up to direct the underground work inside Hungary. These 'home-based' committees or secretariats were frequently reorganized by the Central Committee, especially following the arrests of members. In 1922, the Secretariat, then led by Ernö Gerö, managed to publish such clandestine communist papers as *Kommün* and such Communist youth newspapers as *Ifjú Proletár* (Young Proletarian) at more or less regular intervals. One committee, headed by Károly Öry, Kató Hámán and Ignác Gögös, continued its activities even after the dissolution of the Viennese Central Committee in 1922.[8]

Between Vienna and Moscow

During this first half of the 1920s, the real centre of activity of the Hungarian party leadership shifted gradually from Vienna to Moscow. Most of the leaders, and even the rank-and-file militants, settled in the capital of international Communism, where they met comrades who had been released from Horthy's prisons or exchanged against Hungarian officers in Russian prisoner-of-war camps.

In due course, other Communists were to join the Hungarian group in Moscow – people fleeing repression in Hungary and later escaping from the German Nazis. The history of that emigration is little known, especially as the new immigrants, arriving in successive waves from Hungary, Austria and Germany, mingled in the Soviet Union with former Hungarian prisoners of war who had stayed behind and had been dispersed all over that immense country.

According to a report published by Endre Rudnyánszky, secretary of the Hungarian section (Vengsektsiya) of the Bolshevik Party, his office maintained contact with 3,500 Hungarians, including, as we have mentioned, several hundred who were sent back to do undercover work at home.[9] Some 2,500 to 3,000 stayed behind, and it is impossible to tell how many of the tens of thousands of prisoners of war eventually opted to settle in the

USSR. In view of the smaller number of prisoners of war from other Central European countries, and the much greater ease with which German and Austrian prisoners could return home, it seems likely that the Hungarians constituted the largest group of emigrants in Soviet Russia.

An unknown, but probably very large, number among them became integrated into the life of their adoptive country. Workers, peasants and soldiers settled and founded families with Russian wives, losing all contact with the political émigrés who continued to gravitate round the Hungarian party. Others sought their fortune – or misfortune – in the service of the Soviet state. Yet others became scholars, artists or writers, better known in Russian than in Hungarian circles. Here we shall dwell on only some of the personalities who played an important role in the elaboration and implementation of the party's policies.

Béla Kun was undoubtedly the most important of these, especially after the defection of Rudnyánszky, who decamped with the party funds and later set up a watch business in Rumania. On his arrival in Moscow in 1920, Béla Kun, held in high regard but also severely criticized as the hapless leader of the Hungarian Soviet Republic, was sent on various missions that, for a time, separated him from the Hungarian party. He fought on the Southern Front, negotiated in his capacity as member of the Soviet Military Council with the anarchist Makhno, and was among those responsible for the massacre of several thousand White officers captured in the Crimea. In 1921, Kun resumed his leading role in the Hungarian party, organizing the repatriation of militant prisoners of war expected to engage in illegal work at home. Then he 'disappeared' to Germany, where he led the notorious 'March action', that abortive revolutionary attempt which was to earn the opponents of this adventure, and notably Paul Levi, head of the German Communist Party, harsh condemnation from the Comintern and from Lenin in particular. Kun himself did not emerge unscathed from the adventure: although opposed to Levi, he drew Lenin's thunder for this 'putschist' attempt, which moreover earned him the title of 'Turkestani' in more circumspect German party circles. The Third Congress of the Comintern, held in June–July 1921, ended with a condemnation of the so-called offensive policies of Kun and his associates, and of 'Leftism' in general.

Meanwhile Kun had resumed his activities in the Hungarian party, in particular the repatriation of militants. The faction he led, and which implemented these policies in the face of fierce opposition from Landler, was called the 'party builders' wing'.

As we have mentioned, the internecine conflict duly elicited repeated interventions from the Comintern. After a first warning in 1921, the leaders of the two factions were summoned back to Moscow a year later by the Executive Committee of the Communist International. Following several meetings held between 17 March and 1 April 1922,[10] the Comintern appointed a new Central Committee of the Hungarian Communist Party, consisting of Hirossik, Seidler and Szilágyi, thus excluding the leaders of the two opposed factions, namely Landler and Kun. Kun also lost his place on the most important body of the Comintern, the Restricted Bureau (*Engere Büro*) of the Executive Committee.[11] He was sent on special duty to the Urals, whence he returned to Moscow in the summer of 1923, to do a variety of jobs.

After these setbacks, Kun's fortunes seem to have revived. The Fifth Comintern Congress, held in the summer of 1924, again elected him to an important body, the Organizational Bureau (*Orgbüro*), where he held office for five years. During a visit to Vienna, he was arrested in the company of other Hungarian communists, brought before a tribunal and then released. He was back in Moscow in July 1928, at the very moment when the Sixth Comintern Congress was meeting. The congress elevated him to the highest post: it made him a member of the Executive Committee by the side of Bukharin, Manuilsky, Stalin and Togliatti. Kun, who at the beginning of the 1920s found it so hard to admit the 'error' of having united his party with the Social Democrats, had become one of the most rampant leaders of the campaign against the Social Democrats, or 'social fascists' as they were now termed in party circles. Until the middle of the 1930s, Kun adhered strictly to this sectarian approach and found it hard to swallow the party's next turnabout: support for a Popular Front. It was then that he was first beset with the troubles that were to prove much more serious than anything that had gone before and which culminated in his arrest in 1937 and in his subsequent execution.[12]

While, as the reader will discover shortly, his leading role in the Hungarian Communist Party was connected with his misfortunes, we should not neglect his personal involvement in the ideological and also personal conflicts which, for twenty years, continued to shake the Comintern and the Bolshevik Party. The case of Béla Kun is but one of many examples of how entangled the infighting in Soviet Russian and Comintern circles was with the infighting in the various foreign parties. Kun's position, like everyone else's, depended on personal relations with the Russian leaders. Close to Zinoviev, not greatly esteemed by Trotsky and on bad terms with

Manuilsky, Kun felt the buffetings of Soviet domestic struggles no less than the other foreign militants did. To the extent that the Soviet leaders transformed the Comintern and its subsidiary parties into instruments of their own policies, internal Russian conflicts were bound to have repercussions not only on personal lives but also, beyond them, on the policies of all foreign parties.[13]

Inside the Hungarian party, however, Béla Kun's authority remained extremely strong, the more so as the Comintern and the Soviet leaders, while often keeping him on the sidelines, always saw him as 'one of us' and a 'historic leader' of the 1919 Hungarian revolution. Jenö Landler, his chief rival and unquestioned captain of those opposed to Kun's sectarian and adventurist policies, never enjoyed the same degree of influence or became so involved in the intrigues of the Comintern, from which he held aloof. Landler's death in 1927 (or at the beginning of 1928) after a long illness, rid Kun of the only person capable of threatening his position. Georg Lukács who, with young József Révai, took over the leadership of the old Landler faction, lacked the requisite weight and, from the early 1930s, after several fruitless attempts at stemming the dominant sectarian trend inside the party,[14] devoted himself to philosophy and literature.[15] The brothers Béla and Zoltán Szántó each played a very important role both in Moscow and also in the illegal Communist Party at home, without, however, achieving Kun's fame. Other important figures from the party's early days were all sent on missions that, sooner or later, removed them from the affairs of the Hungarian party. Their ranks included the economist, Jenö Varga, who later became a member of the Soviet Academy of Sciences; the worker and founder member of the party, János Hirossik; as well as Gyula Alpári and many others who spent more time in the editorial offices of *Inprecorr* in Berlin than in the Hungarian Communist Party.

Mátyás Rákosi, who was to become general secretary of the party after the Second World War, rose in the Comintern hierarchy in the 1920s to serve for some time on its executive committee before spending sixteen years in Hungarian prisons; in 1940, he was exchanged for the colours of the Hungarian War of Independence of 1848–9, which had been captured by the armies of Tsar Nicholas I.

Many other leading names could be mentioned, both of activists more closely attached to the 'Muscovite' circle as well as of those who spent more time doing clandestine work at home. It has been possible to identify about one hundred individuals attached at one time or another to the leading sectors of the party, though there were, in fact, at least twice as many. In the 1920s and 1930s, however, their ranks produced no more than ten or so persons of lasting importance, and none strong enough to challenge Béla Kun's leadership. Despite several fluctuations, that situation was to remain unchanged until the middle of the 1930s. Kun kept his authority, and as a result his dogmatic line prevailed despite a slight loss of inflexibility here and there and, above all, a number of internal crises. These, apart from the persecutions and their consequences, were chiefly the result of the harsh alternative the party faced throughout this period: it had to choose between the 'pure and hard' strategic line of a hopeless fight for a 'second Soviet Republic', based on the dictatorship of the proletariat, and policies more in keeping with the true relationship of forces and aiming at the democratic transformation of Hungary.

The First Congress

The First Congress of the Hungarian Communist Party, called originally for the spring and finally for the summer of 1925, was a success as well as a confession of weakness. Since the collapse of the Hungarian Soviet Republic in 1919, the party had been moribund, so much so that in November 1922, at the Fifth Congress of the Communist International, Zinoviev had expressed doubts about its very existence.[16] In reply, Jenö Landler told him that some 200 Communists were about to be tried before Hungarian courts. It nevertheless remains a fact that the Hungarian party was considered to be more of a relic, slightly contaminated by its contacts with the Social Democrats, than a real political force. The Communist International attached little importance to it. Even the HCP's internal crises were more the result of factional squabbles than of a clash of ideas or differences about the international strategy of the Comintern. The '21 Conditions' did not even concern it, seeing that the HCP's break with the Social Democrats had been accomplished long before 1920–1 when other Communist parties were only just beginning to turn their backs on the bitter conflicts inside the various Social Democratic parties, between supporters and opponents of Leninism and of the Communist International. As for the United Front, while it doubtless fuelled debates in the Hungarian Communist Party, it had few practical repercussions on the party's extremely restricted activities. Nor was the Hungarian Communist Party faced with the kind of alternative that, in the 1920s, bitterly divided Czechoslovak communists: the democratic alternative championed by Smeral versus Bolshevik voluntarism imposed by Moscow and championed by the 'bolshevized' leadership under Clement Gottwald.[17]

By holding its *first* congress in 1925, the Hungarian Communist Party also cast doubt on the validity of the seven years of struggle that had gone before. In 1918, there had been no founding congress, and the congress of 1919, held during the dictatorship of the proletariat, had been a Socialist–Communist congress, not a 'pure' Communist Party affair. The First Congress was thus meant to mark birth and rebirth, rupture and continuity. This explains the following statement by Kató Hámán, one the delegates: 'The meeting [held in Vienna] looks upon itself as the first reconstructive congress of the HCP.' Rákosi, another delegate, declared that the 'Communist Party as an organization is not much more than three months old'.[18]

Convened on 18 August as a conference, the meeting constituted itself a congress of reconstruction on the 19th and continued as such until the 21st. Among the twenty-one delegates, five were members of the Provisional Central Committee, fourteen came from underground organizations in Hungary and three came from the Viennese section. Reports were presented by Gyula Alpári, Béla Kun, Jenö Landler, László Váradi, Mátyás Rákosi, Zoltán Vas and Károly Öri. The congress voted for a programme including demands for a workers' and peasants' government and for land reform, but in no way went back on the party's fundamental objective: the dictatorship of the proletariat.

Béla Kun based his report of the political situation in Hungary on a striking thesis. The consolidation of the Hungarian régime would, according to him, culminate in 'the liquidation of Horthy's counter-revolution and counter-revolutionary means of repression'; to the ruling classes, the resulting normalization would also spell 'the liquidation of the revolution'. Henceforth, Kun declared, the latifundia and big capital would be sharing power and round on 'Horthy and the other vestiges of the counter-revolution under the double motto of legitimacy and democracy'.[19] However, during the imperialist phase everywhere and in post-revolutionary Hungary in particular, the Communist Party alone was capable of leading the fight for and beyond democracy. To Communists, the call for democracy and 'the so-called democratic freedoms' was, according to Kun, nothing more than one aspect of revolutionary strategy and of the struggle for the dictatorship of the proletariat.

In fact, the Congress of Reconstruction, while affirming the importance of the changes that had taken place in Hungary following the consolidation of the régime under the government of Count

Bethlen, came forward with the same ideological and political mixture it had served up in the old days. The organizational committee, having done its job, was dissolved, and a new central committee was elected. Included in its ranks were Kun, Landler, Alpári, Gögös, Komor, Mitterer, Öri, Rákosi, Vági, Váradi, Weisshaus, Weisz and four alternate members. The Central Committee then proceeded to the appointment of a Committee Abroad (Alpári, Kun and Landler), a Moscow Committee (Bokányi, Benkö, Jancsik, Karikás, Hamburger and Weisz) and finally a Berlin Committee (Varga, Szántó and Lengyel).

The First Party Congress also paid special attention to the party's legal counterpart, the cover organization or MSzMP (Socialist Workers' Party of Hungary),[20] founded in April 1925, not long before the congress. Thanks to the legal activities of the MSzMP, the Communist Party was able to reach much wider circles, both at home and abroad. The MSzMP claimed, albeit unsuccessfully, the right to contest national elections. It sent delegates to the Congress of the Second International in Marseilles, tried on several occasions to establish a united action plan with the Social Democratic Party, published short-lived periodicals, helped to run campaigns on various social issues and was most active in the countryside, especially in the poorest regions. Yet its Communist nature escaped neither the Social Democrats it wooed nor the authorities. Its history was punctuated with arrests and trials which led to its complete paralysis in 1927.[21]

Trials also marked the history of the Communist Party. The most spectacular trial, that of Mátyás Rákosi and his co-accused, was also the trial of the MSzMP, because several of its leaders were implicated. The court passed twenty-nine sentences. Less than a year later, in February 1927, the police arrested sixty Communists including Zoltán Szántó, a member of the internal secretariat of the Communist Party.

The leadership of the party was as unstable as it had been before the First Congress – the composition of the Central Committee changed between 1925 and 1930, the date of the Second Congress, as often as it had previously. Georg Lukács, who had served on the Provisional Central Committee set up after the collapse of the Hungarian Soviet Republic, was again one of the leading members; another was József Révai, one of his young disciples. The members of the internal secretariat kept changing in the wake of successive waves of arrests. From 1929 to 1931, Sándor Szerényi was the party's first secretary. As for the body which defined the political programme abroad, and which had its official headquarters in

Vienna, it continued to be torn between the pull of two of its most important members: Jenö Landler, until his death in 1927 or 1928, and Béla Kun. The latter, who shuttled between Vienna and Moscow, eventually settled in the Soviet capital and derived his influence from the position he also held in the leading committees of the Comintern.

In reality, however, the Hungarian Communist Party existed in little more than name. At the Second Congress, held in 1930, it had only about a thousand members according to official estimates. Unable with such small numbers to lead important political campaigns, the party was reduced to propaganda activity in the trade-union movement, in the Social Democratic Party, in various publications, in such affiliated organizations as the Communist Youth Movement, or such cover organizations as the MSzMP. While the Youth Movement remained relatively active, even during the difficult 1920s, the cover organizations amounted to very little after the disappearance of the MSzMP.

All in all, therefore, the Communist Party did not represent any great force in the life of the country. Many of its members were individually extremely courageous to the point of sacrificing their lives, but the party as such did not provide a political alternative under the prevailing circumstances. The mouthpiece of a remote idea, it floated in any imaginary world in which the revolution still seemed just around the corner. For the rest, it shared the fate of all weak organizations forced to defend themselves from the police and from informers: self-defence absorbed most of its energies and drove it into stifling isolation.

'Blum's Theses' and the Second Congress

It was in these conditions that Georg Lukács presented the party, at the end of 1928, with his so-called 'Blum's Theses', officially entitled 'Project for a thesis on the political and economic situation of Hungary and on the tasks of the Magyar Communist Party (KMP)'.

'Blum's Theses' are of considerable historical interest. Debated at great length and finally rejected, they reflected a particularly animated period in the history of the Hungarian Communist Party. They were a landmark in the preparations for the Second Party Congress held near Moscow in 1930; their fate casts a garish light on the struggles within the Communist International during these years, struggles that started with the notorious Sixth Congress in June 1928.

The Sixth Congress adopted a formula that allowed for the existence of differences between (1) developed capitalist countries; (2) moderately developed countries; and (3) colonial and dependent countries needing a longer transitional (democratic) period than the other two.[22] The results of the Sixth Congress can nevertheless be summed up by two slogans, inaugurating, and presiding over, an ultra-sectarian period in the history of the Communist movement, namely class warfare and the defeat of social democracy, henceforth labelled 'social fascism' and seen as the chief enemy of communism.

In this context, 'Blum's Theses' must be considered a timid attempt to temper the disastrous effects of this new sectarian approach on the policies of the Hungarian party. This, in any event, was the explanation given, thirty years later, by Lukács himself when, in 1956, back in Hungary, he referred to these theses, long since forgotten, as a milestone in his struggle against Stalinist sectarianism. In fact, the tenor of the document hardly allows one to consider it a particularly courageous challenge to the mainstream. Rather, it was symptomatic of the Communist spirit prevailing at the time and it would therefore not have aroused much comment had it been put forward by some unknown militant and not by Georg Lukács.[23]

In the 1920s, the author of 'Blum's Theses' (Blum was one of Lukács's pseudonyms) was a very prominent militant and one of the leaders of the HCP. At the time, moreover, his person and his work had already become known far outside party circles.

Lukács's theoretical and philosophical writings triggered off major debates in the Soviet Union and Germany and often earned him the official disapproval of the Comintern. In particular, the publication in 1923 of the German version of his *History and Class Consciousness* (*Geschichte und Klassenbewußtsein*) evoked sharp polemics which persuaded Lukács to revise his position.[24] Nor was this the first or the last time he did so. Lukács was a past master in the art of swallowing his words every time superior forces in the Comintern or the party rounded on him, only to withdraw his self-criticism as soon as circumstances allowed. His monumental philosophical, aesthetic, theoretical and political writings are riddled with contradictions, placing him among the guardians of Marxist-Leninist and even Stalinist orthodoxy at one moment,[25] and at the next on the side of the revisionists or on the fringes of the official party line. As for the originality and depth of his thought, they too seem rather uneven.[26]

Published in 1928 following the Sixth Congress of the Communist International and the First Plenary Session of the Central

Committee of the Hungarian Communist Party, 'Blum's Theses' attempted the impossible, namely to infuse the new Comintern line with a minimum of realism when applied to the activities of the HCP, a tiny party, and one moreover in a state of near-permanent crisis. The 'Theses' were divided into five sections. The first and the fourth retraced the history of the party from the First Congress in 1925 to the plenary session in the summer of 1928, and on until the end of that year. The second section was devoted to an examination of the Horthy régime under the government of Count Bethlen and also to an analysis of the underlying economic structures. In the third section, Lukács ostensibly examined the situation of the working class, though his main thrust was a denunciation of the Social Democrats. In the fifth section, entitled 'The Main Problems of the Current Situation', Lukács tried to introduce the novel idea of 'democratic dictatorship', an idea considered too 'bourgeois' and too 'rightist' by Moscow and one that would invite the most violent attacks on the 'Theses' and on Lukács personally.

Nevertheless, Lukács did not present the delicate subject of 'democratic dictatorship' without first taking the precaution of distancing himself from the 'Right' of the party. His main target was Gyula Alpári, editor of *Inprecorr* in Berlin, a man who, in 1925, had opposed the key concept of the second dictatorship of the proletariat and also the party's anti-Social Democratic line.[27] 'Julius's views', Lukács wrote, 'constitute a consistent right-wing system', inasmuch as they denied the fascist character of the Bethlen régime, Social Democracy being part and parcel of fascism. The party was therefore right, according to Lukács, to reject Alpári's views 'incisively'. 'The Communist Party is the *only* party fighting for democracy.'[28]

After these preliminaries, Lukács came to his main point, namely 'democratic dictatorship', basing himself on the Sixth Comintern Congress, which had placed Hungary among those countries where, during the transition to proletarian dictatorship, democratic dictatorship was an important factor. Here we have one of those elastic expressions of Communist language whose secret lies in their interpretation. Its origins go back to Lenin (unless we wish to go further back to Marx) who, on the occasion of the 1905 Russian revolution, came out with the idea of the revolutionary democratic dictatorship of the proletariat and the peasantry. According to Lukács, a democratic dictatorship could assume several forms and contents. It was the most radical form of bourgeois democracy, but was at the same time the 'battlefield' from which the proletarian revolution must emerge victorious, the reason being that this advanced form of democracy was bound in the end (for not too clearly specified reasons) to become incompatible with the domination of the bourgeoisie and with capitalism, as had happened under Kerensky in Russia in 1917 and under Count Károlyi in Hungary in 1918–19. There was no 'Great Wall of China' between the bourgeois and the proletarian revolutions.

Lukács's conclusions were ambiguous, not to say confused. They were in line with the view of the Communist International that Social Democracy was the 'main prop of fascism'. They rejected the allegedly 'social-fascist' option, namely the view that Hungarian society had to choose 'between fascism and democracy'. Instead, 'Blum's Theses' fully supported the class struggle and the dictatorship of the proletariat (both excluding any compromise and class alliance in the struggle against fascism), and called for the 'democratic dictatorship of the proletariat and the peasantry'.[29]

What precisely did Lukács want? His ambiguities were probably so many deliberate attempts on the one hand to pay lip-service to such Comintern shibboleths as the class struggle and the fight against Social Democratic social fascism, and on the other hand to lead the party along slightly less sectarian lines and to adopt as an intermediate objective some sort of transition (democratic dictatorship) towards the final and unchanged objective: the dictatorship of the proletariat.

The interpretation of texts from that period is the more difficult in that their ambiguity is not exclusively the result of the views of the individuals (Lukács in our particular case) responsible for publishing them. The language of the Comintern was in fact a string of coded messages in which all statements had a double or triple meaning which varied with the decoding system. Thus the key phrase 'workers' and peasants' government', and by extension 'democratic workers' and peasants' dictatorship', could be interpreted variously as a form of transition to the dictatorship of the proletariat, as that dictatorship itself (achieved in alliance with the peasantry but under proletarian hegemony) or again as something extremely vague, namely a kind of 'transition' without any specified duration, a dictatorship of the proletariat on the Russian model, but one that did not speak its name directly.

The interpretation further depended on the antecedents of the person or group that had made the statement, as well as on the external circumstances. In the opinion of the Comintern, the capitalist system had, by the close of the 1920s, entered its 'third period', a period marked by the end of its consolidation and the start of a new phase, that of its final crisis: revolution once again seemed more imminent than it had done during 1922–8. Against this background, 'democratic dictatorship' must have looked a suspect idea, one destined to delay the revolution by the introduction of an 'impure' intermediate phase contaminated by compromise with the 'fascist' bourgeoisie and its no less 'fascist' Social Democratic ally.

Finally, the interpretation of the arguments then raging, including those round 'Blum's Theses', is complicated even further by the successive changes in Communist strategy that took place at the time. Seen in retrospect after the events of 1934–44, the rejection about five years before 1934 of 'Blum's Theses' as expressions of compromise looks absurd and utterly devoid of logic. Nevertheless this is what happened. The same fascist danger that, in 1934, led the Communists to embrace the idea of democratic power, had convinced them five years earlier of the need to speed a workers' revolution and the dictatorship of the proletariat. Translated into concrete political terms, that policy meant overthrowing the 'fascist' Horthy régime together with its no less 'fascist' Social Democratic 'allies', while proclaiming the second Hungarian Soviet Republic, and all by the unaided efforts of a Communist Party with roughly a thousand members.

It is this absurdity which explains the reproving tone used in analyses of the official party line during discussions of 'Blum's Theses' *after* the advent of anti-fascist Popular Front movements. But all that did not come about until nearly thirty years later.[30] At the time, 'Blum's Theses' were violently attacked in the party press and also in the discussions and letters of party officials, who adopted the official position of the Comintern and of the Kun faction in the HCP.

Polemics against Lukács went hand in hand with ostensibly impartial denunciations of both sides engaged in the 'factional struggle', though in fact they were aimed at the right wing which, after an interval, assumed the leadership of the party in exile: in 1927, new conflicts divided the members of the Committee Abroad. At first these divisions set Béla Kun against one of his former intimates, Alpári, who subsequently left the leadership of the party and devoted himself to his work as chief editor of *Inprecorr*.[31] The so-called Landler faction (Landler himself had been taken ill and died at the end of 1927 or the beginning of 1928[32]) was then reconstructed under the leadership of József Révai and Georg Lukács with the participation of several prominent Hungarian militants in Austria and in Germany.

As for the Kun faction, stronger in Moscow than in Vienna, its most prominent members were Béla Szántó, Nándor Orosz, Ernö Müller, Ágoston Krejcsi and several Hungarian officials of the Communist International. The latent tensions between the two groups exploded at the beginning of 1928 in connection with 'Robert's Theses', a document published by Béla Szántó, a member of the Kun faction. Szántó, instead of taking the ultra-revolutionary line of the rest of his group, tried to demonstrate that by virtue of the extreme weakness of the party on the ground, priority should be given to trade-union work and also to a revival of the MSzMP (the Hungarian Socialist Workers' Party).

Béla Kun himself did not attach too much importance to what he saw as a minor lapse on the part of a loyal friend. By contrast, the faction led by Révai and Lukács seized on it as an example of 'right-wing deviationism' by a 'left-wing' adversary. They even managed to have Béla Szántó temporarily suspended from his official duties.

It was following these incidents that, in 1929–30 – the period when discussions of 'Blum's Theses' were being pursued rigorously and when preparations for the Second Congress were being made – that three names and three theses became the main targets in the fight against 'right-wing deviationism': the theses of Gyula Alpári (attacked from all sides, although Alpári left the scene without forfeiting Moscow's confidence), the theses of 'Robert' Béla Szántó (defended, but ultimately abandoned by Kun) and the theses of Lukács. This also explains why Kun seized the opportunity to concentrate his fire on his main adversaries, the leaders of the old Landler wing, above all on Lukács.

The earliest of the many important documents published on this affair was the 'Open Letter to Members of the Hungarian Communist Party' signed by the 'President of the Executive Committee of the Communist International' but mainly written by Béla Kun. Drafted in September–October 1929, the 'Open Letter' was published in the August–November issue of *Uj Március* (New March), the official organ of the HCP. Initially, a special committee instructed by the Executive Committee of the Communist International and including Manuilsky, Philip Dengel and Pavel Reiman, spent nearly three weeks discussing the situation in the Hungarian party. The HCP was represented during these sessions by most of the people concerned – Kun, Révai, Béla Szántó amongst them, but not Lukács, who was altogether out of favour. He was expelled from the Committee Abroad and had to retire practically for good from the leadership of the HCP. It was at this point that the *ad hoc* committee of the Communist International entrusted the publication of the 'Open Letter' to three persons: Kun, Révai and Sándor Szerényi.

This document leaves no doubt about the line adopted by the party. On every question of any importance it marked the triumph of the ultra-sectarian and ultra-revolutionary faction: the fight against 'social fascism' (Social Democracy); the creation of illegal red trade unions; the rejection of all programmes involving the idea of democratic transition.

To some historians of the Hungarian Communist Party this radical veering to the 'left' was, on the one hand, a faithful reflection of the continuity of the party 'line', hard and sectarian as ever, and on the other hand of a piece with the ultra-leftist policies adopted at the Sixth Comintern Congress, reinforced further by the resolutions adopted at the Tenth Plenary Session of the Executive Committee of the Communist International in the summer of 1929. From various accounts and letters, we know that there was a great deal of vacillation in the party all through the spring and summer of 1929, until the expulsion of Bukharin (who, for a short time, had succeeded Zinoviev as President of the Executive Committee of the Communist International).

It was in this climate of radicalization that the party leaders, with Béla Kun at their head, gradually arrived at the violent critique of Lukács contained in the 'Open Letter'. It was also during these months of vacillation that Révai turned against Lukács. When writing to Kun in March, Révai still proposed that the attack on Lukács's theses should not go hand in hand with a personal attack on Lukács. He was against turning Lukács into one of the targets in the campaign against the Right. He also stressed that 'Blum's Theses' had been no more than a project circulated for internal use (in the Committee Abroad) and that they had, in any case, been revised in February.[33] For all that, Révai declared roundly that the Lukács view of democratic dictatorship was 'absolutely false', and could not possibly serve as the basis for a general theory of the transition to the dictatorship of the proletariat. Every democratic dictatorship was a transition, he went on to say, but not every transition was necessarily a democratic dictatorship. Everything depended on the relationship of forces. Lukács, the letter continued, had laid stress on the transition and not on the prospects. In short, his was a theory of the Menshevik type, an *Etappentheorie* (stage-by-stage theory).[34]

Kun, for his part, fulminated against Lukács in a prolific exchange of letters with several persons: Lukács, he argued, was an opportunist; he and not Robert ought to be the first target in the fight against the Right. An undated document in German entitled 'Conclusions of the Report on the Remedy to be Prescribed for the HCP', which was probably a report submitted by Kun to the Comintern for one of their meetings in August 1929, and which served as the basis of the 'Open Letter', was even more crushing. 'Comrade Blum's theses are alien to Bolshevism . . .' According to them, 'the future is democratic and the Communist Party is the party of democratic reform'. To Kun, that was tantamount to the 'liquidation' of the party. Lukács was nothing but an idealist, anti-Marxist, anti-Leninist philosopher. As for Révai, he was also reprimanded, though far less harshly: he was simply an indecisive and unreliable person.[35]

Lukács bowed quietly to the condemnation of his theses, declaring in a letter addressed to the Central Committee on 2 May 1929 that he recognized their 'opportunist' character. Later, at a meeting of the Central Committee of the party held on 17 January 1930, he repeated his recantation and confirmed that he was resigning his offices. He now disowned his theses and, despite being the first to suffer from it, sincerely welcomed the new political trend. The affair, for all that, was far from over.[36]

Soon afterwards, preparations began to be made for the Second HCP Congress, which was due to open on 25 February 1930 in Aprelevka, about 150 km from Moscow, with the participation of some thirty delegates. As far as we can tell, the novelty of that congress lay more in its composition than in the resolutions it passed.[37] The latter, as the published documents show, unreservedly endorsed the ultra-sectarian programme of the Communist International and of the Central Committee of the HCP, dominated by Kun.

However, the preparatory meetings held in January 1930 were attended by a new generation of militants who had arrived from Hungary and who were very dissatisfied with the way the Committee Abroad had been running the party and also with the factional struggles that had been tearing it apart for years. At this congress, the old members included Béla Kun, Georg Lukács, József Révai and Béla Szántó, while the younger members included Márton Lovas, Ferenc Boér, Ernö Normai and Pál Sebes, together with Sándor Szerényi, Ernö Müller, József Bergmann and Imre Nagy. Among the old leaders, only Kun and Révai presented reports: Kun on the political situation and Révai on the agrarian question. Szerényi reported on the trade unions, and Normai, Hugó Kiss, Márton Lovas and Janka Brück also submitted papers. The composition of the Central Committee elected at the congress also reflected the new spirit. Of the newly elected members (fifteen members and six alternates), sixteen were workers and five were intellectuals, most of them from Hungary itself.[38] Lukács, Alpári and Béla Szántó were no longer on the Central Committee.

These changes reflected the wishes expressed by numerous young rank-and-file militants in Hungary, opposed less, as we have said, to the *political line* of the party than to being *led from abroad*. Another, even more serious, complaint bore on the mistaken application of the conspiratorial method: scores of emissaries from the Committee Abroad were smuggled into Hungary with orders to take over the leadership of the clandestine organizations and their lack of prudence or weakness posed a grave threat to the working-class militants.[39]

These young militants became known as the 'Sas and Barna Group' – so called after the cover names of Sándor Szerényi ('Sas') and József Bergmann ('Barna'). Márton Lovas, Ferenc Boér, István Rostás and Ernö Normai, among others, also belonged to this group which for some time, during and after the Second Party Congress, managed to play an increasingly important role in the leadership of the party. For the rest, from the moment they arrived for the Moscow congress, Kun went out of his way to win them over; but then the members of the opposite faction did likewise, so much so, in fact, that at the preparatory meetings, held under the auspices of the Comintern (represented by Philip Dengel, soon afterwards to be replaced by Eugen Fried, a Czechoslovak Communist of Hungarian origin and a future emissary of the Communist International to Maurice Thorez), the Young Turks clamoured for Béla Kun's head. At the meeting of 17 January, Szerényi ('Sas') accused Kun of sabotaging the implementation of decisions embodied in the famous 'Open Letter' largely written by Kun himself. Dengel, mouthpiece of the Communist International, called Kun an individualist, even while accusing the young rebels of provincialism.[40]

Despite everything, agreement on the adoption of principles was reached, at the preparatory meetings no less than during the congress itself; there was unanimous condemnation of the Right, the 'rightists' themselves condemning their own deviationism. By contrast, the campaign against Kun failed, the Executive Committee of the Communist International declaring Kun's continued presence to be essential.[41] The resolutions passed by the Congress merely rubber-stamped these conclusions.

The era of the new leaders did not last very long. We have been able to identify fifteen names among the fifteen members and six alternate members elected by the congress, namely: József Berg-mann, Ferenc Boér, Zoltán Fürst, Miklós Juranovszki, Hugó Kiss, Béla Kun, Márton Lovas, Pál Nagy, Ernö Normai, József Pothor-nyik, József Oancz, István Rostás, Pál Sebes, Sándor Szerényi and Antal Tisza. Few of them remained at their posts for long.

At the beginning of 1931, the following year, the Communist International appointed a new Central Committee of eleven mem-bers. With the exception of Béla Kun and Pál Sebes, *none* of the fifteen persons mentioned above was included in this committee. The new members were Sándor Fürst, Géza Gold, Ferenc Huszti, Frigyes Karikás, György Kilián, Károly Kiss, Sándor Poll, Imre Sallai and József Tóth.[42] What became of their predecessors?

Soon after the Second Party Congress, Zoltán Fürst, followed by István Rostás, Béla Juranovszki and József Révai, all of them members of the Central Committee elected at the congress, were arrested by the Hungarian police. Another member, József Oancz, was unmasked by the GPU as an *agent provocateur* and Hungarian police informer and arrested in the Soviet Union. Yet others, whose personal attacks and intrigues Béla Kun could not forgive, suffered a similar fate in 1932: accused, without any grounds, of being agents of the Hungarian police, they were arrested by the GPU. Among them were several members of the Central Com-mittee, including Sas-Szerényi and Barna-Bergmann. As a result, in the words of the Hungarian historian G. Borsányi, 'the Central Committee elected at the Second Congress as good as vanished from the life of the party. Most of its members were in prison, others were put on trial'[43] – be it, we hasten to add, in Horthy's Hungary or in Stalin's Russia.

The fate of the next team was no more enviable. Sándor Fürst and Imre Sallai, two very courageous men, were executed in Hungary in 1932, after being tried before a special (emergency) court. Kilián, who died during the war, was imprisoned in Hun-gary, while most of the others, after passing through Hungarian prisons, finished their lives in some gulag or other.

However, for some years, from 1931 to 1937, one of their members, Ferenc Huszti, provided continuity in the leadership of the party, acting as its secretary until 1937, when he, too, fell victim to Stalin's terror.

−4−

The Years of Crisis:
The Party and the Comintern

The international crisis produced a favourable climate for social and political agitation in Hungary and elsewhere. The Communist Party was quick to seize this opportunity, gaining ground especially among the ever-increasing army of unemployed, but also among agricultural labourers whose association numbered 2,000 members in 1930 and 4,000 members in 1932. Apart from strikes and local protests, many organized by Communists, the party also played an important role in the big demonstration of 1 September 1930.

For the rest, the party's general political line remained practically unchanged throughout the early 1930s and even later. The Central Committee, meeting in Vienna in May 1932, simply reaffirmed that the international crisis was accelerating the 'fascization' of Social Democracy and, simultaneously, 'the revolutionary fermentation' of the masses.[1] The same strains were sounded in a resolution passed by the Central Committee in September 1933 which, inevitably, called for the establishment of a Second Hungarian Soviet Republic.[2]

Despite the explosive social climate, no genuine unity of action between the Communist and the Social Democratic parties could come about in these circumstances. The SDP continued to keep its distance from the CP, not least in order to ensure its own legal existence and to safeguard its various activities, especially its press and parliamentary representation. In 1921, these safeguards were enshrined in a pact between the prime minister, Count István Bethlen, and Károly Peyer, the leader of the Social Democratic Party. The SDP later denounced this pact but maintained its understanding with the government under a different guise. In particular, it continued to reject any form of alliance with the Communist Party. It must also be stressed that the SDP had hardened its anti-Leninist line after the experience of 1919 and in the wake of fierce anti-Social Democratic agitation by the Comintern. The Communists, for their part, while inviting the Social Democrats to co-operate with them, continued to attack their leaders whom they never ceased describing as 'social fascists'. The creation of the ESzE (*Egyesült Szakszervezeti Ellenzék*) (United Trade Union Opposition) only served to increase the dissension between the two parties.

Last but not least, their respective forces were wholly unequal. With its fourteen deputies, the SDP had remained a parliamentary party of some importance; it had kept control of the trade unions, whose membership, though it had dropped to a very low level in 1930 (87,000 as against 200,000 in 1922) was beginning to rise again during the crisis years.

The Communist Party, for its part, had managed to make some headway in intellectual circles, thanks largely to its publications. The journals *Uj Március* (1925–33), *Társadalmi Szemle* (1931–3), the so-called central party paper, *Kommunista* (the party's central organ; 1928–35) and the Young Communist weekly *Ifjú Proletár* enjoyed a fairly wide circulation. A literary review entitled *100%* (1927–30), later joined by the review *Gondolat* (1935–7), reflected Communist involvement in cultural activities, on which, however, the sectarian and dogmatic line of the party imposed limitations. It was because of these that Attila József, then the leading Hungarian Communist poet, was expelled from the party in 1934.

The 1930s proved to be even harder on the party than the preceding years had been. In fact, towards the end of the 1920s, the illegal Communist movement had enjoyed a few brief moments of respite. Emissaries from the Committee Abroad, including József Révai, Georg Lukács, Ernö Müller and János Hirossik took turns in visiting Budapest for three months at a time to direct party activities; clandestine contacts were relatively easy to maintain; the party had safe houses and even ran an office.[3]

The proclamation of martial law in 1931 worsened the situation dramatically. Until then the authorities had, of course, hounded the party, but for more than ten years no Communist had been put to death. From 1931, Communists brought before the special tribunals were in peril of exactly that. A bomb attack on a train in which many were killed, perpetrated by Szilveszter Matuska, who was probably of unsound mind, served as a pretext for the extension of martial law, which had been allowed to fall into desuetude, and to apply it to Communists in particular.

In the summer of 1932, the police rounded up members of the

home-based party Secretariat and other Communists. Their trial brought vigorous international protests signed *inter alia* by Léon Blum, Romain Rolland, H.G. Wells, Bertrand Russell and Upton Sinclair. Two of the accused, Imre Sallai and Sándor Fürst, were nevertheless sentenced to death and executed on 29 July 1932.

After the arrest of its leaders and the execution of Sallai and Fürst in 1932, the Communist Party found itself in a permanent state of crisis. The replacements sent from Moscow, Sándor Poll among them, were all arrested in turn. Thanks to a reorganization in January 1933, new cadres, less well known to the police, were able to take control but without forming themselves into an internal secretariat. At the end of 1933, the HCP still had a Committee Abroad in Berlin or Vienna, under the leadership of Ferenc Huszti; a Central Committee whose headquarters were, to all intents and purposes, in Moscow and one of whose members was delegated to direct the clandestine work in Hungary; a Budapest Committee; and various district committees in charge of local cells. This apparently perfect façade hid a disintegrating and demoralized party. It was unable to profit from the economic crisis so as to strengthen its grass roots or to forge fresh links with the SDP. Its leadership, which kept changing, proved ineffective. Successive arrests decimated its cadres. The party was facing a major crisis which, in 1936, culminated in its dissolution by the Comintern.

We cannot deal with this phase of its history without mentioning the external factors surrounding its internal crisis. After the resignation of Count Bethlen's government and a brief transitional period, Gyula Gömbös, a so-called 'strong man', formed a new government on 1 October 1932. In contradistinction to the liberal Bethlen régime, Gömbös introduced a dirigiste and rightist policy punctuated by a few social reforms. In foreign affairs, he strengthened the country's ties with Fascist Italy first of all and then with Nazi Germany, and also with neighbouring Austria under Dollfuss and Schuschnigg. Gömbös was bitterly attacked by the opposition, even from the centre right, who accused him of having dictatorial and fascist tendencies. He was able to stand up to them all, the more so as his economic reforms and his ideological and cultural platform earned him some laurels, though not enough to allow him to cast off the shackles of the parliamentary system. At his death in 1936, Hungary, now closely linked to the nascent Berlin–Rome Axis, had completed the fateful drift to the right that would, after some vacillation, draw it in 1941 into Hitler's war.

Its second decade underground was therefore full of trials and tribulations for the party. Moreover, it was marked by three major upheavals on the international Communist scene: the official inauguration of the Popular Front policy at the Seventh Congress in 1935, the German–Soviet Pact in 1939, and Hitler's attack on the Soviet Union in 1941. Each of these events shook the small Hungarian Communist Party to its foundations. In this chapter we shall be looking at the most important repercussions inside the party until 1941. In the next chapter we shall try to look more closely at the gradual and difficult gestation of the party's new Popular Front policy during the war. In short, the roots of the party's pre-war difficulties were, on the one hand, the thrust of the Hungarian Right and, on the other hand, the adoption by the Comintern of the Popular Front policy with which the party found it hard to come to terms. To make matters worse, in 1935 and in 1936 fresh waves of arrests cut down its ranks.

In May 1936 the Comintern dismissed the entire Central Committee of the Hungarian Communist Party for having retarded the implementation of the Popular Front policy; it again put the reorganization of the party in the hands of a provisional secretariat with headquarters in Prague, now led by Zoltán Szántó. The Comintern also inveighed against the party's sectarian, bureaucratic and anti-democratic methods, no less than against its leaders' personal squabbles. The dismissed officials were ordered to appear before the International Control Committee of the Comintern. Béla Kun came in for special abuse, the Comintern going so far as to forbid his re-election to any official position.

The last word on these events has not been spoken to this day. According to the study of the development of the HCP we have mentioned earlier,[4] several conflicting resolutions were passed on the topic. At its meetings on 7 and 8 May 1936, the Executive Committee of the Comintern passed a milder resolution than the ones passed six weeks later – on 23 and 26 June – by the Secretariat of the Comintern at special meetings devoted to Hungary. Unlike the Executive Committee, the Secretariat did not propose convening a conference of the HCP for the purpose of electing a new central committee.[5]

For no less obscure reasons, the decision of the Comintern handed down to party officials in Hungary involved the dissolution of the party as a whole and not merely of its Central Committee. Several Communist historians, including Dezsö Orosz and István Pintér, have cast doubt on this version and maintain that the decision to dissolve the party was taken by the new Secretariat in Prague, the Comintern itself having taken no such decision. In corroboration, they quote a report by Zoltán Szántó, secretary of the Prague committee, addressed to the Comintern and declaring specifically that, in view of the circumstances, 'the whole party apparatus must be dissolved'.[6]

It should, however, be noted that Szántó's report was dated February 1938, more than a year after the effective dissolution of the party, and that it in no way establishes which body took the actual decision. Zoltán Szántó himself at no time claimed to have acted on his own authority. His unpublished memoirs are emphatic on this point and incidentally afford a glimpse, however slight, of the decision-making process in the upper echelons of the Comintern.

Zoltán Szántó, born in 1893, had just spent eight years in Hungarian prisons for Communist activities when he repaired to Moscow in 1935. There he was assigned to the offices of the Executive Committee of the Comintern. At a special briefing by the latter, Szántó realized how severe the repercussions of the Kirov affair were being on the Hungarian Party. Manuilsky came out with the official (in fact Stalin's) version, implicating Zinoviev, already in prison, and accusing Béla Kun of having been present at a dinner, attended by Zinoviev and others, during which plans for Kirov's murder were discussed.[7] According to Szántó, Kun did not deny his presence at that dinner but insisted that he did not know anything about such plans.

Nor was this all. József Révai, his future brother-in-law, informed Szántó that the HCP leadership had strong reservations about the Popular Front tactics: they 'do not really consider that the principles adopted at the Seventh Congress apply to the case of Hungary'.

Following these preliminaries, the 'Hungarian affair' entered its official phase: in the spring of 1936, a special committee of the Comintern deliberated on the crisis of the HCP for two months. Consisting *inter alia* of Klement Gottwald, Otto Kuusinen, Wilhelm Pieck, A. M. Moskvin and Togliatti, this committee summoned several leading Hungarian militants to Moscow, among them Ferenc Huszti, the titular (and for the past five years the actual) secretary of the HCP, Imre Komor, Dezsö Nemes, Pál Sebes, Lajos Papp and Szántó himself: all those who were either to answer charges against them or else take over the reins of the party.

In his memoirs, Szántó goes on to quote, in Hungarian translation, the resolution passed by the Executive Committee of the Comintern – or by its Secretariat – at the meeting held on 7–8 May 1936; that resolution seeming to be the result of the labours of the special committee charged with the investigation of the Hungarian party.

The resolution stated that the ability of the Hungarian police to destroy the entire party apparatus during the preceding January cast a merciless light on the party's state of disarray. Moreover, the party had been guilty of sabotaging the resolutions of the Seventh Congress of the Communist International and had done no serious work in the trade unions, while its 'Letter to the Comrades' was so much verbiage meant to gloss over the many grave errors committed.[8] The resolution went on to pillory the irresponsibility of the party in the conduct of its clandestine and conspiratorial activities, its sectarian and bureaucratic character and its refusal to brook criticism. The Executive of the Comintern accordingly called for the dissolution of the Central Committee, for the creation of a provisional secretariat led by Zoltán Szántó,[9] and for a disciplinary inquiry by the International Control Committee.

During June, other meetings were also held in Moscow in connection with the affairs of the Hungarian party: meetings of the Secretariat of the Executive Committee of the Comintern (according to the version mentioned earlier), and meetings of the Control Committee (according to Szántó's memoirs.)[10] In any case, the verdict passed in June was more severe than the one of the previous month. Beyond calling for more severe political sanctions, it also hit out at those personally responsible, according to the Comintern, for the shortcomings of the party, namely Dezsö Nemes, Pál Sebes, Imre Komor and Ferenc Huszti – all of whom were duly punished – and Béla Kun, who was dismissed from office.

It would seem, however, that the dissolution of the HCP was not explicitly mentioned in any of these resolutions. That Draconian measure, fiercely contested by Hungarian Communists, was implemented along administrative channels, mainly by Ercoli (Togliatti). The instructions were sharp and clear: Togliatti warned Szántó of the danger of resuming contacts with the 'illegal cells' and with a party apparatus 'riddled with *agents provocateurs*'. The Comintern subsequently sent instructions to Hungary, via Vienna, to 'dissolve the conspiratorial apparatus'. The bearer of these tidings was a comrade by the name of Lederer: in Vienna he was received by Tibor Szönyi who, in turn, handed the message on to Budapest. Later still, when he was already in Prague, Szántó received confirmation of these instructions through Gyula Tóth, a leather worker who told him that the HCP 'was dissolved in the autumn of 1936'.[11]

Oddly enough, János Kádár would also produce a version of these events, though at the time he was no more than a young rank-and-filer. Himself accused of having dissolved the party in

1943, Kádár in a later article returned to both episodes.[12] He alleged that, in 1936, 'about eight members of the party were kept on in secret' for reorganization purposes. And so, between 1936 and the early 1940s, the party lived under conditions of 'double illegality' – illegality with respect to the authorities and illegality with respect to the party militants – with the exception of eight elected persons.

There is one more witness, Károly Kiss, who was leader of the party after the Second World War, and a young militant in 1936. It was Kiss to whom Szönyi handed the notorious Comintern instructions in Vienna. It was he, as well, who described the final chapter of this long and controversial story: his comrades' disarray and deep despair. Cut off from all 'higher' contacts, the embattled militants were forced to extricate themselves from the mess in which they had been left as best they knew how. 'I failed to understand', Kiss wrote, 'why the party abandoned to their fate the very people whom it had always extolled as professional revolutionaries.'[13]

In fact, about 900 militants were affected, 500 of them in prison. As for financial aid, Vienna sent Kiss a final remittance of 2,000 pengös (the equivalent of 2,000 Swiss francs at the time). After many, difficult enough years, there now began a process of almost total disintegration: the bitter consequences of the Comintern decision were to be felt by the Hungarian Communist movement until the early 1940s.[14]

The only remaining party organization, the Provisional Secretariat, staffed by Zoltán Szántó and two, later four, other members, was set up in Prague in July 1936. It remained there until the day after the Munich agreement; indeed, as far as some of its members, including József Révai were concerned, until the German occupation. Its policy was to strengthen Communist activity in legal working-class organizations, and especially in the SDP. At the same time, the party appealed increasingly to leftist circles of the intelligentsia and to the populist democratic Márciusi Front (March Front). The journal *Gondolat*, representing the 'frontist' approach, was banned by the government in November 1937. The official organ of the secretariat, *Dolgozók Lapja* (Workers' Journal), printed in Prague, came out for one year, from 1937 to 1938. Of the members of the Secretariat in Prague, Zoltán Szántó returned to Moscow; his successor Lajos Papp went to Paris after the Germans marched into Prague in the spring of 1939, while István Friss and József Révai, after several stop-overs, also made their way to Moscow.

It is difficult to assess the effects of the activities of the new party leadership in Prague – a leadership that subsequently became the titular Central Committee and was genuinely committed to the Popular Front idea. On the ideological plane, the Prague team undoubtedly helped to drive home the need to abandon sectarian ideas in favour of an anti-fascist campaign and encouraged sincere collaboration with all democratic forces. We shall be mentioning some manifestations of the new approach, especially the writings of József Révai. The official paper of the committee (*Dolgozók Lapja*), printed in Prague, also helped to propagate the new ideas.[15]

It is less certain whether the Prague committee succeeded in getting its message across to the rank and file, that is, to the cells cut down by waves of arrests and subsequently broken up on Comintern orders.

What contacts there were between the committee in Prague and militants in Hungary came down to just a few meetings in Prague, in Austria and in France. In particular, Ferenc Donáth and Géza Losonczy, Communists involved in the democratic March Front,[16] encountered Zoltán Szántó, Gusztáv Krejcsi, István Friss and later Lajos Papp, all of them emissaries of the Prague committee. Until 1939, the party had no proper organization in Hungary. On instructions by the Prague committee, several militants were charged individually with the establishment of Communist groups. Gyula Kulich set up a Young Communist Movement; until his arrest in the autumn of 1937, György Vértes assembled a group of intellectuals round the review *Gondolat*; Sándor Zöld, Ferenc Donáth and Géza Losonczy worked inside the March Front and its offshoots;[17] József Turai worked among the metal-workers.

The most important organizational work fell to Ferenc Rózsa, who was charged in 1938 with putting the party back on its feet. According to the *History of the Revolutionary Workers' Movement of Hungary*, a political directorate was set up in Budapest in 1939 with Rózsa, László Gács and István Kenéz at its head. This body was in contact with Kulich, Donáth and also with Ferenc Házi, József Turai and others. However, according to Károly Kiss, there was no centralized party organization in Budapest until 1940. In fact, the period of confusion was to continue for many years. After the Germans entered Prague, so putting an end to the work of the committee that had tried to reorganize the Hungarian party, the last secretary, Lajos Papp, settled in Paris. However, at the beginning of the war he lost contact with the Hungarian militants and also with Moscow.[18] As for Rózsa, who had been working with István Kenéz and László Gács on instructions from Paris, he was left for a whole year without orders or assistance from abroad. Resolutions passed in Moscow in 1939 and again in January 1940 concerning the reorganization of both the Central Committee of the party and also of its rank-and-file organizations, mostly in Budapest, probably failed to reach the Hungarian underground movement. In September 1940, a new resolution by the Comintern stressed the need for establishing party organizations under a central control apparatus, but one based not on the groundwork so patiently carried out by the militants themselves, but on new men flowing into Budapest following the recent return to Hungary of territories under the terms of Hitler's Vienna awards and thanks to annexations by the Hungarian government.[19]

The main cause of the party's disarray, however, was the signing of the German–Soviet Pact on 23 August 1939. The Soviet press, the Comintern papers, its leaders, including Dimitrov, all changed their tune in the autumn of 1939. The Popular Front tactic was as good as forgotten, the idea of a united anti-fascist campaign robbed of substance. The new line was once again struggle against the Social Democrats, 'united action' now being confined to co-operation at lower levels in accordance with the old 'single front' motto.

One telling document is the analysis of the pact by Ferenc Rózsa and his brother Richárd Rózsa, two Hungarian Communists working illegally in Budapest in the autumn of 1939. Entitled 'The German–Russian Pact and the collapse of Poland' and intended for the use of other underground militants, this text frankly asked the question: 'Has the Soviet Union become fascist or has Hitler become a communist?' 'Neither,' the authors replied. The pact was simply a bit of *Realpolitik*, a consequence of the Munich agreements. The authors of the document also put the same question in different form: 'Is Russia's attitude treacherous?' 'No,' they replied; Hitler's aggression was bound to be 'displaced' westward as a result.[20]

Another interesting document is mentioned in an unpublished study by the Institute for Party History, namely a resolution taken on 3 January 1940 by the Communist International in the form of 'Instructions to the Party of Hungarian Communists'. In it, the Comintern warned the Hungarian party against the head of the Hungarian government, Count Teleki, whom it accused of duplicity, and went on to insist that the Popular Front had to be created 'from below'. The Comintern further asserted that 'revolutionary change is the order of the day'. There could no longer be any question of a democratic *transitional phase* but only of the need for a democratic *movement*.[21] In short, very little indeed was left of the Popular Front policy, opposition to which by the HCP had led to its dissolution in 1936. And the party had not, of course, been given nearly enough time to join in singing the new Comintern tune before the German–Soviet Pact changed the song all over again.

No wonder that there is a paucity of contemporary documents recording these facts or the party's reaction to them, and this interlude continued until the spring and summer of 1941 when the reorganization of the party began to bear fruit, and when Hitler's war on the Soviet Union clarified the situation almost at a stroke.

Papers and books published in Hungary after 1945 also make little mention of the disappointment and disarray caused by the change of tack in Soviet policy in August 1939. Even pamphlets written for various cadre training schools in the 1950s – at the height of the Stalin period – adopt discretion when referring to this question. 'Thanks to this pact,' we are told in one of them, 'Stalin's sagacious policy was able to safeguard the peace of the Soviet people for a time . . . The signing of the pact . . . helped to improve relations between the Soviet Union and the Hungarian government. Our party was able to take advantage of these developments by popularizing the Soviet Union by legal means.'[22]

It needed a truly ingenious author such as Gyula Kállai to assert that 'the Hungarian Communist Party considered the German–Soviet non-aggression pact an act of great importance, not only for the Soviet Union but also for Hungary'.[23] More discreet, but also closer to reality, the authors of the *History of the Hungarian Revolutionary Workers' Movement*, while defending the Soviet policy, nevertheless conceded that 'at the beginning an important section of the working class greeted the unexpected news of the pact with incomprehension . . .; it caused temporary consternation even among some Communists who did not grasp the need for, and the correctness of, this step until later'.[24]

The German–Soviet Pact also had more directly advantageous effects for the party: the establishment of diplomatic relations between the Soviet Union and Horthy's Hungary; the circulation of Soviet books in Hungary; the opening of a Soviet stand at the Budapest International Fair; the exchange of Mátyás Rákosi for the colours of the Hungarian War of Independence of 1848–9.

During this period, thanks to easier communications with Moscow, the party was also able to redeploy its forces.[25] This work was done, during the short breathing space it had, by a team consisting of Zoltán Schönherz, József Skolnik and Sándor Szekeres. In January 1941, they established a Central Committee, with Skolnik as its first secretary, followed by the other two. Ferenc Rózsa, László Gács and Mihály Tóth were also part of this new leadership team until mass arrest by the police in the spring and summer of 1942 struck another decisive blow at Hungarian Communism.

Party historians often stress the fact that the Central Committee set up in January 1941 was the first to be established on national soil since 1919. It also put an end to the traditional 'double leadership' shared between committees with headquarters abroad and others in Budapest.

As far as that double leadership is concerned, we must nevertheless add that it was not the new team which cut the influence of the 'Muscovites' but the outbreak of war between Germany and the Soviet Union. The Muscovites had been greatly weakened by the savage purges of Hungarian émigrés in Moscow following Béla Kun's arrest in 1937. This is a point to which we shall return. In any case, the brief 'independence' of the Central Committee in Hungary was more a consequence of external circumstances than of any desire for autonomy, unlike what had happened during the revolt of the Young Turks in 1930.

The fact that the Central Committee was set up in Hungary and not, as before, in Vienna, Moscow or Prague, calls for further comment. The Schönherz–Skolnik–Szekeres team was, in fact, appointed by the party leadership in Moscow and included persons practically unknown in the Hungarian Communist movement. Veteran members of the HCP in Czechoslovakia, they had repaired to the Soviet Union after the German invasion, whence they were sent to Hungary with instructions to assume leadership of the party. It was a mission they undoubtedly carried out with courage and devotion. Skolnik suffered police brutality after his arrest and Schönherz, having first built a team of young militants round his courageous and charismatic personality, sacrificed his life for the cause – he was executed in 1942 during a massive assault on Communists which involved hundreds of arrests. Ferenc Rózsa, the other young leader of the party and first editor of the illegal *Szabad Nép* (Free People), was tortured to death during the same wave of repressive measures. After the disappearance of this team, the sad cycle of replacements and new arrests continued for the rest of the war. Among those who took charge in 1942 were several of the party's future leaders, including János Kádár. During that period, the party had already started a new chapter of its history. Hungary's declaration of war on the Soviet Union, while making life harder for the Communist Party, also clarified its position. The anti-fascist propaganda of the Communists as well as their attempts to organize a democratic peace front gained greatly in credibility, though they still had little success. Its reassumption of a role in the anti-fascist front allowed the party to emerge from its ghetto and sectarianism. Retracing the individual steps of that transformation will be our concern in the next chapter.

−5−

From Sectarianism to the 'New Democracy'

Trusting as they do in a world revolution, a revolution without frontiers, Communist parties invariably have great difficulty in adjusting to national circumstances or to the changing imperatives of Soviet *Realpolitik*.[1] The Hungarian Communist Party, for one, found it very hard to come to terms with the new Popular Front line. Everything stood in its way: the party's past, traditions, sectarianism, leaders and composition.

More than its brother parties, it was steeped in its illustrious past, in the achievements of 1919: it could not stoop to a policy so blatantly at odds with that of the heady days of the Soviet Republic and the dictatorship of the proletariat. Measured against that past, the call for a bourgeois democratic republic was tantamount to a historical retreat. And Béla Kun, the most prestigious of the party's leaders, was one of the least prepared to take such a course. In one area, certainly, he had proved more far-sighted than many of his detractors: he had been convinced all along that the Hungarian Communist Party would have achieved nothing in 1919 had it not joined forces with the Social Democrats. Even so, he had never renounced his predilection for violent change and proletarian dictatorship. His role in the Comintern, and especially in the attempted German *coup d'état* of March 1921, clearly brought out the 'Blanquist' aspect of his personality. Again, as the writings we have quoted show, Kun continued to stick firmly to his 1919 position during all the factional polemics and fights that shook the party throughout the 1920s. Party publications, moreover, assert that, as late as 1936, 'he had difficulty in breaking with his old sectarian ideas and obstructed the necessary changes' in party policy.[2] Admittedly, he did not do so for long, because the GPU made sure that the party was rid of its former hero. But in the wake of

Landler's death by 1928 and Kun's relegation in 1936,[3] the Hungarian Communist Party was left without a leader, without a programme and without a rudder to steer a new course. Lukács's arguments ('Blum's Theses' of 1928) lay buried in the archives and were, in any case, inaccessible to minds conditioned by the terror. It was not the party's custom to resurrect officially discredited theses, even though time and developments may have vindicated them.

Moreover, even had such a *volte face* been possible, Lukács was banished from any position of authority in the party during 1935–41 and therefore in no position to reiterate his old theses. And so what little progress the Communist Party made along the anti-fascist and democratic road was confined to the Committee Abroad in Prague and to its paper, the *Dolgozók Lapja* (Workers' Paper).

In August 1939, the German–Soviet Pact again blocked any chance of creating an anti-fascist Popular Front. While Communist historians have tried to gloss over these 'difficulties', most of them have been forced to admit that the elaboration of the new Popular Front line 'took years'; they also let it transpire that the Hungarian Party was unable to introduce real changes until the German attack on the USSR.

Before that crucial turning-point, a few unusual events marked the beginning of a Communist Party adaptation to the Popular Front line, among them the abandonment of the separatist trade-union movement in 1936 and the return of Communist militants to the official trade unions. A change in tone was also struck in several party publications. Some writers, especially József Révai, began to apply the new Comintern spirit in articles on philosophy, aesthetics, politics and literature. One of Révai's studies, entitled *Marxism, Populism and Hungarianism,*[4] published in Prague shortly before Hitler's troops marched into the city, is particularly interesting in this respect: the author redefined the future line of the party as one of support for the 'new democracy' and, at the same time, offered a reasoned appreciation of the so-called 'populist' movement founded by Hungarian intellectuals close to the peasantry.

After the fall of Nazism, Révai envisaged a transformation of Hungarian society that would have 'neither a socialist nor a bourgeois-democratic character in the usual sense of these words'. Thus, while it would be bourgeois-democratic in the way it tackled the agrarian problem and introduced a democratic policy, it would transcend the bourgeois-democratic stage when it came to dealing with monopoly capitalism and allied phenomena.

As for the 'populist' movement, Révai, while criticizing it in the light of his own Marxist-Leninist philosophy, nevertheless stressed that Communists had many points in common with the populist writers so that there were good reasons for a rapprochement. This study, written in 1938 but not published until 1943 under a pseudonym and under a different title,[5] was followed in 1939 by another study on the same subject published in the journal *Új Hang* (New Voice) in Moscow; it was part of a series of studies of Hungarian literature during the political and cultural reforms that had taken place from the beginning of the nineteenth to the twentieth century.[6] Among Hungarian Communists working illegally under the Horthy regime, very few read these writings but, thanks to journals published in Hungary, the 'new spirit' did make some headway among sympathetic intellectuals and fellow travellers.

The journal *Gondolat* (Thought), in particular, reflected a less sectarian spirit during its brief existence from 1935 to 1937 than did other Communist periodicals.[7] It was founded in 1935 by its editor Lajos Nemes-Nagel, the future director of the Nagel Publishing House in Geneva. Its contributors included such brilliant left-wing writers and journalists as György Bálint, Endre Gelléri, Zsigmond Reményik, Péter Veres, such poets as József Fodor, Gyula Illyés, Attila József and Zoltán Zelk. During its second year, in 1936, the review was edited jointly by Tibor Déry and György Vértes, then from the second issue of that year onwards by Vértes alone. Although latterly linked to the Communist Party, *Gondolat* remained a legal publication and did not disclose its Communist Party affiliation. Of a high literary and intellectual standard, the journal devoted many articles to political events, especially to the Popular Front and the Spanish Civil War.

Between 1936 and 1939, there also appeared the brilliant *Szép Szó* (Fair Words). Inspired by the Communist poet Attila József, by Paul Ignotus and François Fejtö, the future historian of the People's Democracies, it was an independent periodical without links to the Communist Party; on the contrary, it was often critical and infused with the spirit of Social Democratic political and cultural renewal.[8]

The middle 1930s, though marked by the thrust of the Right, were particularly brilliant in the intellectual, literary and artistic fields. These were the years of the rise of Béla Bartók and Zoltán Kodály in musical life, the renewal of modernism in art, the proliferation of literary journals and periodicals of all tendencies. Right-wing agitation provoked left-wing defensive reactions, even a leftist counter-offensive. While there was nothing like a popular front in Hungary during the 1930s and not even the vaguest overtures by what had become a completely marginalized Communist Party to a suspicious Social Democratic Party and vice versa, the idea of common anti-fascist action was nevertheless alive among leftists in general, and among writers in particular. Thus, though the field open to Communist ideas was very narrow, the Communist message could nevertheless be spread, through newspapers, journals, exhibitions and plays – though, of course, the forbidden political affiliations of those responsible had to be kept dark.

The party's cultural activity was further shackled by its sectarianism as the expulsion from its ranks of the poet Attila József showed only too clearly.[9] Its relationship with the novelist Tibor Déry was equally capricious, as was its attitude to Communist writers or writers close to the party in the regions annexed following Hitler's awards, for example to the writers associated with the excellent journal *Korunk* (Our Time), published in Transylvania.

The German–Soviet pact, as we saw earlier, caused a harsh breach in these modest political and literary developments. The 'new democracy' was allowed to fall by the wayside and only a timid rapprochement with the 'populists' was to survive these years of crisis.

Communists and 'Populists'

Relations with the Social Democratic 'fraternal enemy' have absorbed most of the energies of Communist parties throughout the world and also provide us with a yardstick for assessing their attitude to the working-class movement at large. This is particularly true of the HCP between the two wars.[10] Nevertheless, in the 1930s, the relationship between the HCP and another political and intellectual trend, the 'populist' movement, also marked its history, less so perhaps in the field of political action than in the intellectual sphere. At all events, the intellectual landscape of Hungary during those years, as well as the specific characteristics of the Hungarian Communist movement, cannot be understood without reference to this factor.[11]

The beginnings of 'populism', in the wider sense of political and intellectual identification with the interests of the peasantry, go back at least to the beginning of the first post-war period. The movement involved several groups and individuals, especially writers, concerned with the fate of the '3 million beggars' – the peasantry crushed by the latifundia system. To mention only two great novelists associated with this trend, Zsigmond Móricz on the 'left' and Dezsö Szabó on the 'right', both described, after the First World War, the peasant scene with all the power of their genius. Such leading poets and writers as Gyula Illyés, László Németh, József Erdélyi and many others drew their deepest inspiration from the same sources in the 1920s and 1930s.[12]

However, it was a new generation of populists, that of the 1930s, which was to provide a fresh impetus and confer the character of a 'movement' on the populist trend: the 'movement of village explorers' with its 'village-exploration literature'. Young people such as Zoltán Szabó, Imre Kovács, Ferenc Erdei, slightly older ones in their thirties such as Gyula Illyés, Géza Féja, Péter Veres, János Kodolányi and others, were to create an entirely new genre, half-literary and half-scientific, called sociography, which quickly gained a large audience among socially aware people.

At the same time, the purely literary output – novels, poetry and plays – of the populists also made great strides. Moreover, other groups and professions, often older than the populist writers, also joined the movement: ethnologists, sociologists, musicologists, artists and academic associations. At Szeged and at Debrecen, then the second and third largest Hungarian cities, large groups were formed under separate leaders but under the same ideological and cultural banner. A great intellectual movement was born.

It did not take the populist 'village exploration' movement long to assume a more explicitly political character, not least because of the rise of Nazism. The March Front was born on 15 March 1937, during the annual commemoration of 15 March 1848, the day of Petöfi and the other Forty-Eighters.[13]

Before we consider the consequences of this event, a short comment about the participants is needed. Their political influence remained very small. They nevertheless, and often without realizing it, constituted the nucleus of a new political class destined to take the lead in the fight for a democratic transformation. This was because, except for the Social Democrats, a few liberal groups and a wing of the Smallholders' Party, no organized movement offered a democratic alternative to the system dominated by the traditional Right. In fact, the political and cultural élite that emerged after 1945 comprised several hundred persons who had been associated more or less directly with the populist movement, a dozen ministers and secretaries of state among them. Other leading populists from the 1930s, by contrast, went over to the extreme Right during the war and later disappeared from public life.

The new start of the populist movement which began with the foundation of the March Front in 1937 also proved important by virtue of the links later to be forged between the original, non-Marxist nucleus of young populists and the Marxist groups that made common cause with them. Foremost among these groups was unquestionably the one in Debrecen, the Protestant city in north-east Hungary. Its members included Géza Losonczy, a deputy minister after the war, a minister during the 1956 revolution and a victim of the repression; Szilárd Ujhelyi, one of the most brilliant Communist intellectuals; Sándor Zöld, secretary of state after the war and a victim of persecution under the Rákosi régime; Ferenc Donáth; Miklós Vásárhelyi; Gyula Kállai, a future prime minister; Lajos Fehér, member of the Politburo under the Kádár régime; and many others who rose to the top only to be toppled again, some surviving and others going to their deaths. Of the Communist members of the March Front, Ferenc Donáth was the driving force behind those anxious to forge closer links with the Communist Party.

The activities of the March Front in its original form lasted a little longer than one year. But the spirit survived, particularly in the National Peasant Party and its paper, *Szabad Szó* (Free Speech) founded in 1939 by populist writers. In addition, a host of literary and political initiatives on the eve of, and during, the Second World War bore its imprint, the most famous being the large get-together in 1943 of intellectuals at Szárszó on the shores of Lake Balaton.[14] The left wing of the populist movement, inspired by the spirit of 1848, also took part in the political and intellectual resistance to fascism and the war.

Among the numerous ramifications of the movement, special mention needs to be made of the opening in 1939 of Györffy College, so called after the great ethnologist who had been anxious to mould a new democratic élite sympathetic to the peasantry. Györffy College and Eötvös College were to become the seed beds for nurturing intellectual cadres in post-war Hungary. Numerous ex-pupils were to hold important posts after the war, not only in peasant and democratic parties, but also in the Communist Party.

Left-wing populism in fact represented an alternative to the Horthy régime, a régime steeped in a form of conservatism more suited to an earlier age and increasingly swamped by the extreme Right. The left-wing populists thus added a 'third force' to the stark alternative between capitalism and Communism, namely a platform for peasant democracy under the slogan of 'with the people, for the people'. Moreover, they were staunch anti-fascists and patriots. Unlike the right-wing populists, they refused to have any truck with the idea of a Nazi-fascist revolution.[15]

All in all, therefore, Marxist populists, most of whom had turned into Communists, had enough ideological affinities with the March Front to maintain, indeed to reinforce, the links existing between them. Needless to say, there was also a great deal of friction but, despite the differences, there were many occasions when the two joined forces during the war to organize the Resistance and to pave the way for a better future. Such legal opposition parties as the Social Democratic Party and the Smallholders' Party certainly provided stronger and politically more important factors in the creation of a national front, but the small populist group nevertheless proclaimed a more original message and one, in a sense, closer to the 'frontist' programme of the Communists.

It was partly for that reason that the involvement of Communists in various populist actions left a permanent trace on the post-war Hungarian Communist Party, and especially on the 'People's College Movement'. Its contacts with populism, and particularly with the March Front, gave even the HCP an original stamp, one that flew in the face of its sectarian tradition. It also provided the HCP with cadres drawn from various rural strata and hence with perceptions other than those of the cadres recruited from the working class or the petty bourgeoisie, partly Jewish, which made up the nucleus of the party at the end of the war.[16]

The Activities of the Communist Party 1941–1944

The Hungarian Communist Party recovered gradually and with difficulty from the double shock of the dissolution of its organizations in 1936 and the political and psychological effects of the German–Soviet pact in 1939. Its militants, dispersed and left without contacts or instructions, now concentrated their efforts on the trade unions, Social Democratic organizations and academic circles. Police reports often compared these activities to Communist actions in the French and Spanish Popular Fronts.[17] Thanks to Ferenc Rózsa (in 1939)[18] and to Zoltán Schönherz (who returned to Hungary in January 1940 for a spell of two months and again from December 1940 until his arrest in July 1942), the party could once more boast a central leadership and especially, as mentioned earlier, a new Central Committee (from January 1941).[19] From 1941, a party propaganda committee operated as well, run by Ferenc Földes, Gyula Kállai and Aladár Mód. Despite the undeniable efficiency of these new bodies, the work of the party rested essentially on the individual activity of its militants. In the early 1940s, Gyula Kállai, then a journalist on *Népszava* (Voice of the People, the organ of the Social Democratic Party) and Ferenc Donáth, like Kállai associated with a movement that had sprung from the March Front, played an important role in these activities, as did Géza Losonczy, Szilárd Ujhelyi, Lajos Fehér, Ferenc Hont, and such writers close to the party as György Bálint, Miklós Radnóti, József Fodor and dozens of others, especially in annexed Northern Transylvania.

Such future leaders of the legal Communist Party as János Kádár, István Szirmai, Márton Horváth, Sándor Zöld and Sándor Haraszti – to mention only a few – also played prominent roles, as, in other spheres, did Gács, Kenéz, László Orbán, Turai, Ságvári, László Pataki and many more. If we include militants in Czechoslovak, Rumanian and Yugoslav territories returned to Hungary, we can put the number of active Communists (many of them in prison for months or for years) whose names appear in various documents, memoirs and studies covering the history of the party during the first half of the 1940s, at between 200 and 300. Together with militants whose names we do not know, this would bring the strength of the party to about a thousand members, again including hundreds who were arrested in successive waves during the same period.[20] It is, however, difficult to determine which of them were actual party members and which of them were 'fellow travellers'. Again, documents and other writings published after 1945 are very sparing with information about Trotskyist militants or adherents of other 'heretical' factions – so much so that the figures given above cannot be considered to be more than approximations.

Among all these militants, a small group of a few dozen persons was involved in the organization and co-ordination of party activity, a few dozen more in purely regional or local activities, while by far the largest number of identifiable militants worked in youth organizations, trade unions, university and college groups, and on such legal newspapers and journals as the Social Democratic *Népszava* and the Peasants' *Szabad Szó*. The party, as such, is mentioned much less frequently in these publications than are its front organizations, the bodies it had infiltrated and the various anti-fascist and patriotic organizations which, its official history would claim, in 1945, were all fathered by the Communist Party. Until the summer of 1941, in any case, the party seems to have been paralysed, and it continued to lie low until the spring of 1942. Writing about the spring of that year, a Hungarian historian attached to the Party Institute of History has pointed out that the pamphlets issued by the party at that time were 'the first [of their kind] to appear after an interval of five years'.[21]

True, the leadership of the party had sown the seeds of this renewal with the creation of the 'independence front' in the spring of 1941,[22] and after June 1941 with the difficult launching of an anti-German national unity movement. Let us also note that the propaganda broadcasts by Hungarian émigrés in Moscow, especially over Radio Kossuth, inaugurated on 1 September 1941, were very slow in coming to terms with the new situation created by Hitler's attack.[23] Among the difficulties of adopting a broad anti-fascist programme we must also mention, quite apart from reservations expressed in the Communist Party itself, the reluctance of the Social Democrats. The latter, after a spell of collaboration with the Communists in the summer of 1941, developed second thoughts and preferred to act with prudence lest they jeopardize the legal existence of their own party and press. There were further objections from some dissident Communist groups, relatively important and influential in certain industrial sectors, who, for an even longer period, refused to adopt a frontist programme on the grounds that it ran counter to the spirit of class struggle. That was the view of the group round Pál Demény.

As far as we can tell from the records, the new line did not really get off the ground until the autumn of 1941, and then in theory more so than in practice. In a resolution dated 1 September 1941, the Central Committee invited 'the [home-based] leadership of the party to make contact with the most important bourgeois parties, including the leaders of the ruling party, for the sake of achieving national anti-German unity'.[24] It went on to invite the bourgeois parties concerned 'not to consider the Communist Party as an enemy but, on the contrary, as an ally'. In return, the Communist Party promised to keep within 'the limits of the Constitution' for the period of the proposed collaboration, and to make no attempt to 'change by the use of violence the existing political and social order'. The Party of Hungarian Communists, the document continued, 'will direct all its activities, its influence among the masses and its organizational strength against the common enemy, until such time as the common national objectives have been achieved'.[25]

The document refers to earlier resolutions, taken on 3 October 1940 and 2 April 1941 in particular, which are said to have been infused with the same spirit, but the existence of these resolutions has not so far been corroborated.[26] In any case, the resolution of September 1941 marked a new beginning, albeit a hesitant and difficult one. To the difficulties inherent in the sectarian character of the party must be added the lack of communication with the Soviet Union. To the best of its ability, Moscow did try to send emissaries to Hungary, among them Zoltán Schönherz, who returned to Budapest in 1940 to take charge of the new Popular Front line. After Schönherz's arrest and execution in 1942, others took over, among them Endre Ságvári, Gyula Kállai, János Kádár, László Rajk, Ferenc Donáth, Márton Horváth and other militants who had stayed in Hungary. These men, however, had lost all contact with Moscow. Moreover, throughout the war, the party's action programme and its future plans were being fashioned independently in Moscow and Hungary. The reconciliation of the resulting ideas and the co-ordination of party activities was to prove impossible in practice.

The testimony of militants shows even so that, in the autumn of 1941, the party became fired with the new spirit. Among the most important demonstrations of this new spirit, party historians cite the famous 'Christmas 1941 edition' of the Social Democratic *Népszava*. For the first time, this official working-class paper opened its columns to patriots as diverse as the Communist Gyula Kállai (who, of course, concealed his Communist identity), the conservative historian Gyula Szekfü, the future Resistance hero and martyr Endre Bajcsy-Zsilinszky, who had changed over from the Right, and several Socialist writers and journalists.

According to Gyula Kállai, the initiative came from the Communist Party and, though he does not actually say so, from himself. There is no reason to doubt the words of a man who helped to lead the Communist Party into the anti-German Resistance front. But which of his words are we to believe?

In the 1946 edition, Kállai still claims that the impetus had come from an agreement between the Communist Party and Árpád Szakasits, editor of *Népszava*,[27] but in the 1955 (the fourth) edition, the Social Democratic leader is no longer mentioned. The left-wing Social Democrats were by this stage labelled 'internal saboteurs' of the anti-fascist cause, men who had merely joined it as a subterfuge under the pressure of popular forces.[28] Yet, in a more recent autobiographical work, Kállai again emphasizes the crucial role of the editor of *Népszava*. When all was said and done, it was *Népszava* which had published the 1941 Christmas edition.

Communist historians place special emphasis on a second anti-German initiative, the foundation of the 'Hungarian Historical Memorial Committee' in the spring of 1942, and a third, the production and wide distribution of a badge commemorating

Petöfi, the poet of the 1848–9 Hungarian revolution and war of independence. In both cases (and also in the case of other, less widespread actions) the organizers invoked the independence struggle fought in centuries past.

The non-Communists on this committee included a number of personalities who were to play a part in the 1945 Hungarian democratic coalition government, among them the future prime minister Ferenc Nagy, the future president of the Republic Árpád Szakasits, and the renowned conservative historian and future ambassador to Moscow Gyula Szekfü. The Communist Party had ceased to concentrate its efforts on setting up front organizations for its underground activities or on infiltrating such legal organizations as the trade unions. Having emerged from its cocoon, the party began to fight openly for a place in post-war Hungary.

Many questions about its precise role in all these actions nevertheless remain unanswered. According to Gyula Kállai, the real initiative came from 'an illegal meeting with Rózsa',[29] accompanied by József Skolnik and Zoltán Schönherz. In fact, Rózsa's main task lay elsewhere: he had been instructed to set up a paper, the *Szabad Nép*, as the organ of the clandestine party. Its first issue appeared on 1 February 1942. The organization of various anti-German actions, such as the establishment of the Hungarian Historical Memorial Committee and the celebration, on 15 March 1942, of the anniversary of the 1848 revolution, fell to a group of artists and journalists, all of them regulars at a small restaurant, the Kulacs. In response to an invitation from that group, other persons, representing various trends, also joined the campaign. After several setbacks – the first application for a permit was turned down by the minister of the interior – the Historical Memorial Committee was founded in the middle of February. Its members comprised one or two Communists apart from Gyula Kállai, none, of course, revealing his true allegiance. Nor did they have much choice in that matter: apart from the danger they ran personally, they would have been endangering the lives of all the other non-Communist personalities who had signed the committee's appeal. Nevertheless the question remains to what extent this may be seen as a genuine manifestation of a united front between Communists and anti-fascist patriots, when its non-Communist committee members had no knowledge of acting in concert with members of an illegal party! According to Gyula Kállai, some of his associates, Endre Bajcsy-Zsilinszky among them, were anxious to know 'to what extent the united national-democratic front represented the political interests of the proletariat, the peasantry and the intelligentsia of Hungary, and to

what extent it represented the political line of Communists returned [secretly] from Moscow'.[30] Moreover, if Zsilinszky was, at
the time, told about Schönherz's mission 'to organize the independence movement in accordance with instructions from Moscow',[31]
Kállai says nothing about it.

From February to May 1942, there appeared four illegal issues of
Szabad Nép edited by Ferenc Rózsa (the paper would reappear in
September 1944). While declaring that the party was not strong
enough to play a leading role in the political life of Hungary and
that its political programme called for an 'independent, free and
democratic Hungary', the paper also insisted that the national unity
movement must be placed under 'the leadership of the working
class'. In another issue, *Szabad Nép* – which bore the subtitle 'The
paper of Mátyás Rákosi' – declared that 'it is we who carry the
March banner' (the banner of national independence representing
the spirit of March 1848).[32]

Such an approach was not very reassuring for non-Communist
patriots or, for that matter, for the Social Democrats who could not
have wanted to fight under the banner of Mátyás Rákosi and his
party. Luckily for the Communists, the other members of these
patriotic committees remained naïvely unaware of what *Szabad
Nép* was putting out as well as of the political affiliation of their
Communist associates. The police, by contrast, were exceedingly
well informed. In May 1942, the Communists were hit by the wave
of arrests which culminated in the murder of Rózsa in prison, the
execution of Schönherz and the conviction of numerous other
militants. The Memorial Committee was dissolved and, for two
years, until 1944, no comparable venture was started.

The HCP was never to recover from the blow it was dealt in
1942 and from the successive arrests. After its most prominent
leaders – József Skolnik, László Gács, István Kovács and others –
had disappeared behind prison walls, militants such as Ferenc
Donáth and Lajos Fehér were able to continue disseminating propaganda among intellectual circles and in some legal organizations.
The leadership now passed into the hands of János Kádár, secretary
of the party since the beginning of 1943 and of two new members
of the Central Committee: István Szirmai and Pál Tonhauser.

In 1943 the Hungarian Communist Party was put under another
strain: the dissolution of the Comintern on 15 May. Already out on
a limb, the party was thrown into total disarray. Its leaders felt that,
in the wake of the dissolution of the Communist International,
there was no justification for the party's further existence, at least
under its former name and form, that is to say as a section of the

Communist International. And so, at the beginning of June, the Central Committee decided on the dissolution of the HCP.

In the absence of any written sources, it is extremely difficult to reconstruct and evaluate the importance of this decision, the more so as Communist historians have given conflicting interpretations. According to the *History of the Hungarian Revolutionary Workers' Movement*,[33] the dissolution was purely cosmetic, the party reconstituting itself in June as the Peace Party. The *Historical Dictionary of the Workers' Movement*[34] gives the same version of the events but mentions a different date, namely July 1943. The then secretary of the Communist Party, János Kádár, as quoted in Gyula Kállai's memoirs, spoke of 'a break of several weeks in the activities of the party'. Kállai himself mentioned two meetings of the Central Committee in June without, however, specifying the agenda of either.[35] These facts suggest that, at the first meeting at the beginning of June, the old Central Committee declared the dissolution of the Communist Party and that at the second, a few weeks later, the foundation of the Peace Party with an enlarged Central Committee, including – in addition to János Kádár, István Szirmai and Pál Tonhauser – Gábor Péter, Ferenc Donáth and László Orbán.[36]

Following its dissolution, the party published a pamphlet explaining that by this act it hoped to facilitate 'the co-operation of other anti-Hitler parties and groups with the Communists'.[37] A sixteen-page pamphlet setting out the resolutions of the various Communist parties on the dissolution of the International produced a version similar to the one just given. By its dissolution, we read there, the Hungarian Communist Party 'facilitates the struggle against Hitler's Hungarian lackeys.' It also facilitates 'the union of anti-German forces . . . who considered our membership of the Comintern to be an obstacle.'[38]

However, in contradistinction to these texts, a number of extracts quoted in Kállai's memoirs, and also in the *History of the Hungarian Revolutionary Workers' Movement*, suggest that the party pamphlet announcing the dissolution was no more than a blind meant 'to conceal the Communist nature of the [new] party' the better to foster co-operation with other anti-German forces. Only access to the original document can enable us to clarify these contradictions; in any case, it seems strange that the party should have declared *publicly* in a pamphlet that it had dissolved itself purely for appearance's sake, the better to conceal the Communist nature of the Peace Party. This version of the events sounds like an amalgam of the resolutions passed and published in the pamphlet itself and of explanations issued for internal use only.[39]

One question accordingly remains unanswered. Did the party dissolve itself at the beginning of June without reconstituting itself under another name (in which case the decision to establish the Peace Party must have been taken several weeks later), or did the party decide to turn itself into the Peace Party there and then? This question would be of no more than incidental importance had it not given rise to numerous controversies at the time and also on several subsequent occasions.

According to Kállai's memoirs, the party's decision threw party members into disarray. In the end, however, everyone is said to have agreed that it was a decision that increased the chances of collaboration between the various anti-fascist forces.[40] On the other hand, this was not the view of Mátyás Rákosi or of the Moscow group. Even before their arrival in Hungary, they had criticized the decision by the Hungarian Communists to replace the HCP with the Peace Party in broadcasts transmitted over Radio Kossuth from the Soviet Union.[41] As will become clear to the reader, their objections would have a decisive influence on subsequent developments because, as soon as they returned from Moscow, they took over the leading posts in the Hungarian party. At the first subsequent party conference, Rákosi again directed his attacks against the leaders of the clandestine HCP who had 'dissolved our party and replaced it with another, called the Peace Party'.[42]

The historian Dezső Nemes, an influential member of the Politburo for many decades, condemned the decision to dissolve the party even more severely, calling it a 'liquidator's resolution'. In the second edition of his work, he toned down his condemnation and described the dissolution as a 'mistaken political act', rather than a destructive one, since, as he explained, the Central Committee dissolved the party only to set it up again in the same breath, albeit under a different name. He nevertheless pointed out that this explanation is not corroborated by any documents written at the time, and that the correction was only added in 1956 – according to the testimony 'of comrades who took part in the decision to dissolve the party'. Among these comrades, the first and foremost was undoubtedly János Kádár, secretary of the party at the critical juncture of the dissolution in 1943, imprisoned by Rákosi in 1951, freed and rehabilitated in 1954, first secretary of the party from November 1956 to May 1988. Dezső Nemes's own correction dates back to 1960.[43]

János Kádár was to pay dearly for the error of taking a different view of the dissolution of the Comintern from that of his comrades in Moscow. In 1945, he was brushed aside, and though he recovered, he was later packed off to prison. After his rehabilitation, he gave his version of the 1943 affair to the Central Committee and again in a published review of party history.[44] In addition to the known arguments – including the fact, according to Kádár, that the Communist Party and the Peace Party were a continuous whole – he cites the weakness of the Communist Party as a further explanation. He asserts, as already mentioned, that after the big wave of arrests in the summer of 1942, only ten or twelve Communists among the 400 to 500 party members remained in contact with one another. With great difficulty, their number was subsequently raised to between seventy and eighty, but after the arrest of the two party secretaries – Skolnik in December 1942 and István Kovács in February 1943 – the party had once again disintegrated. Kádár also draws attention to a point of the utmost importance: in 1941, all communications between the Hungarian Party and Moscow were cut, and continued to be so until the Red Army entered Hungary in 1944.

In these circumstances, the dissolution of the HCP and its transformation into the Peace Party seemed to Kádár and to his comrades the only way of ensuring the survival of a hard-pressed organization whose existence had become purely symbolic.

Dissolving the party, however, had meant breaking a taboo. Reconstructing it under a different name was at best undoing half the damage. This was where Kádár's error lay in the eyes of Moscow, and even in the eyes of those Communist historians who continue ritually to decry his mistake. Police repression, according to István Pintér,[45] was not decreased as a result of the dissolution, because the authorities quickly discovered that the Peace Party was nothing but the Communist Party in a different guise. Moreover, Pintér adds, the party did nothing by its metamorphosis to further the cause of the anti-fascist national front. 'Only large-scale mass actions could have forced the right wing of the independence movement to act in unison with the Communists.' And again: 'This task could not be accomplished by a mere change of name.'[46]

In reality, throughout this period, the Communist Party was as insignificant a force in Hungarian political life as ever. With ten militants, or even with ten times that number, it remained quite incapable of organizing 'large-scale mass actions'. Nor did anyone else wish to join the HCP in a common national campaign. It lacked both weight and credibility. Even after the victorious battle of Stalingrad, the Red Army was still too far away from the Hungarian frontier to make the Communists look like desirable political partners. Moreover, the party's conversion to the idea of national democratic unity, and the renunciation of its revolutionary plans, were still too recent and too faltering to look credible to parties which sought above all an end to the war and to the alliance with Hitler. Finally, the international situation was not favourable to the party either. The Allied landing in Sicily, the fall of Mussolini in 1943 and the armistice between the Allies and Italy led to a redoubling of efforts by the Hungarian government – then presided over by Miklós Kállay, who had succeeded László Bárdossy in 1942 – to reach agreement with the Anglo-Saxon powers. The prime minister stepped up diplomatic and semi-official representations in Rome, Berne, Stockholm, Lisbon and elsewhere.[47] He had no success, however, because his hands were tied by the threat of German intervention (which came in March 1944) and also because of his reluctance to offer military and political guarantees acceptable to the Allies. For all that, a growing section of public opinion had come to favour a rapprochement with the Western Allies; but not with the Soviet Union. In these circumstances and especially in view of the incompetence of Hungary's political rulers and the reluctance of the Allies, and the Americans in particular, to press for the liberation of Central Europe, the Communist Party simply stood no chance of making its voice heard.

All it could do was to build up the appeal of its national antifascist programme, its image as a possible partner and its propaganda against Hitler's war. A dozen or so pamphlets published by the Peace Party in 1943, the appearance of its official organ, *Béke és Szabadság* (Peace and Freedom) in March 1944, the redoubling of contacts with other parties and political personalities, the organization, above all in rural areas, of peace committees, bear witness to some revival of party activities. Outside Budapest, the party ran a clandestine press at Kolozsvár (Cluj). While its new line was impeccably patriotic and anti-Nazi, the party nevertheless failed to realize that only the established political forces were capable of extricating Hungary from its terrible plight. Moreover, by calling ceaselessly for the overthrow of the Kállay regime,[48] the party cut itself off from the consensus that had begun to be forged between the opposition parties and pro-Allied government circles. Contact with these circles, including the prime minister, would be all the more important as Horthy's entourage supported this current of opinion.

What with these conditions and the prevailing balance of forces, the most fruitful initiative came, in the spring of 1943, from two important opposition parties: the Social Democrats and the Smallholders. In two successive memoranda, the two parties tried to persuade the government to withdraw from the war and to adopt a policy of strict neutrality. Their common efforts culminated on 19 August 1943 in the signing of a pact: the two parties promised to act in unison all along the line, parliament included. The pact excited great interest in the press and among other democratic parties and groups. A common front was born.

The Peace Party also welcomed the initiative; yet it deplored the lack of militancy and its own exclusion from the front. Relations between Communists and Social Democrats were by this time at their lowest ebb. According to János Kádár, Árpád Szakasits, the secretary of the Social Democratic Party – the only Socialist leader to maintain contacts with the Communists – insisted that co-operation was contingent on a Communist renunciation of illegal activity. In the Smallholders' Party, the Communists' only contact was Endre Bajcsy-Zsilinszky, and then only through Gyula Kállai who did not reveal his Communist affiliation until the autumn of 1944.[50]

The creation of a national anti-German front led by the HCP was therefore never on the cards. The available documents suggest, moreover, that the Moscow group of Hungarian Communists was much more enthusiastic and understanding about the agreement between the two opposition parties than were their comrades at home, and that the comrades in Moscow even called for an extension of the nascent common front to include the Christian 'Right' as well as the Communist 'Left'.[51]

It should also be noted that, from the summer of 1943, under the influence of the Soviet victories on the Eastern Front and the Allied successes in Italy, the extreme Right lost support, while the trade unions and the Social Democrats gained considerably in strength.[52] This led to the radicalization of some of the rank and file (especially among the miners) a process that, however, went hand in hand with an increase in anti-Communist sentiments.

In his brief account of the origins of the Peace Party, János Kádár also declared, with a touch of humour, that the Peace Party succeeded in making contact with other anti-fascist parties and personalities 'less because of its change of name' than 'thanks to the German occupation' of Hungary.[53] Indeed, when Admiral Horthy returned from a stormy meeting with Hitler on 19 March 1944, he discovered that his German ally had furtively occupied his beloved country: Kállay was dismissed; General Sztójay, the former Hungarian ambassador in Berlin, was instructed to form a new pro-German government. This time, quite apart from most of the

Communists still at liberty, aristocrats bearing historic names, democratic and Social Democratic politicians, Poles who had fled to Hungary in 1939, anti-German officers and even, a little later, Miklós Kállay, the former prime minister, himself were arrested. The operation was directed by the Gestapo relying on a list drawn up in Berlin. All opposition parties were dissolved – and joined the Communists in the world of underground politics.[54]

Despite the difficult conditions, a Hungarian Front emerged in May 1944, as a forerunner of the National Front born in the following December. The Hungarian Front originally comprised the Social Democrats, the left wing of the Smallholders' Party, Communists from the Peace Party and the League of the Patriarchal Cross, a monarchist anti-fascist organization. At first, the National Peasant Party was not admitted because of objections from the Smallholders' Party, but it was allowed to join in September 1944, as were representatives of organizations from the Catholic and the Protestant Resistance movements. Árpád Szakasits was elected president of the executive committee of the Hungarian Front at the beginning of September 1944.

In September, events followed one another in quick succession. The second Ukrainian Front of General Malinovsky entered Transylvania and crossed the Hungarian border. Rumania, which had fallen the month before, signed an armistice with the Soviet Union on 12 September. Admiral Horthy had decided to do the same on the 10th but it took him a whole month to get as far as putting his name to a preliminary armistice (in Moscow on 11 October), which he followed up, on the 15th, with an ill-prepared public declaration; it led to his overthrow and a bloody seizure of power by the Hungarian fascists, the Arrow Cross Party, about whom we shall be hearing more.[55]

In September and early October 1944, a less tragic outcome had still been on the cards. To the Communists, the situation had seemed hedged with fears yet full of hope: fears long expressed in party newspapers and pamphlets that, by making concessions, the Horthy régime might yet save its skin and survive; hope that negotiations with the Soviet Union might facilitate the re-entry of the Communist Party into Hungarian political life. Cut off as they were from Moscow, the Hungarian Communists could not have known that neither was on the list of Soviet priorities. The resuscitation of the HCP was the least of Moscow's worries as, on the one hand, it would have to come at the end (not the beginning) of the armistice negotiations and, on the other hand, it should take place in Moscow and involve the Moscow group of Hungarian

Communists rather than the minuscule illegal group inside be-leaguered Hungary, about whose very existence the Soviet leaders knew nothing. The quick succession of events during October and November in Moscow, and later in eastern Hungary (to be examined in the next chapter), shows that this was indeed the scenario envisaged by Stalin and Molotov and also by the command of the Red Army.

Nor did the Soviet leaders share the Hungarian Communists' fears that the men of the 'old régime' might yet manage to save their own skins. On the contrary, for military as well as for tactical reasons, Stalin wanted Hungary to move into the anti-German camp, preferably without a break in political and legal continuity. A direct result of this wish was that such hostile countries as Rumania and Hungary were in a better position to hang on to their institutions than were such friendly German-occupied countries as Poland or Czechoslovakia. Hungary had no government-in-exile to demand the reinstatement of the legal government deposed by the Germans; nor did Hungary suffer the same institutional and administrative void as existed in, say, Poland. It was accordingly with the existing régime if not with the existing *men* that Moscow wished to reach an agreement. On this specific level, there was an appreciable gap not only between Soviet realism and Hungarian Communist make-believe, but also, as we shall see, between the Soviet leaders and Hungarian émigrés in Moscow. For the latter, seeking an agreement with Horthy's men was utterly out of the question.

If there had been an anti-German insurrection in Hungary, would it have altered these attitudes? It is impossible to say but, in any case, the uprisings in Warsaw, Prague and in Slovakia demonstrated the limited prospects of such heroic endeavours together with the determination of the Soviets to have the last say on all military and political initiatives. Helping or encouraging a national insurrection at the risk of promoting the emergence of an autonomous national political force was not something the Soviet government favoured, any more than they wished to see (at least outside Poland) an insurrection of the revolutionary type able to raise the Communist Party into a dominant position before Moscow thought the time was ripe and in the face of strong protests from the Allies. All these factors combined inclined the Soviets to look for an agreement with Horthy's representatives.

Moreover, theoretical considerations apart, an insurrection was not a realistic option, firstly because of the internal weakness of the Hungarian Communist Party and secondly, as we saw, because of the external circumstances. In September 1944, two months before the tragic death of the military leaders of the Resistance, the party, abandoning its cover name, published several proclamations and manifestos to announce its return to the political scene under the name of Communist Party (and no longer Party of Hungarian Communists, Section of the Communist International, as it had been called in full immediately prior to its dissolution in 1943). At the same time its clandestine paper, *Szabad Nép*, reappeared, now in cyclostyled form. Meanwhile Kádár had fallen into the hands of the police without his identity becoming known; but several other militants managed to go to ground, with the result that in September a small nucleus was able to constitute a party Central Committee. At its head was László Rajk, a veteran of the Spanish Civil War, a man who had just come out of prison. According to Gyula Kállai's memoirs, the new Central Committee also included Bertalan Bartha, Ferenc Donáth, Márton Horváth, Károly Kiss, László Orbán and Gábor Péter.

The party programme was attuned to what was to become the dominant political line: the concentration of all efforts on opposition to Hitler and on strengthening the united resistance movement. As a member of the Hungarian Front, the Communist Party was a co-signatory of two memoranda addressed to Admiral Horthy, who in the end received the representatives of two of the signatory bodies, those of the Smallholders' Party and those of the Social Democratic Party. The audience took place on 11 October in Budapest, four days before Horthy announced from the capital the end of hostilities against the Red Army.

The Communist Party had been given no opportunity of attending the armistice negotiations being conducted simultaneously in Moscow. It is difficult, perhaps impossible, to determine whether the party was left out because of its weakness or because of its unyielding opposition to the Horthy régime. In any event, the documents are full of contradictory statements. In its manifesto of September 1944, the party, under its new name, violently attacked the 'see-saw' policy practised by Kállay before March 1944, and also that of General Lakatos, appointed by Horthy to get rid of the pro-German Sztójay and so call a halt to the national catastrophe. Even if the Communist Party did eventually moderate its attitude to Horthy it missed no opportunity to issue such battle-cries as 'Death to the German occupiers! Death to the Szeged crime syndicate and to the nation's assassins!' The allusion was clearly to the 'Szeged idea', the anti-Communist crusade of which Horthy had made himself the standard-bearer in 1919.[56]

In his account of the events of October 1944, Gyula Kállai nevertheless deplored the fact that the regent did not agree to receive, with the representatives of the democratic opposition parties, that of the Communist Party which was thus being 'isolated'.[57] Let it be noted, however, that László Rajk, though snubbed by the regent, nevertheless had contacts with Horthy's entourage, and that the Communist Party helped, through other members of the Hungarian Front, to pave the way for Horthy's attempt on 15 October to declare the end of the country's participation in the war.

Let it also be recalled that at the same time, in October 1944, the small group of clandestine CP leaders succeeded in reaching an agreement with Árpád Szakasits which included a call for the common struggle of the two workers' parties against fascism and expressed a wish for formal unification in the future.[58] This document has given rise to a number of controversies, some Social Democrats questioning its authenticity, others its claim to be representative, on the grounds that it was signed by only one leader of the SDP, namely Árpád Szakasits, the other signatory being Gyula Kállai for the CP.

The events of 15 October plunged the country into tragedy and chaos. Badly drafted, Horthy's declaration over the radio had no positive results. The army, the pride of the Horthy régime, chose not to follow the orders of its 'supreme war lord', to whom it was bound by a solemn oath of loyalty and obedience. A few hours after the regent's declaration, the Hungarian Nazi Party, the Arrow Cross, with Ferenc Szálasi and a few other diehard supporters of Hitler at its head, seized power. Next day, Admiral Horthy, surrendering to German blackmail, withdrew his armistice declaration, signed his abdication and appointed Szálasi prime minister. The manhunts began, the deportations of Jews were speeded up, men dressed in green shirts and Arrow Cross armbands committed unspeakable atrocities. The Gestapo, with the help of its Hungarian faithful, took over the functions of the police and took reprisals. At the same time, the *Wehrmacht* prepared to turn Budapest into a fortress: the German war machine was determined to hold back the Soviet Army in the face of all reasonable expectations – at Pest, on the left bank of the Danube until mid-January 1945, and at Buda, on the right bank, until mid-February. Inside this city, incinerated and bled white during four months of a siege bereft of reason, the future was being prepared. But what future? With whom? For what alternative?

The only certainties were the collapse of the régime on the one hand and the irresistible advance of the Red Army on the other. The Second Ukrainian Front of Marshal Malinovsky and the Third Front of Marshal Tolbukhin were preparing to converge in a pincer movement on the Hungarian capital. The Hungarian state and administration had to all intents and purposes ceased to exist. Power was in the hands of assassins, the Hungarian Army in the grip of the *Wehrmacht*, Horthy himself a captive of the Germans – in short, Hungary had become a political vacuum.[59]

The Soviets, however, as will appear when we come to look at events in Moscow during those months, were not over-concerned about these conditions and continued to negotiate with the handful of representatives of the crumbling régime who happened to be in their midst, either as members of the armistice delegation, or as those very few senior officers who had gone over to the Soviet side in accordance with orders issued on 15 October. We shall return to them in the next chapter.

Inside Hungary, all that was left of the anti-Nazi resistance movement, apart from a few resistance pockets, was a handful of politicians in the legal opposition parties who had earlier set up the Hungarian Front with Communist Party participation. They had little to hope for from Horthy and his entourage. Because of the intensity of the Nazi terror, all contacts were difficult and dangerous. Nevertheless, amid all the disorder of 15 October, several prominent opposition members, detained since the country's occupation on 19 March, were released or managed to escape from prison, and hastened to strengthen the ranks of the Resistance. The strongest personality among them, Endre Bajcsy-Zsilinszky, took over the organization of the armed resistance struggle. At the end of November, the National Front set up under his chairmanship the Liberation and National Insurrection Committee with the support of a handful of determined men, including several high-ranking army officers. Caught in an ambush, they were all arrested and put to death.

Hunted and cut down, many members of this heroic but ineffective Resistance movement nevertheless survived. We shall find them back in the institutions and the political life of post-war Hungary, first at Debrecen, the provisional capital, and later in liberated Budapest.

-6-

From Moscow to Budapest

During the whole of this period, the future of Central and Eastern Europe, and hence of Hungary, was being decided against the backcloth of the Second World War: by military operations and at inter-Allied meetings in Teheran, Moscow and Yalta.

While the Communist Party and its political partners in Budapest joined forces in the Hungarian Front to shape their country's future, Churchill and Stalin shared out their respective spheres of influence in the region at their famous meeting in Moscow on 9 October 1944.[1] We shall return to this matter.

This bargain – reflecting the fortunes of war that had raised the Soviet Union to the position of supreme arbiter – explains just one aspect of a vast and controversial question, namely that the bargain merely defined the 'maximum' and 'minimum' military and political concessions either side was prepared to make.[2] It seems unlikely that Stalin and his advisers had drawn up a clear-cut and consistent line of approach for all the countries in the region. As a result, the Hungarian Communist Party, and above all its Muscovite wing, were unable to draw up plans based solely on ideological or national considerations; the future of Hungary was being examined separately in the Kremlin and in the Hungarian party, the latter trying to adapt itself as best it could to Moscow's political and military interests and to put itself into the most advantageous possible position.

The 'Muscovites'

This page in the party's history is still to be documented satisfactorily. Hungarian-language books and journals published in the Soviet Union, including the journal *Új Hang* (New Voice) (1938–41) tell us practically nothing about the elaboration of the policies to be pursued after the liberation of Hungary. The news and commentaries broadcast by Radio Kossuth, the Hungarian station opened in Moscow in 1941 before being moved elsewhere, have not been published. The memoirs of Hungarian émigrés in the Soviet Union devote little space to politics. Decimated and stunned by the purges that took a hundred times as many lives as the anti-Communist repression in Hungary after the end of the White Terror in 1919–20, the Muscovite émigré group counted its losses while angling for the best position against a return to Hungary after the war.

It is impossible to put figures to what survived, during this period, of a once large and flourishing Hungarian Communist colony. Let it be recalled that, of the tens of thousands of Hungarian soldiers fighting with the Red Army in 1918, 3,000 to 4,000 had had regular contact with the party's central organization,[3] that many others subsequently followed suit and that a great many militants left Hungary for Russia after the disaster of 1919 and during the next twenty years. Even if we allow for many hundreds returning to Hungary to carry out clandestine work or for other reasons, the Hungarians remaining in Moscow were still to be counted in their thousands.

Hungarian Communists in general fell victim to various 'blood-lettings'. Apart from the several hundreds sent on clandestine missions, 400 to 500 Hungarians fought with the International Brigades in Spain. Others – we cannot tell how many – fought Hitler in the ranks of the Red Army. Finally, old émigrés, militants and simple citizens of their adopted communist fatherland, soldiers back from Spain and, later, from the Second World War, were swallowed up by the Stalinist terror in vast numbers. There are no precise figures, only estimates. What is certain is that the 'political class' among the émigrés, those who gravitated round the Comintern and the Muscovite centre of the HCP, were more vulnerable to the repression than those Hungarians who had become simple Soviet citizens or were employed as ordinary workers or in lowly jobs. There is very little information about this aspect of the history of the HCP in Moscow – it would be necessary to assemble all the documents pertaining to the rehabilitation of purge victims together with hundreds of individual biographies to reconstruct it. But even if that were done, the fate of hundreds of others, of simple militants without title or rank, would still be left out of account. As for the better-known of the Hungarian émigrés, certain details about them are to be found in the biographical notes to such publications as the *Selected Documents from the History of the*

Hungarian Workers' Movement, in several monographs and in the *Historical Dictionary of the Workers' Movement*.[4]

There is also some literary testimony, for example the fictional and autobiographical work of József Lengyel, a writer who returned to his native Hungary in 1955, after seventeen years as a deportee. One of the most interesting accounts can be found in the second volume of Endre Sik's autobiography, published in Budapest in 1970 but later withdrawn from circulation.[5] In the first pages we are told of the arrest of Lajos Magyar, the famous sinologist and expert on the Asian mode of production; in nearly every other chapter, we learn about the disappearance of other comrades who were never to return after the purges: Károly Hisma, János Matejka, Sándor Barta, Frigyes Karikás, József Madzsar (a physician and former chief editor of the party's theoretical journal), Ignác Sorger, the orientalist, and many more. Sik's book also gives us some idea of the fear, suspicion and denunciation rife among émigrés, indeed among all foreigners – be they of Hungarian, German or other origin. The testimony of Sik, who was to become Hungary's minister of foreign affairs in the 1960s, throws a great deal of light on these dark years, but he too was acquainted with no more than a small number of cases. Only a fraction of these émigrés worked in the Comintern apparatus, in its schools, in the Marx-Engels Institute and in other well-known central institutions. Now, it is the names of these prominently placed men which keep cropping up, as they do in Sik's book, in a host of biographical notes to recently published books, all ending with the stereotyped rider: 'In 193—, he fell victim to the unlawful acts committed during the Stalinist period.'

In his memoirs, Zoltán Vas quotes an appeal by Hungarian émigrés in Moscow, exhorting the people of Hungary to fight for their country's independence. This appeal was signed by Béla Balázs, László Dienes, Andor Gábor, Sándor Gergely, Gyula Háy, Béla Illés, Julia Kenyeres, Sarolta Lányi, Endre Lilienthal, Ferenc Szabó, Jolán Szilágyi, Béla Uitz, Dezsö Vozáry, Erzsébet Andics, Gizella Berzeviczi, Elek Bolgár, Béla Fogarasi, Ernö Gerö, György Lukács, József Révai, László Rudas, Jenö Varga, Mária Csorba, Dr Andor Havas, István Hunya, Dr Rezsö Kertész, János Lakota, Ferenc Münnich, Imre Nyári, György Nyisztor, Dr Zoltán Pártos, Mátyás Rákosi, László Sajó, Zoltán Szántó, Zoltán Vas and Mihály Farkas. As Vas explained, several others, including István Friss, György Kilián, Elek Borkanyuk, Richárd Rózsa, Ferenc Pataki, Ferenc Biró, Rezsö Szántó and Imre Nagy were unable to add their signatures because they were away on special duty.[6]

The list also includes names – for instance those of several writers – that do not appear on pages devoted to the political history of the party. We could add many others, but even so the list would remain far from complete.

Some were more at home in the Soviet Union than in their native Hungary, among them the famous economist Jenö Varga and the painter Béla Uitz; others were too much out of favour to obtain authorization to return to Hungary, including Béla Kun's family; Ernö Czóbel, Ryazanov's former associate and a brother of the painter Béla Czóbel; and the engineer Gyula Hevesi, a people's commissar during the life of the Hungarian Communist Republic.

The war offered a new chance to old émigrés and also to the 'second generation' born or raised in the Soviet Union. They were detailed to see to the welfare of Hungarian prisoners of war, to be their teachers and interpreters, and to staff 'anti-fascist schools'. The foremost of these, at Krasnogorsk, situated in a large POW camp for several nationalities, was used to train future German, Rumanian, Hungarian and other cadres. The training of prisoners earmarked to serve as partisans was also actively pursued. Many members of the younger generation of Hungarian émigrés, moreover, were specially trained to serve on missions with the army, the intelligence and propaganda services in the Soviet Union and also, after the war, in their native land.

All these activities were part and parcel of the plans of a belligerent power preparing to enter a foreign country and to take political control for what was, in theory, an interim period. This task demanded a large staff: hundreds of adequately trained, Hungarian-speaking persons. The actual policies they were expected to implement were, of course, elaborated at a higher level where there were a very small number of Hungarian émigrés. It was from this select group that the future party leaders and highest government officials were recruited.

For so important a group of political émigrés these higher posts were few in number and mostly reserved for faithful hacks rather than for politicians of any stature. Was it that Stalin, anxious to still the fears of his allies, tried to avoid swamping Hungary with men of real ability? At all events, the staff was necessarily made up of those who had escaped the purges which had virtually wiped out the party's élite. The magnitude of these purges reflected the size of the Hungarian emigration. In addition to thousands of 'unknown persons', nearly all political figures of any note had disappeared.

In 1929, some twenty Communists, all of them prominent members of the Hungarian Club in Moscow, were arrested –

following a denunciation by Béla Kun who, in order to get rid of awkward opponents, had accused them of being involved in a Trotskyist plot. Luckily for them, Kun's real motives were discovered and the accused were released.[7] Next came Kirov's assassination, on 1 December 1934, and the subsequent arrest of Lajos Magyar. After that, the entire Hungarian élite was cut down in successive waves and practically annihilated during the wave of 1937–8.

Béla Kun's case is just one among many, but it serves as a good illustration of the methods employed. His own importance, moreover, justifies a brief account of his ultimate fate. Though often criticized, Béla Kun remained, until the middle of the 1930s, *the* historic leader of the Hungarian party, and also one of the best-known figures in the Communist International.[8] His eclipse started in 1934 when, as a member of a Comintern sub-committee charged with preparing the Seventh Congress, he adopted attitudes that were increasingly hostile to the party's new Popular Front Line, a radical departure of which few members of the sub-committee had had the least inkling, certainly not before the summer of 1934. Dimitrov was still calling for a Communist-led anti-fascist front. By July, however, he had tabled the prickly question of closer ties with the Social Democrats on the agenda. Kun refused to go along with this and preferred to stick to his 'sectarian' view of the Social Democrats. Nor did he apparently appreciate the connection between the Franco-Soviet non-aggression pact and the need to revise his attitude towards the Socialists. On 14 November 1934, in a memorandum addressed to the secretariat of the executive committee of the Comintern, Kun attacked an article by Thorez and the declaration of the French party published in *L'Humanité* on 7 November. According to Kun, the new policy was tantamount to a rejection of the dictatorship of the proletariat and nothing more than 'vulgar coalition politics'.[9]

In any case, at the meeting of the Seventh Congress on 25 July 1935, Kun's eclipse was demonstrated in a spectacular way: he was not invited to join leading Comintern officials on the platform. And so he sulked in the corridors and in the buffet. Worse still, back in a hall which rose to its feet when Manuilsky walked in, Kun remained seated. Kun's speech, while expressing no clear opposition to the new policy, proved to be lacklustre and superficial. He was allowed to keep his post on the executive committee, but was not elected to the presidium.

After the congress, Ferenc Huszti, head of the Hungarian delegation and Béla Kun's loyal comrade, called on Manuilsky to seek an explanation for the snub Kun had received. He was given several: Kun had defended Lajos Magyar who was arrested after Kirov's assassination; he had criticized Manuilsky's line after Manuilsky had succeeded Zinoviev; he had attended a soirée given by Kamenev, who had been expelled from the party; as early as 1926 he had proposed rescinding Trotsky's expulsion; he had opposed the French Popular Front programme.[10]

The charges against Kun were at one and the same time charges against the Hungarian party which, like Kun himself, was proving sluggish over the adoption of the new Popular Front Line. The 'Kun affair' had only just begun. In March 1936, Kun still received two visits from André Malraux accompanied by Herbert and Ervin Sinkó. They talked about literature and music following two attacks on Shostakovich by *Pravda*. However, by then Kun had grown afraid of making his views public.[11]

In May, the executive committee of the Comintern decided to dissolve the Central Committee of the Hungarian Communist Party, a decision which, as we saw, threw the party into disarray.[12] Kun was expelled from the party leadership and ordered to appear before the international control committee of the Comintern, as were Ferenc Huszti, Pál Sebes and Imre Komor. All these three were arrested; the first two died in prison.

Kun himself continued to walk free. As a member of the executive committee of the Comintern he was entitled to appear before that committee's secretariat, consisting of Dimitrov, Togliatti, Gottwald, Kuusinen, Manuilsky, Marty and Pieck. His case was heard in September 1936, but it is not known which members of the secretariat – beside Dimitrov and Manuilsky and a few alternate members including Arvo Tuominen – were actually present.[13]

In addition to the complaints voiced by Manuilsky after the Seventh Congress, almost the whole of Kun's life was passed in review: his sectarian attitude, his methods, his factional tendencies, his errors, his irresponsibility. Utterly broken, he then confessed to everything except for a number of particularly insulting charges. He was stripped, not only of his position in the Hungarian Party, but also of his post in the Comintern.

According to two depositions, that of his widow and that of his physician, Kun was nevertheless still received by Stalin, Molotov and Kaganovich, all of whom promised to find him a new post. Eventually, after having been kept waiting for several months, Kun was appointed editor of a publishing house. In the meantime his old friends Kamenev and Zinoviev had been sentenced and executed. Then, in June 1937, several papers in Hungary and elsewhere

announced Kun's arrest. However, all these reports were premature. According to Mme Kun, Stalin even telephoned Kun and
asked him to issue a denial of this false piece of information. A few
days later, on 29 June, Kun *was* arrested. The date and circumstances surrounding his death are not known. He probably died on
30 November 1939, or even before according to more recent
information.

After Kun's arrest, Romain Rolland, to whom Ervin Sinkó had
sent an appeal to intervene, returned an evasive reply: he hoped
others would feel free to comply and that Kun might yet be able to
prove his innocence. Rolland added that he was reading Mathiez's
books on Robespierre and that the two periods and the two
situations looked similar to him, down to the infiltration of the
Committee of Public Safety by foreign agents. The only difference
was that at the time of the French Revolution there had been no
powerful nation on whom one could count as one could on Russia
at the present time.[14]

Béla Kun was a complex man, difficult to judge from his writings and from the conflicting reports about his actions and his
character. It is also not easy to appreciate the effect on him of the
long years he spent in Comintern circles and in the famous Lux
Hotel. Though he had the courage to stand up to the men in power
(Lenin, Manuilsky) from time to time, in the end the Comintern
apparatus broke his resilience. Vain and ambitious, he tried to
please, to succeed whatever the cost. There is no doubt that he was
a gifted man, full of good intentions, intelligence and idealism,
qualities that enabled him, at the age of thirty-three, to command
the attention not only of his Communist comrades but also of
many Hungarian Socialists of the old school. At the time, he
appeared as an energetic leader and a kind of 'moderate extremist',
capable of swaying crowds but also of conducting skilful political
and diplomatic negotiations, of seeming implacable, indeed cruel,
even while attempting to contain the terror and to avoid excesses.
Kun's main faults were therefore those of a whole generation of
revolutionaries who believed they could change the course of
history by copying the methods of the Russian Bolsheviks. This
also explains Kun's doctrinaire attitude, his extravagant language,
his outbursts, his inability to appreciate the incongruity of his
position: a petty bourgeois of Jewish descent bearing the mantle of
a revolutionary leader. To maintain his position, be it for only a
few months, he needed a hefty dose of exaltation.

It was in Moscow above all that other traits of his personality
began to appear. Mistrustful, suspicious and scheming, he dis-

patched hundreds of militants on hazardous missions, waged war on the Landler wing without scruple and resorted to denunciation. His authority was undermined as a result, but he nevertheless continued to be held in some regard, though probably not as a really great man. But then he had never been more than a middle-ranker with a remarkable past, a proven organizer, a leader of men and an acknowledged polemicist. In addition, he was full of seductive charm and personal magnetism, qualities, in short, that did not necessarily reflect great strength of character or above-average intellectual powers.

After the disappearance of such 'historic figures' as Jenö Landler, who had died much earlier, and Béla Kun's liquidation in 1937, the Hungarian party was left leaderless. It ceased to play a role of any importance in the Comintern and failed to throw up any figures of greater renown than Manuilsky's secretary Ernö Gerö, Jenö Varga, József Révai, Béla Szántó and other minor party bureaucrats.

The official HCP representative in the Comintern was Sándor Poll until his death in 1937, followed, in 1938, by Zoltán Szántó, who had been dismissed from his post of secretary of the central committee,[15] and, in 1940, by Ernö Gerö. People holding that post in the Comintern were not necessarily the real leaders of the HCP. Neither were the titular party secretary Lajos Papp, who lived in Paris, or his predecessors considered the true leaders. That distinction had been tacitly reserved for Béla Kun, at least until his downfall. After Kun, no Hungarian Communist, with the exception of Rákosi languishing in a Hungarian gaol, would be included in the executive committee of the Communist International nor would any be looked up to as the leading comrade.

Admittedly, Gerö had acquitted himself well in the eyes of the Comintern, acting as their agent and that of the Soviet secret service, especially in France,[16] and later during the Spanish Civil War, and being appointed Manuilsky's secretary on his return to Moscow. As a result, he did acquire considerable authority in the Hungarian party while a power vacuum continued to exist. He was, so to speak, the party's caretaker chief.

According to Zoltán Vas,[17] who arrived in Moscow in Rákosi's company at the end of 1940, Gerö was besides being Rákosi's stand-in – he handed over the reins to Rákosi in 1941 – also his rival and the party's *éminence grise*. Thanks to his close contacts with the Comintern, the Soviet party and the police, Gerö was said to enjoy access to many doors that remained closed to Rákosi. Thus, even while accepting the fact that he was officially no more than No. 2, Gerö retained a crucial say in affairs of the utmost importance. He is even supposed to have given daily instructions to Rákosi himself. According to Vas, Gerö, more so even than Farkas and Rákosi, officially in charge of police affairs, was the real 'brain' behind the so-called 'conceptual' case against Rajk.

But to return to 1940–1, the arrival of Rákosi at the beginning of 1941 changed the situation in Moscow, though Rákosi's promotion was neither immediate nor obvious. It is not known precisely when and thanks to whom – Stalin, Dimitrov or Manuilsky? – Rákosi ended up as leader. In 1941, he replaced Gerö in the Comintern, having been one of its honorary leaders since the Seventh Congress had elected him, Horthy's prisoner, to the executive committee. Another omen: *Szabad Nép*, the party paper published illegally in 1942, called itself the 'paper of Mátyás Rákosi'. In any case, several witnesses have declared that, soon after his arrival in Moscow, he was able to secure control of the HCP. And he was well placed to get to the top: assistant people's commissar in 1919, Comintern delegate to the 1921 congress of the Italian Communist Party, member of the executive committee of the Comintern, a man who had spent sixteen years in Hungarian prisons, far from party factional fights and Comintern intrigues. Persistent rumours about his having broken down after his arrest under Horthy – he is supposed to have betrayed party secrets and the names of comrades – were not, it seems, held too strongly against him.

It so happens that all these allegations were based on Rákosi's having admitted some of his activities to the Hungarian court, including the fact he had represented the Comintern at the Italian Party congress in Livorno. Notwithstanding the allegations in several publications devoted to the subject, however, most of these 'secrets' had been leaked by the Hungarian press well before his trial; no evidence of more serious lapses has ever been produced,[18] so much so that, once he had explained his position in Moscow, it was decided to let the whole matter drop. Needless to say, the dossier containing the charges against him, slender though it was, was retained, to be used against him should the occasion arise.

In Moscow, Rákosi's associates, besides Gerö and Révai, though at a lower level, were his former prison comrade Zoltán Vas, one of the party's most energetic officials, and Mihály Farkas, alternate member of the executive committee of the Comintern and until 1943 secretary of the International Young Communist League.

With their petty bourgeois or bourgeois Jewish backgrounds, few of these new leaders had the ideal qualities to recommend them to their compatriots once the war was over. They were neverthe-less placed, with one or two exceptions, at the head of the party in 'liberated' Hungary. They owed their promotion to their links with the Comintern, with Soviet leaders and with Soviet institutions. The same was true of the stratum immediately below them: Zoltán Szántó, József Gábor, Lajos Bebrits, Géza Révész, Sándor Nógrádi, Endre Sik and others. Some of these party officials, for instance Elek Bolgár and István Friss, had moreover spent relatively few years in Moscow. In the upper echelons, no more than one, Imre Nagy, had a peasant background and did not belong to the Comintern establishment. None was of proletarian origin. Such was the composition of the leading group that left Moscow to take charge of the Hungarian Communist Party in Szeged, then in Debrecen and finally in Budapest, behind the lines of the Red Army racing towards Berlin.

Their policies were a variant of the Popular Front line: a broad anti-fascist alliance of parties and classes and a call for a so-called advanced democratic society, that is one that went beyond 'formal' bourgeois democracy but not nearly as far as the dictatorship of the proletariat. The great revolutionary, proletarian and socialist design of old had apparently been consigned to the Greek calends; the new project was a people's or a 'new' democracy.

Yet this project left too many questions open to be applied immediately and universally. Despite Stalin's promise to his allies (the Soviet system was not for export to Eastern Europe), there was great uncertainty about the precise complexion of the future. Was the people's democracy really to be a permanent structure or was it merely a transition to the dictatorship of the proletariat, that is, to a Soviet system under another name?

Many purely practical problems were similarly left unanswered. There was to be an alliance of parties and classes, but precisely of which ones? In Hungary, to start with, could such an alliance possibly embrace Horthy's conservative, anti-Nazi, Right? What then was to be done with the regent and those of his ministers and generals who were prepared to turn their backs on their former German ally and to adapt to the new political constellation? A whole series of matters concerning the economy, the constitutional form of the State, the property system depended or seemed to depend on the answers to all these questions. Moreover, would the 'new democracy' be a parliamentary democracy, with political parties as its mainspring, or would it be run from the bottom upwards, through local committees, councils, and so on, as the direct representatives of the will of the people?

The question of collaboration with the anti-German wing of the political class round Horthy would, as may readily be seen, resolve itself automatically as a result of the vacillation of these circles. Solutions to the other problems, as may be seen just as readily, were harder to find.

The Final Preparations

The attempts by the regent, Miklós Horthy, and his set to extricate Hungary from Hitler's war impinged no more than remotely on the history of the underground Communist Party (the Peace Party).[19] The party's immediate objective was to organize resistance to the war and to the Horthy régime, *inter alia* by strengthening the Hungarian Front. The latter was designed to allow for the inclusion in the provisional government of other democratic forces and of the army. We have already mentioned the two memoranda to the regent written in this spirit. Meanwhile the Communist Party and the Hungarian Front concentrated their efforts on anti-German resistance and on the elaboration of a seventeen-point programme for the democratic transformation of Hungary.[20] For all that, neither organization was invited to be present during the peace negotiations with the Soviets.

These negotiations started very late in the day and following a great many hitches.[21] The regent and his set only resigned themselves to parleying with the Soviets as a last resort, after numerous fruitless attempts at direct negotiations with the Western Allies. By that time, Rumania and Finland had already broken with Germany. On 22 September the Red Army crossed the Hungarian border.

It was at this point that the first semi-official delegation left Budapest with instructions to discover what conditions the Soviets were likely to put forward. The Hungarian Communist Party refused to be associated with this delegation, but a few days later, on 28 September, another delegation of three, this time official and authorized by the regent to open negotiations, left for the Soviet Union. On 11 October, in the presence of Molotov, its members attached their signatures unilaterally to a document setting out the conditions to be met before the Soviets would sign an armistice with the Hungarian Army command.

During the final phase of the armistice negotiations, Churchill arrived in Moscow. Even though it may have been pure coincidence, it is worth recalling that Churchill discussed the division of zones of influence with Stalin on 9 October and that, on 10 October, Eden started negotiations with Molotov. Originally, Hungary was to be cut in two; on 10 October, the British conceded that the USSR could extend its sphere of influence to 75 per cent of the country. By 11 October, when the Hungarian delegation signed the preliminary armistice agreement, at least 75 per cent of Hungary was already a Soviet 'protectorate'.[22]

Because several senior Hungarian officers had gone over to the Red Army on Horthy's instructions as regent, the negotiations continued until the middle of November, that is, even after the collapse of the Horthy régime; Horthy himself was eventually placed under arrest by the Germans and moved to Germany.

Documents and studies devoted to this subject do much to reveal the Soviets' main objectives.[23] On the military level any disengagement of Hungarian troops, however minimal, was clearly to their advantage. On the political level, they favoured the signing of an armistice with representatives of the regent the better to maintain continuity and to preserve existing legal channels. On 11 November, *Pravda* and *Krasnaya Zvezda* still published a declaration by General János Vörös, who had gone over to the side of the USSR, ending with: 'Long live free and democratic Hungary under the leadership of Regent Horthy'.[24] The general was pursuing the same aim: maintaining continuity.[25] The Soviets, including Molotov in person, then started negotiations on the formation of a provisional government with the Hungarians. It was to be presided over by General Béla Miklós de Dálnok, an Army Corps commander and János Vörös from among the Horthyists in Moscow. The discussions with Molotov about the composition of the future Hungarian government in Debrecen throw light on the Soviets' third objective. They sought a government with three components: military and civilian personnel from Horthy's set; representatives of the democratic parties in the Hungarian Front (especially Szakasits and Tildy); and Hungarians in Moscow, meaning Communist émigrés. And this, in fact, is what came about in Debrecen a little later.

No document exists to help us determine the Soviet leaders' attitude to the 'Horthyist' element in the new government. Did they consider it a permanent component in a coalition or a purely transitional phenomenon that would make way for a 'frontist' alliance of all the parties they had labelled 'democratic', namely the Smallholders' Party, the Social Democratic Party and the Hungarian Communist Party, with at most one or two representatives from the small groups of the Centre Left?

The course of these negotiations in the autumn of 1944 has no direct bearing on the 'internal' history of the Hungarian Communist Party. At no time was the participation of 'home-based'

Communists raised by Molotov and the senior Soviet officers. And yet, as we have said, there was a Hungarian Front in Budapest with the participation of local Communists even while the Moscow committee of the HCP was preparing the way for the creation of a national independence front (later called the People's National Independence Front and later still, in 1954, the People's Patriotic Front).

In the winter of 1944, before the liberation of Budapest, two 'fronts' thus existed side by side. The provisional government soon afterwards set up in Debrecen included Muscovite Communists from the second 'front', that is to say the front they themselves had founded. Communists from inside Hungary were not included until later.

The Moscow committee was far from happy about the negotiations with Horthy's men. Because the Communists in this committee had not been present at the negotiations from the start, their attitude and that of the Soviets to the men of the old régime were divergent.[26] While Soviet newspapers, including the official *Pravda* and *Magyar Ujság* (Hungarian Gazette – a Hungarian paper published by the Red Army with Béla Illés, the writer, as its chief editor) were strongly in favour of collaboration with Horthy, the Hungarian leaders in Moscow kept up their anti-Horthyist stance to the very end: their papers and their radio station, Radio Kossuth, kept on calling for the continuation of the fight against the regent. Recent work helps to clarify the various stages in the elaboration of the Muscovite Communist action programme.[27] Three meetings were held in Moscow on 13 and 28 September and on 7 October 1944 respectively, with between twenty and twenty-five participants and chaired by Mátyás Rákosi. Those present included Vas, Révai, Gerö, Friss, Zoltán Szántó, László Rudas, Erzsébet Andics, Dezsö Nemes, Béla Fogarasi, László Háy, Zoltán Lippay, György Lukács, Gyula Háy, Sándor Gergely, Béla Uitz, György Nyisztor, István Hunya and Rezsö Szántó. There were also additional meetings, either with the same or with such other participants as Béla Szántó, József Fazekas, István Kossa and Sándor Sziklai. Then, between 22 October and 1 November, the Moscow committee again discussed the action programme with József Fazekas, Kossa and Sziklai together with three others: Sándor Nagy, Gyula Rácz and Kerekes.[28]

The original draft of the action programme, prepared by József Révai under Ernö Gerö's supervision, underwent several modifications during these successive meetings. *Inter alia*, the violently anti-Horthy tenor and the demand that the regent and his former ministers be brought before emergency tribunals (Point 9 of the original draft) were dropped. At the end of October, the modified action programme was submitted to Dimitrov, director of the 'Institute' whose task it was to take over several activities of the dissolved Comintern.

The first Communist leaders to return to Hungary on 26 October 1944 (Gerö, Nagy, Révai and Farkas) were instructed to apply this programme. With the approval of Dimitrov and Manuilsky, they also turned themselves into a Central Committee and changed the name of the party back to Hungarian Communist Party. The programme was, however, to undergo yet further changes in the course of discussions with Communists in the previously liberated territories (especially in Szeged, on the River Tisza, and once again in Moscow at the beginning of December 1944).

These Moscow discussions put the finishing touches to a programme that was meant to be the basis of the institutional system of the Hungarian People's Democracy and to determine the nature of the provisional government.[29] Between 1 and 5 December, there were several meetings including two or three with Molotov, Dekanozov and Pushkin and with the intermittent participation of Stalin.[30] On the Hungarian side, these meetings were attended by Ernö Gerö and Imre Nagy, who returned expressly from Hungary. Mátyás Rákosi, who had remained in Moscow and had not yet obtained Stalin's authorization to return to Hungary, joined his two comrades. Two or three working sessions were attended by the Soviet representatives, by the three Hungarian Communist leaders and by members of the armistice delegation – two Hungarian Army Corps commanders and Kuznetsov's Army Corps commander and staff. Other persons, especially high-ranking Hungarian officers, were also involved in one way or another.

Two distinct yet interconnected aspects of these protracted negotiations, which continued from September to December, deserve our special attention. Molotov's chief concern, confirmed by the sporadic interventions of Stalin, was to ensure the creation of a transitional régime that would alarm neither the Allies nor Hungarian public opinion. The Soviet proposals, which merit a closer study, were aimed at establishing a fresh *legal basis* for the new régime. The French precedent – recognition of General de Gaulle's Consultative Committee (General de Gaulle was also in Moscow at the beginning of that December) – was frequently mentioned. The composition of the provisional government needed, as we have said, to reflect both *continuity*, very slender in the event, and also a *break* with the Horthy régime by means of the inclusion of ministers from the National Independence Front, two of whom had to be Communists. Stalin and Molotov also insisted on the democratic, indeed (without calling it so) bourgeois democratic, look of the nascent régime: no revolutionary fervour, no seizure of private property, respect for traditions.

It was all meant to convey a picture of a 'wise and moderate' Stalin, and above all of a Stalin not over-anxious to seize Hungary. After all, Hungary was not Poland. It was just one more piece in Stalin's game and a secondary one at that. Once Hungary had been drawn into the Soviet orbit, its sovietization would follow in due course. And so Stalin and Molotov dampened the ardour of the Hungarian Communists and obliged them to accept several compromises with what the Hungarians felt to be the forces of reaction.[31]

The composition of the coalition and its immediate programme both reflected the new government's public face. Moreover, from September to December, the Communist Party's action programme was moderated as well.[32] It now involved no more calls for the dismissal of the old officials, the trial by special tribunals of all former ministers who had been in office since 1941, the demolition of the old administrative machinery and a radical programme to break the hold of monopoly capitalism. On this last point, the programme was confined to the nationalization of mines and public enterprises and to the introduction of state – rather than workers' – control of financial institutions and trusts.

The 'home-based' Communist Party, while also welcoming a democratic transformation in the spirit of the Popular Front, turned out to have more radical ambitions than the Moscow contingent.[33] One must, however, agree with the authors quoted that there were few real differences to choose between the two. Both groups wanted to base the new democracy on a 'democratic workers' and peasants' dictatorship', with the Communist Party as the leading force. An analysis of the documents published in the winter of 1944 nevertheless justifies the conclusion that even this ideological programme was abandoned in the wake of the moderation demanded by the Soviet leaders. At the same time, the party, and especially the veterans of 1919, preserved some of the old revolutionary fervour, which was to surface in a number of their interventions in the Moscow discussions and also during debates in Hungary, especially at Szeged.

Those protesting against what they considered excessive moderation included several Hungarian Communists who expressed the fear that the party might be forced back underground or might have to content itself with playing the role of an opposition. Such fears were, however, confined to no more than a handful of militants. The Soviet leaders, for their part, knew perfectly well what they wanted, at least in the short and the medium term. While demanding moderation from the Hungarian Communist Party, they made it crystal-clear to their military allies that Communists would have to be included at all levels of government. With the Red Army at the gates of Budapest, there could be no question of driving the Communist Party back underground or into the opposition. The shape of the new democracy was thus moulded more by the combined presence of the Red Army in the country and the presence of the Communist Party in the government than it was determined by ideological considerations or by social programmes.

After the emergence of a Provisional National Assembly following elections in the eastern, liberated part of Hungary, the new government was duly appointed on 22 December. Its president was Horthy's former commander of the First Army, General Béla Miklós de Dálnok. The eleven ministers included Imre Nagy, Communist, minister of agriculture; József Gábor, Communist, minister of trade and transport; Erik Molnár, officially said to be 'without party' but a Communist all the same, minister of social security. Three Communist portfolios out of eleven was still a long way from unshared Communist power, but the march had begun.[34]

−7−

The Totalitarian Road

The four Muscovite leaders who were the first to reach Hungary constituted themselves into a provisional Central Committee on 5 November 1944 at Szeged; in December they moved on to Debrecen, where a Provisional National Assembly and a Provisional National Government were set up on 21 and 22 December to continue until March 1945. Meanwhile, on 19 January, another Central Committee was formed in Budapest under Antal Apró, Bertalan Bartha, Márton Horváth, János Kádár, Gyula Kállai, Károly Kiss, István Kossa, István Kovács, Gábor Péter and Zoltán Vas. With the exception of Vas, all of these were 'home-based' militants, people who had stayed on in Hungary to work underground. László Rajk, the party secretary, who had been arrested in December 1944, was still in prison. The two Central Committees merged on 23 February, with Rákosi as secretary.

The number of party members who did clandestine work is disputed – 3,000 according to one of Rákosi's declarations; between 100 and 200 or even fewer according to other sources. The party had been bled white by repression in Hungary, by the purges in the Soviet Union, by the war, by the deportation of Jews and by the harsh conditions imposed by living the life of a militant. Many had died, from Karaganda to Madrid, passing through Budapest and Buchenwald. The Resistance had claimed other victims, but not in very large numbers because Hungarian resistance during the war was confined to fairly isolated attacks and acts of sabotage. Suffice it to say that the Communist Party lost some of its bravest militants in the Resistance: Richárd Rózsa, György Kilián and Endre Ságvári.

It is, moreover, of little relevance to establish whether the party had ten active members at the liberation of Hungary, or a hundred, or even ten times that number. Once the constraints of clandestine life were gone, it experienced a dramatic new influx, though not nearly as vast as that which occurred a few years later when its ranks swelled to 1 million members in a country of 9 million inhabitants. The party's prospects depended on such factors as the Soviet presence, the course of inter-Allied relations and, inside Hungary, on its own political skill and on the reaction of the people.

The Party and the Nation

In 1945, when the Communist Party tried to present itself as a national movement fit to govern the country, it was standing on familiar ground. Despite minor changes between the two wars, Hungary had remained a predominantly agrarian country, with a relatively small middle-ranking peasantry, a fairly large number of workers and poor peasants, and a middle class more powerful than before, but still dominated by the nobility.

Inter-war Hungary had been neither fascist nor feudal, but the conservatism of its upper class and the collective mentality of its so-called 'seigniorial and Christian' middle classes kept it in a state of stagnation which the dynamic and modern sectors of society had been unable to alter.

Hungary had also been a country out on a limb. Its irredentist aspirations had alienated its neighbours, countries in which about one-quarter of all Magyar-speaking people had lived before the First World War. Most of these Hungarians were restored to their homeland during the Second World War following annexations of previously Czechoslovak, Rumanian or Yugoslav territories, but nothing seemed more uncertain than their fate at the close of hostilities.

Because Hungary, in addition to its other disadvantages, was a vanquished country, 'Hitler's last satellite', it was thrown back to within its 1920 frontiers. These it now shared with a new neighbour, the Soviet Union which had established itself in Ruthenia, once part of Hungary, of Czechoslovakia after the First World War and again Hungarian during the Second.

Hungary's participation in Hitler's war also forced it to pay a heavy tribute in human and material resources, in reparations and in various other forms, for instance through having to meet the occupation costs. According to Iván Berend and György Ránki, 20 per cent of the capital invested in agriculture, more than 50 per cent of Hungary's transport stock and more than 45 per cent of its industrial machinery were destroyed, over and above the total or partial destruction of more than a quarter of the capital's housing stock. All in all, about 40 per cent of Hungary's assets had vanished.[1] Reparations to the victorious Allies came to 300 million US dollars on top of occupation costs representing a total of 30 per cent of the gross national income for several years. Although the Soviet Union agreed to substantial reductions (officially about two-thirds of the reparations), the overall weight of the damages to be paid pushed devastated Hungary to the very limits. Joint Soviet–Hungarian enterprises added to this burden. The Soviet Union gained control of several leading sectors of the economy – a control that continued until after Stalin's death.

In a recent article, the Hungarian historian Mihály Korom tackled the difficult task of computing the losses in human lives Hungary suffered during the war. These calculations were difficult for at least three reasons: territorial changes, the disappearance of large sections of the population (Jews in German concentration camps, prisoners of war in Russia, the exodus of numerous refugees and so on), the impossibility of ascertaining the number of persons who had returned. For all the Hungarian territories, the losses came to about 700,000 to 750,000 persons; for the territories assigned to Hungary after the war, to about 450,000 persons out of a total of about 9 million inhabitants.[2] According to Mihály Korom, half the number of the dead or missing were Jewish victims of the persecution; in addition 125,000 soldiers fell during the war and 44,000 civilians were killed by bombs (mostly in Budapest). Some 850,000 to 900,000 Hungarians were taken prisoner of war, most of them (550,000 to 570,000) by the Red Army. According to Korom, 40,000 prisoners died of diseases or epidemics in various camps.[3] In fact, the losses were probably even greater but the available data do not allow us to say by how much. The same is true of the Jews. According to the figures just quoted, some 225,000 Jews from what is now Hungary fell victim to persecutions and deportations, which means that about the same number must have survived. Yet Korom, like R. L. Braham, to whom he refers, put the number of Jewish survivors in Hungary in 1946 at no more than about 143,000. The fate of some 80,000 to 100,000 Jews therefore remains unknown: some of them may have returned later, others concealed their Jewish identity, yet others disappeared without leaving any trace in the statistical records.

To these figures must also be added losses resulting from the transfer of populations: the expulsion of about 180,000 Germans, the voluntary emigration of about 73,000 Slovaks and the emigration of other categories. These losses were, however, offset by the expulsion into Hungary of about 100,000 Hungarians from Czechoslovakia, of several tens of thousands from Yugoslavia and by the voluntary immigration of several more tens of thousands from other neighbouring countries.

Despite losses adding up to about 5 per cent of the population, Hungary recovered its previous population level fairly quickly: it could count just over 9 million inhabitants by 1949. Since then, demographic growth has slowed down (to give a total of 10,700,000 inhabitants) for various reasons: the exodus of 1956; the decline in the birth rate (1.3 per cent in 1981 as against 2.6 per cent in 1949); the increase in the natural death rate (1.3 per cent in 1981 against 1.1 per cent in 1949), resulting in 1981, for the first time, in a net shortfall in the natural reproduction rate: 144,757 deaths against 142,890 births. Of the deaths, 4,800 were the result of suicide.

The 1949 figures, however, gloss over the fact that the half a million or so persons who had disappeared during the war had been drawn from the most active classes, and that the exodus of successive waves of emigrants emptied the country of a high proportion of its educated elements. Moreover, the 1949 figures also hide the fact that those who returned home, notably the prisoners of war, took several years to do so, and this during the difficult period of reconstruction of 1945–9 when the country was suffering acute shortages in manpower and particularly in brainpower. As for social, political and moral conditions in Hungary at the end of the war, assessments can at best be approximate.

In respect of its ethnic composition, Hungary after the Second World War, even as after the First, became once more a homogeneous country – only small pockets populated by other nationalities were left, with the exception of the German minority in Transdanubia. As a result, present-day Hungary has no problems with national minorities.[4] By contrast, three million Hungarians from the old kingdom continue to live, after 1945 as before, in neighbouring countries.

A little less than two-thirds of Hungary's population is Roman Catholic, less than a third is Protestant; the number of Greek Orthodox is very small, that of Jews relatively low. In pre-war Hungary, Jews made up about 5 per cent of the population (6.2 per cent after the First World War; 5.1 per cent in 1930 not including converted Jews). Among the survivors of the Holocaust, as we already saw, only some 140,000 were to be identified as Jews; and in the light of a more recent study, no more than 100,000 can be considered as such nowadays.[5] However we look at it, the fate of some 100,000 more persons – Jews or converted Jews – remains unknown. The antagonism between Catholics and Protestants seems to have long since been resolved. By contrast, there still exists a 'Jewish question' in the guise of latent anti-semitism and also in attitudes to Jewish members of the Communist Party, a point to which we shall return.

The population density is very high in the capital with 2 million inhabitants, and also in several other urban centres: it varies between 40 and 100 per square kilometre in the countryside. Hungary has always been a primarily agricultural country and is poor in mining and energy resources. Some industrial sectors, however – for instance, engineering, transport, optics, chemicals, textiles – underwent rapid development between the two wars, though it needs to be stressed that about 56 per cent of the population still lived from the land at that time. To appreciate the importance of the party's agrarian policy, we may look again at some of the figures mentioned in Chapter 1. One thousand persons owned estates larger than 600 hectares, making a total of about 2.7 million hectares, or 30 per cent of all cultivable land; about 10,000 other persons owned between 60 and 600 hectares each; 12,064 large landowners held some 48 per cent of all the agricultural land, while 1,622,000 peasants had to share the other 52 per cent.

Wartime destruction caused damage estimated at five times the annual national income. Hence the immediate post-war economic objective was the reconstruction of a devastated country whereas, from 1949–50 onwards, the primary objective was to turn Hungary into an industrial country. In the interval, two socio-economic changes had a great impact on the rural areas. In 1945, the new government, under Communist and left-wing peasant pressure, introduced land reforms long awaited by agricultural workers and poor peasants. As a result, 1,875,000 hectares of land were distributed to 642,342 persons, who thus received an average of 2.9 hectares each. At the same time, the new state proceeded to the expropriation of just under 1.9 million hectares of forest, pasture and uncultivated ground. The reforms did not affect owners of land under 60 hectares, except for war criminals, members of the German *Volksbund*, and so on. At a stroke, seigniorial or 'semi-feudal' Hungary had been turned into a country of small and medium-sized holdings. In 1949, about 25 per cent of peasant farms measured between .6 and 1.7 hectares, 21 per cent between 1.7 and 3 hectares, 32 per cent between 3 and 6 hectares, 17 per cent between 6 and 12 hectares and 6 per cent 12 and 60 hectares. This new system was to disappear during the second upheaval: the collectivization of agriculture begun in 1949.[6]

Anticipating those events, let us add that, apart from the old agrarian structures, two other foundations of pre-war society felt the impact of change, namely the state machinery and, to a lesser extent, the upper middle class. Though receiving no mortal blows, all the old leading classes found the ground caving in under their feet with the arrival of the new democratic régime. This was largely the work of the Communist Party, in agreement – even if that agreement was not always easily obtained – with its coalition partners. It also helped to lay the political, social and moral groundwork on which the party built its programme until the final seizure of power in 1948.

The land reforms, promulgated in Debrecen at the beginning of 1945, earned the party the gratitude of the rural poor and the respect of intellectual circles close to the peasantry, while the anti-capitalist measures, still very moderate, and finally the democratization of the state helped the party to gain a foothold among other strata, especially the working class and the petty bourgeoisie.

With its early slogan of 'Land, Bread, and Freedom', the Communist Party was trying to woo the whole nation, and by throwing itself enthusiastically into the work of reconstruction, to gain recognition as a national party with a broad appeal to the electorate. Active, dynamic, catalytic, the party also tried to sound reassuring. The presence of the Red Army, the conquest of key positions in the state machinery, first and foremost in the police, as well as highly skilful political manoeuvring did the rest to ensure the party's rise to undivided power within the short space of three years.

Salami, Hammer and Sickle

At first, the Communist Party consisted, as we have seen, of just a handful of people led by a 'Muscovite' team, together with a vastly reduced group of 'home-based' militants who had emerged from twenty-five years of clandestine existence. True, the party grew rapidly: 30,000 members in February 1945, 150,000 in May, half a million towards the end of the year – a point to which we shall return. For all that, it remained a minority party, as its electoral record showed on 4 November 1945, when the Communists received no more than 17 per cent of the votes cast, or a total of 793,600 votes, not much more, that is, than the number of its active members.

Three years after these elections – the first and at the same time the last free elections held after the war – the party seized sole power. By what road and by what means did it manage to reach this position? For some close to the party, the Communist success is chiefly explained by the social and psychological changes in the nation during these three years. For others, the presence of the Red Army and Soviet determination to bring Hungary into the Soviet camp were the crucial factors in allowing the Communists to seize power at the very moment when the ratification of the peace treaty, signed in Paris on 10 February 1947, fully restored Hungary's sovereignty. The instruments of ratification were to be deposited 'in the shortest possible time' (Art. 42) and 'upon the coming into force of the present Treaty, all Allied forces shall, within a period of 90 days, be withdrawn from Hungary, subject to the right of the Soviet Union to keep on Hungarian territory such armed forces as it may need for the maintenance of the lines of communication of the Soviet Army with the Soviet zone of occupation in Austria' (Art. 22).[7] The year 1947 was, in any event, to be a turning-point in the history of the country, not least because the intensification of the Cold War turned Hungary into a counter in the global conflict.

According to yet another interpretation, the Hungarian 'turning point' was largely the result of very skilful political manoeuvres by the Communist Party which, enjoying the strength afforded by Soviet support, cut back its adversaries 'slice by slice' like a salami, following the time-honoured tactics of *divide et impera*.

These different hypotheses, far from being mutually exclusive, are, in fact, complementary. In any case, they raise the question of whether the developments were the enactment of a carefully written scenario reflecting the expansionist character of the Soviet Union or whether they were based on a pragmatic approach leaving some room for chance and improvisation.

The course of events and the readjustment of the balance of forces took place, by and large, in three stages: (1) from the emergence of the new provisional government until the elections in the autumn of 1945; (2) from the elections until the party's offensive against the Centre Right in 1947; and (3) from the final offensive in 1947–8 until the election, on a single list, of the new Parliament and the creation of a Communist-dominated government in May 1949.

During the first stage, the tactics of the party were still those adopted in 1944. Governmental pluralism – confined to the four big parties of the National Independence Front – was maintained with some important modifications that helped to consolidate the position of the Communist Party. In May, Ernö Gerö, previously promoted to membership in the Supreme National Council, was appointed minister of trade and transport; in July, Mihály Farkas was appointed secretary of state to the minister of the interior. These nominations reflected the party's determination to concentrate its efforts, over and above the land reforms, on a revival of economic life and also on gaining control of the police, especially of the political branch. Gerö, who subsequently became a kind of super-minister of economics, ably seconded by Zoltán Vas, enhanced the party's reputation by supervising the work of reconstruction, the normalization of political life and of public transport and the stabilization of the currency,[8] while Farkas, the future boss (with Gábor Péter at his side) of the political police (AVO/AVH), ordered the first wave of arrests and repression, acting in concert with Soviet intelligence. The police action was ostensibly directed at war criminals, collaborators and fascists, but numerous perfectly innocent 'suspects' were also subjected at best to intensive interrogation and at worst to long stays in internment camps or prisons. The aura and machinery of the future police system were thus created during the first hours of the new régime.

The collaboration of the various parties in the democratic coalition, however, still continued, and if this was not without its misunderstandings it was at least without major clashes. Though the Yalta Conference had tolled the knell of Polish democracy, it left the new pluralist Hungarian democracy intact. Indeed, what is best remembered about it is the Declaration on Liberated Europe and also the arrangements for holding free elections. In August 1945, Marshal Voroshilov himself had invited the Hungarian provisional government to attend. A little earlier, in March, the brutal intervention by Vishinsky, the marshal's opposite number in Rumania, had carried the pro-Communist government of Petru Groza to power in Bucharest – a step which had not gone unremarked but apparently had no other consequences. The hour of spectacular change had most certainly not yet sounded for Hungary.

Relations between the Communist and the Social Democratic parties remained close, though it is true to say that this was thanks largely to successive expulsions of the old right-wing Social Democratic leaders, including Károly Peyer, and the emergence of a team in favour of closer collaboration with the Communists. Some of these Social Democrats were even accused of being in the pay of the Communists, or, in any event, under Communist orders.[9]

The National Peasant Party, too, presided over by the writer Péter Veres, was divided between its 'leftist' and 'rightist' wings,[10] but it remained by and large the Communist Party's most faithful ally, at least until it, too, suffered the fate reserved by the CP for all its partners: marginalization followed by dissolution. From the start, people had suspected the Peasant Party of being a branch of the CP, created by the latter to offset the weight of the very strong Smallholders' Party.

Self-assured, the Smallholders' Party dominated the immediate post-war political scene. It was the main beneficiary of the refusal by the occupying authorities to allow the resurrection of the other traditional parties, including the Christian Party.[11] The old political classes, clergy, businessmen, a large section of the petty bourgeoisie, not to mention the peasantry, marched behind its banner. Many local and national agencies of the administration supported it as well. It was probably this fact that persuaded the Communist Party to come down heavily in favour of a centralized state apparatus while assigning the role of 'councils' to the municipalities, a point to be looked at more closely in due course.

The first test of the balance of forces came in the autumn of 1945, during the Budapest municipal elections. Under the pressure of the Communist Party and of its own left wing, the Social Democratic Party decided to fight these elections by presenting a common list with the Communists. The votes were counted on 7 October 1945. The two working-class parties combined received 42.76 per cent of the votes, the National Peasant Party just over 6 per cent, the Smallholders' Party emerging as the clear victor with more than 50 per cent of the votes cast. In the country's proletarian citadel, this result was a crushing defeat for the parties of labour.

And so, following the elections, the President of the Allied Control Commission, Marshal Voroshilov in person, tried to persuade the other parties to join the Communists on a single list during the coming parliamentary elections, with the percentages fixed in advance.[12]

This proposal having been rejected and the Social Democratic Party also having decided to go it alone, the members of the National Independent Front presented themselves separately at the national elections of 4 November 1945. The Communist Party attracted 17 per cent of the votes, coming third after the Smallholders' Party – the clear victor with 57 per cent of the votes, and the Social Democratic Party with 17.4 per cent of the votes. The National Peasant Party maintained its score of 7 per cent, and the 80,000 or so remaining votes were shared between two small parties: the Bourgeois Democratic Party and the Radical Party.

Strong because of its absolute majority, triumphant because of the support of more than 2.5 million voters giving them 245 parliamentary seats out of a total of 409, the Smallholders' Party could now, by the rules of parliamentary democracy, have formed a government on its own. But there was no question of it doing so. Both before and after what were perfectly fair elections, the Soviets let it be known that they would not tolerate the exclusion of the Communist Party from power. The coalition was consequently preserved, but this time without any of the generals and politicians associated with the Horthy régime. The new government formed by Zoltán Tildy included nine ministers from the Smallholders' Party (Tildy among them), four Communists, four Social Democrats and one member of the National Peasant Party. Among the portfolios held by the CP were the interior (Imre Nagy) and transport (Ernö Gerö); Mátyás Rákosi became minister without portfolio and so did the leaders of the other two big parties, István Dobi and Árpád Szakasits.

Added to this distribution of portfolios, which favoured the losers more than it did the winners, was the fact that the Social Democratic ministers came from the left of their party and that at least two ministers from the Smallholders' Party, Dobi and János Gyöngyösi, the minister of foreign affairs, were so close to the CP as to have been described as 'moles'.

Until the municipal elections during the previous October, the Communist Party had hoped to do better at the polls, though it had expected a Smallholders' victory. After the municipal defeat, it could not possibly have expected a good result at the parliamentary elections in November. The CP accordingly tried to put the best face on it, stressing that, for a party that had only just emerged from twenty-five years underground in a country saturated with anti-Communist propaganda and with so solidly entrenched a Social Democratic Party, its own score was most creditable. Creditable also because – and this was a factor the CP could not parade in public – of the presence and aid of the Soviet Union.

In a sense, Soviet support was the trump card in the hands of the Communist Party. As a defeated country, Hungary had been placed under the supreme authority of the Allied Control Commission presided over by Marshal Voroshilov.[13] That presence alone ensured that the party was unassailable.[14]

The Soviet authorities did everything they could to help the party: they gave it material assistance (food for distribution, transport, a press and newsprint). Zoltán Vas, for instance, a state commissioner and later mayor of Budapest, was able to curry popular favour by distributing potatoes to the famished population using Russian military vehicles. As like as not, these same potatoes had been requisitioned from peasants in neighbouring villages, and naturally the two-faced character of such actions did not go unremarked. Had not the Red Army taken whatever it needed and had many Soviet soldiers not committed whole strings of crimes?[15] The Communist Party, for its part, was provided with offices, lodgings, food and even clothing by the Russians. In all fairness, however, the Soviets also rendered aid to the Communists' political partners and the population at large.

The direct intervention of the Soviet occupation authorities as well as the controls they exerted were perhaps most strongly reflected in police affairs. Soviet security officials made numerous arrests, and ordered deportations and political interrogations, not to mention the taking of hostages and the abduction of thousands of civilians as so-called prisoners of war.

At the highest level, however, Moscow's attitude and that of its Hungarian allies did not change appreciably with the elections. The strategic line remained the same; it was simply that the tactics changed as the CP prepared to secure a stranglehold on Hungarian politics.[16]

Following the elections and throughout the next year, the party remained in a politically vulnerable state, if not actually on the defensive. While it could, in theory, have been ejected from the government, any of its partners contemplating such a step would hardly have been showing great sagacity in an occupied country about to face its conquerors at a peace conference. The party's isolation, on the other hand, could have placed it in a precarious position if its coalition partners – or at least large sections of the Social Democratic and Populist deputies – had joined forces with the massive Smallholders' bloc. This was a possibility considered very seriously by both sides. The party's first concern was therefore to prevent such a union, the next objective being to split the ranks of its adversaries.

The means of exerting pressure and intimidation, and even the police methods used by the CP, are known from the books and memoirs of such protagonists as Ferenc Nagy, Dezső Sulyok and Imre Kovács.[17] Moreover, Rákosi, the leader of the Communist Party, himself explained that his party's policy was to press claims, moderate enough at first to prevent its adversaries from mobilizing their forces against the Communists, and then little by little to raise the stakes. 'This step-by-step approach was known as the "Salami tactic", and thanks to it we were able, day after day, to slice off, to cut up [bit by bit] the reactionary forces skulking in the Smallholders' Party.'[18]

Not, of course, that there was no resistance. All the great

political, institutional and economic decisions of the new régime aroused the more or less open opposition of the conservative factions in the majority party. Such responses were provoked by the Communist Party's proposals for land reforms, by the first nationalization decrees, by the purges of the state machinery, by the abolition of the crown and by the subsequent proclamation of a republic. The resulting arguments and conflicts enabled the Communists to declare that the only threat to the new and still fragile democracy came from the reactionary Right. The gradual destruction of the Smallholders' Party thus took place under the banner of 'the struggle against reaction'. This made it possible to mobilize, especially in Budapest, all the supporters of the Communist Party and of the 'Bloc of the Left' (set up on 5 March 1946 by the three minority parties and the Trade Union Council) against the Smallholders' Party.

The Smallholders were meanwhile subjected to constant exhortations to purge themselves of their right wing. Between the election of 1945 and those of 1947, this large and heterogeneous party never stopped tearing itself apart, no doubt as a result of external pressures, but also by virtue of its heterogeneous character. As early as March 1946, some twenty deputies left the Smallholders (some voluntarily, the majority by expulsion) to found, after many vicissitudes, a new political organization called the Freedom Party, the first real opposition party to appear after Hungary's liberation. And this was only the prelude to a veritable proliferation of opposition parties drawing candidates and voters away from the big majority party. Needless to say, the spectacle of the fragmentation of their adversary delighted the Communists.

The attack on the Smallholders' Party also involved several large police operations. On 5 January 1947, a communiqué issued by the minister of the interior announced the uncovering of a 'plot' hatched by an organization called the 'Hungarian Community', presided over by a committee of seven. A few days later, a minister, Endre Mistéth, and several deputies of the Smallholders' Party were implicated in the affair and arrested. In February, the Smallholders' Party, under Communist pressure, ordered the expulsion of its secretary, Béla Kovács, who was arrested soon afterwards, not by the Hungarian police but by the Soviet occupation authorities – after Parliament had upheld his parliamentary immunity and refused to deliver him into the hands of the police.

The affair caused an uproar, not only in Hungary but throughout the world, eliciting numerous protests from the Western Allies. All was in vain: Béla Kovács was to spend ten years in Soviet detention and would not return to Hungary until the eve of the 1956 revolution.[19] Nor did the discovery of alleged 'ramifications' of the plot stop there. Several deputies, including Zoltán Pfeiffer, left the Smallholders' Party under protest, others were expelled, and its most prominent leader, Ferenc Nagy, then prime minister, was accused of complicity. Away on foreign travels, Ferenc Nagy was ordered – by a telephone message from Rákosi – to resign. On 31 May Lajos Dinnyés took his place at the head of a radically altered government.

As for the 'conspirators', their leader, György Donáth, was sentenced to death and executed while his 'accomplices' received long prison sentences.

The true history of this 'plot' has yet to be written. According to the most reliable witnesses, the 'conspiracy' charge was based on purely presumptive evidence. The 'Hungarian Community' did, in fact, exist as the successor to a clandestine network formed during the war – against the German occupiers. After the war, its members were in the habit of meeting from time to time, but had neither the means nor the intention of fomenting a 'plot against the state', as the tribunal which sentenced them alleged against them. As for the 'ramifications' involving the prime minister, they were probably more of a social than of a political nature.

But the aim of the police campaign and of the whole legal charade was precisely to make the accused look like conspirators, and this for the express purpose of compromising the circle round the prime minister. That aim was plainly attained. The Smallholders' Party was decapitated, thinned out and disabled to the point of becoming incapable of putting up any serious resistance. In the wake of the affair it lost not only Béla Kovács, its general secretary, but also its most important political leaders: Ferenc Nagy, the prime minister; Béla Varga, the president of the National Assembly; József Kővágó, mayor of Budapest; and several parliamentary deputies. Zoltán Tildy, Ferenc Nagy's predecessor, who had meanwhile been elected President of the Republic, and many other prominent members of the party were destined to follow them either into exile or into prison.

Meanwhile the right wing of the other coalition parties also became weakened, while the Freedom Party was dissolved. By contrast, two other important parties were authorized to keep up an appearance on the political scene, the better to accentuate the division within the non-Communist camp.

On 31 August 1947, 5 million Hungarian electors went to the polls. The Communist Party reaped the fruits of its 'salami' tactics and of its 'pluralist' policy designed to split its rivals: it came first with 21.8 per cent of the votes, having polled a total of 1,113,050 votes. Four other parties – the Smallholders' Party, the Social Democratic Party, the Popular Democratic Party and the Hungarian Independence Party – each obtained between 14 and 16 per cent of the votes; the National Peasant Party received 8.6 per cent, the Independent Democratic Party 5.1 per cent and three other parties the remainder. The coalition parties together thus received a little over 60 per cent of the votes.

The Communist Party's satisfaction at coming top proved to be threadbare as well as illusory. To begin with, the party had hoped for more. This was to be the Communists' last chance for a long time to base their legitimacy on an electoral victory worthy of that name. Secondly, the elections, while ostensibly respecting all legal formalities, had been compromised by pressure and fraud. At least 100,000 votes came from Communist militants who cast their vote *several times* thanks to a system of 'blue voting papers' issued freely to sick persons and persons absent from their electoral district – by Communist officials. The 'blue paper' affair was to cause a scandal, tarnishing the party image and compromising what could otherwise have gone down in the annals as a free election.

It was an illusory satisfaction, finally, because the CP and its weakened partners in the 'Bloc of the Left' did not even have a parliamentary majority. To obtain one, they would either once again have had to come to terms with the Smallholders' Party or else put an end to parliamentary democracy, which, proceeding by several stages, was what they did over the next two years.

Following the elections of 31 August 1947, the coalition formed a new government under Lajos Dinnyés of the Smallholders' Party. The other sixteen members of the government included five Communists, among them László Rajk, minister of the interior, and Erik Molnár, minister of foreign affairs.

In November, one of the main opposition parties, Zoltán Pfeiffer's Independence Party, was dissolved and its forty-eight deputies stripped of their mandates. The Popular Democratic Party lived on for another year, to be dissolved in February 1949.

Meanwhile other political figures, including Zoltán Tildy, the President of the Republic, were, 'slice by slice', banished, exiled, arrested, or at best dismissed from office. As a result, not only the opposition, but also those factions in the coalition that had proved less than amenable to Communist demands, disappeared from the scene. Thus, by the beginning of 1948, the independent existence of the Social Democratic Party had become a fiction which was to survive until the great merger due to be decided in June at the founding congress of the Hungarian Workers' Party.

Pluralist democracy had likewise become a fiction. The coalition of the parties in the Hungarian National Independence Front was nevertheless formally maintained until the transformation of that front into the Hungarian People's Independence Front on 1 February 1949 and even beyond that date until the elections on 15 May. The parties of the new front presented themselves at these elections on a single list which received 96.27 per cent of the votes; the government to emerge from these elections being already a Communist government in all but name. It included thirteen ministers from the MDP (Communist Party united with the Social Democratic Party), two ministers from the Smallholders' Party and two ministers from the National Peasant Party.

To crush resistance and opposition, the police activity and intimidation unleashed by the Communist Party were now extended to other fields, notably to the churches. The Protestant churches did not escape, losing bishops and pastors to the repression which, most notably, claimed the eminent Calvinist Bishop László Ravasz. The main enemy, however, was seen as the powerful Catholic Church and its spiritual and political head, the indomitable Cardinal József Mindszenty, Archbishop of Esztergom. Sentenced to life imprisonment in February 1949, József Mindszenty was released by the insurgents in 1956 and, after the crushing of the revolution, sought refuge in the United States embassy, which he did not leave until a few years before his death in exile.

Church resistance, too, was broken by the well-tried 'slice by slice' method. Stripped of their lands, their funds and their leaders, the churches finished up, one after the other, signing concordats with the state by which their activities were strictly confined to the narrow exercise of their spiritual ministry. The subjugation of intellectual life was accomplished by the same method, highlighted by several spectacular incidents such as the Déry and Lukács affairs, to which we shall turn our attention shortly.

By its forceful interventions on the social and economic planes, the party, as we have seen, scored many, often striking, successes. Thanks to a cautious and gradual approach to private enterprise and above all to the urban and rural petty bourgeoisie, the party managed to keep on the right side of these large strata of the population. The post-war famine, the privations during the period of reconstruction and inflation affected everyone alike, and this fact enabled the CP to make political capital and to blame all shortcomings on speculators, on clerical propaganda, on the forces of reaction and on all sorts of other enemies. By contrast, the CP took full credit for the – undeniable – progress that was being made in the work of reconstruction, for the restoration of order, for the stabilization of the currency. It skilfully mobilized the mass of its supporters, bringing women and workers out into the street in support of a variety of demands. And it was above all able to present itself, in keeping with its policy of national unity, as a party defending not merely the interests of a single class but of the entire nation. None of its partners in the Independence Front would have dared to use nearly as much nationalistic bombast as the Communists invoked.

There remained however one great shadow over it all: the setbacks Hungary suffered at the Paris Peace Conference. These setbacks, admittedly, were shared by all the other parties in the coalition government, and *a fortiori* by the old régime for whose errors Hungary was now having to pay so dearly. There was little hope of recovering the territories lost through Hitler's arbitrations in Vienna or the Bácska (Bacsa) region in victorious Yugoslavia. Budapest nevertheless hoped to regain a few scraps here and there, especially the whole or at least part of northern Transylvania. The CP leaders tried to enlist Moscow's support and continued to feel confident until the signing of the treaty in February 1947. In the event, it would seem, their hopes were frustrated by one of Stalin's asides, made at the last minute.

The author makes no claim that he has been able to arrive at an objective assessment of the results of the first years of post-war Communist activity, the less so as he himself was involved in that activity as a propagandist – for better or for worse. Much that, with forty years of hindsight, looks like an omen and a pointer to a totalitarian dictatorship, impressed many people at the time as a salutary sign of progress, as one among the first steps towards a new Socialist democracy. The relegation of the old upper class, land reform, reconstruction, the democratization of the civil service, the promise of local autonomy, the democratic reform of education and the encouragement of learning and popular culture were some of the many early achievements of the new régime.

Were all of these gains forfeited as a result of the party's degeneration? Was this development inevitable? It is to the party's history from 1945 until the advent of full Stalinism in the 1950s that we must look for a preliminary answer to these questions.

The Emergence of a Totalitarian Party

The rise of the Communist Party to power poses a whole series of questions concerning its internal structure, its tactics and its operations. The rapid growth in membership, from a few hundred to half a million within one year, then to double that number after the party's fusion with the SDP, provides no more than a partial explanation for its dramatic climb to the peak of power. Was it tactical success that brought it these numerical reinforcements? Or was it rather the giddying increase in the number of members that ensured the party's rise? The weight given by numerical strength was doubtless an essential factor, but the party's real attraction and power lay elsewhere.

First and foremost, as we have pointed out, it lay in the presence of Soviet forces: a presence that was both productive and counterproductive, but whose positive and negative aspects cannot possibly be separated out. It nevertheless remains a fact that by virtue of its strength and its victory over Germany, the Soviet Union held great fascination for an unspecified number of individuals of all classes. Even with all the factors narrowed down to that one effect, the party would have been able to fulfil its 'contract' with Moscow: to secure and hold a bridgehead while waiting for better days.

In addition, the novelty of a legal Communist Party also proved an undeniable attraction. Here, too, the advantages and disadvantages of the situation cannot be quantified. On the one hand, starting as it did from scratch, the party lacked an organization, experience, cadres and supporters; on the other hand, precisely because of its novelty, it represented an alternative that many Hungarians of the younger generation were willing to try. Their view of 1919 was unsympathetic, but those events had in any case involved the older generation. For lack of sociological studies of the electorate, it is impossible to tell what age groups voted Communist in 1945. What we do know is that the party itself had a fairly 'young' composition during the immediate post-war period and that even in 1948, before its fusion with the SDP, 18.9 per cent of its members were under the age of twenty-four, and 63 per cent between the ages of twenty-four and fifty.[20]

Finally, there was the attraction of a young, dynamic and disciplined party, a party of the working class and yet of the whole nation, revolutionary yet moderate – an image the party worked hard at trying to convey. Internal discipline and the inseparable notion of 'belongingness' (*partiinost*) undoubtedly played their part as well. They all conferred on the CP a cohesion, a mobilization potential and a force without precedent in the political life of Hungary, over and above its undeniable seductive charm.

The party's tactics were controversial. Numerous witnesses and historians have cast doubt on its sincerity. But sincere or otherwise, the party had a declared policy which it proclaimed in public and put into action, and this alone earned it the support of a relatively large proportion of the population. The same was true of its loudly trumpeted nationalism.

The front-building tactics were continued throughout 1945–8, despite the many blows the Communists delivered to the 'national contract'. And so what was according to some no more than a temporary expedient (and seen in retrospect it was just that) had the appearance of a long-term strategy.

The balance of forces changed constantly in favour of the CP thanks to the success of its 'salami tactics': all adversaries were eliminated 'slice after slice'. The CP continued to claim that its objective was 'a free, democratic and independent Hungary', in other words a 'new democracy' or a 'people's democracy' led by a government representing all the democratic forces. The CP thus presented itself as a committed partner in a large-scale national project and not as a Marxist-Leninist revolutionary and purely proletarian party.

The term 'dictatorship of the proletariat' was not even mentioned, and the Party's spokesmen, with Mátyás Rákosi at their head did not stop castigating those 'old sectarian comrades' who hankered nostalgically after the Soviet republic of 1919. That republic's errors and excesses, and particularly those of Béla Kun '& Co.', were held responsible for its failure – a solution all the more appealing since Béla Kun had been rotting in a pauper's grave of some GPU prison for ten years, not to mention the moral vault reserved for 'deviationists' by the Comintern in general and by Stalin in person. In short, to put it at its mildest, Rákosi's CP distanced itself from sectarians of all kinds – a convenient way of lumping together 'Kun & Co.', the leaders of different factions such as Pál Demény and Aladár Weisshaus, the vanished members of the International Brigades, the 'deviationists' in the clandestine CP and also the innumerable victims of the Moscow purges buried in the vast collective tomb into which the Communist movement had been turned.

The CP also took further tactical steps to brush up its new image. As a sponsor of land reform, it gave the misleading impression of having hit upon a genuinely democratic solution to the agrarian problem, presented under the battlecry of 'Land to the Peasants'. Anyone talking of the collectivization or nationalization of land was immediately labelled a 'leftist' or a 'sectarian'. On the cultural plane, Georg Lukács was promoted into a kind of literary 'Pope', one who was admittedly rather dogmatic in the eyes of writers inhabiting a poetic universe and unwilling to help with the construction of a new society; but nevertheless an unexpectedly liberal and broad-minded 'Pope' in comparison with such men as Zhdanov or even Bertolt Brecht. Lukács's cultural platform – held up by József Révai – proved a wonderful boost to the 'one-nation' policy of the CP and was even an integral part of it. In fact, in Hungary more than anywhere else, politics and culture were intimately, indeed inseparably, linked by tradition. A political party making an appeal to the living roots of the nation would certainly have failed to convince anybody had this not gone hand in hand with a cultural programme harking back to the country's great literary traditions and inviting all artists, writers, scholars and intellectuals to follow the example of Petöfi, Ady and Attila József and to come out of their 'ivory towers'.[21]

Until 1948–9, few writers or artists were subjected to persecution. Several writers close to the anti-semitic extreme Right were imprisoned (including some, such as the great poet József Erdélyi, who were later released and rehabilitated); others were condemned to silence. A number of 'bourgeois conservative' writers and intellectuals close to Horthy and his circle, among them the famous Ferenc Herczeg, were left completely in peace. Others less compromised by sympathy for the old régime even continued to publish their writing, to exhibit their works of art, to make films. Few of them, and similarly few academics, doctors or lawyers, chose to go into exile before 1948 or 1949.

Quite obviously, the world of political ideas was put under closer constraint than the world of art and letters. The 'transition' period nevertheless allowed some revival even of political thought and threw up several remarkable personalities. At debates in the Forum Club, and also in journals and reviews, there was a clash of sharp minds; and while one could not come out with everything, one could at least discuss the nature of society, the past and the future. It was not only such party ideologists as Georg Lukács, József Révai, Márton Horváth and Géza Losonczy who took part in these debates, but also such non-Communist thinkers as István Bibó.[22]

When it came to national traditions, no one extolled, or dared to extol in the presence of the Red Army, the heroes of Hungary's independence struggles as loudly as did the leaders of the CP. In their writings and speeches, the 'new Hungary' and her 'new democracy' were represented as the direct heirs to Prince Rákóczi's national uprising and of Kossuth's war of independence in 1848. A 'Forty-Eighter' was apparently blowing across Hungary but not even the slightest gust from the east.

Among the many aspects of this national line, perhaps even tainted by a touch of chauvinism, special mention must be made of the party's great project to raise a new élite. To that end, people's colleges were set up to train not only young workers' and peasants' cadres, but also cadres of bourgeois origin, in a basically democratic and national spirit. In these colleges, under the control of NEKOSz (the National League of People's Colleges) and under the patronage of László Rajk, the Communist minister of the interior, nothing was castigated as vigorously as sectarianism and all other forms of 'left-wing deviationism'.[23]

The party's attitude to the churches was, like most other things, a mixture of moderation and violence. At first, the CP refused rigorously to adopt the anticlerical and atheist approach of old. Mátyás Rákosi, the party's general secretary, had himself photographed at scores of baptisms and became godfather to hundreds of children during electoral and propaganda tours of the provinces. There were some areas, however, where the party was not prepared to compromise with the churches. To begin with, it stood firmly by the expropriation of church lands, especially those owned by the Catholic Church, one of the biggest landowners. Similarly, tolerance of church schools proved to be of short duration. Most of the measures taken to dissolve the religious orders also affected the teaching orders. The secularization of education, approved by most democratic parties, followed soon afterwards. Finally, though the CP tempered the atheist and anticlerical zeal of its most radical followers, it was not nearly so temperate when it came to cracking down on 'clerical reaction'. There is no doubt that such a reaction did exist – to certain prelates, the defence of the church was inseparably bound up with the preservation of various political ideas from the past. Such was the case with Cardinal Mindszenty and other less well-known church dignitaries. Their hostile attitude gave the CP a convenient pretext for condemning all clerics of insufficient docility and to prepare the way for the police repression that followed soon afterwards.

Let us next look at the party's attitude to the so-called national committees. To explain it, however briefly, we must first set out the differences between 'national committees', 'workers' councils', 'the council movement' and allied terms.[24]

At the end of 1944 and the beginning of 1945, Hungary once again gave rise to a movement advocating self-government, but under a new name and in different circumstances. Whether it happened spontaneously or as a result of prodding by the Communists (and in some cases by the other parties), 'national committees' sprang up in various places as expressions of the people's will and as organs of public administration. The Provisional Government established in Debrecen, soon to move to Budapest, granted them statutes which were, however, modified a little later. At the same time, 'factory committees' appeared and were charged to take control of the management. These two types of committee therefore had quite different functions from those of the national committees. But before we examine the role of either, we must first answer the following question: why 'committees' rather than 'workers' councils'?

The Communists (and for that matter the non-Communists) were obviously anxious to avoid all reminders of the councils of 1919, not only because of the unpleasant memories many Hungarians had of their Soviet Republic, but probably for reasons of international diplomacy as well. On the eve of Yalta, at the height of inter-Allied collaboration, Moscow would hardly have appreciated the creation of a council movement that could easily have been interpreted as a Soviet movement, a wish to sovietize Hungary. And so the term 'council' was proscribed during the 'transition' years, only to resurface again as a term applied to local administrative bodies after the party's seizure of power.

In 1944–5, therefore, it was *committees*, not councils, that sprang up everywhere and took charge of local affairs. At first, they acted as local authorities and administrations, and as such they were genuinely self-governing. Wherever the public authorities of the old régime had disintegrated, the new committees took their place; wherever the old administration continued, they subjected it to their own control and political domination.[25] But not for long.

In January 1945, the Provisional Central Government began to strip them of their administrative powers and vested them, as in the past, in state or municipal administrative agencies. Shortly afterwards, in March–April, the committees lost what remained of their original prerogatives, to become purely consultative bodies with no real powers. The fate of the Budapest national committee illustrates these successive changes clearly.[26] Set up on 21 January 1945, the Budapest committee was a genuine municipal government, indeed a political structure of national importance because of the weight of the capital, and remained so for several months. Then it began to lose its influence until finally it disappeared in April 1946. This happened because, in the meantime, the traditional municipal agencies in the capital had been reconstructed under Zoltán Vas, the mayor of Budapest.

Local committees everywhere else were subjected to a similar amputation of their functions. Thus, following a decree issued on 4 January 1945, they were reduced to mere 'associations of local democratic parties', while the traditional administrative machine was everywhere re-introduced. The committees, having no right to meddle in the affairs of that machine, gradually faded away.[27]

Why did the Communist Party allow these committees to fall by the wayside? To answer this question, we have to go back to the discussions in Moscow in the winter of 1944, before the return home of the Hungarian Communist leaders. In the course of these discussions, several views were expressed about the nature of the committees the party intended to create, not only to supplant the old administration but also as 'revolutionary organs' capable of nudging the future government in the 'right' direction. The Muscovites were afraid that this government would prove too half-hearted by virtue of the partly Horthyite composition imposed on it by the Soviet leaders. The future government of Hungary, they thought, would turn out to be less democratic (read: less pro-Communist) than the Bulgarian government.

The Communist leaders accordingly decided to make use of committees but did not really know how. That, Révai explained, would depend on the class struggle. The party did not, in any case, want to be landed with 'dual power' (central government and workers' councils as in Russia in 1917). The problem, Révai went on to say, was to decide 'what is better: for the government to control [the national committees] or for the latter to control the government. Which would give the party greater influence? We could not give the answer in advance.' George Lukács was of the same opinion: 'Everything depends on the circumstances, on [the answer to the question of] where our strength will lie.'[28]

As it happens, the 'circumstances' were quick to provide the answer. Because the national committees had been built on a quadripartite basis (each one being a 'coalition government' on a local scale), the Communists were in most cases in the minority. They accordingly preferred to reduce the committee's role in favour of the central power – the government and its administrative arms – which the CP, although in a minority at this level as well, could control better and bend to its own interests more readily than it could a multitude of locally run bodies.

In short, as the Hungarian historian Bálint Szabó has pointed out, 'the leaders of the Communist Party failed to realize that the national committees could have embodied the new form of the workers' and peasants' dictatorship and later the dictatorship of the proletariat'.

Actually, only the National Peasant Party favoured a new state based on popular, self-governing institutions.[29] The CP, for its part, quickly came down in favour of the restoration of centralized state power. László Rajk's appointment as minister of the interior completed this move towards a strong centralized government in which the Communists held the key positions while waiting to lay their hands on the rest of the state machine.

The factory committees outlived the national committees. They had never had any real political power, and simply served as outposts for CP attacks on the employers and the Social Democrats. After the nationalization of factories and the absorption of the SDP, the CP no longer had need of these committees either. In the summer of 1947, the trade unions took over the running of the factory committees, all of which became trade-union committees in 1948. Their disappearance put an end – until the fleeting 1956 revolution – to all self-governing projects, and indeed to the idea of workers' control.

A final question arises: were there any differences within the party about the political line to be adopted in the immediate post-war period? Various writers have suggested that there were three distinct conflicts: first, a conflict between those who hankered after the 1919 Soviet republic and the 'frontist' leaders who favoured co-operation between the different classes and non-Communist democratic parties; second, a conflict between the Communist 'Left' and those upholding the 'official' party line; third, a conflict between the men who had returned from Moscow and the 'home-based' – and until then clandestine – leadership of the party.[30]

There is no doubt that some party members in Moscow as well as in Hungary hankered after the 1919 dictatorship of the proletariat and the republic of councils. The first group, however, had learned from their own sad experiences that it was neither prudent nor sensible to oppose the official Comintern line.

The case of the several hundred survivors of 1919 who had stayed behind in Hungary was not so very different. The new party

leadership gave them to understand very quickly that their protestations of revolutionary fervour would henceforth be considered
so many left-wing and sectarian deviations.

The case of another set of Communist 'leftists', however, was
different. They were pilloried as Trotskyists and deviationists by
the 'official' party. The two largest and best-known of these groups
were led respectively by Aladár Weisshaus and Pál Demény, members of the 'official' party until the end of the 1920s. Subsequently
they distanced themselves from the party for different ideological
reasons and set up clandestine Communist groups of their own.
Their influence among the workers and young people was relatively large: the number of supporters in the industrial centres was
larger than the official party membership. As just one example of
their importance, and of that of Pál Demény in particular, we need
only mention that his group vied for influence with the Communist
Party on the eve of the liberation of Budapest, and that, according
to the *Historical Dictionary of the Workers' Movement*,[31] the group had
to be invited to sign a special agreement with the 'official' party, as
a consequence of which the Demény group renounced its partisan
activities. The majority of the group, we are told in the same work,
loyally adhered to this agreement and several joined the Communist Party.[32]

In his memoirs,[33] Pál Demény mentions several meetings, in
1944, between representatives of his group and those of the 'official'
party led by László Rajk. The last of these meetings, before the
arrival of the Red Army, was held on 6 November in the presence
of Rajk, Gábor Péter and three other members of the Central
Committee of the illegal Communist Party. According to
Demény, 'general agreement' was reached to merge the two organizations. Demény also recounts how, after the entry of the Red
Army, the painter Sándor Ék, back from Moscow, came to look
for him accompanied by a Soviet officer and conducted him to a
place outside Budapest already liberated by the Red Army. Here he
was asked to help the party with its propaganda campaign. A day
or two later, Gábor Péter came for him, ostensibly to take him to
Ernö Gerö. In fact, Péter took Demény to a police station as 'a
prisoner of the party'. He found he was not the only one in the
cells. Among the other 'party prisoners' he met József Skolnik,
former secretary of the illegal Communist Party. For the rest, after
a brief period of privileged treatment, these 'party prisoners' suffered the same fate as fascists and other detainees. Demény was not
allowed to leave his 'hosts' until twelve years later, in 1957. He has
lived in Budapest ever since.

The itineraries of other 'deviationists' were more or less the same. The party quickly got them out of the way, even though they posed no threat to the powerful organization the party had become thanks to the support of the Soviet sister party.

A tenacious legend about a cloak-and-dagger conflict within the party is linked to the name of László Rajk, a former secretary of the illegal party who became minister of the interior and finally minister of foreign affairs. A thoroughgoing Communist, he is said to have been executed in 1949 in order to rid the leadership, dominated by Rákosi and his coterie, of the strongest personality in the 'home-based' group.

However plausible this allegation may seem to be, it is not supported by a single verifiable fact. Over the past forty years, no credible information has leaked out about possible dissensions in the Politburo, other than the problems already examined, such as Imre Nagy's 'deviation' regarding the collectivization of agriculture. In any case, documents, speeches, witnesses all suggest that Rákosi, far from considering Rajk a threat at that stage, held him in some esteem and that the feeling was mutual.[34] The party leader's distrust, if distrust there was, must therefore have been induced much later and not immediately after the war, that is to say at the time when the alleged conflicts or dissensions were supposed to have occurred.

What then remains of these dissensions? The only tangible fact, which we have already mentioned, is that on their return home the 'Muscovite' leaders rebuilt the party without bothering to involve members of the illegal party they had left behind in Budapest or its Central Committee, in other words without the best-known 'home-based' militants. However, after the liberation of Budapest in February 1945, the two committees merged and, after his return from fascist prisons (between December 1944 and May 1945), László Rajk was also co-opted.

The proceedings of the first national conference of the Hungarian Communist Party, on 20–1 May 1945, bear out this version of the facts. It elected a Central Committee of twenty-five members,[35] seven of whom were Muscovites and eighteen of whom were 'home-based' militants, and this despite the fact that, in his address, Rákosi alleged that 'the gravest fault of our party is its left-wing sectarian disorder' and that most of the veterans of 1919 were as unsuited to the role of party leaders as were some of the younger militants in the 'home-based' party. The resolution adopted by the conference also underlined the danger of the 'sectarian spirit', condemned the dissolution of the party in 1943 and added that, because of oppression by the forces of reaction, many Communists had been prevented from absorbing 'the teachings of Marx, Engels, Lenin and Stalin'.[36]

While this severe criticism had no repercussions on the composition of the Central Committee, it did much to justify the packing of the Politburo and the higher party echelons with former émigrés. Thus five of the eleven members of the Politburo were 'Muscovites',[37] and in the Secretariat three – Rákosi, Farkas and Révai – were Muscovites while only two – Kádár and Rajk – were 'home-based' men.

At the Third Congress of the Hungarian Communist Party (29 September to 1 October 1946), the Central Committee was enlarged to thirty-one members, the Politburo to nine: Rákosi, Farkas, Gerö, Imre Nagy and Révai from the Muscovite group and Apró, Kádár, Kossa and Rajk from the 'home-based' party.[38]

There was therefore a successive shift in decision-making power in favour of the Moscow group. In particular, the weight of the four most prominent 'Muscovite' leaders – Rákosi, Farkas, Gerö and Révai – made itself felt increasingly in the Politburo and the Secretariat, as we know from the unanimous reports of several witnesses.[39]

Personal testimony also confirms that a large proportion of the 'home-based' militants welcomed the 'seizure of power' by their experienced comrades from Moscow enthusiastically and with relief.[40] What, if any, other reservations did they have?

Sándor Nógrádi, himself a returnee from Moscow, has come out with these severe strictures: 'The Committee Abroad [i.e. the Muscovites] imagined that they alone had the competence to lead. That is the truth of the matter'; and he goes on to say:

> A group of Communists in the Soviet Union had decided from the outset that, after their return to Hungary, they would secure the leadership of the party over the heads of the militants and cadres left inside the country and above all without bothering to ascertain whether they themselves were sufficiently familiar with the situation there . . . When they realized that their 'local' comrades were beset with an inferiority complex, they rejoiced and concluded that the others still had a long way to go before they acquired the necessary leadership skills . . . Having first underestimated them, they very quickly pushed them to one side, then manufactured charges against them and finally destroyed them.[41]

According to some sources which, however, lack documentary corroboration, a strong 'leftist' current persisted among the internal party leadership until the beginning of 1945.

A look at the discussions that took place during the foundation of the party early in 1945, first at Szeged and then in Budapest, supports this interpretation: several speakers came down firmly in favour of the dictatorship of the proletariat.[42] It should not, however, be forgotten that the new party 'line' had only just been put forward by the 'Muscovites', that the first conference adopting the new programme was not held until May, and that a few differences of opinion do not entitle us to infer the existence of a strong leftist current. It is rather in the home-based militants' difficulties in 'updating' their views, so as to fall in with the Muscovites (who, in turn, were under pressure from the Soviet leaders) that we must seek the root of the differences; the militants were even asked to stop calling for socialism and the dictatorship of the proletariat. This aspect of the debate was to continue until it was brought to a precipitate halt at the end of the conference in May 1945, even though, for expediency's sake, the party continued its anti-leftist witch hunt. In fact, the 'home-based' leaders (Rajk, Kádár, Apró and Horváth) were quick to rally to what would henceforth be the sole and unchallenged 'line', namely the policy of a democratic alliance. This they did the more readily as the illegal party and its paper *Szabad Nép*, which had reappeared in 1944, had already adopted a similar line with this – large but purely tactical – difference: the paper continued to proclaim the party's socialist objectives.

Inasmuch as the paucity of sources allows us to draw any conclusions, we might put it that many old militants (including those flung back into the arms of the party by recent events) were to the 'left' of the ultra-moderate new line without being genuine 'leftists'. What dismayed them was not so much the positive side of the programme of class alliances and the counsels of moderation, but the leaders' exaggerated professions of democratic fervour and patriotism, and their insistence on hiding the past and disguising their real objectives.

The campaign against the 'Left' was still in full cry when the next turnabout was already being enacted, leading, albeit gradually, to the restoration of the 'authentic' Communist programme: the seizure of power and the dictatorship of the proletariat, two idols only just consigned to the flames.

Portents of this current also appeared both in the hardening of the party's attitude to the forces of 'reaction', under which term they lumped together all sorts of tendencies; and in the economic sphere, where they tightened the screw on the bourgeoisie; and finally in the ideological sphere. In fact, the Third Congress of the

Communist Party went well beyond the customary speeches about the party's ultimate Socialist and hence anti-capitalist objectives.[43] To some, for instance a journalist on the Smallholders' *Kis Ujság* (Small Paper), this was, if not a declaration of war, then at least a warning shot.[44] As for Rákosi, though he did not offer the same interpretation at the time, he nevertheless declared later that 'it [the Third Congress] adopted a militant programme and militant tactics of moving towards the Socialist revolution'. Some historians, including Dezsö Nemes, have taken the same view; others have questioned this interpretation.[45]

In any case, the party entered a more combative phase in the autumn of 1946, and in 1947 stepped up its campaign against right-wing smallholders and the Catholic Church. The next crucial step would be taken a year later in the struggle for monolithic power.

Immediately after the war, the two workers' parties, the Communists and the Social Democrats, had renewed the pact of co-operation they concluded in October 1944, but this time they had left out, *inter alia*, the hotly contested paragraph concerning the prospects of the future unification of the two parties.[46]

However, the idea of unification had not been completely shelved by the Communists. For various tactical reasons, some not entirely rational, they periodically refloated the call for a merger, thus upsetting not only the Social Democratic 'Right', which was hostile to them, but also the partly pro-Communist 'Left'.

Thus in 1947, and particularly after the autumn elections, the CP launched yet another reunification campaign – this time successfully. Why on that date? One obvious reason was the relative weakness of the CP, despite its share of 21 per cent of the votes (which made it the leading party). The other fundamental reason came from outside. The Cold War was at its height. The Communist push into Eastern Europe had been 'contained' at the frontiers of Greece and Turkey by the Truman Doctrine, in France and in Italy by the ejection of the Communists from government, and finally in 1948 by the Allied stand at the demarcation line in Berlin. The Marshall Plan had come in 1947.

As I have tried to show, developments in 1947 also had crucial repercussions on the international status of Hungary. The peace treaty stipulated that all foreign troops stationed in Hungary must first be withdrawn. It added, however, that the Soviet Union reserved the right of 'retaining on Hungarian territory what armed forces might prove necessary for maintaining the lines of communication of the Soviet Army with the Soviet zone of occupation in Austria' (Art. 22) – a right not surrendered until 1955, after the signing of a treaty with Austria, when it was immediately replaced with a bilateral agreement. Despite this stipulation, the eventual withdrawal of the bulk of the Soviet Army was a source of great anxiety for the CP, which was left stranded on the shifting sands of an unpredictable balance of forces.

The final assault on the Social Democratic bastion was not to be delayed. It was launched during the election campaign in the summer of 1947 with speeches – by Rákosi and others – demanding the unification of the two parties. All speakers referred – for the first time it seems – to the agreement of 1944 recommending such a merger.

This campaign not only aroused the fury of the Social Democratic Right, but also of such Social Democrats on the Left as Bán, Szakasits and even Marosán, who felt that the insistence of the Communists was 'counter-productive'. Antal Bán, until then close to the Left even though he had never played the Communists' game, now turned his back on them. Szakasits, for his part, declared that 'you cannot move a party with a million supporters like a pawn on a chess board'.[47] He was to be proved terribly wrong.

Next, much as they had done before the elections in the autumn of 1947, the Communists resorted to a double tactic designed to break all resistance in the fraternal party. One the one hand, they started a Communist recruiting campaign in the ranks of the SDP; on the other hand, they unleashed their supporters inside the SDP against the right and centre for the express purpose of stifling all opposition to the merger.[48]

Concerted attacks on the 'Right' had, as it happens, already been practised by fellow travellers in the Smallholders' Party, followed by demands for the expulsion of one 'awkward' person after another. In the case of the SDP, the Communist objective was not to persuade the left-wing faction to break away, but rather to achieve the complete disarray of that large party. To that end, the Left in the SDP, and Marosán in particular, also used the 'landslide' argument (referring to the mass conversions of SDP members to the cause of Communism). For this they blamed the Right of the SDP, so much so that they felt justified in mounting a *putsch* against them. In the absence of Szakasits, Marosán managed to persuade a group of 'centrist' leaders to get rid of a number of 'rightists', including Anna Kéthly, Szeder and Szélig. On 18 February 1948, Marosán made public the resignation of these SDP stalwarts.

As expected, some 300,000 to 400,000 Social Democrats applied to the CP for membership the following day, in a veritable atmosphere of panic. The rest was no more than pure formality. Once 'purified' in this way, the SDP dismissed thirty-two of its parliamentary deputies. The date of the unification congress was fixed for 13 June 1948, following a ceremony to be held the previous evening.

But let us return to our analysis of the strategy and tactics of the CP at the beginning of the post-war period. One conclusion is inescapable: violence was never ruled out. In fact, appearances notwithstanding, CP tactics and strategy did not overlap. Had the party had no aims other than those it proclaimed, it would have renounced violence and waited calmly for its 'national' and reformist policies to bolster its electoral fortunes. But the semi-success – or semi-failure – of free elections had a radicalizing effect, and persuaded the party to harden its approach. The tough stance was stiffened even further as relations between the Allied powers deteriorated. And so violence came to resume its place in the party's tactics, with just one difference from the past: now it was backed by a foreign army. However, after 1945, as before, the party remained a heterogeneous organization lacking real social cohesion. Let us devote a few lines to this aspect.

Though it held all the trumps, the Communist Party's room to manoeuvre was severely restricted. Its alien genealogy cannot be stressed too strongly. Despite its noisy nationalistic protestations, the party was widely considered to be a Russian and Jewish party, the torch-bearer of a foreign ideology. Now, Hungary was of old a hot-bed of Russophobia and anti-semitism and latterly of anti-Communism as well, all of them deeply entrenched in the collective consciousness, not least among the peasants and workers, let alone the 'Christian and seigniorial class' which set the tone. To understand the origins of the anti-Communist mental attitude, we have to go back to 1919: the Red Terror, and the arrogance of the Communists, most of whom were Jews into the bargain. Russophobia was rooted in the memory of Russian intervention in the 1848–9 war of independence: many families fervently treasured the memory of the poet Petöfi, mortally wounded by a Cossack lance and writing the word 'Liberty' in the sand with his blood. Myth and reality combined in this legend and were fanned further by the anti-Bolshevik propaganda of the Horthy régime. The resulting resentment, hatred and mistrust would undoubtedly have been less virulent in Hungary than in Poland, and might have faded away in time, had it not been for the war on the Russian front, the routing of the Hungarian army and the Soviet occupation. Soviet support for the CP, as we have seen, was largely held against the

Communists, so much so that an old and forgotten expression was resurrected: like the traitors of 1849, the Hungarian Communists became known as 'Muscovite guides'.

The party was given a second chance after the hardships of the war and the immediate post-war period: pillage and theft ceased, the Soviet control and occupation authorities became more discreet, and over half a million prisoners of war started to return from the USSR. Then, after a lull of approximately two years, the party threw itself into a violent political offensive coupled with attacks on the church, on social institutions and on the middle classes. Once the truce was over, the Communists turned from being 'Muscovite guides' into 'Muscovites' pure and simple, agents of a system detested by the great majority of the population.

An anti-semitic reaction was not long in coming. Hungary had admittedly witnessed violent and bloody anti-Jewish excesses but on an incomparably smaller scale than Poland. The survivors of the Holocaust had felt perfectly secure until anti-Communism became tainted with anti-semitism when the party's brutal climb to power began to strike many Hungarians as a Jewish plot.

In fact, as in all East European Communist parties, the Jewish rank and file, once so strong, had been radically cut. The party had become 90 per cent 'Christian'. Moreover, Communists of Jewish origin did not broadcast their ethno-cultural identity, let alone their religious roots. A Communist was an atheist – and a Magyar; or so the party directed. For most Jewish Communists, moreover, this approach was no imposition. Hungarian Jews, converted or not, had been assimilated to the Hungarian way of life ever since the nineteenth century. It nevertheless remains a fact that their Hungarian compatriots, while not actually practising discrimination against them, nevertheless drew a line between Jews and non-Jews, so much so that it was very difficult for a Jewish Communist to 'cross over'.

The mere presence of tens of thousands of Jews in the ranks of the party would not have elicited such hostile reactions had so many Jews not occupied such prominent positions. The men at the very top of the hierarchy were of Jewish extraction almost without exception, and the same was true, in somewhat smaller proportions, of the Central Committee, the political police, the press, publishing, the stage, the cinema. The deliberate and incontestable promotion of working-class cadres could not mask the fact that the decision-making power lay, in very large measure, with Jewish comrades sharing a petty bourgeois background. The top brass – and Rákosi in particular – were fully aware of this situation and tried to alter it. But nothing came of the attempt. In the end, the party leadership remained unchanged.

The successive elimination of non-Jewish leaders did not help matters. With the removal of Rajk in 1949, one of the most prestigious leaders of the 'home-based' party vanished. With Sándor Zöld's suicide, the party lost one more. János Kádár, imprisoned by Rákosi in 1951, was another of the handful of Communists of popular origin. Others, such as Géza Losonczy and Szilárd Ujhelyi, were to share a similar fate. The case of Imre Nagy was even more extraordinary, because this top party official of peasant stock, twice disgraced and finally executed after the 1956 revolution, was the *only* 'Muscovite' leader to enjoy genuine popularity. His second 'disgrace' and his expulsion from the party in 1955 explain to some extent, if not the roots, at least the immediate causes of the events of 1956. But that is to anticipate.

Besides these victims of fratricidal repression, there were other marked men, in fact a very much larger number of them, who shared the origins of the team in power. But that made little difference to the masses. Scandalous as it may be, the first group was looked on as scapegoats by the majority of the population, and the second as small fry devoured by the bigger sharks.

The Meaning of the Great Turning-point

In one of his exultant speeches, Mátyás Rákosi declared that 1948 was 'the great turning-point' in the history of the Communist Party and of Hungary, over which the CP henceforth intended to rule alone. In fact, the party had been dominating the political scene since the summer of 1947, though the finishing touches would not be applied until 1949, when the Rajk trial also put an end to all forms of 'deviation' within the ranks of the party. The turn of agriculture came later with mass collectivization in 1950–1, a date when cultural life, too, was placed in a stranglehold.

All the same, the leader of the CP was not mistaken when he called 1948 a turning-point: it effectively imposed unmitigated Stalinism for the next five years. Five years of Stalinism, five years of totalitarian rule, may seem a brief interlude in a history covering nearly three generations. However, these five years left indelible scars and shocked the country too deeply ever to be forgotten. They not only went with a legacy and a daily routine overhung with menace, but also spawned the most absolute form of Communist rule.

Were all these developments expected, prepared and minuted in Moscow, as the supporters of the so-called blueprint theory claimed? Or did the CP enter uncharted waters in 1945 ready to steer the course of democratic fronts until a favourable tide happened, quite unexpectedly, to put it on course for a seizure of power? Historians remain divided on this point and until such time as documents jealously guarded in the Kremlin can be examined, it is impossible to give a definite answer. There is, however, one factor to make the author of this study and other historians incline towards the second alternative:[49] in 1948 the CP leadership was patently taken unawares by the course of events. The proof is the 'self-critical confession' of Mátyás Rákosi, and more explicitly of József Révai, that they failed to appreciate the correct meaning of 'people's democracy'. We were wrong, they declared in substance, to consider the new democracy as a permanent political and social structure different from that found in the Soviet Union. In fact, a people's democracy was but one expression of the dictatorship of the proletariat, only distinguished from that prevailing in the Soviet Union by the absence of soviets.[50]

But why did this 'ideological correction' need to take the form of self-criticism? It would seem that the leaders of the Hungarian CP were expected to shoulder responsibility for what was in fact a change in policy decided by Stalin himself in 1948. That change was first mooted publicly during the Comintern conference in the autumn of 1947, but probably not as unequivocally as people have since claimed, the less so as the Yugoslav Party, which excelled by its revolutionary zeal, had just been censured by Stalin for its leftist excesses. We shall be looking at this matter in closer detail. The Hungarian team may well have been led to believe that, while they were expected to accelerate the tempo of change, they must neither adapt tactics to force the pace nor abandon the 'frontist' approach.

The new interpretation of the meaning of 'people's democracy' by Rákosi and Révai was to be followed by such other 'adjustments' as the refutation of Lukács's theses concerning the new democracy. These adjustments were made fairly late in the day, which further confirms the impression that there was uncertainty in leading party circles about the future of people's democracy. In short, there are several indications to suggest that, from the close of the war to at least the end of 1947, the CP anticipated a long – and perhaps a very long – 'transition' period. This is not to gainsay the fact that it at no time relinquished its 'final aim' of establishing a Communist society at some future date. But that is not where the problem lies. Acting on the assumption that the 'transition' might last, not three, but, say, thirty years, the party could well have been justified in basing its 'strategy' on the frontist and new democratic approach; in which case, the seizure of power – suddenly in Prague or more gradually in Budapest – would have come as a sudden interruption to the anticipated course of events. On the contrary assumption, of course, a *coup d'état* must have been planned from the outset and meticulously prepared many long years in advance. But might there perhaps be an intermediate explanation? The policy of 'wait and see', of living in expectations and making the best of circumstances is not, after all, an exclusive Anglo-Saxon prerogative – Communists of all types have applied it more than once in their history.

> The dictatorship of the proletariat emerged during the development of people's democracy, the *History of the Hungarian Workers' Movement* tells us. However, there was no ideological explanation of how that had happened when the party leaders had stuck to their policy of attaining socialism through a people's democracy but without a dictatorship of the proletariat. At the end of 1948, the leaders of the people's democracies, raising the question with Stalin, discovered that a people's democracy already fulfilled the function of the dictatorship of the proletariat and that, consequently, a dictatorship of the proletariat already existed in their countries.[51]

This is a revealing text not only because of its language, but also because of the information it contains. If the gist is correct, then it must indeed have been *Stalin's new directives* that obliged the leaders of the satellite Communist parties to 'proclaim' the dictatorship of the proletariat retroactively and hence to fit the facts to the fiction.

In 1949, on the occasion of the critical debate directed against Lukács, József Révai, as ideological leader of the party, made an astonishing declaration, some of which merits being quoted at length:

> We do not reproach comrade Lukács for proclaiming a 'literary united front', the fraternal collaboration of all democratic writers in 1945–6. Nor was his error his failure to call for socialist realism in 1945. His error was to oppose socialist realism by and large in 1949. This stems directly from his false concepts regarding the people's democracy and these false concepts determined his theory of literature in the framework of people's democracy.
> 'Because the key to the situation' – Lukács wrote in 1946 – 'lies precisely in that a new democratic culture is emerging all over Europe without any change in the material base, the capitalist mode of production . . .' 'The principle of people's democracy' – he wrote in

1947 – 'first of all in our country, but elsewhere, too, is only beginning to be applied and even if it should attain its objectives, it does not aim at eliminating the capitalist mode of production, hence it cannot strive to establish a classless society.'

I could continue to quote similar views, but I don't think it is necessary. Are they mere slips of the pen? Or is it simply that comrade Lukács failed to clarify those problems of the nature and development of people's democracy which at the time – in 1945–7 – even the Party did not completely clarify? If it were only this, it would scarcely be worth mentioning comrade Lukács's false concepts in the context of a literary-theoretical debate. But the point is not this. A people's democracy which does not even aim at creating socialism, that does not even wish to touch the capitalist mode of production – such a concept means more than a certain lack of clarity regarding the problems of development toward socialism. Comrade Lukács took a transitional and temporary situation for an absolute and final state of affairs. He supposed that the people's democracy as such, as distinct from bourgeois ('formal') democracy, can survive and perpetuate itself on a capitalist footing. There is no need to prove that this is nonsense in theory and in practice a harmful and opportunistic concept. Where do these concepts stem from? From the fact that comrade Lukács, while fighting against fascism, forgot about the struggle against capitalism. From the fact that – not only in the last 5 years, but long before – in his struggle against imperialist decadence he was contrasting the old plebeian, populist revolutionary forms and traditions of bourgeois democracy to fascism, generalizing and transforming them into myths . . .

Is it pure chance that Lukács (see his critique of Tibor Déry's novel *Unfinished Sentence* in January 1948) regards the illegal communist movement in Hungary 'sectarian' as a whole? . . . It appears to comrade Lukács to be 'sectarian', because he considers the pre-popular front communist policy, with its strategic aim the dictatorship of proletariat, to be sectarian. He considers communist policy correct only since the advent of the anti-fascist struggle, of the popular front policy, from the adoption of people's democracy as strategic goal. He overlooks the fact that this is only a diversion forced upon us by fascism and not the exchange of an overall incorrect, overall sectarian policy with correct popular policy.[52]

This text proves several things. On the one hand, it confirms and corroborates the other declarations and excuses concerning the belated – hence culpable – 'awakening' of the Communist leaders. On the other hand, it shows that the latter, unlike Lukács, had never been serious about their allegiance to the Popular Independence Front. Throughout the 'transition', they had kept their attention fixed on relations between Moscow and the Western allies, relations they knew to be precarious. Hence they had sat back and waited for the bubble to burst, at which point the HCP would at last fulfil its 'contract' with the Communist world, make common cause with the Soviet Union and align itself with the Soviet system.

The 'Prague coup' in February 1948, moreover, was intended to make it perfectly clear that all the countries in the region, be they former friends or enemies of the USSR, were destined to go in the same direction. It is in this light that the seizure of power must be viewed, rather than in the light of ideological considerations, as some Western historians have naïvely contended.

It is in this light, too, that we must interpret the 'dialectics' of the Communists' alliance policy on all levels: the alliance between the Soviet Union with the other Big Four at the international level; the alliance between the CP and its partners at the party and 'local' government level. In other words, it is idle to pose the question in terms of sincerity or duplicity. The Kremlin practised its policy of alliances, and subsequently its policy of breaking with its former partners, as sincerely as its interests dictated. The Communist parties simply followed suit. All that was needed was to judge the right moment for each coup.

The 'theory of circumstances' put forward by some American revisionist historians, who argue that the Kremlin's 'satellization' of Eastern Europe was nothing but a response to American acts of hostility, has the ring of being as false as the theory of premeditation. Stalin and his advisers 'premeditated' and 'planned' just one thing: not an inch of conquered territory in Europe must be allowed to escape their net. This is a factor, incidentally, which also explains the Finnish exception. For the rest, the precise moment and the form of the seizure of power hinged very largely on a combination of external and internal circumstances. Instead of imagining a universal scenario written by an omniscient and machiavellian Stalin, we would do better to consider that the Soviets envisaged and elaborated several scenarios with a view to securing an optimal hold on each of the countries concerned.

The formula for a pluralist people's democracy was therefore not an alternative, but no more and no less than a 'wait-and-see' policy. It was the springboard from which the party prepared, throughout the long years of transition, to make the great leap into the Stalinist system.

Finally, there are three more questions, all of which impinge on the origins of this interpretation.

The first concerns the Cold War. All our hypotheses converge on this one point, that the Cold War as a global confrontation made no more than a marginal impact on Hungary. While it is true that the country did not fall definitively into the Soviet camp until the famous 'turning-point' of 1948 – that is until the period of the great clashes round the Truman Doctrine, the Marshall Plan and the Berlin crisis – it is equally true that by that stage the signposts were already in position.

These signposts, though clearly perceived by British and American diplomats, elicited no energetic reactions from London or Washington. The British had abandoned Hungary to its fate well before Yalta; the Americans had never seen Hungary as a political counter. By all accounts, the policy of containment and the Marshall Plan did nothing to change this situation. No one lifted a little finger to try to save Hungary's pluralist democracy.

A further argument used to support the contention that circumstances alone changed the course of history in the different peoples' democracies is the claim that all Communist leaders declared that this democratic period would continue over a long period. In support of this claim, various writers have quoted Rákosi, Révai, Márton Horváth, Jenö Varga and even Dimitrov, who in 1946 spoke of the 'Bulgarian way'. Gomulka and Gottwald are quoted as sharing this opinion with regard to their own countries and so, we are told, did Giorgio Amendola in his discussion of the tendencies of Italian capitalism.[53] All these quotations have been seen as evidence in favour of the credibility of the thesis that the 'frontist' form of post-war Communist policy was simply an extension of the frontist policy of 1935–9, conceived with a view to a long period of collaboration between Communism and democracy, or even as an actual replacement for the old policy of embittered class struggle culminating in the dictatorship of the proletariat.

In fact, none of the quotations prove anything else than that such speeches were in fact being made by Communist leaders from Paris and Rome to Budapest and Warsaw, and even as far as Moscow. To keep them in correct perspective, we must remember that Stalin himself was making similar speeches. He missed no opportunity to assure the Allies that there was no question of foisting the Communist system on a liberated Europe. The 'democratic' language used by Communist parties immediately after the war was the product of a co-ordinated policy whose main lines were decided in Moscow, by Moscow, and imposed, as during the life of the Comintern, on all Communist parties without exception. Similarly the change that came in 1948 sprang from a policy again determined by Stalin and imposed in like manner on all fraternal parties.

The speeches themselves thus prove nothing at all. At best, we might frame the hypothesis – fragile and impossible to prove – that the first version of the party's policy, still democratic and pluralist, gained the consent of a number of European Communist leaders and rank-and-file militants. So much is possible, even likely, but it does not entitle us to speak of any democratic current within the Communist movement, let alone, as certain historians do, of a 'rearguard action' by the supporters of this current against the official line, a rearguard action they ostensibly fought from the meeting of the Cominform in 1947 until the final 'turning-point' in 1948 or even in 1949. In fact, the change of line proclaimed in high places was as unanimously accepted – with or without reservations or afterthoughts – as Stalin's order to drop the revolutionary programme of traditional Communism had been four years earlier. All ranks, caught by surprise or otherwise, fell in without demur.

That does not, of course, gainsay the existence in the various parties of minor currents opposed to one tactic or another; in the Hungarian Party it mainly took the form of comrades hankering after the 1919 revolution.

Why then should there be all these uncertainties and debates about the interpretation of the 1948 'turning-point'? One of the reasons is that all our knowledge about the direction-changing decision reached by the HCP leaders in concert with Stalin comes from such second-hand sources as the *History of the Hungarian Workers' Movement*. Moreover, if that book is right, then Stalin must have summoned his subordinates unceremoniously to Moscow to issue them with their new instructions. It goes without saying that every Communist Party with the least self-respect would have preferred to give the impression that Moscow, far from issuing instructions, never did more than proffer advice, the national parties themselves deciding whether or not to take it.

There is yet a third factor to contribute a measure of uncertainty. In the opinion of many historians,[54] it was at the inaugural meeting of the Cominform in September 1947 that the new directives were issued. This version is certainly correct – we have only to read the Cominform journal *For a Lasting Peace, for a People's Democracy* to have it confirmed. In particular, Zhdanov informed the Cominform that the era of the 'two camps' had begun, that henceforth the capitalist and the socialist worlds would be quite distinct and hostile to each other. It was in the Cominform that the Yugoslavs criticized the French and Italian parties for their lack of revolutionary ardour. It was from the Cominform platform that Kardelj decried as parliamentary cretinism the policy of forming coalitions with other parties. It was there, equally, that 'certain shortcomings' of the Hungarian party were exposed and criticized.

None of this alters the fact that the Hungarian Communist Party had gained approval for its alliance policy; that the first meeting of the Cominform still left open the possibility of pursuing the lines adopted immediately after the war. At the time, only the Yugoslavs continued to champion the radical-revolutionary approach, and this earned them some influence in the Communist world – it was only later that they began to be accused of all sorts of crimes and deviationist lapses. Then, at the end of 1948, Stalin himself saw fit to adopt the ultra-radicalism he had recently condemned so virulently.

The last question raised by the 'turning-point' of 1948 is how the party on the one hand and public opinion on the other were made to swallow it.

According to some authorities we have quoted above, the Third Party Congress held in September 1946 had already shown premonitory signs of a political sea change. The Hungarian historian Ágnes Ságvári is nevertheless right to dwell on a significant phrase in an article by Márton Horváth in the 7 November 1946 issue of the party paper, stating that 'the Hungarian development will involve a long period of popular democracy',[55] that is to say, in the language of the day, of pluralist people's democracy. Despite several sabre-rattling utterances, the Third Congress did not, in effect, give any signal for radical change. That was to come, as already pointed out, during the second half of 1947, with the concentrated attack on the Smallholders' Party, and even more forcefully at the end of the same year in the wake of three events: the implementation of the peace treaty and the consequent reduction of the Soviet presence; the somewhat disappointing outcome of the autumn elections in which the CP attracted 21 per cent of the votes, a figure that failed to place it in a dominant position unless it could destroy its rivals; and finally the establishment of the Cominform.

In this connection, Ágnes Ságvári quotes several premonitory passages from a document meant for internal use, in which the Hungarian delegation proffers an evaluation of the importance of the founding congress of the Cominform. The latter, the document states, 'has elaborated important modifications to the political and tactical line adopted by the Seventh Comintern Congress'.[56] 'The policy of the leaders of the MDP [the HCP]', Ágnes Ságvári goes on to explain, 'was not based on an analysis of the real situation, but on theoretical considerations interpreted and applied in a mechanistic manner. [Their] dogmatism was wholly based on the resolutions of the Cominform Bureau.'[57]

Moreover, while stressing that the Cominform meeting of 1947 was not at that stage as unmistakable a landmark of the new approach as were the anti-Titoist resolutions of the following years, Ágnes Ságvári nevertheless sees signs of an incipient reorientation, but one that would not come about until 1948, especially following Stalin's directives at the end of that year. She sums up the views of her Hungarian colleague Bálint Szabó as follows: the policy of the party until the summer of 1948 'was characterized by the search for a [new] path'.[58]

Szabó would probably not repudiate this succinct résumé. However, he attaches less importance to the chronology of events than to an analysis of the ideological speeches proffering various interpretations of 'popular democracy'. With the help of a representative number of addresses by different leaders, including a great many by George Dimitrov, Bálint Szabó shows that these leaders were anxious to demonstrate, in 1945 and in 1946, that a pluralist people's democracy was fully compatible with a socialist objective. What had changed was simply the method of getting there: henceforth it was thought possible to attain the objective without revolution or the dictatorship of the proletariat.[59] Even so, Bálint Szabó doubts the importance of these theoretical elaborations and shows that in several Soviet analyses produced at the time (for instance in an article by the philosopher Fedoseyev, published in *Bolshevik*, vol. 14, 1948), only the first possibility – socialism without *revolution* – was endorsed, but not the second, socialism without a *dictatorship*.[60]

It was not, however until the end of 1947 or the beginning of 1948 that the party drew the conclusion, and did so in the elaboration of its new economic directives, especially the collectivization of agriculture, and in moving more openly towards the adoption of socialism, the dictatorship of the proletariat and the single-party state. That reorientation, moreover, was opposed by Imre Nagy. According to Bálint Szabó, the use of the term 'people's democracy' became synonymous with 'construction of socialism'.[61] By contrast, it was apparently not until after a great debate in the Central Committee, in November 1948, that 'people's democracy' came to be identified with the 'dictatorship of the proletariat'.[62]

Only the last word now needed to be spoken: the official proclamation of a people's democracy in the form of the dictatorship of the proletariat, naturally followed by the retrospective interpretation of the preceding phase as the elaboration of that dictatorship. In other words, it had to be argued that the party's objective, even during the pluralist phase, had been nothing less than the dictatorship of the proletariat which Karl Marx, followed by Lenin and Stalin, considered to be an indispensable step in the progress of all Communist parties.

That last word was duly spoken, outside Hungary to begin with, by those preparing the Prague coup in February 1948, by Bierut in Poland on 15 December 1948, and finally by Dimitrov on 18 December. Soon afterwards, on 26 December, Ernö Gerö, in a letter, enjoined the Secretariat of the Hungarian Communist Party to draw the lessons of 'Comrade Stalin's last and very important theoretical demonstrations'. He went on to admit that, along with the other Hungarian leaders, he himself had 'tampered with the essence of Leninism to some extent by declaring that socialism could be built without the dictatorship of the proletariat'. (The historian must note, in parentheses, that 'these demonstrations by Comrade Stalin' have not been recorded.) We may take it that Bierut and Dimitrov consulted Stalin before the congress (at Warsaw), where Gerö must have been told which way the wind was blowing.[63] We have already described the sequel: following in the footsteps of their Bulgarian and Polish comrades, the Hungarian leaders, Rákosi and Révai chief among them, published several self-critical papers in 1949 and afterwards, deploring their failure to appreciate the true nature of people's democracy. As far as that particular turning-point is concerned, everything therefore points to the fact that the final impetus came at the end of 1948 or the beginning of 1949; and to Stalin.

Public opinion was to learn of the consequences of these successive reinterpretations with consternation. To the man in the street, the leaders' theoretical explanations were so many obscure lucubrations. As far as he was concerned, the alleged functions of a people's democracy – whether or not it was identified with the dictatorship of the proletariat – mattered little; what did matter was the hardening of the party line not only in words but also in deed. And hand in hand with the 'transition' to the dictatorship of the proletariat went tough measures during the year that had ushered in the new 'turning-point', and continued throughout the long Stalinist dictatorship – from 1949 to 1953.

–8–

Stalinism in Action

The SDP proved incapable of resisting the pressure of the Communist Party. It finally gave in and, on 12 June 1948, at a congress held at the same time as a Communist Party congress, voted for union, whereupon the two congresses merged. A new party was formed, and between then and the events of 1956, bore the name of *Magyar Dolgozók Pártja* (Hungarian Workers' Party). From 1945 to the merger of the two parties, the composition of the CP leadership had remained largely unchanged: nine members of the 1945 Central Committee made up the Politburo; the rest joined what became an enlarged Central Committee. In the Politburo appointed at the end of the Third Congress of the HCP, the Moscow team had accounted for five posts out of nine; the Muscovites had also dominated the General Secretariat and the Organization Committee in charge of the dedicated and strictly controlled party apparatus.

In the unified MDP, the 'leftist' Social Democrats were given a number of leading posts, but the old HCP organizational principles and the real leadership remained unchanged. Árpád Szakasits may have been made president of the new party, but Rákosi was its general secretary.

At cabinet level there were frequent changes. In August 1948, Rajk was appointed minister of foreign affairs, while János Kádár took over his place as minister of the interior. Several ministers from the Smallholders' Party were gradually eclipsed but, during a complete cabinet reshuffle in December of the same year, Lajos Dinnyés was replaced by István Dobi, another Smallholder, who was asked to form a new government largely dominated by ministers from the united MDP.

Virtually in sole control, the Communist Party began to adopt an openly Stalinist line. Nationalizations,[1] forced industrialization projects, the collectivization of agriculture, purges and mass arrests – Hungary was following the same path as the other people's democracies.

In 1949, when nearly all the former leaders of the Socialist Left in the unified party joined the veteran leaders of the democratic parties in prisons or graves, the elimination of 'dangerous' or 'awkward' Communists began. The Rajk trial in October 1949 gave the signal for a long series of liquidations within the Communist Party.

The Rajk Affair

On 23 December 1948, Cardinal Mindszenty was arrested; predictably he was found guilty at the end of his trial, on 8 February 1949. József Grösz, Archbishop of Kalocsa, followed him into prison soon afterwards, as did other Catholic and Protestant clergymen. Rigged trials of leading personnel from several industrial companies representing American or British interests were staged, such as that against the directors of the Maort Oil Company and the Standard Electric Company. Dozens of former parliamentary deputies from the 'coalition' parties were flung into prison, while their more fortunate comrades were merely banished from political life. On 10 September 1949, as a presage of the Rajk affair, Zoltán Horváth and Pál Justus were expelled from the party for supposedly being agents of the imperialist powers. In addition to men in the public eye, tens of thousands of 'small fry' were goaled, tortured or, at best, placed under house arrest.

In short, in 1949 a veritable Red Terror descended on Hungary, succeeded by fresh waves during the following years. No one has yet taken full stock of this dark period in which, according to the most cautious estimates, several tens of thousands of Hungarian citizens were subjected to police and judicial repression on political or economic grounds.[2]

In this orgy of terror, the Rajk affair did not excite Hungarian public opinion to any greater extent than had the trials and internments of priests, Social Democratic deputies, Catholics or, more generally, people's next-door neighbours. Indeed, many Hungarians welcomed the arrest and execution of the former minister of the interior, the man nicknamed the 'fist of the party', as a hopeful sign that the Communists were about to finish one another off.

In the history of the party, the Rajk trial was nevertheless set apart from the general terror, inasmuch as it was the first of a host of trials and purges of Communists and Social Democrats in the unified party. The arrest of László Rajk was announced in an official communique on 16 June 1949. His sentence and execution came on 24 September, the charges against members of the military implicated in the affair being referred back to a military tribunal.

On 24 September, Tibor Szönyi and András Szalai were also

sentenced to death, and in October the military tribunal sent György Pálffy, Béla Korondy, Dezsö Németh and Ottó Horváth to the firing squad. Others implicated in the Rajk affair received heavy prison sentences, the Yugoslav Lazar Brankov and the former Social Democrat Pál Justus among them. As already mentioned, several other trials, held *in camera*, were to follow in 1950: those of General László Sólyom, the Hungarian Army Chief of Staff, of Géza Losonczy, the former deputy minister of culture, of his father-in-law Sándor Haraszti, of the brilliant scholar Szilárd Ujhelyi, and of hundreds of other prominent personalities, including János Kádár.

What were the charges against László Rajk and his associates? What was the reason for their trial?[3] Of these two questions, the first, oddly enough, merits less attention than the second. The trial was rigged from start to finish – not a single charge, not one admission bore any relationship to the truth. The confessions were extorted by a mixture of torture and 'persuasion', the nature of which went far beyond the fiction so powerfully presented in Koestler's famous novel *Darkness at Noon*. The police agents who staged the affair were not lacking in imagination, even though the Budapest trial was largely modelled on the Moscow trials in the 1930s of the former heroes of the Great October Revolution, namely Zinoviev, Kamenev, Radek and Bukharin.

One of their first objectives was to vilify the accused. This was done by transforming every stage in their dedicated lives into so many acts of treachery against the party, against the revolutionary cause and even against their comrades. Thus Rajk was painted before the tribunal as a forty-year-old villain who had been a spy all his life, a traitor who had been in the pay of every imperialist and fascist police force in Europe, from his native Hungary to the French Deuxième Bureau and not omitting the Gestapo. One of his former comrades in the Spanish Civil War produced a long list of Rajk's anti-communist and treacherous activities, first in the International Brigades and then in the French internment camps. According to other witnesses, all the accused had belonged directly or through intermediaries to an American spy network set up in Switzerland during the war by Allen Dulles and one of his agents, a man named Noel Field.[4] Most of the depositions and 'confessions' bore on the alleged links between Rajk and Titoist agents, including Ranković, the Yugoslav minister of the interior, in person. They were said to have conspired to overthrow the people's democracy in Hungary.

From the individual charges – the accused, presented as craven cowards, were alleged to have been police informers, *agents provocateurs* and spies – the state passed on to charges of collective treason, the individual cases having simply laid the foundations for the 'Great Plot' indictment. The latter was meant to demonstrate that the felonious activities of the individuals concerned had but one criminal objective: the subversion of the Communist cause. At this collective level as well, the trial tried to establish a logical progression of events: it was only to be expected that Horthy's humble police agents of the 1930s should become agents of the Deuxième Bureau and of the Gestapo during the Spanish Civil War and the Second World War. From being spies for Allen Dulles, the path then led quite naturally to service with the imperialist Yugoslavs. Everything was finally thrown into the same melting-pot of universal imperialism, of a gigantic conspiracy against the Communist world.

In fact, the Rajk trial was but one move in a campaign extending throughout Central Europe. It was part of a series to be continued in Rumania and then in Czechoslovakia.[5]

As many observers and historians have stressed,[6] the trial had a marked anti-Titoist character. Péter Jankó, the president of the tribunal, and Gyula Alapi, the public prosecutor, made no secret of it. In his indictment, Alapi argued in particular:

> It is not just Rajk and his accomplices who are facing us over there in the dock, but also their foreign instigators, their imperialist masters in Belgrade and in Washington . . . All these facts . . . throw fresh light on the entire past of Tito, Kardelj, Ranković and Djilas, and above all on their role in the Yugoslav partisan struggles. Through the British and American intelligence officers attached to the partisan staff, Tito and his men sided, even during the war, with Anglo-American imperialism, and worked with it against the Soviet Union, at the very time when the Soviet Army was shedding its blood for the liberation of Yugoslavia.[7]

The Rajk affair may also, of course, have had secondary objectives. This possibility is strongly suggested by (uncorroborated) private information to the effect that the initiative came, not from Moscow, but from Akadémia Street in Budapest, the headquarters of the Hungarian CP. According to my informant, the then Soviet Security Service, the MGB, initially adopted a reserved attitude to the trial 'project' put forward by Mátyás Rákosi and his circle, and only came round after some hesitation and then on Stalin's orders. Whatever the truth of the matter, Rákosi and his closest colleagues at the time – Ernö Gerö, a Soviet intelligence veteran, and Mihály Farkas – had good reason to display and prove their anti-Titoism, precisely because neighbouring Yugoslavia had exerted a very strong influence over the Hungarian party before Yugoslavia's expulsion by the Cominform in the summer of 1948. Many people still remembered Tito's triumphal reception by the Hungarian Communist Party on his visit to Budapest, shortly before his break with Moscow. Moreover, it seemed quite likely that Budapest would have been deeply involved in Tito's project to form a confederation of Yugoslavia and Bulgaria, followed by Rumania and, who could say, perhaps by Hungary as well.

There is no knowing the full extent of the attacks on the leaders of the Hungarian party originating from the Cominform and, in the background, from Stalin and his entourage. Rákosi made a passing allusion to the matter in his article on the 'delay' of socialist development in Hungary, in which he also confessed that his view of the dictatorship of the proletariat had been mistaken. Behind Rákosi's anti-Yugoslav fervour, many have, in any case, seen an attempt to make a public recantation of earlier lapses.

Finally, Rákosi had a special motive: to demonstrate that the party machine inherited from clandestine days was infested with criminals and foreign agents, and that only the vigilance of the leaders who had returned from Moscow was capable of unmasking and eliminating them. And who embodied that illegal past more conspicuously than Rajk, followed by Kádár? In any case, the list of accused (and of those who had to face subsequent trials) shows beyond doubt that, apart from various 'agents' who had never been party members, it was only 'home-based' Communists who were dragged before the tribunals. Rajk, Szönyi, Pálffy, Szalai, Béla Szász, György Heltai, Frigyes Major, László Marschall, László Sólyom, Sándor Haraszti and Géza Losonczy, to mention just a few, were all veterans of the 'home-based' party. By contrast, not a single 'Muscovite' was ever implicated.[8]

The evidence remained unconvincing. Many of the charges were obscure, confused, suspect, contradictory. But then so was the whole trial with its implications of collaboration with the various foreign secret services. The confessions completed the picture – the accused pleaded guilty. Despite its shaky foundations, the trial did serve some purpose. It aroused keen debates in the West – the correspondents of several leading newspapers having been admitted to court – and the Communists were not alone in believing at least some of the charges. In any event, in Hungary, where a veritable poison campaign was unleashed so that all might learn the 'proper' lessons of the trial, it became imprudent to cast the least doubt on the justice of the verdict. Needless to say, the denials of the foreigners who were implicated were never made public in Hungary, nor the doubts expressed in most foreign papers. And when all was said and done, had not the whole matter been a test of faith for Communists and fellow travellers? To cast doubt on the Rajk trial was not the same as casting doubt on the trial of President Kennedy's assassin or of Ben Barka's kidnappers. In the Rajk trial, the whole régime was involved, and involved to the hilt. To cast doubt on the trial was tantamount to challenging not only the legal institutions and the police, but also to call in question the entire party leadership which had publicly endorsed the trial. To believe in Rajk's innocence, moreover, meant to give the lie to the Cominform and to Stalin himself, quite apart from lending criminal support to Titoist and imperialist forces at a time when the Cold War was at its height. All in all, to defend Rajk meant certain disaster.

Police terror did the rest. Those who courted eternal damnation for their disbelief – and their numbers turned out to be vastly greater than those of the believers – quickly realized that they had best keep their opinions of the trial to themselves. Thus, for five years, nobody spoke about the Rajk affair unless it was to justify the successive disappearance of hundreds of people indirectly involved in the trial. This was because of a decision by the authorities that it would be best to prevent, not just the accused, but also the witnesses for the prosecution and even many whose names had merely been mentioned at the trial, from speaking about it – and so they were until 1954.

We have already mentioned, with some reservation, private information to the effect that the Rajk affair was initiated by Mátyás Rákosi and his circle, or more precisely by his Hungarian secret police, that is to say by the AVH of Gábor Péter, one of László Rajk's old friends, rather than by Soviet Intelligence. It nevertheless remains a fact that the preliminary investigation was carried out under the direction of the same Soviet intelligence unit led by General Byelkin as, according to Béla Szász, also organized the trial of Kotchi Dzodze in Albania, of Kostov in Bulgaria and of Slansky and his co-accused in Czechoslovakia. It was Byelkin who dug up the accusation of Trotskyism against people whose age was such that Trotsky's name, to them, was no more than a chimera from the past.[9]

In any case, Moscow directed and obviously approved of the Rajk trial as it did of the whole wave of terror that was let loose on the Communist Party and the people of Hungary. Such 'advisers' as General Byelkin exercised a grip on the Hungarian political police, the military intelligence and counter-espionage services, the ministries of the interior and of defence, the central administration of the party and on economic, scientific, educational and cultural organizations and institutions.

Moscow's vigilant eye henceforth watched over everything, the party's affairs no less than those of the Hungarian government. In addition to presiding over sensational political trials, the Soviet advisers also oversaw the immense purges resulting in tens of thousands of arrests, internments and dismissals in every field: party, police, army, public services, education, publishing, art, literature, economic affairs, agriculture – nothing escaped their long arm. Five years of sovietization left Hungary battered, bled dry, stripped of its cadres and its most experienced hands, frightened and shaken to the core.

The End of a Society

Many books and eyewitness accounts have retraced the political upheavals suffered in the 1950s by Hungary and the other people's democracies on all of which the Soviet model had been imposed by force and in identical manner. The trials, persecutions and exactions ordered by the Communists in power, culminating in the 're-education' of every last shop foreman and village schoolteacher, are well known. Stalinism bore down relentlessly on one and all: on industry, agriculture, arts and letters.

In 1945, the Communist Party had gained a decisive say over the running of the economy. While nationalization had proceeded at a moderate pace until 1948, the three-year reconstruction plan coupled to workers' and then to state control of all enterprises had led to a general collapse of capitalism.[10] The new nationalization measures introduced after the party's seizure of total power had put a rapid end to whatever vestiges of capitalism survived. In March 1948, the government had decreed the state control of all enterprises employing more than a hundred workers. Thanks to this one measure, 83 per cent of all industrial workers passed into the state sector. The credit policy favouring this sector accelerated the process until finally, with the First Five-Year Plan which began on 1 January 1950, the hold of the state over the economy became absolute.

The First Five-Year Plan was speeded up at the beginning of 1951 but mitigated again by a more moderate economic policy in June 1953 – in the wake of impressive but not easily verifiable results.

Industry, which had by and large regained its pre-war level at the end of 1948, undoubtedly experienced a spectacular growth. Its part in the gross national product (1950 = 100) was 67 in 1938 and 146 at the end of the plan in 1954.[11] The plan was originally intended to increase the gross national income by 63 per cent, capital investment by 127 per cent and the standard of living by 35 per cent. Half of the 35,000 million forints set aside for investment was earmarked for industry, 89 per cent of it for heavy industry. These inordinate ambitions ensured that the population in general and the peasantry in particular were put through a great deal of suffering and that the production of consumer goods remained drastically restricted.

At the end of 1949, soon after the adoption of the plan, it was decided, for the express purpose of laying the foundations of socialism, that Hungary must be equipped with a redoubtable military machine, so much so that the plan, ambitious as it already was, needed to be greatly 'expanded' – in other words revised upwards. Resolutions to this effect were passed at the Second Congress of the MDP, held from 25 February to 2 March 1951.[12] One single figure must suffice to demonstrate the trend: the volume of investments set first at 35,000 million forints and then at 50,000 million in 1949, was stepped up to 85,000 million, representing a further increase of 67 per cent. According to the 'expanded' plan (to use the official term), heavy industry must now reach in two years the objectives originally set to be reached in five.[13]

As it happened, this forced growth had to be cut back, but such cuts did little to repair the cruel lack of consumer goods, to improve the appalling lack of investment in agriculture, or to prevent the standard of living dropping by about 20 per cent during the life of the plan.

There was more money than there were goods in the country. People had to queue for consumer goods of every type: provisions, industrial products, simple shoe repairs. To extirpate 'capitalism' in all its forms, the government had even closed down tailors, cobblers, plumbers, together with tens of thousands of small shops in the high streets, following the nationalization of the foreign and wholesale trades.

The collectivization of agriculture was to have even more catastrophic consequences, less on account of the number of holdings actually nationalized, which was smaller than is generally realized, than because of the policy of 'dekulakization' and its economic and psychological repercussions. Thus in 1949, in a country with 9,200,000 inhabitants, 63.2 per cent of the population lived in villages. The active agricultural population (2,200,000) made up 53.8 per cent of the overall active population, as against 21.6 per cent engaged in industry and construction combined. During the same period, agriculture provided about a third of the national income. The disruption of rural life therefore had an effect on the greater part of the population, and on the rest as well, if only indirectly and psychologically. The devastating results showed the futility of all efforts and exactions employed to foist the collectivization of agriculture upon an unwilling peasantry.

The number of individual holdings declined from about 1,440,000 in 1949 to 1 million in 1953. At the same time, the number of collective farms rose from 500 to more than 5,000, their total area from 39,000 to almost 1.2 million hectares. Correspondingly, the membership of the collective farms (*kolkhozes*) rose from 13,000 in 1949 to 376,000 in 1953.

Approximately 20 per cent of all peasants had therefore been incorporated into the co-operative sector.[14] During the same period, the state agricultural sector also grew appreciably. Altogether a third of the agricultural population became dependent on the state and co-operative sectors. As for the mediocre results, they were common to all the sectors.

Ten years later, when János Kádár's régime proceeded to much more sweeping collectivizations, he succeeded because he avoided the worst mistakes of the first campaign. Between 1949 and 1953, everything went badly. The main objective having been more political than economic, the most experienced peasants – those 'kulaks' who owned more than fifteen hectares of land – were crushed by taxes or forced off their land without being admitted to the *kolkhozes*. Moreover, even those described as 'middle-ranking peasants', meaning peasants who owned around ten hectares of land, were often described as 'kulaks' and subjected to the same punitive fiscal measures and system of forced deliveries. In short, the most capable peasants were persecuted and penalized, the weaker abandoned to their fate, and the peasantry at large driven to the wall. And it was this distressed form of agriculture that was expected to feed the towns and to finance the party's extravagant industrialization policy! No wonder Hungary found itself on the brink of a famine in 1952: empty shops in the towns, empty granaries in the villages.

These catastrophic results merely served to fan the determination of the authorities. Recalcitrant peasants who put up any form of resistance to being driven into the *kolkhozes* were not only punished with extra taxes and impositions but had their land sequestrated and were often arrested and beaten up into the bargain. Instead of provoking the expected clashes between poor peasants and kulaks, these repressive measures helped to unite all rural classes in opposition to the régime. And so the battle for socialism in the country-side ended in almost total failure. At the first sign of moderation shown by Imre Nagy's new and reformist government in 1953, and again at the first sign of revolution in 1956, a large section of the co-operative movement disintegrated.

However, the balance of the earlier years was not entirely nega-tive. Cultural policy, for instance, produced some positive results. Here we cannot take stock of this aspect in full. Suffice it to point out that the government made determined efforts to encourage (needless to say, under state control) the spread of culture. A writer whose books were published (we shall ignore what criteria he had to satisfy) earned more money than he had in the past, not least because of the increased circulation of all written works. Books were relatively cheap, book sales boomed, and so did the stage, the cinema and art exhibitions. Moreover, culture had ceased to be the prerogative of the leisured classes, or of people living in large cities. Theatres sprang up in small villages almost everywhere; films were shown by thousands of cultural associations; permanent or travell-ing libraries sprang up; popular song and dance ensembles prolifer-ated in the countryside and in factory cultural societies.

Despite all this effervescence, however, cultural life, and edu-cation in particular, also knew dark periods between 1949 and 1953. Religious education was abolished in practice, inasmuch as no one dared to enrol a child for a type of education that was barely tolerated. Secular education was almost completely in the hands of the state, which had only to 'purge' the teaching staff to have its way. The only figures we have in this sphere are that, in 1948, 6,505 schools with a staff of 18,000 teachers were nationalized. It is certain, however, that many teachers lost their posts, were forced to take early retirement or were downgraded. The workforce of the nascent socialist society was recruited not only from peasants driven out of their villages, but also from middle-class people who had lost their social status.

Schools were perhaps even more profoundly affected by the process of ideological reconstruction. The so-called feudal and reactionary spirit the régime set out to extirpate made way for a different if no less conservative approach: Marxism-Leninism. Henceforth every subject, from social science to physics, had to be taught in accordance with the Soviet model. Whereas the con-servative and nationalistic character of the old educational system had been offset, at least in part, by the political and cultural pluralism of social life, nothing comparable was allowed to happen under the socialism of Stalin's disciples. The least deviation from the official canons was severely punished, with the unforeseen result that, except for party zealots, teachers and pupils were drawn together in covert complicity: teachers showed that they did not believe what they taught and pupils learned without bothering to remember. One illustration of this process was provided by the obligatory teaching of Russian, a language that, despite its beauty and practical importance, most pupils refused to master. Another example was history. One kind was taught at school, another remembered: that one transmitted at home, full of living memories and national legends.

As a result there were, so to speak, two schools and two cultures, one public and one private, the second carefully nurtured in the closed circle of the family and other small and elusive groups. The resulting collective spirit escaped the grip of the state. Two schools, two cultures and also two languages: one for public consumption, the other private and suffused with the traditional mores.

The most spectacular and hence the best-known state measures were those designed to control literary and artistic life. Whereas, until about 1948, some kind of cultural plurality had been allowed to persist, all this was to change at the beginning of the 1950s. We have already mentioned the astonishing 'Lukács affair'. It was neither the first nor the last of its kind. Western readers know about some of them from eyewitness accounts and from several books that have reached them in translation.[15]

The Déry affair was one of the most famous, and also one of the most important, because, apart from involving a prominent Communist writer, it served as the starting-point for a second *Gleichschaltung* of literary life, following the prior elimination of awkward non-party writers. This time it was the turn of recalcitrant party authors to be put on the carpet. With József Révai as their mouthpiece, the party inveighed bitterly against all those poets and writers who had not yet grasped – it was 1952 – that the times had drastically changed over the past three years, and that it was high time for literature to adopt the Soviet model of Socialist Realism.[16]

Let us briefly recall one less well-known aspect of this campaign. The various literary and artistic 'affairs' were all played out in the context of the Hungarian writers', painters', sculptors' and composers' associations.[17] It so happens that these associations were not run on the same lines as technical associations, let alone of trade unions. But all of them had one thing in common: they were formed on the Soviet model for the express purpose of keeping tabs on everybody. They represented a veritable grid map of society. Nothing and nobody could escape from the net of associations enclosing society vertically as well as horizontally – by sex, age, address, place of work, profession, even of hobbies (reading clubs, sports associations, hunting, fishing, chess). The aim was a double one: while ostensibly there to defend and promote professional and cultural interests which were not, in principle, subject to state intervention, the new network served to control them all the more effectively. Cultural and social associations in Hungary during the Stalinist years were nothing but a gigantic network for the surveillance of everyone by 'reliable' men placed at the head of every one of these societies.

Here we shall not dwell on them in detail. If we mention the problem at all, it is only because the course of events after Stalin's death revealed not only the depth but also the futility of this type of framework. As the reader will see, the effervescence that seized Hungarian society and led to the revolution of 1956 would be centred precisely on these associations, from such smaller ones as the writers' union to the trade unions, not to mention university and youth associations.

Did Hungary therefore become a totalitarian state during the dark years of Stalinism? The answer depends on one's criteria. During the past two decades, Western political scientists have constructed a multitude of theories that question the very concept of totalitarianism and, *a fortiori*, its practical relevance.[18]

But do purely practical considerations force us to modify the theory of totalitarianism in the light of the uprisings, revolts, reforms or changes that have taken place in Eastern Europe or in the Soviet Union itself over the past few decades?

In any case, if we adopt the criteria put forward by Hannah Arendt or Raymond Aron, the countries of Eastern Europe have been the arena for the implementation of totalitarian plans akin to pure Stalinism. And public opinion in the countries concerned would fully subscribe to such a view. Even if we admit – and this is a question to which we shall be returning – that these plans were only half completed, the people, especially of Hungary, were unquestionably subjected to a totalitarian dictatorship and experienced it as such. It needs no training in political science to identify and name its constituent elements. Stalinism was totalitarian in Hungary because it imposed a single party, an omnipresent political police force, compulsory nationalization, an invasive ideology and the state control of all information; because it flouted traditions, spread terror and lies, disrupted social structures and ensured the intrusion of the state into private life. Admittedly, totalitarianism experienced with one's own skin resembles only in part the formulas of political scientists. The changes that came after Stalin's death have undoubtedly altered, if not the basis of the system, at least the foundations of everyday life. But they have not, for all that, been able to efface the traumatic effects of Hungary's totalitarian experience.

–9–

Imre Nagy and the 1956 Revolution

In October 1956, Budapest witnessed an event unique in the annals of Communism: a popular uprising leading to the overthrow of the Communist régime and replacing it, for two weeks, with a pluralist system under a veteran Communist – Imre Nagy. Before we describe and evaluate this unprecedented happening, we must retrace our steps to 1953.

After Stalin's death in March 1953, the entire Communist world expected that there would be at least minor changes. A new, joint team had taken over in Moscow and, though it included such well-known old-timers as Molotov and Voroshilov, it also comprised such less familiar figures as Mikoyan, Malenkov, Khrushchev and Beria, the chief of police.

The new leaders, headed by Malenkov, were undecided about what measures to take. While they hesitated, all ruling Communist parties were given directives to steer a 'new course'. East Germany was the first to respond, but there the measures intended to reassure the population went hand in hand with economic directives – an increase in production norms – so unpopular that the 'new course' finished up by enraging the masses. They revolted on 17 June 1953.

That day the workers of East Berlin took to the streets, especially concentrating on the Stalin Allee, to demonstrate their opposition and to press their claims. Soviet tanks were needed to restore order. Must this protest be attributed to tactlessness or rather to provocation on the part of the German Communist leaders? All that is known is that the position of Walter Ulbricht, the head of the party, was compromised, not only in Berlin but also in Moscow.

At the time of the Berlin insurrection, a series of reforms had already been initiated in Hungary. As in Germany, the initiative had come from Moscow in the spring of 1953 – most probably in April – with the intention of easing the tensions created by the hard Stalinist line. Budapest, like Berlin, was set on a 'new course', but in Hungary the process was probably accelerated by an unexpected event.

The Era of Reforms

In June 1953, the leaders of the Hungarian Communist Party, including Rákosi, Gerö and Farkas, were summoned in disgrace to Moscow in the company of Imre Nagy, one of their comrades.[1] The Hungarian delegation was received in the Kremlin on 13 and 14 June by the full Presidium of the Soviet party: Beria, Khrushchev, Malenkov, Mikoyan and Molotov. The upshot of the meeting was the break-up of the whole system built up by Rákosi and his men. The Soviet comrades came down hard on those who had been responsible for imposing Stalinism on Hungary, and instructed them to 'correct their errors' right down the line.

The tone was harsh, even brutal, Beria going so far as to refer to the leaders of the Hungarian party as 'that Jewish gang'. A dumbfounded Rákosi was stripped of half of his party and state offices. Imre Nagy, an almost unknown quantity, returned home as president designate of the Council of Ministers to inaugurate a new era of reforms.

The new policy was officially adopted by the Central Committee and became known as the 'June resolution'. The full text was not published until 1985, when it surfaced in Budapest in the *samizdat* publication of Imre Nagy's secret report in *Beszélö*, republished in the French journal, *Communisme* (No. 9, December 1986). Previously, all that was known of this document had been based on extracts quoted by Imre Nagy himself, or on versions that had been circulating among party militants. In his memoirs, Zoltán Vas states that there were in fact two June resolutions, the first adopted by the Central Committee, then withdrawn; and the second drafted, then watered down, by the Politburo. According to Vas – who is quoted here with reservations – the first resolution was not only violently critical of Rákosi's and Gerö's leadership, but also strongly anti-semitic inasmuch as it incorporated the abusive terms used by Beria at the Moscow meeting.[2] (Some of these terms are quoted in Imre Nagy's memoirs.[3]) The first resolution was allegedly dropped following the news of Beria's dismissal on the very day the Hungarian Central Committee met. The second version is then said to have served as the basis of the address Imre Nagy, the new prime minister, was due to deliver in Parliament on 5 July 1953; it was this version that became known as the 'June programme'.

And so the era of reforms was born. It was marked by an improvement in the economic situation, a lowering of tension, the release of thousands of political prisoners – and continuous infighting between the Stalinist wing and the liberal faction led by Imre Nagy.

The story of the eighteen months during which Imre Nagy attempted the first experiment in 'Communism with a human face' has lost some of its lustre in the meantime. In retrospect it looks like no more than a bit of tinkering with the lunatic 'iron and steel' economy; a slackening of the reins of a collectivized and totally bankrupt agricultural policy; a bit of 'magyarization'; a bit of humanization. After the events of 1956, after the Prague Spring, after Solidarity, it all seems rather tame.

The era of reforms nevertheless did have some lasting effects, not so much in practical terms as in the less palpable field of ideas. With his address to Parliament on 5 July 1953, Nagy managed to create a climate of confidence and to shine a ray of hope into a thick fog of fear and humiliation. His personality made as much of a contribution to that result as did his reforms. It would probably be incorrect to describe Nagy as a charismatic personality: he had a jovial temperament, the stocky build of the peasant and the reflective look of a professor as he forever toyed with his pince-nez. Everything considered, he radiated the assurance of an honest champion of his people. It was not long before they were calling him 'the old man'.

Born to poor parents on 6 June 1896 in Kaposvár, in eastern Hungary, Imre Nagy spent the First World War fighting on the Russian front; having been taken prisoner, he joined the Bolsheviks in the Lake Baikal region. He fought against Kolchak and stayed on in Russia for several years before returning to Hungary. A rank-and-file member of a clandestine and persecuted party of about a thousand members, Nagy took part in several political campaigns, then emigrated and settled in Moscow in 1930. During fifteen years in the land of the revolution, holding modest posts, especially in Bukharin's Agrarian Institute, he never became involved in any of the conflicts between the Comintern bosses and the Hungarian party. Because he kept so low a profile, he evaded the purges, the internment camps and the firing squad. Attached to the propaganda section, Nagy slowly climbed the ladder to find himself, in 1944, one of the militants chosen to lead the party and the government in liberated Hungary. As the future Hungarian minister of agriculture, Nagy was received by Molotov in that November. A not very well known but characteristic episode marked the occasion. Stalin walked into the room and, with the studied gesture of a monarch, turned to Nagy and said: 'I congratulate you, Comrade, on the liberation of your native Kaposvár'. The Red Army had marched into Kaposvár that very day.

In Hungary, Nagy had the good fortune of seeing his great dream – the land reforms that would put an end to the latifundia system – being fulfilled. He went on to take up a series of important posts, then was eclipsed for a time. In 1949, he was dismissed from the Politburo for his opposition to the 'great turning-point', that is to say the dictatorship of the proletariat and the forced collectivization of agriculture. In 1951, however, he resumed his rise on the party ladder.

That rise has been the subject of controversial interpretations. According to some, Nagy was nothing but a traitor, an opportunist who took advantage of circumstances the faster to climb to power. To others, he was a sincere man, romantic and weak, one who let himself be carried by the current. For yet others, he was a man torn between his old Communist convictions and patriotic sentiment who, when the time came – in 1953, in 1956 and then during his trial in 1958 – offered proof of unquestionable political ability and a true greatness of spirit.

What is certain is that Imre Nagy did not show the full measure of his personality until the turmoil of 1953–6 and later before the tribunal. Few could have guessed beforehand that this party apparatchik, this veteran Communist hack, was destined to make history. He tried, at a particularly dramatic moment, to reconcile his loyalty to his people with his loyalty to the cause he had served all his life long. This duality was a hallmark of Imre Nagy himself. In the end he foundered. He might justifiably be accused of being slow to make up his mind and somewhat clumsy in the way he implemented his policy – grave faults indeed in a statesman confronting an extraordinary situation. But in the circumstances he would have foundered no matter what his skills as a politician. For all that, his tenacity, his determination to save the situation, and even his hesitations, reflected the tragic character of an event that, without being able to produce the slightest tangible result, has nevertheless come to be engraved in the popular mind as one of the great moments in Hungary's long history.

In 1953, counting on public support and confidence as well as on Moscow's approval, Nagy refused to organize his supporters into a separate political group, even as he refused to set up a separate reformist apparatus within the administration. Unfortunately, the success of his initiatives depended on the balance of forces in the Central Committee and in the Politburo, in other words on an apparatus hostile to any form of change. The 'June programme' was thus at the mercy of the slightest contrary wind. On 6 July 1953, following Nagy's presentation to Parliament of his programme,

Szabad Nép, the official organ of the Communist Party, launched a covert assault on his policy. It was to be the first in a long series of attacks.

On 11 July, the day after the official news of Beria's liquidation broke, a triumphant Rákosi – convinced that Beria had been the main instigator of the new Soviet line – denounced Nagy's programme before a meeting of party militants. Imre Nagy also spoke. In measured tones, and choosing his words with care, he restated his views of the Five-Year Plan, of the marked fall in the standard of living, of the illegal acts committed against the peasants and especially against the kulaks: views diametrically opposed to those of Rákosi, who had been the first to address the meeting. Rákosi had argued, in particular, that the 'the standard of living is far higher than it has ever been' and that it was time 'to shut the kulaks up'. It is impossible to judge who won this particular debate.

In public, Rákosi and his supporters seemed conciliatory and even to favour Nagy's initiatives. Behind the scenes, by contrast, they put up all sorts of obstructions and, in particular, encouraged the party machine to oppose Nagy's policies.

In January 1954, there was a new trial of strength, probably initiated by Nagy when he became incensed at Rákosi's sabotage. The Hungarian leaders appeared once again before the Kremlin arbitration committee. This time, too, Nagy came out on top, Rákosi being showered with even more reproaches than he received during his first summons.

> On that occasion, Khrushchev stated that, in June 1953, we raised justified objections about the leadership of the Hungarian party. These objections still held. There was little purpose, he went on to say, in putting all the blame on Beria, as Rákosi kept doing . . . Political prisoners were not being released fast enough, he added, and that was clearly Rákosi's fault.[4]

On his return from Moscow on 23 January, Nagy presented Parliament with a glowing account of his six months in office. Prices had fallen by 13.3 per cent, the peasantry had had its burdens reduced,[5] 8,000 tradesmen had been given permission to reopen their workshops, internment camps had been abolished, persons forcibly moved to various parts of the country had been authorized to return and a number, many of them elderly, were already back in their homes in Budapest. Nagy also announced a rise in the standard of living and the resumption of economic relations with capitalist countries. Finally he attacked those 'sabotaging the government programme', a remark obviously aimed at Mátyás

Rákosi who sat by Nagy's side in one of the red velour armchairs reserved for ministers and high dignitaries, a broad smile on his face.

The battle raged on without public opinion ever being told what was really happening. Information took the form of leaks, rumours, the interpretation of signs. 'Things are going badly for Imre Nagy,' some thought on 5 March when the front page of *Szabad Nép* carried a photograph of Stalin on the first anniversary of his death. Others were quick to reassure them: *Pravda*, for one, had carried no such picture, and its commemorative article had been briefer and more reserved than that of the Hungarian paper. The whole thing was no more than an isolated show by local Stalinists. That sort of thing could do no harm so long as Moscow did not endorse it.

Other comforting signs also appeared. On 13 March, the papers announced that General Gábor Péter, head of the AHV and hated torturer of democrats, Socialists and in the end of Communists – especially of László Rajk and János Kádár, found guilty at the end of their rigged trials, had himself been given a life sentence.[6]

On the following day, new party regulations were drawn up. These stipulated that there would no longer be two levels of discipline in the party, one for ordinary members and another for the leadership. Self-criticism would henceforth have to be practised 'regardless of person'. The party congress, the only body entitled to adopt the new regulations, was however adjourned for five weeks: the Third Congress was not convened until 24 May 1954.

This delay was apparently imposed by the Soviet leaders, themselves divided and incapable of solving the thorny Hungarian problem. Preoccupied with the Geneva conference on Korea and Indo-China (April to July), the Soviets decided to compel Nagy and Rákosi to settle their differences. But that was easier said than done. Rákosi's and Nagy's speeches, which had to be ready and translated before the congress opened, kept going through revisions under the pressure of the Central Committee and then of Marshal Voroshilov. The latter, as head of the Soviet delegation to the congress, had arrived in Budapest with the mission of closing the gap between the leaders of the two factions. While he failed to do so, he was at least able to save appearances. The two leaders' speeches were moderate and conciliatory: Rákosi approved of the 'new stage', while Nagy refrained from dwelling on the errors and crimes of the past.

All the same, in the autumn of 1954, Nagy launched a last attack on behalf of the new current (before its defeat) against the old régime. In fact, October 1954 saw a general anti-Stalinist offensive by the supporters of the 'June ideas' and of the politics of reform in the press and in literature, at party meetings from small cells to the Central Committee, and at public rallies and congresses. It was at the October meeting of the Central Committee that Nagy launched his direct attack on his 'opponents', the Rákosi–Gerö group which had drawn up an economic austerity plan designed to undermine the June programme, and in doing so used arguments of unprecedented boldness. Next day, on 20 October, in an article in the party paper,[7] he put his arguments to the country at large, thus making the nation privy to the debates that had been raging in the Central Committee behind closed doors. He accused the old leaders of dogmatism, of a lack of scientific understanding, even of anti-Marxism, in the way they had planned and run the economy. 'The old economic policy', Nagy declared, 'was based on a false interpretation of socialism. It took account neither of man nor of society, and limited the idea of socialism to a maximum increase in iron and steel production, to super-industrialization'. Referring to something Gerö had said in support of the austerity measures, Nagy went on to ask: 'Who is living it up, then? No doubt some people have been living it up, but not the working people.'

Nagy's stand was no less firm on the political front. 'Members of the party', he declared, 'are not mere tools for the implementation of party decisions. They also have an important role to play in the framing of party policy.' And turning his attention to the burning question of rehabilitation, Nagy went on to demand the release from prison of 'all who are not guilty', and stated categorically that the crimes inflicted on innocent people in the past must 'never be repeated'. At the congress of the Patriotic Popular Front, opened on 23 October in the Budapest municipal theatre, Nagy, addressing an audience of 2,000, went straight to the essential problem of political power when he called for the restoration of the front's leading political and moral role.

The gulf between Nagy's proposals and the reality of the situation was plain to see. He was balancing on a knife edge. He could not go one inch beyond the limits the Kremlin had set; worse still, the slightest backsliding by Moscow into Stalinism would be more than likely to undo whatever the Nagy government had already achieved. This was borne out by the temporary hardening of Soviet foreign policy after the signing of the Paris agreement,[8] and its repercussions on the internal policy of all the Eastern Bloc countries.

At any event, in October 1954, the Nagy government was riding the crest of a wave from which one fatal step was all that was needed to topple it. That fatal step was not long in coming. After Malenkov's fall in February 1955, Rákosi seized the opportunity of getting rid of 'his own Malenkov'. In April, Nagy was dismissed, then expelled from the party. A cloak of silence and fear once again descended over the country. But not for long.

The Writers' Republic

After a short interval, intellectual ferment once more began to grip Hungary. Conditions were favourable. Outside, the freeze continued, Tito was more or less forgiven, and in February 1956 Khrushchev denounced Stalin's crimes before the Twentieth Congress. The new wind of change only served to accelerate a variety of crises in Rákosi's 'restalinized' Hungary: a supply crisis, a political crisis, and a moral crisis.

The return home of the survivors of the rigged trials, including János Kádár and Anna Kéthly, was to play an immensely important role in this critical situation. In 1954–5, hundreds of political prisoners were disgorged from the gaols, having been tortured and maimed – so many living witnesses of the régime's iniquity. But that was only the tip of the iceberg, a relatively small number of 'regrettable errors'. In fact, tens of thousands of men and women, including veterans of the Spanish Civil War, former Resistance fighters, democrats, Socialists, ministers and simple peasants, intellectuals and manual workers had all been cast into the Hungarian gulag. And though the full scale of the crimes was yet to be appreciated, though the survivors of the Slansky affair continued to suffer great hardship, though Solzhenitsyn was still in the first circle of his hell – the shock felt by the Hungarian people was indescribable. One of the most remarkable acts at that time was the presentation to the party's Central Committee of a memorandum signed by fifty-eight leading writers and artists, all of them party members, protesting against the arbitrary measures which had sapped the country's literary and artistic life.

Another source of popular indignation and revolt that filtered down right into the ranks of the party was an outraged national spirit. The Twentieth Congress in Moscow had done no more than open the floodgates. Thereafter a wave of protests swept the country. The role of intellectuals, writers, scholars and artists in this fight for change, for renewal, for the rehabilitation not only of human beings but also of moral values is well known. For many Communists the associated guilt feelings proved an overwhelming emotion.

As for Imre Nagy, the man on whom Hungary had pinned its hopes, he saw only a handful of close friends and proceeded to write, with his habitual calm, his voluminous and famous memorandum, which he was to present to the Central Committee in the autumn of 1956.[9] But in the meantime his name had become willy-nilly identified with the call for national renewal and his person had been turned into its rallying-point.

The Writers' Association, associations of journalists, of artists, *Irodalmi Ujság* (Literary Journal) and later, the Petöfi Circle which was an offshoot of the Young Communist League, took up the struggle pending Nagy's return to power. This movement, punctuated by events no less important than the ferment after the Twentieth Congress in Moscow, the dismissal of Rákosi in the summer of 1956 and the long-delayed funeral of Rajk on 6 October 1956, was to spread to all sections of the population. The party itself responded to the scorn in which it was generally held with an irreversible process of disintegration.

Rákosi's dismissal, which came during the session of the Central Committee of 18–21 July, has been reported down to the last detail in every book dealing with this period in Hungarian history. It is a well-known fact, for instance, that it took the personal intervention of Mikoyan, dispatched to Budapest by the Kremlin, to persuade Rákosi to resign. According to some sources, Rákosi even insisted on telephoning Khrushchev for confirmation. In any case, the consequences of his forced resignation proved more important than the picturesque details: his relegation sent off a shock wave not only through public opinion but also through the party apparatus. Until that moment Rákosi had seemed completely irremovable.

A whole myth – albeit a fairly seedy one – collapsed with his departure. At the same time, the Central Committee decided to drop Mihály Farkas and to expel him from the party. As part of the same move, György Marosán, a former Social Democrat imprisoned under Rákosi, and János Kádár, who had also emerged from Rákosi's prisons, were elected members of the Politburo. János Kádár was appointed secretary of the Central Committee. These measures might have been greeted with greater enthusiasm had Rákosi been replaced as first secretary of the party by a new face or at least by one not too compromised. The leaders had actually thought of handing the post to András Hegedüs, the relatively young prime minister, but Hegedüs declined. The choice then fell on Ernö Gerö, a man almost as detested as Rákosi himself.[10]

On 6 October 1956, at the funeral – deferred for seven years – of

László Rajk and his brothers-in-misfortune, including two generals, a crowd of approximately 150,000 formed a cortège behind empty bronze coffins, torches and officials with obsequious expressions. It was thought by many that only a spark was needed to transform the funerals into a riot. But the crowd dispersed in silence. The igniting spark was not to appear until a fortnight later. It originated in Poland.

The Insurrection

On 19 October 1956, Poland experienced one of the dramatic moments marking its chequered history.[11] This was the rise to power, despite the threat of Soviet intervention, of Wladislaw Gomulka, a 'revisionist' Communist.

In Hungary, the new wave had similarly started under the banner of moderate reformism,[12] led by university students who had formulated their demands variously under twelve or fourteen points couched in the style of the 'Forty-Eighters'. In response to their message, a crowd assembled on 23 October at 2 p.m. in Petöfi Square, waving banners, intoning the *Internationale* and other rousing songs and chanting: 'Independence, freedom, we want Imre Nagy!'

A procession began to move off. Swelled by workers leaving their factories, a crowd of some 250,000 to 300,000 wound its way through several miles of road and across the Danube bridges. No incidents, not one window was smashed. At the end of the day, everyone expected some gesture from the party leadership. But the Hungarian Communist Party was not as willing to listen as its Polish counterpart had been.

At 8 p.m. Gerö, having just returned from a visit to Tito, delivered an imperious and dogmatic speech in which he refused to promise the least change. This amounted to a blatant provocation of a whole people. Then came an even graver incident of provocation: at nightfall the whine of a bullet could be heard over the radio while students at the broadcasting station were trying to read their 'points' into the microphone. There followed a second, a third – a fusillade. The revolt had begun.

Meanwhile, at party headquarters, the panic-stricken leaders implored the Soviet Union to come to the aid of Socialism and to send their armoured divisions into the capital. After the stick came the carrot: they asked Imre Nagy to join them and to serve as prime minister.

A revolution was under way, one that the party felt compelled to interpret as a challenge to Communist power and the whole system of socialism in the Soviet mould, to 'eight years of imbecility and terror', as Jean–Paul Sartre called it. The facts are known. Learned analyses can add but little.

The opposing camps were formed that very night. By dawn a whole nation stood up to the foreign occupier and his henchmen. In that sense, the movement was a national insurrection. But it was also, as Raymond Aron has put it, an 'anti-totalitarian revolution', the first in history. A whole society had risen up to recover its fundamental rights. The events invested the insurgents with the authority of a popular mandate. The Hungarians voted with their arms or with their unflinching support of those who fought on their behalf.

And so the battle lines were drawn. There were two camps, of course, but there were also slight disagreements in the popular camp about the best practical steps to take and about the future prospects. All in all, four main forces entered the arena during the first hours:

1 the insurgents out in the street, few in number but fortified by the active support and solidarity of the civilian population at large;
2 the workers' and national councils – veritable organs of local power, of self-government;
3 two Soviet armoured divisions, turrets closed, firing almost at random. They had neither plans nor orders;
4 the party: a handful of leaders in complete disarray. We shall be watching them at work during the critical days to come. Their pride, the pride of this organization of almost a million members, was broken during these early hours. All they were left with was a small number of militants ready for action and a few paralysed political police detachments.

And then, one man, Imre Nagy – the focus of everyone's attention. For the insurgents and most of the public, he embodied hope and change. For the obtuse and obstinate leaders of the old régime, he was a life raft, a reprieve – that might enable them to carry on without or with only little change.

Imre Nagy: an almost invisible man surrounded by a small band of faithful friends. A voice over the radio. Never before had a medium of communication affected the course of events as profoundly as happened in this case.

An Imprisoned President

Nagy's attitude while he remained in party headquarters during the next four days remains shrouded in controversy. In fact, except for a few slight differences, he accepted the party's view. 'A small number of subversive counter-revolutionaries', he said on the radio on 25 October, 'has started an armed rebellion against our people's republic.'[13] It is true that Nagy did not sing the praises of the Soviet forces brought in by Gerö and Hegedüs and admitted quite frankly that the situation was the result of 'the grave errors' committed in the past. Nevertheless he called for the insurgents' unconditional surrender, while promising the withdrawal of Soviet forces and magnanimity towards the rebels. According to some versions published in the press at the time, he had by then been made a prisoner of the party, the political police literally holding a gun to his back. The reality seems to have been dramatic in a different way and far more complex into the bargain.

Faced with the *fait accompli* of the insurrection and with armed Soviet intervention, surrounded by members of a practically unchanged Central Committee,[14] Nagy was undoubtedly in a precarious situation, but being the *only* Communist leader with any credibility, he allowed himself to be made a hostage to fortune.

The roots of that miscalculation lay both in the history of a sixty-year-old man who had been a card-carrying party member for forty years, and in the history of a movement that was incapable of facing up to the disastrous consequences of its own policies. Nagy was admittedly not as blinkered as the rest. He thought that, by introducing his reformist programme, he could manage to appease the popular movement, having first isolated those 'hostile elements' inside the party who were the reason why dormant popular discontent had erupted into open insurrection. But it was far too late for that kind of solution. The mediator faced a hopeless task in trying to convince either side during the four crucial days left to him.

Nagy, like all the other Communist leaders, had misjudged the popular movement. 'We are up against an unknown force', the philosopher Georg Lukács told a young poet. 'That unknown force', the young man replied, 'is the Hungarian people.' It took Imre Nagy four days to realize the truth of this answer.

What Nagy still believed in, 'the party', had turned into an empty shell, a concoction of verbose ideas and myths, the flotsam of a detested police force and a handful of leaders shut away in the headquarters of the Central Committee. Within a single day, all their awesome power had disintegrated. There was hardly anyone in the whole of Hungary who was prepared to defend this derelict band by force of arms. Several documents refer to the creation of a military committee under Antal Apró, standing by to launch a counter-attack.[15] Other sources mention clashes between army and police units and the insurgents. The party itself certainly did not lack the political will to survive. Although disorganized, a section of the Central Committee and the rest of the apparatus continued to uphold Gerö's 'line' on the need to crush the insurrection – even after Gerö was replaced by Kádár. Yet all these attempts at consolidating their position failed for reasons we shall examine shortly.[16]

As for Imre Nagy, he overcame his reservations and arrived at the momentous decision that was eventually to earn him world renown. The key date was 28 October, after what had often been stormy discussions with colleagues,[17] workers' delegations and the insurgents. It also followed the replacement on the 25th of Gerö as head of the party by Kádár and the arrival of Mikoyan and Suslov, Moscow's emissaries, on their first reconnaissance tour. Clearly, the Kremlin's wish to defuse the crisis weighed heavily with Nagy. And so on that day he left party headquarters, moved into the parliament building and took a series of measures that, though admittedly inadequate and belated, were nevertheless to change the political face of his country. The Soviet military and security forces were to stop firing and start their withdrawal from the capital; the political police (AHV) was to be dissolved; the cabinet was to be reshuffled. The effects were not slow in making themselves felt. The fighting stopped and life began to return to normal. Nagy had just six days ahead in which to complete the work.

The Reprieve

It was during these six days that Nagy showed the true measure of his personality. Recovering his energy and his full authority, he was able to carry nearly all the forces involved with him on to a platform of national unity. On 30 October, he set up a coalition government.[18]

Though the actions of the various parties, churches and associations, and the speeches of the many protagonists, certainly merit attention, however limited their scope, we shall focus attention on two socio-political forces in particular: the insurgents and the movement of councils and committees, for these were to have the most telling effect on the course of events.

The insurgents came from every possible circle. Some of them (for instance Colonel Maléter and István Angyal) were Communists; others were Socialists or Catholic Democrats; yet others were ordinary men and women, workers, students – all imbued with the spirit of patriotism. They were not a large group, just between 2,000 and 3,000 at the start, perhaps double that number or a little more by the time of the second Soviet intervention.

While operating as the fighting wing of the revolution, the insurgents also gave unstinted support to the work of consolidation Nagy had set in motion. Those discordant voices which tried to destabilize the situation came from outside and particularly from Radio Free Europe.

A full account of the complex movement of workers' councils and national committees would take up too much space. Suffice it to say that self-governing bodies sprang up spontaneously throughout the country, and especially in the towns. Although not particularly well co-ordinated at a national level, they exerted a tremendous influence on government policy. Agreed on a national action programme, they nevertheless represented several divergent tendencies. In a number of admittedly rare declarations, they expressed reservations about all the existing political parties which, they alleged, were more likely to divide than to unite the country.

In that sense the Hungarian Revolution was indeed a 'revolution of councils' rather than of parties; of councils, however, that are not to be confused with the self-managing works councils or factory committees of old. Unlike the latter, their main function was to organize the strikes and the political struggle. Should they therefore be seen as genuine organs of self-government? The provincial ones in particular took charge of local administrations. Like the national committees that sprang up in 1945 after the liberation, they stepped into the shoes of the disintegrated local apparatus of the Communist Party. As Claude Lefort has put it, their original and common characteristic was 'democratic improvisation'.[19] As non-institutionalized institutions, and as networks of intercommunication and consolidated action, they embodied an unarticulated form of popular power, one that existed side by side with the political parties, the armed forces, the government, religious bodies and professional groups. Within the space of six days, civil society was being reborn from its own ashes.

Budapest–Moscow: The Unequal Confrontation

The amplitude of the 1956 Hungarian explosion took the whole world by surprise. Indeed, at first there seems to have been no plan for the Russian tanks placed at the disposal of the panic-stricken Communist leaders. On both sides, playing it by ear seemed the rule of the day during a march into the unknown that continued for five polar nights. One may venture to suggest that the Kremlin was genuinely trying to find a political solution by making concessions in Nagy's spirit. This would explain the replacement of Gerö, the chief obstacle to change, by János Kádár on 25 October, during Mikoyan's and Suslov's first visit to Budapest, and also the cease-fire declared unilaterally by the Soviet military and security forces.

The now famous article published in *Pravda* on 30 October confirms that many changes were approved, but the implications went even further. It was admitted that the Soviet Union had made many mistakes and errors in its dealings with the peoples' democracies, and declared that 'the Soviet government is ready to enter into negotiations' with Budapest and the other capitals of the Warsaw Pact countries concerning the presence of Soviet troops on their soil.

The article admittedly incorporated a warning that may be seen in retrospect to have foreshadowed the 'Brezhnev Doctrine'. It nevertheless remains the only published document to suggest a radical transformation of relations between Moscow and the satellite countries at that time.

The *Pravda* article appeared during the second meeting of Nagy and other Hungarians with Mikoyan and Suslov on 30 and 31 October. We have not been able to see the minutes of these meetings or the report the two Soviet emissaries submitted on their return home. However, all the Hungarians present have stated that the two representatives of the Soviet Politburo voiced their approval of the second series of political changes initiated by Imre Nagy. The latter, moreover, was confident enough to announce these changes over the radio at 2.28 p.m. on Tuesday, 30 October, and to confirm them the following day. The three main points were the formation of a multi-party cabinet, an official announcement that negotiations for the withdrawal of Soviet forces from Hungary were in hand, and the 'abrogation of the obligations imposed upon our country under the terms of the Warsaw Pact'. Negotiations, Nagy went on to declare in his address on 31 October, had started 'this very day'. 'Today is the first day of our sovereignty and independence', he proclaimed. Just a few hours later he would learn that Soviet reinforcements had crossed the Hungarian frontier. The longest night of the Hungarian Revolution had begun.

Next day, on 1 November, Nagy summoned Y. V. Andropov, the Soviet Ambassador, to demand an explanation. None was given. Soviet troops continued to pour into the country. At 6.12 p.m., a government communiqué announced that the Warsaw Pact had been abrogated and that a telegram declaring Hungary's neutrality had been sent to the United Nations. For thirty years, this step has remained the most controversial issue in the history of the Hungarian Revolution. Some historians consider the 1 November decision 'to cross the Rubicon' as having been the real cause of the massive intervention by the Red Army three days later.

There is no official document to confirm or deny this view. Only the night before, Nagy had announced the start of the withdrawal of the Warsaw Pact forces. The only new factors were his unilateral denunciation of the pact and the declaration of Hungary's neutrality.

Now, his decision to take up the Soviet challenges was not lacking in political logic. As head of the Hungarian government, Nagy had little choice. To give in to the Russians would be tantamount to throwing in the towel and opening the floodgates of anarchy. Doing nothing would mean standing by with folded arms while the country was invaded. Squaring up to the Russians while pledging, as a seasoned Bolshevik, that his country, though neutral, would remain a friendly ally had become the only chance of salvation, slender as it seemed. János Kádár himself also took this line on the eve of 1 November, the date of his mysterious disappearance, several days before returning in the wake of Soviet tanks to head the new government appointed by Moscow.

The processes by which the Soviet leaders arrived at their final decision have never been fully clear. Khrushchev's comment on 29 October on the possible 'Finlandization' of Hungary, *Pravda*'s memorable article on 30 October, Mikoyan's and Suslov's visit and, above all, the withdrawal of Soviet forces from Budapest, all suggest that Moscow had been concerned to defuse the crisis by making substantial concessions.

Does this suggest that the Hungarians went too far, and that Mikoyan and Suslov did so as well? The realities were probably even more complex. Apart from the dissension that almost certainly existed in the ranks of the Soviet leadership and the 'backsliding' of the Hungarians, a whole series of external factors contributed to the hardening of the Soviet line. Peking, hitherto favourably inclined towards Nagy, did a sudden *volte face*.[20] East Berlin and Prague prodded Moscow towards intervention. But it was another, totally unforeseen event that seems to have tipped the balance, namely the Suez crisis. Tension in the Middle East had, of course, preceded the Hungarian insurrection. However, on 22 and 23 October, during secret talks in Sèvres, 'D-day' was unexpectedly advanced to 29 October, when the Israelis launched their attack, followed by the Anglo-French operation (D + 2) on the 31st. Cynical calculation or pure coincidence? The fact remains that the explosion of the bombs in the Sinai peninsula wonderfully muffled the noise of the tanks rumbling across the Carpathians – and vice versa.

There remained just two unknowns: Tito's reaction and that of the United States. The definitive document, the paper proving beyond any doubt that Washington had promised non-intervention, cannot be said to exist with certainty. But the United States' lack of energy and initiative gave Moscow the green light. As for Belgrade, its true role would lie buried under a veil of myth for a long time. There is no doubt that armed Soviet intervention was a source of concern to Tito, but less so than the changes taking place in Hungary. The attractions of the 'Yugoslav model' were in danger of being overshadowed by the appeal of a pluralist model.

Veljko Mičunović has since cast a great deal of light on these events.[21] On 2 November, Khrushchev and Malenkov came to Brioni to meet the Yugoslav leaders. Their impromptu visit continued into the night, but agreement on one essential point was quickly reached: Tito, too, gave the green light to Soviet intervention. Khrushchev's memoirs put it even more bluntly: Tito presented the visitors with a pleasant surprise by declaring that the Soviet Union was well within its rights and advising the speediest possible intervention by the Red Army.[22] These matters having been settled, the Soviet and Yugoslav comrades went on to discuss nothing less than the composition of the future Hungarian cabinet. János Kádár was proposed as the leader of the party and of the régime.

The Crisis and Dissolution of the Party

The Hungarian Communist Party had literally fallen apart on the night of 23 October 1956. The party officials remained ensconced in Akademia Street, the headquarters of the Central Committee. A number of committee members had also repaired there in haste to deliberate on the turn taken by of events and the best way to tackle the crisis. They decided that Nagy, who had been expelled a week before, was to be readmitted as an ordinary member. But before the night was out, he had been co-opted to the Central Committee, elected to the Politburo, and invited, with the agreement of the head of state, to form a new government.

In the purely theoretical and retrospective opinion of a number of observers, the party made a mistake in acting as it did. Instead of appealing to Imre Nagy, it should have gone into battle and smashed the 'counter-revolution'. That it failed to take such action was no doubt the result of something more than a fleeting sense of panic.

As mentioned earlier, paralysis prevented the mobilization of party militants to defend a discredited régime or to set up the military dictatorship which some advocated.[23]

Everything suggests that the Communist Party simply lacked the means to stand up to the 2,000 insurgents who took to the streets during the first hours. Yet it remains true that in the barracks of the AHV there were several times that number of men loyal to the party, if only because they had no choice in the matter. Similarly, thousands of militants or party members could well have been prepared to come to the defence of the régime out of pure self-interest if not out of love of the cause. Finally, despite the demoralization of the army, the Communist generals should have been able to muster a few officers' units superior in strength to, and more disciplined than, the insurrectionist force. This was obvious from the fact that the Soviet tanks summoned to the rescue of the Communist Party and the government found themselves facing no more than a handful of rifles and Molotov cocktails.

No, the cause of the party's impotence was not material or numerical weakness. Nor was it the result of political miscalculation or a mistaken analysis of the situation. The party's malaise was a moral one. Its roots lay in total demoralization. It was not the relatively feeble pressure of the insurrection, but the weight of the past which prevented the party from standing up to the incensed populace. Similarly, the call to Imre Nagy to join the Central Committee was based not on a true assessment of his political qualities but on the fact that he was the only existing link with the people on whom the party could continue to call.

The party's crisis must therefore have triggered off an infinitely greater crisis amongst the Communist leadership. The collapse in 1956 was the direct outcome of a whole series of crises, conflicts and shortcomings that had manifested themselves more or less acutely throughout the preceding decade. It had all begun with the Rajk affair and the other rigged trials of thousands of party militants. The vicious attacks on all forms of heterodox thought, notably that of George Lukács, were, to say the least, further signs of a profound malaise. Finally the horrors of Rákosi's régime became increasingly clear in 1953–6, following a spate of revelations concerning police brutality, denials of justice and continued Stalinist attacks on the reformers, including Imre Nagy and his collaborators.

Of all these factors, the hateful police system was undoubtedly the main cause of the party's downfall. The political police, the AVO and later the AVH (State Protection Authority), originally confined themselves to investigating activities likely to threaten the security of the new democratic state, and more specifically to looking into the activities of fascist war criminals. However, as the Communist Party stepped up the fight against the conservative parties and later against its reluctant democratic partners, the political police became an extremely useful and powerful tool in the party's hands. This was because the political police quickly rid itself of any elements the party considered unreliable, and particularly of officers brought in by the other coalition partners. Gábor Péter, deputy chief and later chief of the AVO/AVH, was answerable to only the 'big four' of the Communist Party and very often took his orders directly from Mátyás Rákosi. Among the ministers of the interior, ostensibly in charge of the political police, László Rajk, who held that post from 1946 to 1948, was the only one entitled to call the police to account. As for Péter, this veteran party militant, a tailor by trade, and a colourless personality of mediocre intelligence, he was devoted body and soul to Rákosi who, in turn, looked upon Péter as his chief ally and helped to make him one of the most feared men in all Hungary. Péter surrounded himself with men and officers to his liking. Many of them came from a Jewish petty bourgeois background, which merely served to aggravate what was already a highly charged Jewish problem.

So long as the AVO/AVH confined its activities to the persecution of non-party members, persistent rumours about its brutal methods and use of torture did not excessively trouble Communist consciences. Most of the militants simply stopped up their ears or explained 'irregularities' away with references to the hardness of the struggle, first against the fascist reaction, then against the clergy, and finally against the many others who fell successively from grace: moderates, Social Democrats and kulaks. Even during the thaw, Imre Nagy was the first and practically the only leading Communist to acknowledge and deplore the illegal acts committed against non-Communists.

The Rajk affair had meanwhile provided the first clear indications that all was not well inside the party either. The arrest, trial and execution of the former minister of the interior and his fellows-in-misfortune proved a shock so great that it did not die down until after Stalin's death, and then very slowly. In other words, for five long years not only the population at large but also a majority of Communists had continued to live in an atmosphere of terror constantly boosted by fresh waves of arrests.

As in the Stalinist trials, the accused all belonged to the party élite. A large proportion were of Jewish origin. All without exception had been part of the 'home-based' party; none were 'Muscovites'. The obvious intention was to destroy whatever had remained of the illegal Communist apparatus, to tear up its patents of nobility, so to speak. Frequent references to close ties between the accused and Tito strengthen this impression, while highlighting the painful excommunication of the Yugoslavs, formerly the pride of international Communism. Who could hope to avoid becoming a suspect, who was safe from arrest and imprisonment when such great men as these could tumble from their pedestals? Whether or not they believed in the charges, all Communists found themselves living with a permanent sense of fear and apprehension.

This underlying sense of unease mixed with strong guilt feelings first came into the open in Hungary in 1953–6, when the doors of prisons and concentration camps had been flung open and hundreds – perhaps thousands – of Communist survivors of a terrible ordeal returned home.

The diabolical 'mechanism' of the purges is too well known and the Hungarian example resembled the others too closely to merit yet another description. The only slight difference between the Hungarian case and the rest was that the thaw began earlier in Hungary than elsewhere – in 1954 – and that the revelation of the full horror whipped up a tempest of indignation and remorse. The Hungarians were unique among Communists in immediately raising the question of the responsibility of the party and of its leaders. The sacrifice of a few scapegoats did not suffice to appease disturbed consciences. Later, and particularly after Khrushchev's revelations at the Twentieth Congress of the Soviet Communist Party, Hungary witnessed a veritable explosion of political and moral demands. These included the unequivocal rehabilitation of László Rajk and his companions, a review of all the trials and the punishment of all responsible for the many miscarriages of justice, not least Mátyás Rákosi himself. An even harder blow for the party leaders was the fact that the internal challenge to their authority, previously confined to party intellectuals, had spread to other

Communist circles including the army and even to those at the periphery of the party apparatus. As for the 'hard core' bound to the leadership for a variety of reasons, they had all been forced on to the defensive: they had lost their old self-assurance and were exceedingly anxious and disorientated.

We have deliberately ignored such other aspects of the crisis as economic mismanagement, the total alienation of the peasantry, the increasing grip of the Soviet Union. The importance of these factors is obvious, and so is their repercussion on the party, now seen as the main cause of the country's catastrophic situation. It nevertheless seems preferable to dwell more on the country's growing demoralization from 1949 onwards, and its culmination in the collapse of the party at the very moment when the people, until then so many dumb actors in the wings, flocked to speak out on the political stage. To the militants, here was the revelation of a truth they had vaguely come to expect: the party they had served had lost its credibility and its standing.

Dissolution and Re-formation

While the destiny of Hungary was being played out in the streets of Budapest and became the subject of keen discussions in Moscow, Peking, Belgrade and other capitals, the Hungarian Communist Party was once again dissolved. But then, if truth be told, very little of it was left to dissolve.

On the ruins of the old Hungarian Worker's Party (MDP), there arose a new party, the Hungarian Socialist Worker's Party (Magyar Szocialista Munkáspárt – MSzMP), a name it retained until 8 October 1989. The event was announced over the radio by János Kádár on 1 November 1956 between 9.40 and 10 p.m. It was in this famous address that he called what was happening a 'glorious uprising of our people', one that had led to the 'liberation of our people and the independence of our country without either of which there is no socialism or ever can be'.[24] Kádár also mentioned the danger of Hungary's suffering the same fate as Korea and declared that 'the new party breaks with the crimes of the past'.[25] The old leadership was replaced with a steering committee which immediately set about organizing the MSzMP and making preparations for a founding congress. Its members were Ferenc Donáth, János Kádár, Sándor Kopácsi, Géza Losonczy, Georg Lukács, Imre Nagy and Zoltán Szántó. Two of these, Kádár and Szántó, were former secretaries of the Communist Party and three – Lukács, Nagy and Szántó – were old 'Muscovites'. Lukács and Szántó were, moreover, two founding fathers of the Hungarian Communist Party and of the 1919 Hungarian Soviet Republic. Nagy had been a member of the Politburo in 1945 and again in 1953. Six of the seven had been members of the Central Committee at various times. As a replacement for *Szabad Nép*, the party launched a new paper, the *Népszabadság* (People's Freedom).

−10−

The Kádár Régime

Like East Germany, János Kádár's Hungary knew a measure of economic success. Although this was relative, it was nevertheless an indisputable improvement both over the past and over most other countries in the socialist camp. (This chapter is written from the viewpoint of the 1960s and 1970s, and subsequently from the perspective of the first half of the 1980s.)

The economy has been one of Budapest's main concerns since 1956 and *a fortiori* since the introduction of the 'new economic mechanism' in 1968. However, economic success, reflecting the Hungarians' innovatory spirit, is by no means the only characteristic of the experiment presided over by János Kádár and his team during the past three decades. The Hungarian party, while adopting Stalinist methods of oppression during its difficult inaugural period, has since turned into a kind of 'model', and as such has received a good press in the West, enjoyed some popularity at home, and been an object of envy and criticism in other Communist countries.

The interval between the emergence of the Kádár régime and its most recent major reforms is long enough for the historian to be able to sit back and take stock. Such a detached approach to the 'Kádár phenomenon' seems the more fitting as, in contrast with the preceding decades, Hungary has become a serene country during the past thirty years. Even so, the dictum that 'a happy people has no history' does not really apply to the 'Goulash archipelago' which, while admittedly abounding in consumer goods, continues to suffer incurable ills that look as though they are inherent in the system. But what happiness there is has produced a climate of relative calm and serenity: the ruling party has been able to govern the country without spectacular ups and downs, and since the 1960s there have been few upheavals worth mentioning.

Our analysis will be confined to structural and political problems. But even in these areas it will be neither definitive nor comprehensive. The difficulty of gaining access to the sources and the lack of studies made in Hungary itself place severe restrictions on all such analyses. We are in the same boat as historians inside

Hungary: they, too, are frustrated by an inability to lay their hands on documents kept under lock and key.

The Emergence of the New Régime and the Trial of Imre Nagy

During the night of 1 November 1956, after his public announcement of the birth of the MSzMP, the new Communist Party, János Kádár disappeared, not to return until a few days later in the wake of the Soviet army – as head of a new government.

His mysterious disappearance has caused much ink to flow, but the main course of events can nevertheless be reconstructed. I know from several personal communications that Ferenc Münnich, one of Kádár's comrades, after having contacted the Russians, went to fetch Kádár in the parliament buildings and escorted him to the Soviet embassy in Budapest. From there, Kádár was taken to the airport and flown to one of the nearest Soviet villages in the Carpatho-Ukraine, where he met the Soviet leaders. Khrushchev himself was to recall their meeting during an official visit to Hungary. According to recent information this meeting with Soviet leaders took place in Moscow, allegedly in the presence of Mátyás Rákosi and some other Hungarian Stalinist leaders.

In a broadcast over a weak transmitter (probably in Szolnok), Kádár then announced the formation of his new government. It included Ferenc Münnich, as vice-premier, György Marosán, Imre Dögei, Antal Apró, Sándor Rónai, Imre Horváth (foreign minister) and István Kossa. We do not know whether all of these were present at the proclamation of the government on foreign soil or whether they joined it subsequently. The party newspaper in Budapest did not publish the news until a few days later, and István Dobi, the prime minister, also did not confirm the appointment of the Kádár government until 12 November. Imre Nagy's government, its legitimacy thus challenged, took refuge in the Yugoslav embassy, never having tendered its resignation.[1]

From his first days in office, János Kádár addressed the nation as head of the new, so-called 'revolutionary workers' and peasants' government' rather than as the first secretary of the MSzMP, the party he had helped to found a few days earlier. The position of the MSzMP was confusing to say the least: the party had set out with an appeal to the members of the MDP (the old Communist Party) to join its ranks. A new Central Committee was appointed, and all the members of the previous Central Committee, Kádár excepted, were eventually sent into exile.

The new MSzMP, 'János Kádár's party', set up following the Soviet intervention on 4 November 1956 was to have great difficulties in imposing itself as the leading political force, as the sole repository of socialism and as sole guardian of the nation's destiny. In 1956, before the October events, the Communist Party had counted some 860,000 members, or almost the same number as during the preceding five years. On 1 December, the records showed a membership of 37,818, or less than 5 per cent of the old figure. According to the official estimates, the real number was slightly higher – between 50,000 and 60,000 – which would have raised the level to 7 per cent.[2] Either way, the losses were severe. Thereafter the number of Communists grew rapidly to 120,000 in mid-January 1957, to 345,000 in June, to more than 400,000 during the following year and to more than 500,000 in 1966 – ten years later.

The original collapse had several causes. The party had lost its credibility and authority, not only with a majority of the nation but also with its traditional supporters. Moreover, Kádár and his team inspired the old Hungarian Stalinists with little confidence and the supporters of Imre Nagy – who felt betrayed – with even less. Suspicions were mutual: the MSZMP never invited the support of Nagy's 'rightists', and at the same time distanced itself from the dogmatic and Stalinist wing of the old party. A few veteran Stalinists, leading officials of the Rákosi and Gerö régime, were kept out; others were expelled, especially those who had served in the secret police. Most of the old apparatchiks nevertheless retained their places, though some heads of department were replaced.[3]

More important changes in the party leadership were to follow during successive reshuffles at the national conference held from 27 to 29 June 1957, the Seventh Congress held from 30 November to 5 December 1959, the Eighth Congress held from 20 to 25 November 1962, the Ninth Congress held from 28 November to 3 December 1966, and at subsequent party congresses.[4]

But let us return to the beginnings of the new party at the end of 1956; its very name clearly reflected a wish to stay within the tradition, to maintain a kind of continuity in discontinuity. Instead of 'Communist Party' or 'Party of Communists' or 'Workers' Party' – all marked with the sectarian and dogmatic stamp of the old leaders – the final choice fell on 'Hungarian Socialist Workers' Party', which contained an echo of the clandestine party of the 1920s.[5]

That choice had been well considered: on 31 October–1 November, during the revolution, Kádár and his comrades needed and wanted to break away from their immediate predecessors, to emphasize the differences rather than the similarities between them. In this way, they wished not only to acknowledge the consequences of the party's collapse but also to provide for a possible recovery of its fortunes within a pluralist framework. That pluralism would, of course, be limited, certainly supervised, by Hungary's mighty neighbour, but pluralism it would be for all that: power shared with other parties and with a kind of 'second power' represented by national committees, workers' councils and a free press.

But the MSzMP, when it surfaced on 4 November, was in no position to do anything about future plans. It had returned in the armoured cars of the Soviet Army, thus trampling from the start on any illusions of national independence. Moreover, by calling itself a 'revolutionary workers' and peasants' government' at the outset (in those early days no distinction was made between government and party), it swept aside, under the protection of the Soviet Army, all hopes of pluralism together with the idea of the separation of party and state. In the judicial vacuum and chaotic conditions which prevailed, the MSzMP seized power and left the question of the party's place in the nation's institutions wide open. The Kádár group thus laid claim to virtually all decision-making powers.

Even so, it did not shut the door entirely on all the forces of the crushed revolution. In his initial declarations over the radio and also in *Népszabadság*, the party paper – declarations carefully omitted from János Kádár's published speeches[6] – the head of the party and of the state still tried to present himself as heir to the old Marxist-Leninist party and to the Hungarian Revolution 'stripped of its reactionary deformations'. He implied that the main cause of the 1956 explosion lay in the errors and crimes of the Rákosi régime, and that Imre Nagy, Géza Losonczy and their friends had committed no more than excusable errors.[7] Indeed, many of those who were close to the new government – parachuted in by the Russians and lacking legality and legitimacy – were still thinking in terms of bringing Imre Nagy back and maintaining the workers' councils of the revolution. Kádár himself seemed in favour of this, stating in particular that Nagy was not under arrest (declaration published in *Népszabadság* on 14 November 1956 when Nagy and his associates were taking refuge in the Yugoslav embassy), and that no one wanted to restrict his freedom of movement. 'It is entirely up to him,' Kádár went on to say, 'whether or not he takes part in political life.'

Nevertheless, the policy of the group in power left few doubts as to its real intentions. Kádár had not broken with Imre Nagy merely to return a week later and then carry on as if nothing had happened. It was from a position of strength based on the Soviet Army that he intended to wield power and if possible to arrive at some accommodation with Imre Nagy or with other persons and trends.

It was on this basis, and not on continuity with the MSzMP he had founded with Nagy, that Kádár was to rebuild the Communist Party swept away by the storm. On the day of Kádár's return to Hungary, the only one to remain of the original leaders of the MSzMP, born on 31 October, was – Kádár himself. Of the other members of the executive committee that had served as the old Central Committee, Imre Nagy, Géza Losonczy, Georg Lukács, Zoltán Szántó and Ferenc Donáth were, as we saw, in the Yugoslav embassy, soon afterwards to be deported to Rumania, from where they would return to Budapest, not as free men, but as prisoners.[8] The seventh member of the Central Committee, Colonel Sándor Kopácsi, head of the Budapest police, would be arrested by the Soviet authorities.

One of the first tasks of the Kádár group, therefore, was to rebuild the party's executive committee: such documents as do exist suggest that this was done on 6 November 1956 when a Provisional Central Committee was appointed. According to some sources, however, this committee was not set up until 11 November,[9] and it seems likely that its original composition was identical with that of the government.[10]

The Budapest committee was also resuscitated: its members included György Aczél and Béla Biszku. The Provisional Central Committee, for its part, met on 2–5 December 1956, but its composition (thirty-seven members),[11] or for that matter that of the Provisional Executive Committee replacing the Politburo, did not become known until February 1957. On that date, the Executive Committee comprised the following ten persons: Antal Apró, Béla Biszku, Lajos Fehér, János Kádár, Gyula Kállai, Károly Kiss, György Marosán, Ferenc Münnich, Sándor Rónai and Miklós Somogyi.

An examination of the list of members of the Central and Executive Committees shows that the new team consisted of the least compromised old MDP leaders, some of whom had been victims of the Rákosi régime. Thus, while appealing to old Communists to join the MSzMP, the Kádár group also hoped to avoid being associated with the Stalinist taint of the old organization.

The same attitude marked their relations with the workers' councils that had sprung up during the revolution. Paradoxically, a government decree published in the *Government Gazette* on 24 November 1956, when repression was at its height, confirmed the legal existence of these councils. They were said to be the 'basis ' of real factory leadership, a form of workers' self-management.[12] For all that, the national committee of the workers' councils could not be convened because its meeting place was surrounded by Soviet tanks.[13] Moreover, it was also to be stripped of its functions by government decree. On 9 December 1956, the Greater Budapest Council was dissolved and its Information Bulletin discontinued.[14] The same decree, on the other hand, stipulated that local factory councils could continue as management committees, which they did for some time to come.

The contrast between the treatment accorded to the central workers' organ on the one hand and the rank-and-file organizations on the other was deceptive. The authorities were anxious to maintain the latter, at least for the time being, in order to revive production which had been completely paralysed by strikes; at the same time they wanted to get rid of the central councils whose aims were essentially political. It did not take long to become clear, however, that the rank-and-file councils sought to interfere with factory management, not to mention with party decisions. In June 1957, János Kádár spoke of the 'struggle between the party organs and the workers' councils'.[15] The latter disappeared soon afterwards. The economic reform projects, which we shall be discussing below, were to bypass completely the workers' councils.[16]

János Kádár's new régime, which initially still showed some inclination to preserve several of the ideas and institutions produced during the Revolution, thus did not take long to slide back into the rut of the old party.[17] It would be a matter of several years before it initiated another partial change of tack, especially in the economic sphere. Between 1957 and the middle 1960s, restoration was given precedence over renewal.

It is worth pointing out that Khrushchev's reforms also suffered a setback during this period: relations between the Soviet Communist Party and Yugoslavia deteriorated, the first signs of disagreement with China surfaced, the programme for outstripping the West within a few years was dropped. As elsewhere in the Soviet Bloc, in Hungary it was likewise a period marked by police repression and also by a hardening of ideological and economic attitudes. The Twenty-First Congress of the Soviet Communist Party moreover signalled a general return to Stalinist methods, and it was not until the Twenty-Second Congress (October 1961) that a new thaw would be announced.

As early as 1957 and 1958, even before the Twenty-First Congress, the Hungarian régime was bearing down on the nation with a heavy hand, all the heavier for being faced with the long, hard and bitter passive resistance that paralysed life in Hungary for several months. Police repression returned with a vengeance; the leaders of the workers' councils and those allegedly responsible for the events of October 1956 were the first victims. Charged with counter-revolutionary activity, thousands of persons were thrown into the same prisons that formerly held János Kádár and Gyula Kállai.

In June 1958, outraged public opinion heard of the execution of Imre Nagy and of three of his co-accused. According to unverified sources, Kádár would never have agreed to this step had he not been coerced into it by the Soviet leaders who were, in turn, under pressure by the Chinese. Perhaps there is something in it, but then other executions took place at the end of trials held *in camera*, without any noise or publicity. Several more trials of notables ended without fatal verdicts. Such celebrated writers as Tibor Déry and Gyula Háy received heavy sentences. It was not until 1962 that most of the ordinary workers, youths, officers and intellectuals gaoled for their participation in the events of 1956 were released following amnesties or the remission of sentences.

The full Nagy story is widely known today.[18] Arrested on leaving the Yugoslav embassy in Budapest, deported to Rumania, Imre Nagy and some thirty others (including women and children) were at first treated as 'guests' of the Rumanian government (although they had never asked to be 'invited'), while negotiations begun in the Yugoslav embassy continued. Emissaries from Budapest tried to persuade the 'guests' to admit their errors and to collaborate with the new régime. After that, all the families were dispersed and the main 'culprits' – Nagy, Losonczy and Donáth – separated from Georg Lukács, Zoltán Vas and the rest. Lukács and Vas eventually returned to Budapest where they were completely excluded from political life and, in Lukács's case, from all academic and cultural activities as well. Lukács died after twenty years of semi-banishment in his native Hungary; Zoltán Vas died as a retired 'pensioner'. The most prominent and active political figures involved in the events of 1956 and such leading personalities associated with their group as Zoltán Tildy, the former president of the Hungarian Republic, were tried before a tribunal in June 1958.

At this trial, nine persons were charged with being the main agents of the 1956 'counter-revolution': Imre Nagy, Ferenc Donáth, Miklós Gimes, Zoltán Tildy, Pál Maléter, Sándor

Kopácsi, József Szilágyi, Ferenc Jánosi and Miklós Vásárhelyi. Of these, Nagy was an old party stalwart, several times a minister of state, twice a prime minister; Tildy had been a prime minister and then president of the Republic; Donáth had been a member of the Central Committee of the party; Pál Maléter was a young career officer who had joined the party and had been made minister of defence in 1956; Kopácsi was a worker who had been appointed Budapest police chief; Jánosi was a former Calvinist clergyman who had joined the party during the liberation, and was Nagy's son-in-law; and finally Gimes, Szilágyi and Vásárhelyi were Communist journalists.

The only absentee was Géza Losonczy. A veteran Communist, one of the party's most brilliant intellectuals, a deputy minister of state, then (like Ferenc Donáth) imprisoned under Rákosi, he died in detention on the eve of the trial, probably at the hands of his gaolers. Szilágyi, too, was killed before the tribunal was able to pass the death sentence on him.

It should be stressed that the Nagy trial, like the Rajk trial in its day, was no more than the visible tip of an iceberg. Thousands, among them hundreds of political prisoners, were sentenced, generally behind closed doors, during the wave of repressions.

However, the Nagy trial had several features peculiar to itself. Rajk and his co-accused had been the victims of a trial based on total obfuscation: the whole thing had been pure invention, one great tissue of lies. The Nagy trial was much the same but in a different way; it was based on the transformation of perfectly normal actions into so many illegal acts. Had there been a meeting at Nagy's place or at one of his friends' homes before the October events? A gathering of political friends was nothing short of conspiracy. Had Nagy, as head of the government, granted an amnesty to the insurgents? It was clearly a plot to destroy the established 'order' of the people's democracy. The same was true of his decision to transform a Communist government into a coalition government, or of his other decision, taken *in extremis*, to abrogate Hungary's adherence to the Warsaw Pact. Nagy and his associates had indeed committed all these acts, not as conspirators but in full agreement with all the country's decision-making bodies: the government, the head of state, the leadership of the Communist Party. The monstrous nature of this trial was that it treated perfectly legal political acts or, at all events, acts not contravening any laws, as so many crimes.

The trial was not only a blatant perversion of justice but became even more monstrous by its moral implications. Behind the accused, the whole Hungarian nation stood in the dock. What the indictment and the tribunal laid at the door of Imre Nagy was nothing less than the *Hungarian Revolution*. In fact, Nagy and his associates had done nothing to foment it; they had merely tried to channel it. The tribunal ignored this truth. It even pretended ignorance of the fact that when Nagy assumed responsibility during a political crisis that was to turn into an insurrection – through the party's own fault – he and his associates were the only ones who could still have saved the Hungarian people's democracy.

On 16 June 1958, Nagy and those of his co-accused who were still alive were sentenced to death and executed. After that, political trials became rare events and police repression abated. Did the Kádár régime therefore succeed in lancing the abscess of the police system? Nothing may be assumed with less confidence. In recent years there have again been stories of police interference with intellectuals, writers and sociologists. One of the victims was dragged before a tribunal and acquitted; others received suspended sentences. It is not the gravity of such recent new developments that makes one cautious about the chances of creating Hungarian communism with a human face in which police methods are disallowed, nor is it the attitude of János Kádár and his closest collaborators. The real problem is that, despite the leaders' formal desire not to fall back into the errors of the past, the infrastructure of the system has not really changed, so that the clock can always be turned back. In particular, the present-day leaders are not really in control of their secret police, which is still dependent on the Soviet secret service acting through Russian 'advisers'. Kádár could well have got rid of that system at the time when Khrushchev was in power, but he did not feel the need to do so at the time, and afterwards it was too late even had he wished to.

In any case, the freedom and sense of security enjoyed by Hungarians and members of the party today, though relative when compared with conditions in the West, nevertheless render life incomparably easier than it was in Rákosi's Hungary or still is in other Communist countries.

A Quarter-century of Relative Political and Economic Stability

After a difficult start and a laborious process of reorganization in 1957, the party was to enjoy a period of relative political and economic stability, which went hand in hand with a remarkable period of growing prosperity. This boom continued until the early 1980s, when stagnation and decline set in again.

The Development of the Party

For many years ahead, the party was to enjoy almost unprecedented stability in its leadership. Until the Tenth Congress in 1970, the Politburo was made up of the 'original' team, that is of members of the 1956 Executive Committee and of members of the Central Committee re-elected at the 1957 party conference and at the Seventh Congress in 1959: Antal Apró, Béla Biszku, Lajos Fehér, Jenö Fock, János Kádár, Gyula Kállai together with György Aczél, L. Czinege, Sándor Gáspár, Pál Ilku, Zoltán Komócsin, Dezsö Nemes, Károly Németh, Rezsö Nyers and István Szirmai, members or alternate members of the Central Committees of 1957 and 1959. At least a dozen or so other persons also remained in key party posts for some ten years, among them the economists István Friss and Miklós Ajtai, such leading party officials as László Orbán and Árpád Pullay, such ministers as Endre Sik and Géza Révész, and several others. As for Ferenc Münnich, Kádár's co-founder of the 'revolutionary workers' and peasants' government', he, like Miklós Somogyi, retired for reasons of age but also because of differences with János Kádár. After 1970, however, the entire original team disappeared.

And so there were fifteen years of stability at the top and, let it be added, also at the centre. This was because all those who stood in Kádár's way were removed, at one point or another, for involvement in so-called 'factional' plots against Kádár's middle course. One of the first to go, Imre Dögei, minister of agriculture in the 1956 Kádár government, was suspended from the Central Committee in May 1960, and expelled from the party two years later. In fact, it appears that Mátyás Rákosi never stopped trying to make contact from his Soviet exile, either personally or through intermediaries, with his old friends, in continued attempts to incite them against Kádár and his circle. Dögei was apparently part of this group of conspirators and so were several less important figures.

Another spectacular case was that of György Marosán, a former left-wing Social Democrat who had rallied to the Communist Party in 1948, had been imprisoned by Rákosi, freed and rehabilitated by Nagy and promoted to membership in the Politburo by Kádár himself. Marosán fell into disgrace in 1962, in circumstances that remain unexplained to this day. In any case, his fall coincided with another campaign against Kádár, this one on a much larger scale than those preceding it. Thanks to unwavering support from Khrushchev, Kádár triumphed once again and the Eighth Party Congress, meeting in the autumn of 1962, endorsed his policy in every respect, and particularly his 'energetic administrative measures' against those who 'by their factionalist attempts had tried to deflect the party from the Marxist-Leninist path'.

The directives issued by the Central Committee of the Hungarian Socialist Workers' Party to the congress stressed the need to pursue the 'battle on two fronts', namely, against right-wing revisionism and against left-wing sectarianism.[19] In reality, it was chiefly the left that was under attack, as witness the concrete measures taken and also some of the resolutions to which we shall be returning.

Mention must also be made of three other grave crises. Khrushchev's dismissal in October 1964 threatened Kádár's position. This may explain why he alone among all the party leaders of the people's democracies felt compelled to criticize, if not the basis, then at least the form in which the decision against his powerful protector had been taken. Nevertheless he was left in charge of his own party, the new Soviet team realizing how useful it was to keep him at the helm.

Four years later, during the invasion of Dubček's Czechoslovakia by Warsaw Pact troops, including Hungarian units, Kádár was once again to play a somewhat enigmatic role. It all began with an attempt to play the mediator: making Dubček 'see reason' while checking the interventionist intentions of Dubček's adversaries. Next came a gesture of disapproval, if only in the form of total silence for several days after the armed intervention of 20 August 1968. Over and above the distress the intervention itself and Hungarian participation in it caused him, Kádár must have feared the repercussions the Czechoslovak affair could have had on his own policies. Was it not the Hungarian party which had practised, well before the Prague Spring, if not a form of 'communism with a human face', at least a policy of respect for the citizen's person? Was it not also the Hungarian Communist Party which had, almost at the same time as the Czechs, introduced the economic reforms known as the 'new economic mechanism', which involved decentralization and profitability? Once again, Kádár survived the crisis and even seemed to emerge from it with an enhanced authority allowing him to get his way all along the line: inside the party, in the economic field, in cultural life, where Hungarians enjoyed liberties unknown among their Socialist neighbours, and finally in the strictly political arena. The only price the party had to pay for

Moscow's indulgence was unqualified support for Soviet foreign policy. It complied as ever. Reformist at home, the Hungarian Communist Party unhesitatingly underwrote Moscow's policy towards Peking, Bonn, Jerusalem and Bucharest.

The Stalinist opposition, however, did not give up the ghost. It merely waited for the right moment to strike at the leading team and at Kádár in particular. Even an important section of the Central Committee elected by the Tenth Congress in 1970 was attracted by the theses of the 'left' opposition, so much so that János Kádár threatened to resign on several occasions, and especially in 1972. Was this a ruse or a sign of genuine exhaustion? Whichever it was, during that year of internal crises, Kádár came out on top once again and issued a new challenge to his opponents. In a speech delivered on his sixtieth birthday he returned to the analysis of the 1956 events he had given fifteen years earlier, stressing not the 'counter-revolutionary' but the 'tragic' character of that great historical moment.[20]

Popular despite the role he had played in 1956, architect of a new, flexible and moderate policy, a skilful politician, Kádár was able to stay in the saddle, but at the cost of numerous compromises. In 1972, the party was forced to put a brake on the 'new economic mechanism' and to restrict cultural freedom. A group of sociologists, with András Hegedüs, Rákosi's old prime minister, at their head, was disbanded, writers were reprimanded and even brought before the tribunals. These were so many signs of a general hardening of the political line, a process that became even more pronounced following the 'ideological conference' of Communist parties held in Moscow in December 1973. In March 1974 Kádár had to put a good face on it when, following a resolution of the Central Committee, he was forced to dismiss some of his closest collaborators from the party Secretariat, including György Aczél, in charge of cultural affairs, and Rezsö Nyers, the real father of the new economic mechanism.[21] In an address he delivered on 28 March, Kádár nevertheless insisted that 'the main direction of our policy has remained unchanged and unbroken'. However, the call for a 'strengthening of the leading role of the working class' in all spheres, including cultural life, suggests that there must have been a readjustment of the party 'line' at the expense of the policy of openness and of the relaxed climate enjoyed by the citizens of Hungary.

The Eleventh Party Congress, meeting from 17 to 22 June 1975, and the policies adopted since that date have finally dispelled many exaggerated fears. Nevertheless, during the congress, there was covert opposition to Kádár's policies, and it is quite possible that potential leaders of a harder line were still counting on his downfall. Kádár himself alluded to the matter in his closing speech. Referring to the country's economic problems, he declared that 'there have been many critics; sometimes I even thought that I was listening to the opposition'.[22] But these critics had in fact confined themselves to such special problems as the lack of iron and steel or the food shortage, and had not questioned the government's general policy. The dismissal, soon after the congress, of Jenö Fock, the prime minister, was probably connected with the economic shortages some of the delegates had mentioned at the congress, but there were no other consequences. Above all, the person and policy of János Kádár were not impugned by the 'opposition' speakers. Sándor Gáspár and Károly Németh, the leaders of that tendency, used extremely moderate terms at the congress. If there was a 'plot', Kádár was able to defuse it once again, thanks to his political skill, the undeniable success of his policies, and finally thanks to the support the Soviet leaders continued to give him, despite his deviations. At the Eleventh Congress, Brezhnev appeared in person to pay tribute to the Hungarian leader.

From then on Kádár's position seemed unshakeable. With the Korean leader Kim Il Sung, the Bulgarian Zhivkov, the Albanian Enver Hodja and a few others, Kádár was the oldest of the Communist Party leaders in power. He had maintained himself there since 1956; compared with him, Gierek or Jaruzelski, Husak or Honecker and also Andropov and Gorbachev were mere greenhorns.

His success has turned Hungary into the most prosperous country in the socialist camp besides East Germany – a country with a more or less contented population. *Incredibile dictu*, the collectivized land system no longer encounters peasant opposition and, thanks to the extraordinary ebullience of the Hungarian *kolkhozes*, the country suffers no food shortages. All this has produced a relatively serene political climate, in contrast to conditions in the rest of the socialist bloc. Disowning Kádár, or worse still, throwing him out of office, would in these circumstances be tantamount to disavowing the *sole* Communist experience that has been less than painful. Neither the opposition to the left of Kádár nor the Kremlin would run the risk of embarking on so dangerous a path. And so Kádár remains at his post and can even allow himself the use of phrases and political manoeuvres that make him the champion of a rather unusual form of Communism. It is not his possible dismissal that threatens this experiment, but something more natural: his age and state of health. Who will succeed him when the time comes? No one can answer that question. There is no obvious successor in his immediate circle, but one thing seems certain: Kádár has his eyes on the younger generation, the new party élite, not on the old revolutionary guard. For the rest, he has allowed Hungarian economists to draft and then to apply the famous 'new mechanism' on which, despite its defects, the relative prosperity of Hungary rests.

The 'New Economic Mechanism' and Hungarian Society

According to Hungarian statistics, the country's national income has quintupled in the space of thirty-three years: the index has risen from 100 in 1950 to 493 in 1983. (It stood at 80, one year before the Second World War.) This result is particularly flattering for the Kádár régime, because the index stood at no more than 117 in 1956 and also flattering for the reforms introduced since 1968 during which period the index rose from 265 to the final figure of 493.[23] The investment index quadrupled from 1950 to 1981, while the industrial output index rose from 100 to 864.[24]

The socialist sector accounted for the lion's share of the gross national product with 95.8 per cent in 1982, of which 68.4 per cent was due to the state sector and 23.6 per cent to the co-operative sector, leaving 3.8 per cent for the so-called 'personal patch' sector run part-time by wage earners, and 4.2 per cent to the fully private sector.[25] The last two sectors thus accounted for a total of 8 per cent as against 92 per cent in the socialist sector proper – state or co-operative. These are the official figures; the real share of the private sector is higher. We shall be returning to this point.

When it comes to the distribution of the national product by branch of activity, industry takes the lead with 45.1 per cent, followed by building with 12 per cent, agriculture and forestry with 18.8 per cent, transport and communications with 9.2 per cent and commerce with 14 per cent. Of Hungary's 10,700,000 inhabitants (in round figures), 5 million are active persons. Of these, 31.7 per cent are employed in industry, 7.5 per cent in construction, 21.8 per cent in agriculture and forestry, 10 per cent in commerce, 7.9 per cent in transport and communications, 10.7 per cent in the health, social and cultural services and 4.7 per cent in the administrative sector.

Let us now look at real incomes. The index, set at 100 in 1950, rose to 342 per head of population in 1981; the consumption index rose to 323 during the same interval. Savings stood at 160,000 million forints in 1981 compared with 300 million in 1950 and 5,500 million in 1960. From 1950 to 1981, the consumption of meat per inhabitant more than doubled (36 kg as against 16.3 kg); that of milk and dairy products rose from 99 kg to 172 kg; that of eggs from 85 to 315 per annum.

It should be noted that the 1950 figures were practically identical with those for 1934 and 1938. Consumption has thus nearly trebled when compared with the pre-war figures.[26] By contrast it has increased very little or stood still since the beginning of 1980. This stagnation or even drop in the standard of living has hit the least fortunate categories of the population hardest. The Thirteenth Party Congress held in March 1985 – in other words at precisely the end of five lean years – was forced to acknowledge this decline: the real wages of workers, other employees and peasants in the co-operative sector fell by 6 per cent in four years.[27]

As far as durable consumer goods are concerned, in 1983, Hungarians owned (per thousand inhabitants): 121 telephones, 262 television sets and 103 motor cars, which puts Hungary ahead of Bulgaria, Poland, Rumania and the Soviet Union, but still behind Czechoslovakia and the German Democratic Republic. The gap between these three leaders and Western Europe nevertheless remains considerable: 1 : 3 for telephones and 1 : 4 for private cars, to name but two items.

Comparing standards of living is always a hazardous undertaking. Nevertheless it is possible to make two broad generalizations. The Hungarian standard of living is among the highest in the Communist world and in the least advanced Mediterranean countries. The average Hungarian lives a much better life than his pre-war compatriot, or for that matter his predecessor in the Stalinist period. In both cases, there has been a leap of 200 per cent. In that sense, we can agree with the Hungarian historian, Iván T. Berend, who, discussing the standard of living, speaks of a definite turning-point in the 1960s following 'a stagnant standard of living and of consumption over two or three generations'.[28]

And so Hungarians entered a period of relative prosperity and did so, we hasten to add, without jeopardizing the future: the funds set aside for the accumulation of capital, for investment and for scientific and technological research have been adequate and obtained without recourse to the extreme measures characteristic of the early 1950s.

Hungary in the reform era owes this largely to a party-state government which has learned from the disasters of the past, setting itself realistic targets and underwriting the successive reforms proposed by a remarkable team of economists. It must, however, be pointed out that all these achievements were bought at the price of an effort which no other country in the socialist camp has so far shown itself capable of making. The performance of East Germany, while often better, was based on a head start and also on special relations with the Federal Republic. The Hungarians started out from a much lower level and arrived at generally satisfactory results by dint of hard work, a spirit of enterprise and even ingenuity. Thus, while fully acknowledging the merits of the government, we must nevertheless attribute Hungary's 'economic miracle' first and foremost to the indefatigable brains and brawn of its people.

A second comment is in order. Without being directly involved in the 'co-prosperity' of the West, Hungary has profited from it. The success of the Hungarian economy is also connected with the unprecedented increase in the West's level of production, technology, commerce and consumption.

These two complementary factors suggest that the vaunted 'new economic mechanism' is one of the causes of Hungary's success, but also a sign of Hungary's relative underdevelopment. Like Austria, Spain and Italy under a free economic system – or with a less ramshackle mechanism – Hungary was able, thanks mainly to its human resources, to join the ranks of the more prosperous countries, leaving its former poverty-stricken condition far behind.

Let us now sum up the successive stages in Hungary's economic development and also the principles and faults of its system. According to Berend, the recent development towards a less rigidly planned and more profitable economy had its origins in the era of reforms under the first Imre Nagy government in 1953–5. On the one hand, some preliminary theoretical and practical conclusions were then drawn from the disastrous policy of forced investments practised during previous years: investment in heavy industry was slowed down and measures were taken to encourage the production of industrial and agricultural consumer goods. In addition, a start was made with the rationalization of the economy and a first step was taken towards far more sweeping reforms. One of the sponsors of the new trend was György Péter, President of the Statistical Bureau, a man who was to die at the hands of the secret police a few years later in mysterious circumstances. In an article published in 1954 in *Közgazdasági Szemle* (Economic Review), Péter outlined the necessary reforms, advocating greater profitability for enterprise, fewer central directives, greater independence based on the creation of autonomous units, a realistic revision of prices and finally a more competitive economy offering wider choices. The attempt to rethink economics in terms of profitability and competitiveness continued throughout the second half of the 1950s.

According to Berend, it was János Kornai who 'X-rayed the way the Hungarian economy really functioned',[29] and most specifically the effects of its 'exaggerated centralization'.[30] His was the germ of the theory subsequently developed by Hungarian economists, namely that the lack of autonomy of enterprise (read 'state manipulation') leads to waste, which in turn engenders and perpetuates poverty. In the late 1950s, the Hungarian economy was in the throes of the second Three-Year Plan (the first having been the post-war Three-Year Reconstruction Plan followed by the first Five-Year Plan). At the beginning of this period, reformist ideas not only percolated to academic circles but also to such agencies as the Planning Bureau and the Price Bureau. The result was a veritable avalanche of new suggestions.

All these reformist attempts were squashed at the end of 1957, partly because of an anti-revisionist campaign in all Communist countries and those associated with Comecon in particular. Soon afterwards, the pipe-dream of outstripping the West put an end to reformist programmes by its exaggerated emphasis on heavy industry and on forced growth. During these years, Tibor Liska was to be one of the few economists to preach real reforms. These were to come in 1964, a period during which the reform movement also took a leap ahead in Czechoslovakia.

Another impetus for reforms came from agriculture. To understand why, we must go back to 1958–61, when the transformation of private agriculture into collective farming was set in motion. To examine this process in detail would take up more space than we have available. The reader may remember that, at the beginning of the 1950s, the régime managed, by force and brutality, to collectivize a quarter of all private landholdings. During the Revolution of 1956, a major part of this *kolkhoz* system was reconverted into private holdings. In the early years of the Kádár régime, the collectivization programme was temporarily abandoned, in part to save the countryside (but also the towns which relied on the countryside for their provisions); in part to spare the unstable new régime fresh vexations. In addition, the party and János Kádár in person were strong in their opposition to the attempts made by certain dogmatic circles to press for further collectivization measures regardless of the fact that these measures were bound to lead to the impoverishment of the peasantry.

For all that, the party-state never turned its back on the idea of collectivization. At the end of 1958, conditions seemed ripe and the collectivization idea was revived. This time, however, it was reintroduced with a few more precautions, though not without inflicting economic and administrative violence on the peasantry. At the beginning of the 1960s, the countryside once again witnessed aggressive and sometimes brutal acts against recalcitrant peasants. By physical violence, sequestration, intimidation and harassment, the peasants were again forced into collective farms and had to make over to them all their possessions.

However, unlike the course events had taken in in the 1950s, the new collectivization campaign – which culminated in the creation of a near-total collective system (apart from small personal plots) – went hand in hand with a series of measures to mitigate its worst consequences. Thanks largely to Lajos Fehér, a former colleague of Imre Nagy and now the Politburo member responsible for agriculture, an attempt was made – not without success – to place co-operative farming on more solid foundations.

On the individual plane, this meant first of all winning the confidence of the middle-ranking peasants instead of relying exclusively on the poorest and least experienced. From the outset, the aim was to establish profitable, prosperous and well-managed farming co-operatives. An effort was also made to avoid turning the campaign into a class struggle (rather than a way of improving agricultural production) by incitement of the poorer peasants against the 'kulaks', many of whom were in fact middle-ranking peasants. This time, after two years on probation, these 'kulaks' even became eligible for leading posts in the co-operatives.

One of the most important new provisions was the principle of co-operative autonomy; the co-operatives were no longer subjected to interference by party or state officials. In principle, they were even entitled to elect their own leaders and to run their farms as they saw fit – technically, administratively and commercially. In practice, however, official interference never ceased. Far from it. The authorities continued to intervene in every aspect of the life of the *kolkhozes*, if less blatantly than in the past.

Three other important innovations must also be mentioned. The distribution of incomes was no longer solely based on the 'working day' (the Russians' *trudoden'*), which guaranteed workers equal wages for equal time regardless of the results of their labour. The new system was much more pragmatic in that it used a number of criteria among which yield, productivity and returns were the most important. Another new measure was the allocation of co-operative holdings – and also, where applicable, of the livestock – to those who actually worked them (generally families) and who thus became the co-operatives' 'tenant farmers'. Finally, the most important new measure was the changed attitude to 'personal plots'. These small allotments – kitchen gardens, farmyards and so on – which, hectare for hectare, proved vastly more productive than the collective sector, were no longer considered a necessary evil. On the contrary, the party's guidelines now favoured a symbiosis between the co-operatives and farmers working individual or family plots.

This brief account does not pretend to cover special cases. There are smaller and larger co-operatives (the state prefers large ones of 4,000 hectares on average), more or less prosperous and more or less fortunate ones. Some extend their activities to semi-industrial or even industrial activities in the food sector; others act as subcontractors for a variety of non-agricultural enterprises. The state, far from trying to stop them, tends to encourage diversity and diversification of this kind. Rural Hungary has thus become an immense agricultural producer with a flourishing market.

However, agricultural production is more expensive than it is in the West. The yield, though higher than it used to be, is still relatively poor when measured by any criteria: by area, capital investment or by working hour. The rationalization of agriculture in this traditionally and structurally rural country is therefore a prerequisite of economic reform.

That reform, prepared for three years, was introduced on 1 January 1968. Ever since, as I have tried to show in brief, it has had a chequered history. What follows merely sketches in its main characteristics.

Underlying the reform are ideas of the economists and the team of party specialists headed by Rezsö Nyers, then a member of the Politburo and still an influential member of the Central Committee. Most importantly he has, for more than a decade, been director of the Economic Institute of the Hungarian Academy of Science which has played a most important role in the elaboration of the economic reform programme and in all the changes that have marked its history since 1968.

The role of these 'brains' cannot be stressed enough, nor the fact that the Kádár governments allowed, indeed encouraged, them to examine the situation in depth and to isolate the causes of Hungary's economic plight without whitewashing any individual. The party allowed 'a hundred flowers to bloom' – at least in the economic sphere – without cutting off their heads afterwards.

Admittedly, the experts' recommendations were never fully implemented. Far from it, but they were nevertheless examined, executed in part and, above all, treated as a reliable *scientific information base*. In Hungary, unlike other countries, telling the economic 'truth' and propounding modern economic theories were no crimes.

Hungary also drew the lessons of the disastrous consequences of planning based on outdated Marxist-Leninist dogma and on a single criterion: the quantity of goods produced. The Hungarian economy is, of course, nothing like the 'socialist market economy' some have claimed it to be. For all that, the market plays a considerable role in the determination of demand and of the 'real price' determined by profit and competition. And while actual economic measures undoubtedly lagged far behind these vaunted principles, the spirit and the approach had clearly changed: economic problems were viewed in the light of late twentieth-century ideas and no longer in that of the political sociology of an earlier age.

Decentralization, restructuring, the autonomy of enterprises were the new principles. Every sector and even every enterprise became a self-managed entity, free, in principle, to use its capacity and resources at its discretion. It invested capital as it judged best, on paper at least it could hire and fire as it saw fit, it bought and sold in accordance with its needs and resources, it made profits and losses in line with its results, in competition with other enterprises. In principle, it was also free to redistribute its revenue to match individual productivity.

The authorities even considered adapting the property system to meet the needs of this new economic order, made up of competing units and (to some extent) subject to the law of supply and demand. In that event, each factory would have been owned by its workforce.

In practice, however, things did not quite work out in this way. Despite a determined effort to allow prices to be set by the imperatives of the market (which, as they said in Hungary, set the 'true price'), the price of many base and raw materials remained fixed by the state. The market and competition were thus out of mesh. Moreover, the state remained the sole importer of raw materials, machinery, manufactured goods and so forth, individual enterprises, in any case, lacking adequate funds and foreign currency to order them on their own.

The state also intervened through the allocation of investment funds and through its general control of the labour market and of wage aggregates. Free in principle, individual enterprises could not hire and fire in accordance with their real needs: the principle of full employment remained almost sacrosanct.

The autonomy of individual enterprises, however relative, did introduce a measure of competition and also rewards for individual and collective success. This applied more to medium-size enterprises, with no more than a few hundred employees, than to the industrial giants employing between 1,000 and 10,000 workers or even more. To the detriment of the entire Hungarian economy, the big enterprises, accounting for approximately 80 per cent of the labour force, remained partly bound up with the old centralized system: if they were in the red, they expected the state to rescue them, and they continued to shelter hidden unemployment 'behind their factory walls'. Innovation in these giants was so slow as to damage the profits from expensive investments, foreign loans and foreign licences.

The national debt also jeopardized the new economic mechanism. With a debt of 7,000 million US dollars (see Preface for update), Hungary shared the honour of heading the list of Communist debtor countries with Poland. Now, per capita debt is not, of course, the sole criterion of a country's economic standing. Its exports, and hence its repayment potential, helped to place Hungary in a better position than a number of countries with smaller debts. Servicing and repaying the debt nevertheless imposed a heavy burden on the Hungarian economy, which, in addition, had to struggle desperately against internal difficulties, against pressure from the Communist bloc and also against the effects of the international fuel and economic crises, the more so as nearly half of Hungary's foreign trade was with non-Communist countries – 34 per cent with capitalist countries and 13 per cent with developing countries.

Economic relations with capitalist countries were not confined to commerce. Hungary practised, albeit on a small scale, a policy of mixed enterprises, in some of which the foreign partner held a majority of the shares. Among the peculiarities of the Hungarian economy, there is one in particular that has provoked a great deal of written comment. With exaggerated emphasis, the Western press often draws the picture of a kind of Hungarian economic paradise to which the private sector is alleged to hold the key. In the absence of detailed statistics, it is difficult here to sift fact from fable. Estimates of the overall value of the production of goods and services by this sector – not including the peasants' allotments – vary between 7 and 15 per cent. It all, of course, hinges on the criteria used in what are exceedingly complex calculations.

The party-state does without doubt encourage some economic activity based on so-called 'personal initiative', a term used to avoid too many references to private let alone capitalist enterprise. This encouragement is unprecedented in the history of East European socialist economies. All of these, including the Soviet Union, admittedly have a black, a grey or a grey-white market and even black or grey or grey-white labour. The proportion of 'parallel labour' – labour that is not black because it either enjoys state authorization or toleration – is in any case appreciably higher in Hungary than elsewhere. People speak of a 'second economy', though, by virtue of the extreme variety of private and semi-private activities, it is impossible to give precise figures. However, the press – Hungarian journalists themselves devote enormous space to this issue – does at least give some idea of these forms of labour and sometimes of their presence in various sectors if not in the economy as a whole.

The 'second economy' covers a whole spectrum beginning with small craftsmen or tradesmen, traditionally a private sector, whose number has become most impressive in the wake of almost unlimited permits: nearly 76,000 independent workers, 14,000 pensioners or retired people and 40,000 wage earners have been issued with craftsmen's licences. These craftsmen give work to 20,000 employees and 5,000 apprentices. Taken all in all, 150,000 persons are associated with this group, as against a few tens of thousands during the period preceding the new economic system. They cover 48 industrial trades, 18 branches of the building trade and 7 service occupations.

It is much more difficult to put figures to the number of private industrial enterprises authorized to employ up to 50 and, exceptionally, up to 100 persons. Overall, there are 148 small industrial enterprises employing a total of more than 12,000 persons, 138 co-operatives employing 6,000 persons, 704 professional groups employing 16,220 persons, 5,399 industrial 'work communities' employing 62,000 persons,[31] 1,684 private 'work communities' employing close to 8,000 persons – all this over and above the craftsmen we have mentioned. To these figures must be added people engaged in the building trade (private and communal) which accounts for 50,000 persons in addition to craftsmen, and also those engaged in agriculture, the service sector and the so-called 'small communities', not forgetting private trade with 19,000 persons and trade under government licence with about 10,000 persons.

Leaving agriculture aside, we thus arrive at about 200,000 persons over and above the 150,000 in the craftsmen's sector. Without counting the liberal professions, the arts and agriculture, the number of persons employed in the private and semi-private sectors (we have seen the variety of forms) therefore adds up to about 350,000 in a total of 5 million active persons.[32]

But this must be well below the real figure, the more so as it is impossible to quantify the number of people who divide their time between wage labour and non-registered, part-time, private labour as a secondary occupation. A joke has it that every Hungarian has two jobs, an official one with the state from which he draws his wages and a private one at which he actually works and from which – this is no joke – he often earns more money. According to some estimates, 75 per cent of all families have some 'private interest' (including allotments) and 25 per cent of all the work done in Hungary comes from this sector.

But no matter what the exact number and the precise role of private employment, Hungary is close to being a country with a mixed economy with, it must be stressed, absolutely preponderant state and co-operative sectors. What counts, however, is not merely the proportion of the various private sectors expressed in absolute numbers or percentages, but also the character of these sectors. It very much looks, in fact, as if these are the most dynamic of the Hungarian economy. The thousands of small craftsmen's, communal and private shops and enterprises adapt themselves most readily to the needs of the market, fill the gaps in industry and the state services, amortize their investments more quickly, and produce higher yields. Thus while the private sector may not be like a heavily laden goods train, it at least represents one of the most efficient locomotives. The question is: how far can it travel?

The prospects are far from favourable. The various private sectors are beset with a lack of capital and with structural and, ultimately, political obstacles. In the very nature of things, the leading enterprises are and remain state-run. Political principles cannot be bent indefinitely. There is an ideological limit which the Hungarian leaders cannot overstep without attracting the wrath of the Soviet big brother.

On the other hand, the state socialist sector of the economy also comes up against structural obstacles. The Hungarian economic mechanism, as remarked earlier, is not really a workers' self-management system. Decentralization has merely introduced a limited degree of autonomy in the *management* of particular enterprises. The reform is thus based on the response of managers who remain salaried officials dependent on the good will of the state and the party hierarchy, even though state intervention is incomparably less heavy-handed than it may be in planned centralized systems.[33] This hierarchic dependency has a host of disadvantages: no enterprise is free to develop its productive and innovative capacities to the full.

In these circumstances, it will prove difficult to escape from the stagnation that has bedevilled the Hungarian economy since the early 1980s. What is still desperately needed is the removal of structural obstacles and political changes accompanied by more radical, more effective reforms.[34] Rezsö Nyers, the 'father' of the Hungarian reforms, has been outspoken on this point. According to him the party is made up of 'two parties': one urging reforms and another resisting them. Which will win out in the end? Perhaps the future is one of endless compromises.

Does the Hungarian Experiment Provide an Alternative?

Since the early 1970s, the Hungarian experiment or the 'Hungarian model' has been giving rise to hopes, controversies and the most varied opinions. Its severest critics are to be found in a group that, in fair and foul weather, pours out its *samizdat* wrath in such journals as *Profil, Beszélö* (Parlour), *Hirmondó* (Messenger) and several others. While collaborating with one another, these opponents reflect several tendencies, including one close to the late Georg Lukács; another is inspired by András Hegedüs, the former prime minister and reformist sociologist; yet others subscribe to an independent ideology, for instance the famous writer György Konrád, or János Kis, György Bence, János Kenedi, Miklós Haraszti and many others. Ferenc Donáth, a former member of the Central Committee who had seen the insides of Horthy's, Rákosi's and Kádár's prisons, was another independent critic until his death, as are István Csurka, the writer, and György Dalos, István Eörsi, Mihály Vajda and György Krassó – intellectuals, some of whom used to be close to the party, together with others unconnected with the Communist movement. There are also some whose opposition is based on an old Hungarian writers' tradition or on the 'populist' movement. The poet Sándor Csoóri is one of their spokesmen. László Rajk's son is (almost openly) engaged in the distribution of various *samizdat* publications edited by Gábor Demszky.

Their development, various actions and, above all, the great range of their political ideas are worth noting. Among them are proponents of self-management, liberals, and reformists with attitudes akin to the revisionism formerly championed by Imre Nagy. Their activities are ideological as well as economic, and they also concern themselves with social problems and the fate of Hungarian minorities in neighbouring countries. It is the last two activities above all that have aroused public opinion and kept gaining them growing support. In this connection, we need only mention public and the numerous protests by opposition groups against the persecution of cultural leaders of the Magyar minorities in Rumania and to a lesser extent in Czechoslovakia. These opposition groups were often harassed by the authorities, but not nearly to the same extent as Czech, Rumanian, East German or Soviet dissidents. None were sent to gaol. Trials and even police intervention have become rare in Hungary, though when they happen they are often still heavy-handed. The opposition has been given a small amount of elbow-room and can even distribute some of its clandestine publications.

This tolerance may be attributed to the fact that 'permanent' opponents are not very numerous, do not enjoy much popular support and practise a considerable degree of moderation, even of self-censorship. Finally, the régime tries to safeguard its tolerant not to say 'liberal' reputation by overlooking oppositional activities confined to mere words, except for certain street demonstrations or commemorative ceremonies.

The aim of the opposition can be summed up in a few words: it is not to topple the régime, but to infuse it with greater momentum; it longs for reforms that go beyond the official reformism. In some fields, it steps into the breach on the régime's behalf, as for instance when it comes to improving the lot of Hungarian minorities abroad or of the poor at home. Needless to say, the opposition also advocates wider human rights, political pluralism, freedom of speech and the right of free assembly.

Does the opposition then constitute a viable alternative to the régime? It is impossible to give any clear-cut answer. It undoubtedly offers an alternative inasmuch as it calls, if not for a change in the régime, at least for a change in outlook and for greater freedom in practice. If for that reason alone, the opposition is a permanent stimulus, one of the guarantees that the voice of the people is heard. This is also its most radical claim because, without saying it in so many words, the opposition poses what is virtually a permanent challenge to the inflexible bases of a Soviet-type Communist system enjoying a monopoly of power, of information and of social organization.

For all that, it is exceedingly difficult to extract a viable alternative programme from the numerous writings of the opposition. Because realism prevents them from turning themselves into a radical movement, the system's opponents confine themselves to denouncing the errors and shortcomings of the régime and to offering piecemeal remedies.[35]

At the other extreme, the régime also has dogmatic critics longing for a return to Stalinism. Do these constitute a large group? That, too, is impossible to say. In the leadership, their number and influence seems to have been decreasing since the crisis of the early 1970s when doubt was cast on the value of the economic reforms and also on the moderate liberalism accompanying them. As I have tried to show, János Kádár was able to cope with that crisis most ably, and nothing more has been heard of the matter. It is, however, quite possible that certain sections of the party and the state apparatus feel uncomfortable with the process of 'liberal' modernization, if only because it threatens their privileges and decision-making monopoly. But the historian may well have to revise his view that the state apparatus is a bastion of rigidity and orthodoxy. In 1985, for instance, it received a double face-lift through the passage of time and also through Kádár's determination to make it an instrument of his policies. As a result, the political class is now recruited from a new generation, whose ranks are most unlikely to shelter an opposition threatening the official line. It is also unlikely that the Soviet big brother poses a serious threat to the new line. Moscow has certainly set limits that are not to be overstepped, but there is no sign that its patience has been strained.

From all this we may conclude, be it only as a hypothesis, that the policy of cautious reforms is in no danger from either the dogmatic 'Left' or from the revisionist and more openly oppositional 'Right'. Does this mean that the Kádár régime enjoys a consensus and that it is a genuine alternative to communism of the Soviet type? Before answering that question, we must first look at some other aspects of the problem.

To take the consensus first, no one could in fact say what sort of government would emerge if the electors were allowed to choose quite freely. Since Hungary is unlikely to see the advent of political pluralism for some time to come, it is hazardous to speculate on the subject. Would the Kádár régime be swept away by public opinion, or would it be able to maintain itself with the active support of the population? There is no way of telling so long as the régime continues to rely on a monopoly of power guaranteed by the massive presence of the Soviet Union across the frontier, by Soviet divisions stationed in the country, and by Soviet advisers in strategic positions.

In addition, while enjoying internal stability thanks to the reforms, the party is careful not to surrender the safeguards of its power by venturing into the quicksands of political pluralism. It has admittedly found it expedient to introduce such changes as allowing several lists of candidates at various, and particularly parliamentary, elections. As a result, the electorate has been offered some choice in the *persons* it can elect, though not of *political alternatives*. The nation has also been offered a choice of social institutions. Nevertheless, there is just one trade-union system and, after the Solidarity experience in Poland, it seems unlikely that autonomous trade unions will be allowed to emerge in Hungary. It is also most unlikely that the workers' councils, buried for almost thirty years, will be resuscitated.

No *major* autonomous institution can thus be expected to emerge, but *minor* forms keep springing up in almost every domain, with or without formal permission: simple religious communities, cultural societies, song and folklore ensembles and also modern music groups.[36] An ecological movement has also been started. Over and above improvements in the standard of living, it is undoubtedly this modest form of social pluralism which explains the stability of the régime and the support it receives from public opinion. This stability is further reinforced by a growing measure of personal freedom, and by freedom to travel in particular. The issue of passports and travel permits is admittedly subject to rules and regulations. However, once they have received an invitation, Hungarian citizens are entitled to one exit visa a year. Without an invitation, that is travelling at their own expense, they may go on foreign travels once every two to three years. In 1983, approximately 5 million Hungarians went abroad, of whom a tenth, 558,000, visited non-socialist countries, going mainly to the West.

Touring in Hungary, or holidaying on Lake Balaton or in other resorts, going to the theatre, seeing Hungarian and foreign films, reading and buying books, playing and watching sports, listening to classical or modern music including Western rock and dance music, dressing in the trendiest or the near-latest fashion, are now within the reach of all but the poorest and most disadvantaged citizens.

However, poverty continues to exist in Hungary. Differences in income are very large. In the artistic, liberal and commercial professions and among craftsmen, there are many *nouveaux riches* with more than comfortable incomes, and there are many more poor at the other extreme – poor as we find them throughout the world: old people living on risible pensions, wage earners at the bottom of the scale, derelicts of all sorts. Included among the poor must be between 300,000 and 400,000 Gypsies, that is, the majority of Hungary's Gypsy population. Public opinion in general is not very favourable to them, ostensibly because other Hungarians are afraid of being swamped as a result of the Gypsies' high birth rate. On the other hand, like all the poor, the Gypsies are strongly supported by such communal organizations as SzETA, the Foundation for Aid to the Poor, mentioned earlier. This type of aid is actually very much frowned upon and often obstructed by the authorities, who are loath to admit either the existence of poverty or of a Gypsy problem. The 'secret' is, however, poorly guarded. We need only mention an article by István Huszár, director of the party's own Social Science Institute, in which he admitted that the conditions in which 12 to 15 per cent of the population lived were 'unsatisfactory in several respects'.[37]

The motto coined by János Kádár in the 1970s – 'Those who are not against us are with us' – seems to have borne fruit. Thanks to improvements in every field, few Hungarians seem to be 'against' the régime, though without necessarily approving of it with conviction.

Apart from the liberal measures passed by the régime, there is yet another element to explain the relative degree of public satisfaction with the powers that be. This is their tendency – deliberate in part and partly without realizing the full implications – to create a middle-class society. The wish to reward those who contribute most to the general well-being is particularly clear in the sphere of collective farming, the authorities having come round to the view that success means encouraging middle-ranking or even formerly rich, but in any case experienced, peasants. The various forms of private and semi-private enterprise – including the work communities created as part of the socialist sector – also encourage the most dynamic and enterprising elements. The same is true of commerce, of craftsmen and finally, *mutatis mutandis*, of the liberal professions.

The criticism voiced by the 'Left' that the new trend favours the best endowed at the expense of ordinary wage earners – who are in no position to 'round off' their earnings – thus seems justified. Despite the government's equalitarian professions, the range of incomes is probably as wide as it is in all bourgeois societies except for the richest. According to official statistics, 1.7 per cent of the active population lives on less than 2,000 forints per month; 12.4

per cent on 2,000–3,000 forints; 63.8 per cent on 3,000–6,000 forints; almost 20 per cent on 6,000–10,000 forints; and 2.2 per cent on above 10,000 forints per month.[38]

This spectrum also explains that, while 5 million Hungarians can afford to visit other countries, only 500,000 of them can afford the costly journey to West Germany, Switzerland or Spain. It also explains – quite apart from the fact that demand greatly exceeds supply – why this fairly prosperous country can boast no more than 1 motor car for every 10 inhabitants, as against 1.5 in East Germany and between 3 and 4 in Western countries.

The state of material semi-satisfaction enjoyed by Hungarians is a source of tensions but also of fresh stimuli. While the standard of living continues to rise and demand keeps growing, the system of half-hearted reforms is likely to remain stable. The threat to the system comes from its inability to meet all the hopes it has kindled and on which it counts. So far, the deepest of these hopes have been disappointed. The government has obviously learned the lessons of the 1956 insurrection and avoids repeating the old mistakes. Its merits may therefore be attributed to three main factors: the Revolution of 1956; the Hungarian peoples' capacity for hard work and innovation; and finally the reformist policies of the ruling team stamped with the remarkable pragmatism of János Kádár. Since, however, the basic political needs of the country – liberty, independence and pluralism – cannot be met by this type of reformism, the consensus rests on material well-being and constant growth. A drop in the standard of living, or its stagnation, over several years may thus snap the fragile consensus and with it the stability of the country.

After this rapid examination, are we now in a position to answer the question of whether or not the Kádár régime provides an alternative to the Soviet model of socialism in the pre-Gorbachev era? Perhaps the question is badly posed. No true democracy – socialist or otherwise – can exist without freedom and pluralism. The present Hungarian régime, as it happens, holds out no prospect of these. For a long time to come, every attempt at fundamental change will probably find itself up against Hungary's membership in the Soviet bloc and the rigidity of a 'model' which, though not identical with the Soviet one, nevertheless sets strict limits to all developments. As a result, the prospects of an alternative future for Hungary remain strictly limited. It might be argued that Hungarian reformism can, at the very most, lead to social and economic, as distinct from political, pluralism. It would thus constitute, if not a true alternative to, at least a model *sui generis* appreciably different from the Soviet model. Hungary has achieved this distinction already, at least to some extent, in the literary and artistic spheres, in which Hungarians nowadays enjoy a great deal of freedom of expression with few ideological restraints. Films, novels and literary reviews often demonstrate this fact in astonishing measure.

But even with these exceptions, the Hungarian experience has produced too few convincing results. It has left too many fundamental demands unsatisfied to earn the unstinting support of public opinion. Only a much more radical reform programme can help to turn it – even in the absence of political freedom, pluralism and independence – into something more than a slightly improved form of Soviet socialism. Any such radical programme is slow in coming precisely because of the system's structural sluggishness, not to mention the external restraints imposed by Moscow and by geopolitical circumstances.

All in all we therefore have to conclude that the Hungarian model is not, or not yet, an alternative to the pre-Gorbachev Soviet one. But is it likely to provide that alternative in the future?

Under the conditions prevailing in the mid-1980s, the success or failure of attempts to arrive at a viable alternative depend largely on the party in power and on its relations with the public, that is on a 'social contract' and on the ability of the social partners to arrive at a system that satisfies the aspirations of society at large while protecting fundamental party interests, subject to well-known constraints. Is the Hungarian Communist Party capable of performing that task?

The Communist Party in the Mid-1980s

Before the Twelfth Party Congress in 1980, there were 811,311 registered party members of whom 28.6 per cent were industrial workers, 7.8 per cent pensioned or retired workers, 34.3 per cent white-collar workers and 6.3 per cent workers in agricultural co-operatives. Of these, 0.8 per cent had joined the party before the liberation, 16 per cent had joined between 1944 and 1948, 9.2 per cent between 1949 and 1956, and 74 per cent after 1956. The great majority was therefore made up of MSzMP Communists, none of whom had been a member of the MDP or its predecessors. As for their respective ages, 9 per cent were below twenty-nine, the remainder being between thirty and fifty-nine except for 14.8 per cent who were over sixty.

Only 11.5 per cent attended school for less than eight years, the great majority having finished secondary or high schools (gymnasia) and 17.4 per cent holding university degrees or diplomas.[39]

Five years later, at the Thirteenth Party Congress held in March 1985, the party had 870,992 members, 7.3 per cent more than five years before. There has, in fact, been a constant growth in membership ever since the 'new start' in 1956. Since then the average membership level has been the same as it was before the Revolution: about 8 per cent of the population.

The party's social composition has undergone few significant changes, but the older groups are, of course, increasingly making way for the younger. In 1980, 74 per cent had joined since 1957; the 1985 figure is 80.3 per cent. Because of the great tenacity of the over-sixties, however, their percentage has increased from 14.8 to 18. The average age has increased from 45.5 years to 46.9 years. The party is old rather than young. Finally the number of members who are secondary-school graduates or hold university diplomas has grown: 31.6 per cent and 21 per cent respectively as against 28.9 per cent and 17.4 per cent.[40]

A new factor: it is now possible to leave the party of one's own free will, and not feet first, or even without being thrown out with all the opprobrium and disaster expulsion used to entail. From 1975 to 1985, 41,473 members resigned from the party. During the same period, 15,567 were expelled 'for grave breaches of discipline', while 35,623 were removed from the list of members for apparently less serious lapses. The reasons given in the reports submitted by the Central Control Commission to the various congresses vary. They range from failure to implement resolutions, through abuse of authority, corruption and drunkenness, to morally reprehensible behaviour.[41] Possible ideological differences are no more than touched upon in these reports (in deference to the principle of freedom of opinion), and we find that 'anti-party and factional activities' have become extremely rare. In the past, as the reader knows, such activities used to be the official reason for the expulsion of four or five times as many members from the MDP.

Apart from minor fluctuations, the social origins of members have changed but little. The educational standard is increasing. The MSzMP is far from being a party with a proletarian majority, a fact that reflects the enormous transformation of Hungarian society and the development of the service sector in particular. Moreover, since the party controls its own growth, this is not a spontaneous composition but a deliberately chosen one. It is the picture the MSzMP wants to present of itself: a party of all classes (even though the statistics still describe 62.4 per cent of the members as being of working-class *origin*), of all professions, of all active age groups. This image is also reflected in the selection of delegates and executive committees. (Except for women: there are only 12 women in the Central Committee of 105 members, and none in the Politburo or the Secretariat.)

As for the composition of these bodies, it is difficult to determine whether or not it has been stable. Immediately after the 1956 Revolution, the Central Committee and Politburo were reshuffled. Only a handful of the old leaders remained, among them Antal Apró, István Friss, Károly Kiss, Dezsö Nemes and Géza Révész. Most of the Central Committees to appear between 1956 and 1966 were made up either of survivors from the purges in the Rákosi era or from newly promoted members.

How many of them remain today in the Central Committee appointed at the Thirteenth Party Congress in 1985? About fifteen of the original team, and not much more of the 1966 team.[42] The explanation is that a new generation has taken over; at present, this 'second generation', too, is in a state of flux. Of 127 members elected to the Central Committee in 1980, more than 50 (including a few who have since died) were not re-elected to the new Central Committee of 105 persons.[43]

These shrewdly judged proportions have provided János Kádár with a Central Committee loyal to him and progressively purged of undesirable elements. The same is true of the Politburo, which now has thirteen members, and of the eight-member Secretariat. Not a single leader from the Rákosi era is left in either. Of the leaders to constitute Kádár's earliest team (the Politburo elected at the June 1957 conference), Kádár himself is the only one to have remained at his post. Thirty years later, it is of course only to be expected that many of the old guard would have died or retired.

A nucleus close to Kádár emerged in the early 1970s. It has continued even after the Thirteenth Party Congress in March 1985. This congress re-elected ten former members of the Politburo and appointed three new ones (shown below in italics). They are: György Aczél, Sándor Gáspár, *Károly Grosz*, Ferenc Havasi, *Csaba Hámori*, János Kádár, György Lázár, Pál Losonczi, László Maróthy, Károly Németh, Miklós Óvári, István Sarlós and *István Szabó*. Four of these – Havasi, Kádár, Németh and Óvári – are also members of the Secretariat together with János Berecz, István Horváth, Lénárd Pál and Mátyás Szürös. János Kádár now bears the title of general secretary (instead of that of first secretary), and Károly Németh has become deputy general secretary. The present team is meant to continue until 1990, the date of the next congress.

The changes introduced at the Thirteenth Party Congress do not seem to indicate a fundamentally new approach. A spirit of continuity is also reflected in the reports presented to the congress, in the debates and in the resolutions passed. The new title conferred on János Kádár does not suggest that he is preparing to retire. He retains his leading position, perhaps delegating some administrative responsibilities to Károly Németh, his deputy, and other members of the Secretariat. The election of new members to the Politburo and the Secretariat did not raise many eyebrows, though the promotion of Károly Grosz and several personnel changes in the party apparatus caused some anxiety because of the rather imperious tones and allegedly 'illiberal' attitudes of Grosz and a number of the newly promoted heads of various services and committees. Is the 'up-and-coming' man, as Grosz is called, perhaps a 'neo-Stalinist' as some fear and others hope? It is difficult to judge at a time when the 'Gorbachev style' still contains so many unknowns. The Secretariat, too, has undergone an important change: György Aczél, though still a member of the Politburo, has left.

The new Kádár team is relatively young: Aczél, Gáspár, Losonczi and Németh are in their fifties, and only Kádár is in his seventies. But old and young alike are supporters of Kádár's cautious reformism. If there is any danger of a counter-current, it will not come from the top of the pyramid. Those who hanker after the good old days no less than the more impatient innovators, such as Rezsö Nyers, have been eliminated long ago. There will be no reform of the reforms, as János Kádár has declared, but neither will there be any ditching of the reforms. Kádár is trying to steer a middle course.

But reform is not everything; it does not embrace all the activities of the party, which extend into dozens of different spheres, from education to improving the position of women, from rural problems to housing and foreign policy.[44] Reform is not everything, but it covers the essential aspects. There is not a single domain, from ideology to such highly technical questions as the revision of the statute book code or the role of history-teaching, that is not subordinate to the main objective: the pursuit of the reform programme.

In other words, Hungary is not devoid of a policy or of perspectives. Though limited, this path confers on the MSzMP a dynamism lacking in most other Communist parties. All decisions are admittedly taken inside the Politburo, if not in János Kádár's immediate entourage, but the lower echelons have ceased to be so many rubber stamps. As a result of decentralization, the local committees (departmental secretariats) have even become a kind of oligarchy with their own dependants. There are genuine public discussions, a kind of political life within the narrow bounds of the system.

What are the place and the function of the party and its apparatus in this kind of political life which, without being comparable to that of the heady days of 1956, is genuine political life for all that?

It would be wrong to say that the party rules but does not govern, leaving it to the government and its executive organs to steer the ship of state. The government remains subordinate to the party, whose policies it faithfully executes. Because Parliament is purely symbolic, the party remains the supreme legislator-cum-executive organ. The difference between the role the party used to play and the one it plays today lies elsewhere. Its legislative role seems nowadays confined to the elaboration of the main directives rather than to their implementation. The latter, of course, remains under the direct control of party members, but the party at large no longer concerns itself with the details. While remaining omnipotent and omnipresent, it does not meddle with everything as it used to in the past, contenting itself with being the supreme arbiter and the country's top-level administrator. Reality or Weber's ideal-type? In either case, our last assertion needs further clarification. By the term 'administrator' we mean a power that controls the great machinery of state while allowing the delegated authorities to do their job, subordinating ideology to efficiency and finally leaving some elbow-room for private life. These three characteristics have enabled the Hungarian party, at the cost of some self-effacement, to avoid unpopularity, to become more effective and to stimulate social and private initiative.

Party membership still implies not simply power and privilege, but responsible action in the position in which one is placed. However, things have become more relaxed. Communists no longer enjoy quasi-impunity, but are also no longer spied upon day and night by their peers and superiors. Moreover, they look more like ordinary citizens than in the past. Their most detested privileges have been withdrawn. The reserved shops of infamous memory no longer exist, quite simply because there are fewer shortages of goods. Disciplinary sanctions are applied when party members fall down on their duties, and no longer for what were often obscure ideological reasons. As mentioned earlier members can also resign from the party; in the past very few would have dared to do such a thing.

Admittedly membership in the Communist Party cannot be compared to membership in a political party in a pluralist society. It involves greater discipline and more responsibility. However, Hungarian rank-and-file Communists do not really wield political power, are not true members of the *nomenklatura*. In Hungary, as elsewhere, the ordinary party member or the minor party official has no real political say. On the other hand, prestige derives from party membership, and so do some other advantages. Party membership is a way to certain promotion, but it is not the only route. In any case, the real political ruling class still consists of a small number of Communists and people whose influence derives from their position or their ability or from both. It is impossible to specify their precise number.

According to a report the Central Committee submitted to the Twelfth Party Congress, Hungary has 24,450 rank-and-file party organizations and some 3,000 higher-level (factory, enterprise, cantonal, departmental, and so on) party committees. The total number of members in the executive committees of the rank-and-file organizations is 110,633. The report does not specify the number of members in the 3,000 higher-level committees or the number of permanent officials in the central and departmental apparatus. If these accounted for no more than 20,000 or 30,000 persons, then we would arrive at a total of 140,000 persons to which must be added the staff of party schools, party publishing houses and so on. But not all of these persons belong to the political apparatus, the true centre of power.

In reality, party members holding positions in the government, at the head of enterprises, in cultural institutions and in mass organizations often wield far more political power than do ordinary propagandists or members of rank-and-file committees. Again, not all leading figures in the economy or the administration are Communists, though most of them probably are. They nevertheless belong to the political ruling class, to the *nomenklatura*. They are not irremovable, but by virtue of the stability of all levels of the political machinery, they are a category apart, one that does all it can to preserve its position and to derive the maximum family benefits (admission to higher schools, issue of travel permits, priority car purchase or priority building permits). The right connections extend a long way and mutual aid, to the point, often beyond the point, of corruption, is typical of the mentality of this group.

For the rest, the party is not hermetically sealed off from the rest of society. Its members feel the influence of the religious, cultural and social environment. It is not enough to be a member of the party, even a local leader; if you want to enjoy social prestige, then you must also fit in with the rules of society at large. Now these rules, precisely because the militant party is no longer presenting itself as guardian of the only true ideology, have become much more like what they used to be before the advent of Communist rule. Unfortunately we lack the space to expand on a theme that demands considerable research into spiritual and cultural life, into the collective mentality of the Hungarian people, their sense of national identity and the rules of communication between them.[45]

It is nevertheless possible to suggest that there must have been some osmosis between Hungary's new rulers and society at large, a search for equilibrium that allows those in power to govern even in the absence of political pluralism, and society to enjoy what is a very relative but nevertheless an appreciable degree of freedom.

This brings us to the end of the golden age of the Kádár era and the beginning of its decline, foreshadowing the 'end of the story'.[46]

Conclusion

A party carried to power by fortuitous circumstances finds it hard to stand back from its past. The Hungarian Communist Party has benefited from such circumstances three times in its history. Carried to power by the sudden collapse of the Austro-Hungarian monarchy and the resignation of Count Károlyi's government, the Communist Party, united with the Social Democratic Party, set up the Soviet Republic and proclaimed the dictatorship of the proletariat. After this short-lived interlude, it remained a prisoner of its original design for twenty-five years of clandestine life, never appreciating the utterly utopian nature of its dreams. It stuck to its guns all the more resolutely because the 'Moscow line' proclaimed by the Communist International left it no other choice, at least not until 1935, which saw the beginnings of the Popular Front policy, to which, moreover, the Hungarian party proved incapable of adjusting. The second occasion was the victory of the Red Army over the Nazis, which propelled the CP back into power and rendered it even more dependent on Moscow than before. Once again, the Hungarian party slavishly followed the 'line' fixed by Moscow, and continued to do so until its third metamorphosis in 1956 when, after having been stripped of the reins of power for a few days during the popular insurrection, it seized them back, once again with the help of the Red Army.

All these new beginnings have left indelible marks and scars, and this despite drastic changes of the party itself and of its active members. These changes were not merely connected with the ravages of time which, over seventy years, wiped out the first and saw the retirement of the second generation of party militants. The persecutions during the clandestine period, and even more so the internal purges, drastically cut down the ranks of the party. From their sojourn in the Soviet Union, no more than a few hundred out of the many thousands of Hungarian Communist militants returned home after the liberation.[1] The rest had become Soviet citizens or had perished in the purges.

In an earlier study I listed 111 militants who, at one time or other, held office in the executive agencies of the illegal party; no more than sixteen of these could be found in the Central Committee set up in 1945; a few more joined their ranks later. Calculations based on the more detailed figures subsequently made available do not show substantially different proportions.

The rank-and-file party membership has undergone similar changes, thanks largely to successive purges, to the total collapse of the Hungarian party in 1956, and finally to the natural ascendancy of younger generations. After the forced merger with the Social Democratic Party, the unified party counted 1,128,130 members; in the wake of the purges, only 880,774 were left. After several fluctuations, the figure settled at about 850,000 just before 1956. Approximately 100,000 of these joined the party rebuilt by János Kádár; that figure rose gradually to above 850,000. However, we may safely say that most of these members were newcomers – only one-fifth of today's Communists were party members before 1956.[2] Bearing in mind the earlier purges, we can take it that some 2 million Hungarians, or one adult in three, have been party members at some time in their lives.

The continuity of the party's history is therefore not based on the continuity of its membership or of its leadership, which has also changed radically on several occasions. At the very top – in the Politburo – János Kádár alone represents the old generation of leaders, while the Central Committee of over 100 members can boast a few more veterans. Least affected by all these political changes has been the 'apparatus' of the Central Committee, that is, the large number of minor party officials. The party's continuity is if anything ideological in character, and this despite its undeniable 'laicization'. In other words, this 'laicization' notwithstanding, the ideological and institutional foundations of the system have changed very little. Nor is there any need to draw up an organizational chart to show that the wheels of power have remained unchanged in János Kádár's Hungary, that 100,000 or so officials and activists make up the actual party, while the 700,000 ordinary members remain, as before, so many supernumeraries. These activists also control the police and the media.

Something has, however, changed since the consolidation of the Kádár régime, and most particularly since the introduction of the economic reforms in 1968. We have mentioned the main economic aspects. Let us therefore merely recall the political maxim exemplifying the change. Whereas the Rákosi régime proclaimed that 'he who is not for us is against us', Kádár declared that 'he who is not against us is with us'. Nothing demonstrates better than this János Kádár's wish to be a faithful administrator and manager of the country's affairs, to be, if not *uti pater familias*, at least a good businessman.

In fact, the change symbolized by the maxim is mainly confined to a reform of the way the system functions – not to social or institutional reforms. But the way a Communist party functions depends on several parameters, which we shall now examine.

The Promethean Myth

Every political party has a programme; each promises a better society either by introducing changes or else by preserving traditional values thought to be under threat. It would be pointless to dwell on the secular aspects of that great revolutionary drive which, at the end of the road or the barrel, is alleged to compel the world of necessity to make way for the world of freedom. Nor is there the least need for us to dwell on the fascination this has had for five generations of Socialists and Communists. In Hungary, that flame of hope survived despite the pragmatism of the Social Democratic movement; this, together with more down-to-earth reasons, explains why the Social Democratic Party was drawn to the Communists' Leninist programme in 1919. The Communist Party itself basked from the outset in the radiant promise of a Promethean ideology, and this all the more so as the Promethean myth appeared to bestow greater legitimacy on it than it did on Social Democratic reformism.

It is difficult to imagine, even nowadays, a Communist party prepared to renounce the promise of that new Jerusalem. Being at the root of its legitimacy, that promise is also the tacit charter elevating the party into an assembly of chosen people, a special race, made, as Stalin put it, of 'unusual stuff'. This feeling of superiority among the holders of the promise and of the historical truth was deeply entrenched in the small sect known as the Hungarian CP. It became one of the mainsprings of its pride and arrogance after the war and after its rise to power. This feeling of superiority went hand in hand with other features reflecting the social isolation of the Communist veterans who had only just emerged from clandestine life.

Let us also note that the Promethean myth helped to feed the suspicion prevalent in the party both before and after the war; those veterans who have published their memoirs, and even Kádár himself in the confidences he imparted to his biographer, have admitted this with surprising frankness,[3] though – not surprisingly – they attribute their suspicion to the conditions of clandestine life, a breeding-ground of police spies and *agents provocateurs*, and also to the paranoiac character of their own leaders: Stalin and Rákosi.

Nor should we forget the collective need to flush out the internal enemy and to reveal his 'impurity' – a phenomenon that many writers, for instance Talmon, Richet and Furet, were also able to detect among the Jacobins. In more than one sensational affair, such as the expulsion of the poet Attila József in the 1930s, or in the Rajk affair, it is difficult to disentangle sectarian suspicions from cold-blooded political calculations designed to eliminate all potential threats to the leader's authority.

The Real Party

A political party of a Leninist inspiration, such as the Hungarian CP, is set up for a single political purpose: to prepare for the great day of reckoning. Whatever reservations we may have about what would be a generalization were it applied to other parties, the Hungarian CP has always been a device, a machine for seizing power. The party's brief and limited experiments with political pluralism ended, on the first occasion, in 1919, in failure right down the line, and the second time round, during the post-war coalition, in the total demolition of all democratic achievements.

In the 'Lukács debate', published in 1950, József Révai has provided astonishing confirmation of this interpretation of the party's role. It merits being quoted here. While fully admitting that the party had qualms about the coalition policy, or the 'transition' period as it was called, Lukács – according to Révai – considered the new democratic period as an embodiment of the 'old, plebeian, popular and revolutionary traditions of bourgeois democracy', and 'elevated these traditions into a myth, forgetting that this kind of plebeian democracy was no more than a transitional system in 1792 [*sic*]'. And Révai added that the reason why the party's clandestine activities struck Lukács as ineffective and sectarian was that he also 'considered as sectarian the policy that the Communists pursued *before the Popular Front* [Révai's italics], a policy whose strategic aim was the dictatorship of the proletariat'. According to Révai, Lukács's mistake was to overlook the fact that the Popular Front policy 'was no more than a historical *detour* [Révai's italics] which fascism compelled us to take'.[4]

Since the dictatorship of the proletariat too,[5] is no more than a 'transition', however long, on the road to Communism, it follows that the only acceptable policy is that reflected in the theory and practice of the Hungarian CP. This presupposes the existence of a lull in political and social life, followed by a 'first transition' period, that is by a frontist coalition, which is simply an extension of the 'detour imposed by fascism', and finally a 'second transition', the dictatorship of the proletariat, prior to the golden age of abundant life and a classless society.

In this approach, political pluralism and social progress are mere irrelevancies. The idea, however orthodox, that a democratic society is a necessary stage in the transition to socialism becomes an empty catchphrase: in the history of the Eastern bloc it served no purpose other than to pull the wool over the eyes of the Western Allies, whose susceptibilities Moscow was still anxious to spare. In fact, the Hungarian CP, supported by the Red Army, could have seized power in 1945 as easily as it did in 1948: the social changes introduced during the 'transition' were not meant to last or to filter down into society at large, as witness the fate of the hapless Hungarian peasantry.

Waiting for the right moment, seizing power, exercising it unshared and holding on to it – these are the successive stages in the party's *realpolitik* stripped of its ideological trappings. The preaching of that ideology, moreover, has been degraded to the role of stereotyped phrase-mongering, has become a language in the service of the 'technology' of power. Indeed, the party's Jacobin-Leninist conception – that it represents the incarnation of the general will and is a vanguard fulfilling History's mythical objectives – have rendered the application of the ideology to real social structures and to public attitudes quite superfluous.

Everything was done at the abstract level, which incidentally explains why the party appealed to so many intellectuals with a love for hair-splitting. Communist 'praxis', or rather mystification, meant concealing the gulf between the declared intentions and actions of a party ostensibly identified with the working class and with society. The 'people' in the abstract were bound to agree, so there was no need to consult them. If necessary, though, as Bertolt Brecht has explained, 'the government can simply dissolve the people and choose another'.[6]

The real party also dispenses with all such trappings of modern politics as the social contract, the separation of powers, elections, representative government and the relative autonomy of private life.

It also does away with the principle of the alternation of power, on the grounds that real socialism is a *civilization* radically different from modern democratic, or if you prefer bourgeois, civilization. This is because while, despite Guizot's claim that, representative government is a form of government in which the victors do not aim at the annihilation of their vanquished predecessors, the Communist system aims to do nothing less. Moreover, to the Communist Party, all failure spells Thermidor, and Thermidor spells failure. This metaphor has been etched into the minds of two or three generations of Hungarian Communists. The party may lose the odd battle on the road to power, but it cannot lose power without losing the war – the Communist Prometheus is enchained to power. It cannot hang back until the next elections; the next day in Jerusalem may not dawn for another 2,000 years. This explains the party's intolerance, haste, fanaticism, violence during and after its rise to power. Politics, in the eyes of the party faithful, is above all the destruction, within and without its ranks, of anybody or anything that can dislodge it.

In these circumstances, it is small wonder that the collapse of the party in 1956 was felt to be a cataclysmic event whose catastrophic consequences could only be averted by Soviet intervention. No more than a handful of leaders, including Imre Nagy and Georg Lukács, were able to conceive of the possibility of, as Lukács put it, 'restarting from scratch' with a new party that could count on attracting no more than 5 or 6 per cent of the votes at the next election. János Kádár said much the same in an interview during the Revolution. This is just one pointer to his mysterious personality, but one that is not without significance.

But much earlier, at the time when the Hungarian CP was still no more than an insignificant party, 'standing by for the universal Communist republic', such considerations did not as yet weigh in the balance. As a humble member of the international Communist system run by the Comintern, the HCP waited its turn, waited for its hour to strike. It mattered little how it survived until the D-Day of the seizure of power. Then things would change radically. Having accomplished this historical function, the party would be duty-bound to fulfil its other function, that of honouring its 'great promise'.

At this point, the function of the 'real party' merges with its Promethean function, albeit in muted form, and also with its administrative-cum-managerial function, the three functions producing a new kind of interaction culminating in the triumphalism of the Rákosi era and subsequently in the managerial realism of the Kádár régime.

The Party as a Sanctuary

A small, persecuted party such as the Hungarian CP, which can look back to twenty-five years of illegal activity, is a clandestine organization *par excellence.*

In January 1919, Hungary counted some 10,000 Communists, and more than a million Socialists and Communists combined during the short life of the Hungarian Soviet Republic. After its collapse, the loss of members was catastrophic. The Social Democratic Party, reorganized and legally recognized, gradually recovered its former strength, but not so the Communist Party, which was banned and persecuted. The few hundred Communists working underground were consequently a group of men with staunch convictions ready to make whatever sacrifices were demanded. But how representative of the nation at large was their social composition?

The party's strength in the factories was, according to almost unanimous testimony, extremely small. Traditional fiefs of the Social Democrats, the factories could boast no more than a handful of Communist workers, and in some of them, moreover, as in the Csepel works, the influence of the ultra-left factions led by Weisshaus and above all by Pál Demény was stronger than that of the CP.

Party membership was no stronger in the countryside, that is, in the ranks of the agrarian sub-proletariat. Most active Communists, if we can call them so without being euphemistic, came from the lower middle classes, from commerce and from the liberal professions, and most were recruited from minority groups: Jews, bourgeois individuals who had broken with their class, or people without a settled profession. All, for one reason or another, had been rejected by society, all or nearly all were in search, not only for an ideal, but also for the sanctuary afforded them by a second identity: that of the party militant. Two categories of these militants, very small in number, escaped this rule: some of the Hungarian combatants in the Spanish Civil War, volunteers fired with anti-fascist fervour, and some persons from the Slovak and Transylvanian territories Hitler had attached to Hungary. In any case, most party members were Jewish tailors, shoemakers, glovers, hairdressers, waiters and shop assistants, together with a few typographers and technicians, not forgetting the fairly large proportion of intellectuals among them.

Hardly any non-Jews or blue-collar workers could be found among the most prominent party militants (successive members of the 'home-grown' Central Committee, Comintern delegates in Moscow or persons involved in the great public trials). Even among these rare exceptions, we find that many had suffered hurts or deep frustrations that drove them to seek a sanctuary and a second identity. A case in point was the celebrated poet Attila József, who experienced a grave identity crisis that eventually caused him to take his own life; another was a deeply sincere Communist born out of wedlock: János Kádár. For the rest, being a Communist, a Jew and at the social and professional fringes of society is not easy in any country. It was particularly hard in inter-war Hungary, dominated by a Christian-national ruling class with an archaic outlook. The party-sanctuary thus fulfilled a double function: it willy-nilly did service firstly as a 'tribal' community and secondly as protective barrier. How did it acquit itself in that situation?, No one may ever be able to tell. Because of the conspiracy rules, members rarely knew one another: the HCP was not, as I put it too summarily in an earlier study, a counter-society, nor yet a real tribe.[7] The communal link was forged in small cells, if not actually in small prison cells, and at the ideological level.

The ideology, as we saw, took unusual sectarian forms, not only in the constantly threatened 'home-grown' party, but also in the ranks of the Muscovite émigrés. A rigid, radical, exclusive and intolerant revolutionary attitude coupled to the real dangers that lay in wait for Communists at every clandestine meeting they attended was bound to engender a climate of suspicion, a world teeming with real or imaginary traitors, so many factors to leave their mark on the party before as well as after the liberation. None of this in any way prevented Horthy's police from infiltrating its *agents provocateurs*, but it did prevent the party from laying the indispensable foundations of trust among its members. The Communist in the illegal party feared the police, the informer, and also his own comrade, whom he was ready to denounce to the party for the least real or imaginary deviation. His suspicions and fears persisted even during the heyday of the Hungarian people's democracy.

The CP in power, with a membership of 800,000, differs fundamentally from the minuscule clandestine group made up of ethnic minorities, people at the fringes of society and misfits in search of ideological and emotional security. The 'party-sanctuary' label cannot be applied to the monumental organization which, expressed on the United Kingdom population scale, would number some 4 million members. However, the main motivation of these members, too, was not so much political conviction as conformism, careerism, or quite simply, without any pejorative connotations, the wish to fit into the established social order. Beyond that, and we shall come back to this point, there was the gratifying and honourable feeling of participating in a relatively efficient administration. One cannot even say that, in 1987 and as a general rule, party membership conferred excessive privileges, over and above the normal job and responsibility rewards.[8]

If the 'party-sanctuary' was thus a thing of the past, some vestiges of it nevertheless survived in practice as well as in the outlook of many members. Suspicion, far from disappearing after the seizure of power, has been redoubled. The facts are known; we have mentioned them in connection with the purges and trials of hundreds of thousands of party members, of former coalition partners, or of ordinary citizens. Such practices have largely, though not completely, disappeared. Even so, it is a fact that, after the war, not only did the scale of repressive measures increase a thousand-fold, but also the consequences became infinitely worse. In the olden days, Communists dragged before the tribunals only had to pay with their lives in exceptional cases; the Communist régime, by contrast, has been responsible for the execution, torture and incarceration of thousands of Communists, not to mention the multitude of its other victims. On top of all that, the concentration of political, judicial and economic power ensured that anyone ostracized by the party, or even under suspicion or thought to be non-conformist, was deprived of work permit and job. Never before had a Communist been so much at the mercy of the people in power. And all this was part and parcel of a new dialectic of power relationships.

The Party and the International Communist System

Those at the centre of the Communist system, from Lenin to Gorbachev, through Stalin, Khrushchev and Andropov, have never had cause to complain about the Hungarian Communist Party. Like all the other parties in the system until the most recent period, it has always bowed to the authority of the Comintern and, after the dissolution of that body, to the secret Institute No. 103 for Inter-Party Affairs, to the Cominform and also to the various Soviet decision-making centres. If it erred, the Hungarian party was quick to repent. Only once did it succeed in escaping from the clutches of the centre, namely during the 1956 Revolution which caught a drifting party in an advanced state of disintegration.

An analyst of the international role of the Hungarian CP might well have left it at that, had there not been, within the limits of a continuous line of obedience, certain gaps in the faithful performance of that role.

Here we shall merely record the first of these: the unexpected situation that thrust the young and unprepared Hungarian CP into power. The adventure of 1919 unfolded, on the plane of external relations, in full accord with the Bolshevik concept of world revolution. The Hungarian Soviet Republic considered itself a natural ally of the Soviet big brother, and this from its very first act. Lenin and Chicherin, for their part, and Zinoviev in the name of the Comintern, expressed the same sentiment. Budapest was, moreover, expected to serve as a staging-post for spreading the world revolution to Austria and Germany.

Once reduced to its bare bones after the debacle of 1919, the Hungarian party was not, throughout its long stay in the wilderness, of the slightest practical use to international Communism, itself in a state of suspended animation. In realistic political terms based on an objective analysis of real conditions in Hungary, a para-Communist Party, such as the ephemeral Socialist Workers' Party of the 1920s ('Vági's Party' as it was called, after its general secretary), had a better chance of exerting however small an influence on the country than an illegal Communist Party. The Vági experiment, however, remained unique; neither the party nor the Cominform made any attempt to repeat it. On the contrary, when the CP was dissolved as a last resort at a time when, according to János Kádár himself, the Central Committee (itself reduced to two or three persons) had contact with no more than eight (!) party workers, it received nothing but harsh reproaches and two severe reprimands – as mentioned earlier. The Peace Party, created to fill the vacuum, did not meet with Moscow's approval either. The Hungarian broadcasts from Moscow ignored it and continued to play up the phantom Communist party. In fact, Moscow's attitude, but also that of the Hungarian émigré leaders, was based on considerations quite distinct from those used by the clandestine party. Moscow cared very little about what so insignificant a party might or might not be able to achieve; all that mattered was that Moscow's creature should *survive*.

There is no need to point out that the main complaint was not against the change of the party's *name*, even though the Communist label had not yet lost its symbolic importance. The unforgivable thing was that the Hungarian leaders had acted without Moscow's prior consent (or, which came to the same, had misread Moscow's intentions), and that they had lopped off one of the dormant arms of international Communism. In terms of Moscow's strategy of conquest, one secretary and eight members could look after Moscow's affairs just as well as a full Central Committee and a rank-and-file membership of several thousands. The continued existence, however fictitious, of the party had to be guaranteed; the rest could safely be left to the executive organs created, trained and then issued with instructions by Moscow.

In the infinitely greater and more complex framework of the post-war Communist world,[9] the role of such parties as the Hungarian CP, now a medium-size organization, became more complex as well, but nevertheless remained insignificant in Moscow's eyes. One episode will illustrate, perhaps better than anything, Moscow's attitude to Budapest.

In June 1953, the new Kremlin leaders, alarmed by a number of disquieting reports, summoned Mátyás Rákosi and several other Hungarian leaders to Moscow. Rákosi, 'Stalin's best Hungarian disciple' entered the room, fully convinced that he had faithfully executed the Soviet leader's instructions. It was for precisely this slavish attitude that he was now taken to task.

Neither would János Kádár's party have escaped this sort of treatment had its economic and administrative efficiency not conferred greater authority upon it. But did the liberalization of the system after Stalin's death also lead to a qualitative change in the relations between the fraternal parties and the centre in Moscow? This question is difficult to answer. The only certainty is that the Soviet grip remained tight: the Hungarian CP, like the rest, remained part and parcel of an international Communist system with a small margin for manoeuvre in respect of managerial methods. The difference between the relatively 'liberal' and internally efficient Kádár system and Ceauçescu's Rumanian system, which had a slight tendency to act autonomously in foreign affairs, is deceptive because, politically and militarily, both remained under the thumb of the USSR. In both systems, the party exercised control over society, though with different degrees of severity.

The Hungarian CP, moreover, also rendered some slight service to Moscow in the complex field of international relations. By way of example, we might mention Kádár's 'overtures' to the Socialist and Social Democratic parties as well as his visit to the Pope, his special relation with Austria under Chancellor Kreisky and his successor. Hungary also rendered technical aid to politically 'friendly' Third World countries, without necessarily committing its resources to the same extent as Czechoslovakia, East Germany or, most outstandingly, Cuba. Showcase and 'model of prosperity', Hungary served the system with discretion and at little cost to itself.

Towards a Managerial Party?

In the past, the party's policy involved a series of administrative, police, cultural, authoritarian and arbitrary measures, alien to what goes by the name of politics in the democratic world, and not propitious to efficient management.

Over the past fifteen years, however, there have been several more or less dramatic changes. The reader will remember that, in power, the Hungarian party has played several overlapping roles. In particular, there has been a dialectical relationship between the party's administrative role and the role bestowed on it by the Promethean myth. The result is a well-known psychological phenomenon: flight into the future. During the illegal period, the building of the new Jerusalem had to wait for tomorrow; it would be created with the act of revolution. After the seizure of power, it was still a project for the morrow, but one expected after only a brief period of rearguard action and sacrifice. Thereafter, every moment and every act needed to bring the day of final accomplishment nearer, every brick needed to be a piece in the grand design under construction. Nothing could any longer justify the relegation of the final aim to the Greek calends or even the least delay in the work of construction. Let it be said in passing that the invention of the ever-present Enemy and the Traitor served as a ready-made excuse whenever delays and setbacks did occur, and also explained the continued need for sacrifice. As long as there were social traitors (not to mention fascists, reactionaries, the Church, kulaks . . .) and such masked enemies within the gate as Rajk and Slansky, was it not 'normal' that the building of the new Jerusalem should suffer so many delays? And while every traitor unmasked was one more step in the accomplishment of the mythical task, the hydra had, not just seven heads but hundreds, indeed, as many as it required. Thus, paradoxically, terror became a permanent feature of the dream and, instead of bringing the great day closer, postponed ever further with the perpetual re-invention of new enemies.

The continuous discovery of new *obstacles* in the path of Communism went hand in hand with what we have called the 'triumphalist' attitude. In order to fulfil its true task, the party had to keep *proclaiming* imaginary successes. It was, as said earlier, propelled forward, into a world of sheer fantasy, by the need to prove itself through results, however fictitious. Anyone seeking such diversion would have no difficulty in demonstrating, by quoting official victory announcements and statistics, that the industrial output of the USSR is at least twice that of the United States, that Hungary is stronger than West Germany, and that Hungarians have a higher standard of living than the Swiss and a more democratic government than the Swedes.

Despite changes in its history, the mythical party thus displayed a remarkable continuity in maintaining its Promethean function. It received its investiture from History herself; it was the midwife of the Revolution, opening the gates to the new Jerusalem. It was the depository of all Knowledge. It was finally the active agent of History determined by necessity. It was the moving spirit and the guarantor of the attainment of the final goal. Hence its entitlement not to share power with anyone else and to scorn all forms of pluralism – temporary alliances, frontist tactics and 'transitional' accommodations under coalition governments notwithstanding.

Have the experiences under the Kádár régime since the early 1970s changed this picture? Is Hungary, in the late 1980s, moving towards a new, essentially managerial communist society?

It would perhaps be best to end the present study with this question mark, because the future is unpredictable and the present confused. Such clichés as 'liberalism', 'consumer society', 'consensus', 'relative efficiency' do nevertheless encapsulate some of the régime's most striking features.

Peasants are producing what the market demands; economic reforms are slow to come, but come they do for all that; private enterprise supplies a substantial part of the GNP. The régime provides consumers with refrigerators, television sets, a growing number of private motor cars. In short, Hungary has become a consumer society without capitalists, or almost so. The 'liberated areas' of public life are being extended into the private, cultural and social spheres, with consequent changes in habit and outlook.

Hungarians realize only too well that this process is reversible. In theory, at least, the party-state can retrace its steps by simple decree. No political force could stop it. If necessary, a Hungarian Jaruzelski can always be produced, even while Jaruzelski himself is trying to become a Polish Kádár. But history pulls strange faces. In the end the dead Kádár might have envied the living Jaruzelski, who in the entirely symbolic chair of president outlived his own epoch . . . it does not matter for how long. But Kádár did not outlive it. With his political and physical death there ended an era which was not only a thirty-year chapter in the history of little

Hungary, but a chapter of world history. (See the Preface to this edition.) But let us return to the period of this culmination's antecedents.

Hungary's relative calm and prosperity are based on a fragile equilibrium. Hungarian 'liberalism', we might say, rests on its own dynamics. The party, without discharging all its ballast, has renounced the mythical logomachy of old, and is trying to meet the country's real needs with real means. It seeks its justification more in concrete achievements than in the utopia of the ideal City. That is what we mean when we say that the directivist administration of *people* is perhaps gradually giving way to the management of *things*. There is no need to stress that Hungary is far from being a free society and a market economy, or, for that matter, from being a system founded on human and civic rights. In every possible sphere, the administration continues to watch, control, intervene, dismiss, fine, punish. The weight of the party and state bureaucracy (the two being one and the same) makes itself felt everywhere, and so, it goes without saying, does that of the Soviet presence. In these pages I have tried to delineate the general tendency underlying the development of the party. It appears that its cautious, essentially economic reformism has been unable to meet many of the spiritual, cultural and national aspirations of Hungarian society.

This study would be incomplete if it ignored these aspirations and also the repressive methods used to squash them. In some areas, as in the instance of the Catholic Church, the tension between the 'official line' and the attitude of nonconformists has reached crisis point and elicited repressive measures despite the authorities' desire not to tarnish their image.

It nevertheless remains a fact that managerial reformism constitutes an indispensable component of the party's stewardship. A return to the past would be catastrophic for the population no less than for the party, which would at one stroke lose its authority, credibility and reputation for efficiency.

On the whole, the interim results of the Hungarian experiment continue to be positive, and so the Soviet Union, contrary to the fears expressed by some because of the 'boldness' of Hungary's reforms, has no need to interfere. Inside the country, however, a workers' opposition has emerged during the past ten years as a reaction to economic tendencies considered to favour peasants, tradesmen and other entrepreneurs at the expense of wage earners.[10]

The consequent pressures have produced a temporary slackening in the pace of the reforms but no decisive halt. In Hungary, the subject is discussed quite openly while the conflict between the opposing tendencies continues. However, the threat to the fragile equilibrium of the system comes, oddly enough, less from the orthodox camp – Russian or Hungarian – than from the repercussions of the West's economic difficulties, and also, of course, from the counter-productive nature of Hungary's economic structures. In times of international prosperity, Hungary, with a per capita debt roughly the same as Poland's, can repay its creditors and meet its need for new investment with the help of its exports. During periods of world recession, things become vastly more difficult and the Hungarian economy goes into a spin without any obvious prospect of a new take-off, however badly one is needed.

János Kádár is unquestionably responsible in person for many of the changes that have taken place. However, quite aside from his role and that of his team, everything now depends on Hungary's ability to introduce innovations, to master advanced technology, to finance the overhaul of its manufacturing and service industries, and to offset the burdens imposed by a bureaucracy and a state industry caught in an ultra-conservative trap.

The age of myths has gone for ever.

The future therefore largely depends on the economic efficiency of the system, in short on reforms. Hungary's 'New Economic Mechanism' has undoubtedly introduced an important element into the 'revisionist' debate by demonstrating that the system is more open to reform than people would have believed possible, especially in Polish and to a lesser extent in Hungarian opposition circles. But is there no more to it than this? The Hungarian experiment has also shown that all economic reforms of the system are bound to founder unless they are accompanied by an equally radical form of political 'liberalization'. This cannot simply mean promulgating a few so-called liberal measures, but reshaping the way the system and its institutions work. A country's creative energies cannot be mobilized unless the authorities and society at large are working in harmony. Society has aspirations that cannot be fully satisfied by the material rewards of economic reforms. Society also aspires to some sort of pluralism, even if it takes the form of social and cultural pluralism in a single party – but one that tolerates divergent tendencies and views.

Sooner or later the party had to come up against new demands that had not so far been expressed except by a few intellectual groups. So can the leopard really change its spots? Perhaps this one can, though it would be rash to insist that it will, not least because of the grip of the Soviet big brother.

For the time being the problem was not especially acute. Reform no doubt involves restructuring the system, but it also has a depoliticizing effect. While Hungarian citizens continued to enjoy a decent standard of living and a tolerable degree of freedom of movement and expression, they were unlikely to follow the Polish example – an example that, moreover, has elicited a lukewarm response from Hungarian public opinion. The rise of a new generation would, on the other hand, accelerate changes in the collective outlook. Counting on the economy is certainly the régime's best bet, but also its weakness, and that not simply because of the hazards the reforms involve. At the end of the war, the party radiated enthusiasm. It was an enthusiasm reflecting a deep desire by part of the nation, and by Hungarian youth in particular, to have done with fascism, to turn their backs on archaic ideas and to build a new society. Successive setbacks have long prevented the party from returning to the sources of its enthusiasm: the people. The reforms and their political repercussions undoubtedly gave the party a second wind. However, the second wind never rose. Instead came the storm that swept away Kádár's successors and, ploughing across the whole of Eastern Europe, brought down the Berlin Wall and the barbed wires of the Iron Curtain. But this, as Kipling would say, is 'another story'.

Notes

Preface to the English Edition

1 See, for instance, Ákos Szilágyi, *Befejezetlen forradalom* (The incomplete revolution) and *Tovább . . . tovább . . . tovább* (Forward . . . forward . . . forward) Budapest, 1987 and 1988; Ágnes Gereben, *Több fényt* (More light), Budapest, 1988; *Csillagforduló. Két és fél év peresztrojka* (The turn of the star. Two and a half years of *perestroika*), a collection of reports by József Barát, a Hungarian newspaper correspondent in Moscow, Budapest, 1988.

2 Imre Pozsgay, born in 1933, and Rezső Nyers, born in 1923, are relatively young men. Pozsgay had been kept out of office by Kádár all along and was therefore a newcomer, but Nyers, the 'father' of the 1968 reforms, whom Kádár removed from the Politburo in 1974, was an 'old hand' who made a comeback to the Politburo in May 1988 following Kádár's downfall. In June 1989 he was voted president of the party, heading a directorate of four members: Nyers himself, Károly Grosz (the general secretary of the party), Imre Pozsgay and Miklós Németh (born in 1948 and prime minister since 24 November 1988). According to a public opinion poll taken at the end of July 1989, the prime minister is the most popular politician, ahead of Imre Pozsgay and also of the leaders of the democratic opposition parties.

3 For all these figures see *Magyar statisztikai zsebkönyv 1988* (Statistical Pocketbook 1988), Budapest, Központi Statisztikai Hivatal (Central Statistics Office), 1989.

4 See particularly the document entitled *Fordulat és reform* (Turning point and reform) presented to a conference of various – including Communist – reformist movements, held at Lakitelek on 27 September 1987. This document, running to about forty printed pages, presented a plan for economic reconstruction based on the adoption of a market economy. Together with several complementary documents, it was published in the journal *Medvetánc* (Dance of the bear), no. 2, 1987. Since then, various other reform projects have been put forward.

For an overall analysis of the economic and political crisis see also a document entitled *Történelmi utunk* (Our historical path) published by a panel of experts appointed by the Central Committee of the Communist Party and chaired by Imre Pozsgay. The director of research was Professor Iván T. Berend, president of the Academy of Science. A first abridged version was published in the Communist theoretical journal *Társadalmi Szemle*, vol. 44, special issue, 1989, and ran to eighty pages. The full document was submitted to the Fourteenth Congress of the Communist Party in the autumn of 1989.

5 See particularly the 1989 issues of the journals *Valóság* and *Mozgó Világ*.

6 See *Országgyülési Tudósítások* (Proceedings of Parliament), 12 Jan. 1989.

7 Cf. *Magyarország politikai évkönyve* (Hungarian Political Yearbook), Budapest, 1989.

8 R. Aron, *Démocratie et totalitarisme*, Paris, Gallimard, 1965, p. 87.

Chapter 1: From Monarchy to Revolution

N. B. For further bibliographical details of the books quoted, the reader is referred to the Bibliography at the end of this study.

For second and subsequent references to each source shortened titles are used in readily identifiable form. The following require explanation:

Dictionary	*Munkásmozgalomtörténeti Lexikon* (Historical dictionary of the Workers' Movement)
Directives	*A Kommunisták Magyarországi Pártja II. Kongresszusának irányelvei* (Directives to the Second Congress of the Hungarian Communist Party)
FRUS, PPC	*Foreign Relations of the United States. The Paris Peace Conference*
PTI	Archives of the Institute for Party History
PTK	*Párttörténeti Közlemények* (Bulletin for Party History)
Resolutions	*A Magyar Kommunista Párt és a Szociáldemokrata Párt határozatai 1944–1948* (Resolutions of the Hungarian Communist Party and of the Social Democratic Party, 1944–1948)
Selected Documents	*A magyar munkásmozgalom történetének válogatott dokumentumai* (Selected documents on the history of the Hungarian Workers' Movement)

1 Among recent publications, see György Litván (ed.), *Károlyi Mihály levelezése, I: 1905–1920* (Correspondence of Michael Károlyi, vol. 1, 1905–1920), Budapest, Akadémiai Kiadó, 1978. See also: Tibor Hajdu, *Az 1918–as Magyarországi polgári demokratikus forradalom* (The Hungarian bourgeois-democratic revolution of 1918), Budapest, Kossuth, 1968; Tibor Hajdu, *Károlyi Mihály: Politikai életrajz* (Michael Károlyi: a political biography), Budapest, Kossuth, 1978. For personal testimony of the utmost importance, the reader is referred to Mihály Károlyi's own writings, including particularly *Egy egész világ ellen* (Against the whole world), which has been republished several times. For a Social Democratic account, see Vilmos Böhm, *Két forradalom tüzében* (In the fire of two revolutions), 2nd edn, Budapest, Népszava, 1946. Among Radical accounts, see the Memoirs of Oszkár Jászi, *Magyar kálvária, magyar feltámadás* (Hungarian Calvary and Resurrection), 2nd edn, Vienna, Bécsi Magyar Kiadó, 1921.

2 Note from Pichon to Franchet d'Esperey on 28 Nov. 1918. Archives of the French Armed Forces Ministry (Château de Vincennes), 20 N 217. The French policy, influencing that of all the other Allies, was clear-cut from the outset. The note forwarded to Franchet d'Esperey via the Ministry of War amounted to a blunt refusal to recognize Count Károlyi's government as anything more than a '*de facto* local government'. Franchet accordingly had no right to sign an armistice with that government or a military convention completing the first armistice (signed near Padua on 3 November). The note stipulated that this convention could·only be agreed 'with delegates of the Austro-Hungarian State endowed with plenipotentiary powers by the authority that had signed the armistice' – notwithstanding the fact that this authority no longer existed in Vienna or in Budapest. The note also specified that the armistice thus concluded (i.e. the second armistice signed with the delegates of the Károlyi government) 'must be immediately revoked'. 20 N 217 also contains a telegram to the same effect dated 1 Dec. and forwarded to Franchet by General Charpy.

The Archives of the Ministry of Foreign Affairs (Stephen Pichon Papers, 281, vol. 7, items 224–30) contain a memorandum dated 16 Aug. 1919 which retraces the events in Hungary since the end of the war and repeats the reproaches

Notes

addressed to Franchet.

The Belgrade affair was not the only complaint against the latter. The 'Clemenceau Papers' handed over in 1930 to the Army Historical Service by General Mordacq and now in the Archives of the French Armed Forces Ministry, include a rebuke about an interview Franchet gave to an Italian paper: 'You have been appointed commander-in-chief . . . not to talk, but to fight' (*Minutes du courrier*, p. 275, 5 Oct. 1918).

Ultimately, however, the Budapest government was granted full recognition by the Allies with Count Károlyi as President of the Republic (see below, n. 4, the note addressed to Count Károlyi in that capacity). As a consequence, the Allies did not question the legality of the Socialist–Communist government that succeeded Count Károlyi's.

For an overall account of Allied policy in Hungary in 1918–19, see particularly: Leo Valiani, 'La politica estera dei governi rivoluzionari ungheresi del 1918–1919', *Rivista storica italiana*, vol. 78, no. 4, 1966, pp. 850–911; Alfred D. Low, 'The Soviet Hungarian Republic and the Paris Peace Conference', *Transactions of the American Philosophical Society*, vol. 53, no. 10, 1963; Mme Zsuzsa L. Nagy, *A Párizsi békekonferencia és Magyarország 1918–1919* (The Paris Peace Conference and Hungary), Budapest, Kossuth, 1965; and also the recent survey by Mária Ormos, *Pádovától Trianonig, 1918–1920* (From Padua to Trianon, 1918–1920), Budapest, Kossuth, 1984.

3 For the 'Vix note', see *inter alia* the account by Captain N. Roosevelt in *Foreign Relations of the United States. The Paris Peace conference* (hereafter: *FRUS, PPC*), vol. 12, pp. 413–16.

4 'General Lobit, provisional commander of the French Army in Hungary to His Excellency, Count Károlyi, President of the Hungarian Republic in Budapest', in Jean Bernachot, *Les armées françaises en Orient après l'armistice de 1918*, vol. 1: *L'armée française d'Orient. L'armée de Hongrie (11 novembre 1918–10 septembre 1919)*, Historical Service of the French Army Ministry, Imprimerie nationale, 1970, pp. 69–112, and also in appendixes 11 and 12, pp. 273–8. See also Sándor Vadász 'Vix és Károlyi' (Vix and Károlyi) in *Hadtörténeti Közlemények* (Military History Review), vol. 2, 1969, pp. 239–63; Peter Pastor, 'The Vix Mission in Hungary, 1918–1919: A Re-examination', *Slavic Review*, vol. 29, no. 3, 1970, pp. 481–98.

5 According to Countess Károlyi, the declaration that the President had resigned and was 'handing power to the Hungarian proletariat' appeared 'under Mihály's name'. But she also declared that, even if Count Károlyi had not signed the declaration himself, he knew perfectly well what was happening and was even trying to convince the conservatives that, in the given circumstances, 'there was no alternative to supporting the Communists and thus defending the country, since the note from the Allies was totally unacceptable'. Mme Mihály Károlyi, *Együtt a forradalomban* (Together in the revolution), Budapest, Europa, 1967, pp. 466–7.

6 Some sources claim that Count Károlyi wanted to entrust the Social Democrat Zsigmond Kúnfi with the formation of a socialist government with Károlyi himself staying on as President of the Republic.

According to the Hungarian historian Tibor Hajdu, moreover, Count Károlyi was not sympathetic to the Communists. Before his resignation, on 21 Mar. 1919, he had not known any Communists personally, and had never wanted to enter into political relations with them. Tibor Hajdu, *Károlyi Mihály*, p. 316.

During the life of the Soviet Republic, Károlyi remained in Hungary and backed the government. He left the country at the beginning of July 1919 and did not return for twenty-six years. Meanwhile he drew closer to the Communist Party and collaborated with the Comintern despite the advice of such friends as

Oszkár Jászi. In 1945, Károlyi was made an honorary member of the Provisional National Assembly and would have liked to participate in the political life of the new democracy but, with the exception of a few loyal friends, nobody wanted him. Rákosi, head of the Communist Party, opposed his return. Károlyi did not come back home until May 1946, and then only for a brief stay. Budapest, beflagged for the occasion, gave him a triumphant reception, and so did the National Assembly on 10 May. He spent the next year dividing his time between Budapest and London, then returned to Budapest for good and, in August 1947, despite the gradual dismantling of the democratic parties, accepted the post of minister plenipotentiary and head of the Hungarian delegation to Paris. He remained at his post for two years. Following the Rajk trial, he broke with the Communist government. He was then 74 years old. After a long life full of contradictions and disappointments, but not without idealism, he died at Vence in 1955 at the age of 80.

7 The respective advantages and disadvantages of Habsburg domination have long been the subject of historical controversy. Among recent Hungarian works, see Péter Hanák, *Magyarország a Monarchiában* (Hungary in the monarchy), Budapest, Gondolat, 1975. See also I. T. Berend and G. Ránki, *Hungary: A Century of Economic Development*, Newton Abbot, David & Charles/New York, Barnes & Noble, 1974, p. 74.

8 Iván T. Berend and György Ránki, *Underdevelopment and Economic Growth: Studies in Hungarian Social and Economic History*, Budapest, Akadémiai Kiadó, 1979, pp. 108–9. Berend and Ránki, *Hungary: A Century of Economic Development*, p. 74.

9 See *Magyarország története* (History of Hungary), Budapest, Akadémiai Kiadó, vol. 8, 1976, p. 770 and vol. 7, part 1, 1978 p. 282.

10 Figures and percentages taken from several statistical tables including ibid., vol. 8, pp. 729–809.

11 'Le deuxième servage en Europe centrale et orientale', *Recherches internationales à la lumière du marxisme*, vols 63–4, 2nd and 3rd quarters, 1970.

12 The workers' movement, in Hungary as in the rest of central Europe, made rapid strides in 1860–70, thanks *inter alia* to the First International. In Hungary, the Social Democratic Party, founded under a different name in 1878, was its largest component, with a membership of about 100,000. Radicalism, for its part, was a predominantly intellectual phenomenon. The celebrated Galilei Circle, founded in 1908, was its focal point. See Zsigmond Kende, *A Galilei Kör megalakulása* (The foundation of the Galilei Circle), Budapest, Akadémiai Kiadó, 1974.

13 According to Berend and Ránki's calculations, inter-war Hungary was among the most slowly developing countries of Europe with a growth rate of 1.5 per cent (or a mere 0.8 per cent if allowance is made for the population increase from 7.9 to 9.3 million during this period). (*Hungary. A Century*, p. 149.) Compared with Hungary's mean growth rate of approximately 3 per cent per annum during the years prior to the First World War, that performance was extremely disappointing; nevertheless, according to the same authors, industrialization received a fresh impetus between the wars, increasing industry's share of GNP from 30 to 36 per cent (ibid., p. 152).

Chapter 2: The Emergence of the Communist Party

1 No authentic documents are available to determine the precise date, place and circumstances of the foundation of the Hungarian Communist Party.
According to a 1956 publication by the Institute for Party History, no such

Notes

documents were available at that date. Later publications have failed to remedy this gap. In particular, the various documents do not agree on the date and place of the first constitutive meeting of the CP.

2 The CP adopted a number of different names which we shall mention as they occur.

3 *A magyar munkásmozgalom történetének válogatott dokumentumai* (Selected documents on the history of the Hungarian Workers' Movement), vol. 5 (7 November 1917–21 March 1919), Budapest, Szikra, 1956, pp. 311f., 351 (hereafter referred to as: *Selected Documents*).

4 György Milei, 'Mikor alakult a KP?' (When was the CP founded?), *Párttörténeti Közlemények* (Bulletin for Party History) (hereafter: *PTK*), vol. 11, no. 3, Sept. 1965, pp. 124–41. See also György Milei, *A Kommunisták Magyarországi Pártjának megalakításáról* (On the foundation of the Hungarian Communist Party), Budapest, Kossuth, 1962.

The date generally adopted is 24 November. See *Munkásmozgalomtörténeti Lexikon* (Historical dictionary of the Workers' Movement), Budapest, Kossuth, 1972; 2nd edn, 1976 (hereafter referred to as *Dictionary*); cf. *Legyözhetetlen erö. A magyar kommunista mozgalom szervezeti fejlödésének 50 éve* (Invincible force: 50 years of evolution of the organization of the Hungarian Communist Movement), Budapest, Kossuth, 1968 (hereafter referred to as: *Legyözhetetlen erö.*)

See particularly *Dictionary*, 1972 ed. In the 1976 edition, Hirossik is mentioned as a 'founding member of the party'. Before that date, Hirossik's name appeared very rarely in party publications, no doubt because he was not a party member from 1933 to 1942.

5 *Selected Documents*, vol. 5, pp. 97–120; *Dictionary*, under Ligeti, Kun, *Szociális Forradalom, passim.*

6 *Selected Documents*, vol. 5, p. 118.

7 According to Sergei Lazo, 80–5 per cent of the foreign combatants in the Red Army were Hungarians (ibid., p. 120). See also Antal Józsa and György Milei, *A rendíthetetlen százezer. Magyarok a Nagy Októberi Szocialista Forradalomban és a polgárháboruban* (The hundred thousand intransigents: Hungarians in the Great Socialist October Revolution and during the civil war), Budapest, Kossuth, 1968.

Mention must also be made of *A magyar internacionalisták a Nagy Októberi Szocialista Forradalomban és a polgárháboruban* (Hungarian internationalists in the Great Socialist October Revolution and in the civil war), documents, 2 vols., Budapest, Kossuth, 1968; and of Zsuzsa Szántó's study, 'Magyar internacionalisták harca Szibériában a polgárháboru idején, 1918–1929, Adalékok' (The actions fought by Hungarian internationalists in Siberia during the civil war, 1918–1920, facts and figures) in *A Magyar Munkásmozgalmi Múzeum évkönyve 1971–1972* (Yearbook of the Museum of the Hungarian Workers' Movement, 1971–1972), Budapest, 1973.

According to the last study, the Red Army ran a recruiting campaign among the half million prisoners of war in Siberia, most of them Germans and Hungarians. The head of the foreign section of the political division of the Red Army in charge of this campaign was the famous Czech writer Jaroslav Hašek (p. 196).

Szántó also claims that the Hungarian section of the Russian Communist (Bolshevik) Party had 6,600 members and candidate members in March 1920, which is a higher figure than that given by Rudnyánszki, head of this section.

8 Béla Kun, *A Magyar Tanácsköztárságról* (On the Hungarian Soviet Republic: speeches and selected writings), Budapest, Kossuth, 1958, p. 135.

9 Cf. the report by the Hungarian Communist group quoted earlier.

10 *A Magyar forradalmi munkásmozgalom története* (History of the Hungarian Revolutionary Workers' Movement), 2nd edn, Budapest, Kossuth, 1970, vols 1 and 2, p. 178.

Notes

11 See Zoltán Horváth, *Magyar századforduló* (Hungary at the turn of the century), Budapest, Gondolat, 1961; György Fukász, *A magyarországi polgári radikalizmus történetéhez, 1900–1918* (On the history of Hungarian bourgeois radicalism, 1900–1918), Budapest, Gondolat, 1960; György Litván, 'Egy barátság dokumentumai: Károlyi Mihály és Jászi Oszkár levelezéséből' (Documents of a friendship. Correspondence between Mihály Károlyi to Oszkár Jászi), *Történelmi Szemle* (Historical Review), vol. 18, nos. 2–3, 1975, pp. 175–210, and other articles by Litván and Tibor Hajdu on Oszkár Jászi, Mihály Károlyi and their intellectual and political circle.

12 Böhm, *Két forradalom tüzében*, p. 83.

13 Also known as the 'Chrysanthemum Revolution'.

14 Böhm, *Két forradalom tüzében*, pp. 79f.

15 Ibid., p. 85.

16 V. I. Lenin, 'The Social Democratic Attitude to the Peasant Movement', 14 Sept. 1905.

17 *Legyőzhetetlen erö*, p. 17.

18 See particularly the proclamations by the Socialist Revolutionaries in *Selected Documents*, vol. 5, and a letter from the writer Lajos Kassák to Béla Kun published in the review *Action poétique*, Paris, 1972.

19 This document is translated from a photographic copy of the signed text published in *A magyar forradalmi munkásmozgalom története* (History of the Hungarian Revolutionary Workers' Movement), vols 1 and 2, p. 219. In his memoirs, the former Social Democratic leader Vilmos Böhm gives a slightly different account based on a 1919 publication of the People's Commissariat of Public Instruction, entitled *Az egység okmányai* (The unity documents). The most striking difference between the two versions is in the paragraph dealing with the exercise of power. According to the photographic copy, 'the representatives of the Hungarian Communist Party will *also* [my italics] share in the leadership of the new party and in wielding political power'. Böhm's version reads: 'the two parties will jointly . . .'

20 The official name of the government was Forradalmi Kormányzótanács (Revolutionary Governing Council).

21 According to the French historian Dominique Gros, 'Les conseils ouvriers. Espérances et défaites de la révolution en Autriche-Hongrie, 1917–1920', PhD thesis, 3 vols, University of Dijon, n.d., vol. 2, p. 335, the Hungarian government had the following composition in March–April 1919:

17 people's commissars: 15 Social Democrats, 2 Communists

13 deputy commissars: 3 Social Democrats, 10 Communists (and allies).

From the beginning of April, the modified Revolutionary Governing Council comprised 34 people's commissars (the title of deputy commissar having been abolished) namely: Garbai, Landler, Vágó, Hamburger, Nyisztor, Vántus, Kun, Böhm, Fiedler, Haubrich, Szántó, Rónai, Ládai, Erdélyi, Kondor, Kunfi, Lukács, Szabados, Szamuely, Ágoston, Pogány, Bokányi, Guth, Kalmár, Székely, Lengyel, Stefan, Varga, Dovcsák, Hevesi, Kelen, and Rákosi. *A Forradalmi Kormányzótanács jegyzökönyve* (Minutes of the Revolutionary Governing Council), Archives of the Institute for Party History (hereafter referred to as: PTI), Section 601f., 1–35.

The names of Artur Illés and of Ferenc Bajaki should be added to the above list, Bajaki having been appointed a little later. Except for one or two changes, the composition of the government remained unchanged until the June congress. According to the Hungarian historian Tibor Hajdu, of the 34 commissars named above, 19 had been Social Democrats and 13 Communists, namely Fiedler, Guth, Hevesi, Illés, Kun, Kelen, Lukács, Rákosi, Szamuely, Szántó, Székely, Vágó and Vántus. See Tibor Hajdu, *A Magyarországi Tanácsköztársaság*, (The Hungarian Soviet Republic), Budapest, Kossuth, 1969, pp. 98f.

A report dated 22 April by General Hallier, head of the French military mission in Vienna, mentions a government of 42 members, 30 of whom were Jews. Bibliothèque de documentation internationale contemporaine (International Document Library), Dossiers Klotz 20, Fo. 223/Res/20, Hongrie (Hungary).

22 The Bolshevik leaders showed exceptional interest in the events in Hungary in 1919. Between 21 March and 1 August, no fewer than 318 messages were exchanged between the Hungarian Communists – almost invariably in the person of Béla Kun – and the Russians – Lenin and Chicherin in most cases. There was a telegraph line between Moscow and Csepel near Budapest. Most of the messages were in German, see Magda Imre and Imre Szerényi (eds), *Budapest–Moszkva, Szovjet-Oroszország és a Magyarországi Tanácsköztársaság kapcsolatai táviratok tükrében* (Budapest–Moscow. The contacts between Soviet Russia and the Hungarian Soviet Republic by means of telegrams), Budapest, Kossuth, 1979.

Lenin's and Chicherin's keen interest is easily explained: the Bolshevik leaders considered the proclamation of the Hungarian Soviet Republic a first step towards the world revolution for which they were clamouring and which remained the basis of their international policy during the first five years of the Russian revolution. The relevant texts published in *Budapest–Moszkva* are of the utmost importance because they cast light on the political preoccupations of Lenin and Chicherin and also on the practical relations between the Soviet Union and the Hungarian sister republic.

23 Böhm, *Két forradalom tüzében*, p. 292.

24 There is a great deal of source material together with many books covering its history. In addition to the documents, addresses and memoirs mentioned earlier, special mention must be made of *Vörös Ujság* (Red Journal); *A Tanácsok országos gyülésének naplója 1919 június 14–1919 június 23* (Minutes of the Proceedings of the National Assembly of Councils, 14 June 1919–23 June 1919), Budapest, Athenaeum, 1919: and also of the detailed and unique testimony of a foreign observer, Guido Romanelli's *Nell'Ungheria di Bela Kun e durante l'occupazione romena. La mia missione, maggio–novembre 1919*, Udine, Doretti, 1964. The most complete general work is Tibor Hajdu's *A Magyarországi Tanácsköztáraság*. For accounts written in English, see Rudolf L. Tökés, *Béla Kun and the Hungarian Soviet Republic: The Origins and Role of the Communist Party of Hungary in the Revolutions of 1918–1919*, New York, Praeger, 1967; Iván Völgyes (ed.), *Hungary in Revolution 1918–1919: Nine Essays*, Lincoln, University of Nebraska Press, 1971. Among writings published on the 50th anniversary of the Hungarian Soviet Republic, see particularly *A Magyarországi Tanácsköztársaság 50. évfordulója. Nemzetközi Tudományos ülésszak* (The 50th anniversary of the Hungarian Soviet Republic. International scientific symposium), Budapest, Akadémiai Kiadó, 1970.

25 *A Magyar Tanácsköztársaság pénzügyi rendszere* (The financial system of the Hungarian Soviet Republic), Budapest, Közgazdasági és Jogi Könyvkiadó, 1959.

26 *A Tanácsok országos gyülésének.*

27 *Történelmünk a jogalkotás tükrében* (Our history through legislation). Compilation of basic laws edited by János Beér and Andor Csizmadia, Budapest, Gondolat, 1966.

28 Tökés, *Béla Kun*, pp. 122f.

29 *Lenin Magyarországról* (Lenin on Hungary), Budapest, Kossuth, p. 109.

30 Kun, *A Magyar Tanácsköztársaságról*, pp. 438–50.
31 Bennett Kovrig, *Communism in Hungary. From Kun to Kadar*, Stanford, Hoover Institution Press, 1979, p. 77.
32 Hajdu, *A Magyarországi Tanácsköztársaság*, p. 251.
33 Ibid., p. 249.
34 György Borsányi, *Kun Béla. Politikai életrajz* (Bela Kun: political biography), Budapest, Kossuth, 1979, p. 145.
35 *A Tanácsok országos gyülésének*, 9th session.
36 Kun, *A Magyar Tanácsköztársaságról*, pp. 438–50.
37 Cf. Valiani, 'Politica estera', p. 893.
38 PTI, Section 601f., 1–35.
39 Imre and Serényi, *Budapest–Moszkva*, item 26.
40 Quoted by Valiani, 'Politica estera', p. 909.
41 PTI, Section 601f., 1–35.
42 Imre and Serényi, *Budapest–Moszkva*, item 25.
43 *Selected Documents*, vol. 6/A, no. 326, p. 328.
44 PTI, Section 601f., 1–35.
45 Archives of the French Ministry of Foreign Affairs, 'Europe 1918–1929', Russia, vol. 669, items 207 and 327.
46 Ibid., vol. 683. This report is confirmed by others not mentioned here.
47 *FRUS, PPC*, vol. 13, *passim*: Paul Mantoux, *Les délibérations du Conseil des Quatre (24 mars–28 juin 1919)*, 2 vols, Paris, Éditions du CNRS, 1955; Zsuzsa L. Nagy, *A Párizsi békekonferencia*. See also Miklós Molnár, 'Révolution, contre-révolution et politique étrangère: Hongrie 1919', *Relations internationales*, vol. 4, 1975, pp. 111–15; György Litván, *Documents des relations franco-hongroises des années 1917–1919*, Budapest, Akadémiai Kiadó, 1975.
48 Béla Kirschner, 'A Clemenceau-jegyzék és a párton belüli nézeteltérések' (The Clemenceau Note and the inner-party disagreements) in *A Magyarországi Tanácsköztársaság 50. évfordulója*.
49 Branko Lazitch, Milorad M. Drachkovitch, *Lenin and the Comintern*, Stanford, Hoover Institution Press and Stanford University, 1972, vol. 1, pp. 110–24; Lucien Laurat, 'Le Parti communiste autrichien', in Jacques Freymond (ed.), *Contributions à l'histoire du Comintern*, Publications de l'Institut universitaire de hautes études internationales, no. 45, Geneva, Droz, 1965; Gábor Sándorné, *Ausztria és a Magyarországi Tanácsköztársaság* (Austria and the Hungarian Soviet Republic), Budapest, Akadémiai Kiadó, 1969.

Chapter 3: The Clandestine Party from 1919 to 1930

1 *Mátyás Rákosi face au tribunal fasciste*, Paris, Éditions sociales, 1952.
2 Annie Kriegel, *Communismes au miroir français*, Paris, Gallimard, 1974, pp. 11–30.
3 Dezső Nemes (ed.), *Iratok az ellenforradalom történetéhez I. Az ellenforradalom hatalomrajutása és rémuralma Magyarországon 1919–1921* (Documents for a history of the counter-revolution, vol. 1; The accession to power and the terror of the counter-revolution in Hungary 1919–1921), Budapest, Szikra, 1956; see also Dezső Nemes, *Az ellenforradalom története Magyarországon 1919–1921*) (History of the counter-revolution in Hungary 1919–1921), Budapest, Kossuth, 1962.
4 Besides Kun and Landler, the committee also included Béla Szántó, János Hirossik and György Lukács. (*A magyar forradalmi munkásmozgalom története*, vols 1 and 2, p. 282).
5 See Jacques Rupnik, *Histoire du Parti communiste tchécoslovaque: des origines à la prise de pouvoir*, Paris, Presses de la Fondation nationale des sciences politiques, 1981, pp. 49–51.

Notes

6 *A magyar forradalmi munkásmozgalom története*, vols 1 and 2, p. 299. On the various attitudes of the party leaders, see also Kun, *A Magyar Tanácsköz-társaságról* and Jenö Landler, *Válogatott beszédek és írások* (Selected Speeches and Writings), Budapest, Kossuth, 1960. Cf. Ágnes Szabó, *A Kommunisták Magyarországi Pártjának ujjászervezése (1919–1925)* (The reorganization of the Hungarian Communist Party), Budapest, Kossuth, 1970. Among the memoirs of former militants, see Nándor Szekér, *Föld alatt és föld felett* (Underground and in the open), Budapest, Kossuth, 1968.

7 For the sequel to this conflict, see below.

8 After the publication of Ágnes Szabó's study of the First Party Congress in the journal *PTK*, May 1962, pp. 1–34, a veteran militant, Nándor Szekér, challenged the official version of the composition of that committee. His article, also published in *PTK*, vol. 8, no. 4, Nov. 1962, pp. 123–6, alleges that the original committee was led by Gögös, Hámán and Aladár Weisshaus. (Weisshaus's name was probably removed from the official version because of his 'Trotskyist' activities.) Szekér also claims that when he returned to Hungary under the *nom de guerre* of Herist, he, Öry and Gögös made up the 'home-based' committee.

9 Borsányi, *Kun Béla*, pp. 253–6; Borsányi mentions the figure of 2,000 without giving his sources. This figure seems most unlikely. A few hundred militants were probably sent back home among the mass of Hungarian prisoners of war exchanged by Soviet Russia for Communist political prisoners incarcerated in Hungary. In this connection, see also Dezsö Nemes, 'Észrevételek Borsányi György: Kun Béla politikai életrajza c. munkájához' (Remarks on György Borsányi's political biography of Béla Kun), offprint from *Párttörténeti Közlemények* (Bulletin for Party History), vol. 3, 1979, pp. 47–8.

10 The committee charged with the examination of the case of Hungary was made up of Radek (rapporteur), Zinoviev, Zetkin, Suvarin, Borodin and some ten other Comintern personalities. Cf. Borsányi, *Kun Béla*, p. 262.

11 We lack the space to describe all the stages of these factional struggles. The most comprehensive work on the period is Ágnes Szabó, *KMP ujjászervezése*. See also Borsányi, *Kun Béla*, chap. 6. Special mention must be made of the publication in 1921 of a 'dissident' paper by the Landler faction under the title of *Vörös Ujság (Wien)* (Red Journal, Vienna), and of the fact that Landler, Lukács and Hirossik resigned from the Central Committee. See Borsányi, *Kun Belá*, p. 261. In 1922, László Rudas, another of Kun's opponents, published a long and virulent attack on Kun in Vienna in a pamphlet entitled *Abenteurer und Liquidatoren. Die Politik Béla Kuns und die Krise der KPU* (Adventurers and liquidators. Béla Kun's policy and the crisis of the HCP), Vienna, 1922. According to Ágnes Szabó, (*KMP ujjászervezése*, p. 143), a Comintern committee convened on 21 Jan. still sided with Kun; Rudas was expelled from the party. Soon afterwards, however, as we saw, Kun himself was removed from the leadership.

12 The best-written and most fully documented account of Béla Kun's life is Borsányi's *Kun Béla*. For the 1920s, see pp. 199–326.

13 For Béla Kun's fall, see Chapter 6.

14 For Lukács's intervention and very slightly 'anti-sectarian' attitude, see the discussion of 'Blum's Theses' at the end of Chapter 3.

15 For Lukács's activities before 1929, see particularly Michel Löwy, *Pour une sociologie des intellectuels révolutionnaires: l'évolution politique de Lukács, 1909–1929*, Paris, PUF, 1976; and Yvon Bourdet, *Figures de Lukács*, Paris, Anthropos, 1972.

16 Ágnes Szabó, György Borsányi and István Pintér, 'A Kommunista Internacionálé és a Kommunisták Magyarországi Pártja' (The Communist International and the Hungarian Communist Party: historical survey), manuscript, PTI, p. 32.

17 Cf. Rupnik, *Histoire du Parti communiste tchécoslovaque*, pp. 41–82.

Notes

18 PTI, Section 500f., 2/76 Oe. See also *A KMP elsö kongresszusa* (The First HCP Congress), Budapest, Kossuth, 1975.

The fifth Congress of the Communist International (June 1924) – the so-called 'Bolshevization Congress' – shouldered the Hungarian party with a new organization committee whose task it was to prepare the First Party Congress. Made up of Kun, Landler and Alpári, this committee later co-opted Rákosi and Hirossik and Aladár Weisshaus. Weisshaus and Pál Demény eventually became associated with the party's new 'factional spirit'.

19 PTI, Section 500f., 2/79 Oe., pp. 2–20; cf. *A KMP elsö kongresszusa*, pp. 121–40.

20 Nowadays the Hungarian Communist Party has an almost identical name, viz. Hungarian Socialist Workers' Party.

21 The trial of Vági, head of the MSzMP, was held in 1927, but 24 party leaders and 273 militants had been sentenced in 1926. For the history of this legal branch of the Hungarian Communist movement, see Ervin Liptai, *A Magyarországi Szocialista Munkáspárt, 1925–1928* (The Socialist Workers' Party of Hungary, 1925–1928), Budapest, Kossuth, 1971. Among the memoirs of former militants, see Károly Kiss, *Nincs megállás* (No stopping), Budapest, Kossuth, 1974; Szekér, *Föld alatt és föld felett*.

22 *Kommunisticheskii Internatsional'* (The Communist International), Moscow, Izdatel'sltvo Politcheskoi Literatury, 1969; Hungarian translation (see chap. 4 n. 21), Budapest, 1971, p. 256.

23 In what follows, we shall be referring to some of these studies and commentaries and also to Lukács's own reservations. The full text of 'Blum's Theses' was published in vol. 4 of the Acad. ed. of Attila Jozsef's *Complete Works* as an appendix. The *Bulletin for Party History* has only published long extracts, the full text – which we were able to consult – being deposited in the PTI, Section 677f., 1/22 Oe.

24 Georg Lukács, *History and Class Consciousness*, London, Merlin Press, 1971.

25 At the beginning of the 1930s, for instance, Lukács upheld a hard realist line against Brecht, Benjamin and other avant-garde members of the Organization of Revolutionary Writers in Berlin.

26 In his *Az elmaradt reneszánsz* (The abortive renaissance), Munich, Protestáns Magyar Szabadegyetem, 1979, an important work on Hungarian Marxism, Tibor Hanák provides a detailed analysis of Lukács's contribution in the Hungarian context. There have also been many detailed studies of certain aspects of, or periods in, Lukács's life, including particularly Miklós Lackó's studies of 'Blum's Theses' in *Válságok – Választások* (Crises – choices: collected papers), Budapest, Gondolat, 1975, and of Lukács's publicist activities in *Szerep és mü* (Role and oeuvre: studies in cultural history), Budapest, Gondolat, 1981. For Lukács's political role in the party, the reader is also referred to various other titles listed in the Bibliography.

For Lukács's development until 1929 and for 'Blum's Theses' see also Michel Löwy, *Pour une sociologie*. According to Löwy (p. 238), the 1928 theses were the culmination of Lukács's long and tortuous intellectual journey; the ultimate stage of his political development; 'the ideological foundation of all the intellectual work he did from 1928 onwards'. Löwy also contends that the theses reflect Lukács's continuous attempt to reconcile Stalinism with a democratic culture (p. 242).

27 After the Nazis came to power, Alpári moved to Paris where he was put in charge of the *Rundschau*. In 1940, the Gestapo arrested him and sent him to Sachsenhausen concentration camp. Goebbels is said to have suggested to him in person that he write his reminiscences of the Communist International for purposes of Nazi propaganda. Alpári refused and was killed in 1944.

28 'Project for a thesis on the political and economic situation of Hungary and on

Notes

the tasks of the Hungarian Communist Party (KMP)'. From the Hungarian original, PTI, Section 677f., 1/22 Oe.

29 See PTI, Section 677f., 1/22 Oe, pp. 10–13. See also extracts from 'Blum's Theses' in *PTK*, vol. 2, no. 3, 1956, pp. 75–94, and vol. 21, no. 2, 1975, pp. 154–206. For a German translation of some of the extracts, see Georg Lukács, *Schriften zur Ideologie und Politik*, Neuwied/Berlin, Luchterhand, 1967, pp. 290–322.

30 The first public debate after the 1930s did not take place until 1956 – in the Petöfi Circle. In his contribution, Lukács freely admitted the dogmatic nature of his theses, even though he called them an 'attempt to break with the dominant spirit of sectarianism in the Communist Party'. He went on stress that the importance of the debate was not purely historical since sectarianism continued to play an important role in the Communist Party. See 'Discussion of Blum's Theses', *PTK*, vol. 2, no. 3, 1956; German translation in Lukács, *Schriften zur Ideologie und Politik*, pp. 703–74. Twenty years later, in reply to an article by Miklós Lackó, Sándor Szerényi, a former leader of the illegal party, claimed that Lackó had exaggerated the importance of Lukács's 1928 theses and appended Lukács's self-criticism first published in 1929. See also *PTK*, vol. 21, no. 2, 1975, pp. 146–53.

Miklós Lackó's study nevertheless remains one of the most detailed analyses of 'Blum's Theses'. It appears that Lukács's ideas were in vogue at the time, especially in the smaller East European Communist Parties, and that the Comintern did not put up any real opposition to them. A rising leftist trend in 1929 nevertheless led to the rejection of 'Blum's Theses' and related ideas. They were to resurface with the Popular Front. See Miklós Lackó, *Válságok-Választások*, pp. 171–93. For a new analysis, see Béla Kirschner, *A Blum-Tézisek* (Blum's Theses) in *A KMP stratégiai vonalának alakulása 1928–1930*, Budapest, Kossuth, 1988.

31 See p. 36 above.

32 The most probable date is February 1928.

33 The present author has been unable to discover an amended version of 'Blum's Theses'.

34 Révai to Kun, 21 Mar. 1929, PTI, Section 500f., 2/221 A.

35 Ibid.

36 Minutes of the plenary session of the Central Committee of the Hungarian Communist Party, PTI, Section 500f., 1/142 A.

37 The minutes and related documents of the Second Congress have not been published, and the author was not given permission to examine them in the PTI archives. Other sources, however, throw light on the agenda of this congress. See particularly *A Kommunisták Magyarországi Pártja II. Kongresszusának irányelvei* (Directives to the Second Congress of the Hungarian Communist Party). Cover: *Irányelvek. Elfogadta a Kommunisták Magyarországi Pártja II. Kongresszusa 1930 májusában* (Directives. Approved by the Second Congress of the Hungarian Communist Party in May 1930), Vienna, Vermy, 1930 (hereafter referred to as: *Directives*). See also several articles and reports in the party papers *Uj Március* (New March) and *Sarló és Kalapács* (Sickle and Hammer). The author has also consulted the very detailed, unpublished memoirs of Ernö Normai, one of the delegates to the congress and a member of the Central Committee: 558-page manuscript in the safekeeping of François Fejtö (hereafter referred to as: Ernö Normai, 'Memoirs'.)

38 Zoltánné Horváth, *A KMP második kongresszusa* (The Second Congress of the HCP), Budapest, Kossuth, 1964, p. 43. Cf. Borsányi, *Kun Béla*, pp. 335–40; Ernö Normai, 'Memoirs'.

39 At the end of December 1926, a member of the Committee Abroad left his briefcase containing secret party documents in a Viennese taxi. Next day, the briefcase was returned to him, but meanwhile the documents had been photo-

graphed and forwarded to the Hungarian police who, in February 1927, rounded up some thirty clandestine party members including Zoltán Szántó, secretary of the illegal organization in Hungary. The Hungarian police did not, however, rely on such windfalls but employed a number of infiltrators and informers inside the party. In 1929, the Austrian police again laid hands on documents belonging to the Vienna committee and sent them on to Budapest, precipitating numerous fresh arrests.

40 Minutes of the session held on 17 Jan. 1930. According to Ernö Normai, the younger delegates to the congress wanted to rid the party leadership of all former members of the two factions. They were only half successful (and not for long) because the Comintern wanted to keep Kun in his old position. Normai also points out that Jenö Fried, who had taken over from Dengel as the Comintern representative, was busy behind the scenes recruiting young cadres newly arrived from Hungary for an activist 'core' that would apply new 'Stalinist leadership methods'. See Ernö Normai, 'Memoirs', pp. 400f.

According to Philippe Robrieux, *Histoire intérieure du Parti communiste*, vol. 1: *1920–1945*, Paris, Fayard, 1980, pp. 304–6 and *passim*, the same methods were used at the time in the French Communist Party with the 'promotion' of the Barbe-Celor Group.

41 See Minutes of Central Committee, 30 Jan. 1930, PTI, Section 500f., 2/263; and Borsányi, *Kun Béla*, p. 336. 'The main problem', Borsányi writes, 'is still how to put an end to the factional struggles. So far without success. All that has happened is that the representatives of the new line have teamed up with those of the old Landler faction, and particularly with József Révai and Georg Lukács; at the same time, the leaders of the Communist International have remained determined to keep Béla Kun in his leading position.'

42 Cf. G. Borsányi, 'Adalékok a Kommunisták Magyarországi Pártja szervezeti fejlödéséhez 1928–1932' (Contribution to the organizational development of the Hungarian Communist Party, 1928–1932), *PTK*, vol. 8, no. 1, 1962.

43 Borsányi, *Kun Béla*, pp. 344–7.

Chapter 4: The Years of Crisis: The Party and the Comintern

1 *A KMP KB 1932 májusi teljes ülésének határozatai* (Resolutions of Plenary Session of the Central Committee of the HCP held in May 1932), Vienna Arbeiterbuch-handlung, n.d.

2 *A KMP KB 1933 szeptemberi határozata a magyarországi helyzetröl és a KMP alapvetö feladatairól* (Resolution of September 1933 by the Central Committee of the HCP meeting on the situation in Hungary and the fundamental tasks of the HCP), n.p., n.d.

3 Kiss, *Nincs megállás*.

4 *Legyözhetetlen erö*, pp. 106f.

5 *A magyar forradalmi munkásmozgalom története*, vols 1 and 2, pp. 437–9.

6 Dezsö Orosz and István Pintér, 'Adatok a KMP szervezeti fejlödéséhez, 1936–1942' (Data on the organizational development of the HCP, 1936–1942), *PTK*, vol. 4, no. 3, Aug. 1958, pp. 56–85.

7 Since Kirov was assassinated on 1 Dec. 1934, the dinner in question must have been held before that date. According to another source, Kun attended a soirée at Kamenev's place after the latter had been expelled from the party. Moscow was trying to compromise Kun and to establish a link between him and Kirov's alleged assassins. One of Kun's friends, the sinologist Lajos Magyar, was also implicated. See p. 86.

8 This letter (also known as Letter from a Comrade) was published in January 1936 by the Central Committee of the HCP in Moscow to herald the change from the sectarian political line in favour of joint action with social democratic organizations, but not with the SDP.

9 The Prague Committee, which was to become the new leadership arm of the party. Its members included Ferenc Bozsóki, Gusztáv Krejcsi, József Révai, Lajos Papp and István Friss (in addition to Szántó).

10 The two versions were identical. In June, the political Secretariat again examined the Hungarian 'affair', and the International Control Committee also met to pronounce on 'former members of the Central Committee of the Party of Hungarian Communists', namely Huszti, Komor, Nemes and Sebes. Two of them – Huszti and Sebes – were arrested soon afterwards and disappeared. Komor spent a long time in prison. Kun's case was examined separately. On 5 Sept. 1936 he was brought before the Secretariat of the Executive Committee which stripped him of all his offices. He was left at liberty for another few months, arrested on 29 June 1937 and executed. See Borsányi, *Kun Béla*, pp. 376–85. For Kun, see also Chapter 6 below.

11 Unpublished memoirs of Zoltán Szántó.

12 János Kádár, 'A Kommunisták Magyarországi Pártja feloszlatása körülményeinek és a Békepárt munkájának néhány kérdéséröl, 1943 junius–1944 szeptember' (On some questions concerning the dissolution of the Party of Hungarian Communists and on the work of the Peace Party, June 1943–September 1944), *PTK*, vol. 2, no. 3, Oct. 1956.

13 Cf. Kiss, *Nincs megállás*, p. 237.

14 According to a work published by the party, viz. *Legyözhetetlen erö*, pp. 108f.

15 The author was able to consult five issues of *Dolgozók Lapja* (Workers' Paper) published between 1 Apr. 1937 and June 1938. The most important directives are found in the editorial of the first of these issues which dealt with principles and tasks of the paper in a tone-setting article on the 'Struggle of the Communist Party of Hungary against fascism and for a democratic Hungary'. The same article denied, moreover, that the party had been dissolved, though it did admit that 'something had happened' as the result of a failure by the former Central Committee to take cognizance of the principles of the Seventh Congress of the Communist International and of the call for a united front. In the Sept. 1937 issue, the paper rounded on 'Trotskyists', especially on Weisshaus, Demény and one Kállai-Sallmayer, who were said to be taking advantage of the Spanish Civil War to pursue their nefarious activities.

16 For the activities of the March Front, see Chapter 6.

17 Information supplied by Ferenc Donáth.

18 Lajos Papp, *Törvényen kivül: Emlékiratok* (Outlawed: recollections), Budapest, Kossuth, 1973, pp. 167–74.

19 Kiss, *Nincs megállás*, pp. 265–9.

20 The document was published in 1979 under the title 'A szovjet-német megegyezés elsö magyar kommunista értékelése' (The first Hungarian Communist evaluation of the Soviet–German Pact) in *A Politikai Föiskola Közleményei* (Communications of the Political High School), Budapest, vol. 2, 1979, pp. 83–93.

21 *A Kommunista Internacionále és a Kommunisták Magyarországi Pártja* (The Communist International and the Party of Hungarian Communists, historical survey), Budapest, 1971, p. 107.

22 *A Magyar Tanácsköztársaság. A Kommunisták Magyarországi Pártjának harca a Horthy fasizmus ellen* (The Hungarian Soviet Republic: the struggle of the Party of Hungarian Communists against Horthy fascism), Budapest, Szikra, 1952, p. 45.

23 Gyula Kállai, *A magyar függetlenségi mozgalom, 1936–1945* (The Hungarian independence movement, 1936–1945), Budapest, Kossuth, 5th edn, 1965, p. 78. See also Gyula Kállai, *Életem törvénye* (My life's law), Budapest, Kossuth, 1980, pp. 142–5.

24 *A magyar forradalmi munkásmozgalom története*, vols 1 and 2, p. 451.

25 It should also be borne in mind that the successive annexations, for which Hitler was partly responsible, of southern Slovakia, the Carpatho-Ukraine and northern Transylvania, appreciably strengthened the Hungarian party with the influx of several hundred communists of proven militancy. See *inter alia* Part 2 of Edgár Balogh's memoirs, *Szolgálatban. Egy nemzedék története, 1935–1944* (On active service: history of a generation, 1935–1944), Budapest, Magvetö, 1981.

Chapter 5: From Sectarianism to the 'New Democracy'

1 For the problems of the French Communist Party in adopting the Popular Front policy, see Robrieux, *Histoire intérieure du Parti communiste*, vol. 1, *1920–1945*, pp. 407–87.

2 *A magyar forradalmi munkásmozgalom története*, vols. 1 and 2, p. 438.

3 Having been ousted from the party leadership in 1936, Kun was arrested in 1937. He died – or was shot – in prison some time between 1937 and 1939 (probably in September 1939). See Chapter 6.

4 József Révai, *Marxizmus, népiesség, magyarság* (Marxism, populism, Hungarianism), Budapest, 1947.

5 Révai's manuscript was first published in 1943 under Gyula Kállai's name and under the title *Népiség, demokrácia, szocializmus* (Populism, democracy, socialism), Budapest, Társadalmi Könyvtár, 1943.

6 József Révai, *Literarische Studien*, Berlin, Dietz Verlag, 1956. This German edition contains Révai's most important literary studies. With the exception of the study devoted to the poet Endre Ady, the essays in this volume were not published in their definitive version until after 1945.

7 Apart from the journal itself, see also Ernö Gondos, 'A *Gondolat*-ról' (On the journal *Gondolat*), *PTK*, vol. 1, 1964. Among the many memoirs referring to the journal at some length, see particularly Gyula Schöpflin, *Szélkiáltó, Emlékezések* (Curlew, Memoirs), Paris, IUS, 1983.

8 Edited originally by Pál Ignotus and Attila József, then by a committee and finally by Zoltán Gáspár, the journal's contributors included many left-wing writers and essayists, among them Miklós Radnóti, Andor Német and François Fejtö. See Andor Német, 'József Attila és kora' (Attila József and his epoch), republished in A. Német's selected writings, *Szélén behajtva* (The dog-eared page), Budapest, Magvetö, 1973; Paul Ignotus, *Die intellektuelle Linke in Ungarn der 'Horthy-Zeit'* (The intellectual left in Hungary during the 'Horthy epoch'), Munich, 1969.

9 After the manuscript of the present work had been completed, the French publishing house of Calmann-Lévy brought out the most important contribution to the intellectual history of that period, namely François Fejtö's *Mémoires. De Budapest à Paris*, Paris, 1986. Cf. Miklós Molnár, 'Un poète entre Freud et Lenine: Attila József', *Cadmos*, vol. 3, no. 12, 1980, pp. 86–106.

10 In addition to the works already mentioned, see István Pintér, *A Szociáldemokrata Párt Története, 1933–1944* (History of the Social Democratic Party, 1933–1944), Budapest, Kossuth, 1980.

11 Gyula Borbándi, *Der ungarische Populismus* (Hungarian populism), Mainz, Hase & Koehler, 1976. See also Gyula Borbándi, *A magyar népi mozgalom* (The Hungarian populist movement), New York, Püski, 1983.

12 The populist movement was not confined to literature or even to sociological studies of peasant life. As it grew, it spread into social geography, ethnology and folklore. It also embraced music and particularly the work and studies of Béla Bartók and Zoltán Kodály, two indefatigable explorers of folk music. Despite its political divisions and heterogeneous character, the movement left a lasting mark on the Hungarian cultural scene thanks to its popular and innovative approach, which was sharply distinct from the 'neo-baroque' ideology of conservative society.

13 Konrád Salamon, *A Márciusi Front* (The March Front), Budapest, Akadémiai Kiadó, 1980.

14 *Szárszó 1943. Elözményei, jegyzökönyve és utóélete. Dokumentumok* (Szárszó 1943: antecedents, minutes and sequels. Documents), Budapest, Kossuth, 1983.

15 Several populists veered towards the Right and some, such as József Erdélyi and János Kodolányi, even towards the extreme (fascist) Right. The role of László Németh, the influential populist writer and ideologist, held in high regard by the present régime and also by the Hungarian public, remains controversial. This study does not pretend to offer an analysis of the populist movement as a whole or of the often dogged conflict between the 'populists' and the 'urbans' who represented several socialist and radical tendencies.

16 Many documents and periodicals mention Communist involvement during the inter-war years in the March Front, in the populist movement, in peasant newspapers and journals and in such peasant organizations as the Peasant Alliance. See Borbándi, *A magyar népi mozgalom*; *Szárszó*; László Kardos (ed.), *Sej, a mi lobogónkat fényes szelek fujják . . . Népi kollégiumok 1939–1949* (Those luminous winds in our banner . . . People's colleges 1939–1949), collected documents, Budapest, Akadémiai Kiadó, 1977. Among the many reminiscences and memoirs, see particularly Lajos Fehér, *Igy történt* (It happened thus), Budapest, Magvetö, 1979; Gyula Kállai's memoirs, *Életem törvénye*. A particularly striking and authentic account can be found in 'Kolostor és barrikád. Beszélgetés Ujhelyi Szilárddal' (Monastery and barricade: conversation with Szilárd Ujhelyi), produced on Hungarian television by András Sylvester on 10–11 Dec. 1981 and published (in 1982) in the Budapest journal *Kritika*. Among the writings of Imre Kovács, see particularly *A Márciusi Front* (The March Front), New Brunswick, 1980; 'Szárszó húsz év után' (Szárszó, twenty years on) in *Uj Látóhatár* (New Horizon), vol. 4, 1963 (Munich).

The author of the present work has also relied on personal conversations with several people involved in the movement and with Ferenc Donáth who acted as a link between the March Front and the Secretariat of the Communist Party.

17 PTI, Section 651p., 6/1936.

18 István Pintér, *Rózsa Ferenc. Életrajz és dokumentumok* (Ferenc Rózsa. Biography and documents), Budapest, Kossuth, 1983.

19 Ferenc Házi, a delegate of the Prague provisional committee, had been dispatched to Budapest as early as January 1938 to oversee the reorganization of one of the executive committees. At the time, a trio consisting of Rózsa, László Gács and Gyula Kulich was acting as a provisional executive. The headquarters of the 'titular' Central Committee were then in Paris, where Lajos Papp had taken up residence. Rózsa was summoned to Paris at the beginning of 1939 for discussions with Papp, who asked him to assume the leadership of the clandestine party pending Schönherz's arrival in Hungary. In the autumn of 1939, Rózsa set up, or reorganized, a 'home-based' political executive with the participation of Gács and Kenéz.

At the same time, however, the Comintern also made decisions about the Hungarian party. A new Committee Abroad was appointed, including Zoltán Fodor, Lajos Papp (still in Paris) and Olexa Borkanyuk, who were subsequently joined by Ferenc Bozsóki, György Kilián, Lajos Domokos and József Révai. At the same time, Ernö Gerö replaced Zoltán Szántó as representative of the Hungarian section of the Comintern. The outbreak of war cut communications – sporadic and unreliable even before then – between Budapest, Moscow and Paris.

To add to the confusion, in the autumn of 1939, the party organization in Kassa (Kosice, chief town of the Czechoslovak territory annexed by Hungary) sent Zoltan Schönherz on a mission to Moscow, while Rózsa's brother Richard also went to Moscow for instructions, as did György Kilián soon afterwards. It appears that the Comintern, who had to redefine their policy in the light of the German–Soviet pact and the war, based their conclusions mainly on Schönherz's report. In any case, Schönherz was ordered to return to Hungary and to continue the work of reorganization with the help of Sándor Szekeres; a third person was to be co-opted locally. Now that person was someone other than Rózsa who had counted on being chosen – personal relations between Schönherz and Rózsa were strained; besides which the two men had political and tactical differences. To escape arrest, Schönherz and Szekeres fled back to Moscow in May 1940; in September they were ordered to return to Budapest and instructed to reorganize – this time with József Skolnik, another Communist from the annexed territories – the home-based executive that had been left in a state of suspension for two years. In December 1940 – this time in agreement with their comrades in Budapest – they established a Secretariat and soon afterwards a Central Committee headed by the three emissaries from Moscow together with Lászlo Gács and Ferenc Rózsa. Skolnik was appointed secretary. See Pintér, *Rózsa Ferenc*, pp. 82–149.

20 According to János Kádár, after the wave of arrests in the summer of 1942, the party was reduced to 450 to 500 members, including just a few dozen active militants. See p. 76.
21 István Pintér, *A magyar kommunisták a Hitler-ellenes nemzeti egységért 1941 junius–1944 március* (Hungarian Communists for national unity against Hitler, June 1941–March 1944), Budapest, Kossuth, 1968, p. 73.
22 During this period, the Independence Front and the National Front were thrown into disarray by the apparent need to obfuscate the anti-fascist character of the Popular Fronts prior to the German–Soviet Pact.
23 It is practically impossible to assess the real effect of these barely audible broadcasts which, moreover, were treated with suspicion by Communist circles in Hungary. According to the manuscript setting out the relations between the Communist International and HCP, Hungarian Communists did not look on Radio Kossuth as a party transmitter.
24 The Committee Abroad addressing the 'home-based' committee. PTI, Section 677f., 1/83 Oe.
25 *Dokumentumok a magyar párttörténet tanulmányozásához 5. köt: 1939 szeptemberétől–1945 áprilisáig* (Documents for the study of Hungarian party history, vol. 5: September 1939–April 1945), Budapest, Szikra, 1955, pp. 58–60.
26 See ibid., editors' note: 'We have not been able to lay our hands on the documents in question.'
27 Gyula Kállai, *A magyar függetlenségi mozgalom* (The Hungarian Independence Movement), Budapest, Szikra, 1946, pp. 6–8.
28 Gyula Kállai, *A magyar függetlenségi mozgalom, 1939–1945*, Budapest, Szikra, 1955 (4th rev. and enlarged edn), pp. 114–18.
29 Kállai, *Életem törvénye*, p. 353.
30 Ibid., p. 387.
31 Ibid.
32 *Szabad Nép*, vol. 1, no. 1, 1 Feb. 1942 and vol. 1, no. 2, 1 Mar. 1942.

Notes

33 *A magyar forradalmi munkásmozgalom története*, vols 1 and 2, p. 508.

34 *Munkásmozgalomtörténeti Lexikon*, p. 383 (hereafter: *Dictionary*).

35 Kállai, *Életem törvénye*, pp. 511f.

36 The Hungarian historian István Pintér mentions discussions lasting several days. Some participants opposed the change in the party's name, but in the end the resolution was adopted unanimously. See Pintér, *A magyar kommunisták a Hitlerellenes nemzeti egységért*, pp. 237f. He also explains that there was 'a conspiratorial interval of a few weeks 'between the June meeting and that held at the beginning of July when, after some discussion, the name of Peace Party was adopted.

37 Kállai, *Életem törvénye*, p. 511.

38 *A kommunista pártok határozataiból, amelyeket a Kommunista Internacionále VB elnökségének a Komintern feloszlatásáról szóló 1943 május 15-i határozatával kapcsolatban hoztak* (Extracts from the resolutions passed by Communist parties concerning the 15 May 1943 Comintern Executive Council resolution on the dissolution of the Comintern), 16 pages, n.p., n.d. The pamphlet contains extracts from the resolutions of about a dozen parties.

39 A collection of documents: *Dokumentumok a magyar forradalmi munkásmozgalom történetéből 1939–1945* (Documents on the history of the Hungarian Revolutionary Workers' Movement, vol. V, 1939–1945), Budapest, Kossuth, 1964, quotes the text of the pamphlet on pp. 414–17. If this is indeed the original document, which seems probable, it is clear that this move was not a mere pretence or show but a genuine dissolution of the party. The Communists, the pamphlet declared, will continue the struggle on a broad national basis, but prefer to disband their organization. 'We cease to exist as a party, but will continue to be present as individuals,' wherever the fight 'for peace, for the nation, for an independent, free and democratic Hungary' is being waged.

40 Kállai, *Életem törvénye*, pp. 512–17.

41 *Tanulmányok a magyar népi demokrácia történetéből* (Studies in the history of the Hungarian People's Democracy), Budapest, Akadémiai Kiadó, 1955, pp. 41f.

42 *Az MKP I. országos értekezlete. Gyorsírói jegyzökönyv, 1945 május 20–21* (First national conference of the Hungarian Communist Party. Stenographic minutes, 20–21 May 1945), PTI, Section 274 (bequests). Documents of the Central Committee of the Hungarian Communist Party; see also *Szabad Nép*, 23 May 1945.

43 Dezsö Nemes, *Magyarország felszabadulása* (The liberation of Hungary), 2nd edn, Budapest, Kossuth, 1960, p. 61.

44 János Kádár, 'A Kommunisták Magyarországi pártja feloszlatása körülményeinek és a Bekepart munkájának néhány kérdéséről, 1943 junius–1944 szeptember' (Some questions concerning the circumstances of the dissolution of the Party of Hungarian Communists and the activities of the Peace Party, June 1943–September 1944), *PTK*, vol. 2, no. 3, Oct. 1956, pp. 20–6.

45 See Pintér, *A magyar kommunisták a Hitler-ellenes nemzeti egységért* p. 239.

46 Note that it is very rare indeed for official historiographers of a Communist Party in power to adopt so critical an attitude to a party leader still in office.

47 *Magyar-Brit titkos tárgyalások 1943-ban* (Secret Hungarian–British negotiations in 1943). Documents collated, arranged and introduced by Gyula Juhász, Budapest, Kossuth, 1978; among the many personal accounts, see particularly György Barcza, 'A svájci misszió' (The mission in Switzerland), in *Uj Látóhatár*, Munich, 1983. See also Péter Gosztonyi, 'Magyarország a második világháboruban' (Hungary in the Second World War), *Katolikus Szemle* (Catholic Review), 2–3, 1983.

48 See particularly the pamphlets appealing to the peasantry in September 1943; another pamphlet, also published in September, calling for the overthrow of the government in favour of a 'national government' that would immediately sue

for peace; a memorandum sent by the Peace Party to the Social Democratic and Smallholders' parties in January 1944; and an editorial in *Béke és Szabadság* (Peace and Liberty) discussing this memorandum on 1 March 1944 – all in *Dokumentumok a magyar párttörténet tanulmányozásához*, vol. 5, nos. 97, 98, 110 and 111.

49 László Gyurkó, *Arcképvázlat történelmi háttérel* (Portrait sketch on a historical basis), Budapest, Magvető, 1982, p. 119.

50 Bajcsy-Zsilinszky then belonged to the most radical anti-fascist wing of his party and did not always have the ear of the other leaders. His party's middle-ranking cadres, by contrast, included several secret CP adherents and also a number of pro-Communist young intellectuals.

51 See *Dokumentumok a magyar párttörténet tanulmányozásához*, vol. 5, no. 94 (9 Aug. 1943).

52 Pintér, *A magyar kommunisták a Hitler-ellenes nemzeti egységért*, pp. 272–86.

53 Gyurkó, *Arcképvázlat történelmi háttérrel*, p. 122.

54 György Ránki, *1944 március 19: Magyarország német megszállása* (19 March 1944: the German occupation of Hungary), Budapest, Kossuth, 1968. See also the reports on the Hitler–Horthy meeting in Klessheim, in *Allianz Hitler–Horthy–Mussolini. Dokumente zur ungarischen Aussenpolitik, 1933–1944* (The Hitler–Horthy–Mussolini alliance. Hungarian foreign policy documents, 1933–1944), Budapest, Akadémiai Kiadó, 1966.

55 The actual armistice was not concluded with Horthy's representatives, although several members of the Hungarian delegation were invited to serve in the provisional government on their return to Hungary. The first chairman of that government, whose appointment was agreed during the negotiations between Molotov and Horthy's representatives in Moscow, was General Béla Miklós de Dálnok. Hungary did not break officially with Germany until 28 December and did not sign the armistice with the Allies until 20 January 1945. See *Treaty of Peace with Hungary, 1947*, Paris, 10 February 1947 (official text in Russian, English, French and Hungarian).

The negotiations conducted in Moscow between October and December 1944 were nevertheless of crucial importance to the creation of provisional institutions in liberated Hungary.

56 'A Kommunista Párt kiáltványa a magyar néphez' (Manifesto of the Hungarian Communist Party to the Hungarian People), Budapest, September 1944, a pamphlet included in *A Magyar Kommunista Párt és a Szociáldemokrata Párt határozatai 1944–1948* (Resolutions of the Hungarian Communist Party and of the Social Democratic Party, 1944–1948) (hereafter referred to as: *Resolutions*), Budapest, Kossuth, 1967, pp. 19–25.

57 Kállai, *Életem törvénye*, p. 585.

58 *Resolutions*, vol. 1, pp. 30–3; Gyula Kállai included a facsimile of the memorandum of agreement in his memoirs; see *Életem törvénye*, pp. 608–11.

59 In a communication to the School of Slavonic and East European Studies (July 1983), the historian György Schöpflin explained that the local political and administrative apparatus in most East European counries disintegrated at the end of the war, which facilitated the rise of Communist parties. See György Schöpflin, 'A kommunista hatalomátvétel fázisai Kelet-Europában' (The phases in the Communist seizure of power in Eastern Europe), in 'Nemzet és demokrácia Kelet-Európában' (Nation and democracy in Eastern Europe), Paris, *Magyar Füzetek* (Hungarian Notebooks) 13, 1984. Nevertheless, the Hungarian situation difffered slightly from that of the rest, not least because the Soviet authorities were interested in maintaining, albeit temporarily, whatever local institutions of the Horthy regime had survived the Nazi *putsch*.

Notes

Chapter 6: From Moscow to Budapest

1 Graham Ross (ed.), *The Foreign Office and the Kremlin. British Documents on Anglo-Soviet Relations 1941–1945*, Cambridge, Cambridge University Press, 1984; Charles Gati, 'Two Secret Meetings in Moscow in October 1944 and the Communist Quest for Power in Hungary', prepared for delivery at the annual meeting of the American Association for the Advancement of Slavic Studies in Columbus, Ohio, n.d.

2 See also Miklós Molnár, 'La révolution importée: Europe de l'Est (1944–1948)', in *Le système communiste: un monde en expansion*, ed. Pierre Kende, Dominique Moïsi and Illios Yannakakis, Paris, Institut français des relations internationales, 1982, pp. 33–52.

3 Cf. Chapters 2 and 3.

4 See *Dictionary*; *Selected Documents*, volumes published before 1973; cf. Branko Lazitch and Milorad M. Drachkovitch, *Biographical Dictionary of the Comintern*, Stanford, The Hoover Institution Press and Stanford University, 1973.

5 Endre Sik, *Viha a levelet* (The Storm Drives the Leaf), Budapest, Zrinyi, 1970.

6 See the manuscript of Zoltán Vas's autobiographical 'Nem a tejes csenget' (It isn't the milkman ringing), pp. 185f.

7 Borsányi, *Kun Béla*, p. 332.

8 Ibid., chap. 7, pp. 319–86. It should be remembered that this biography, which was withdrawn from Hungarian libraries, was the subject of an 80-page critique in *PTK*, vol. 3, 1979 (also published separately). Dezsö Nemes, the author of this critique, refuted Borsányi's interpretation of the facts rather than the facts themselves, except for some minor mistakes.

Among literary sources, see particularly Böhm, *Két forradalom tüzében*; Lajos Kassák's fictionalized memoirs, *Egy ember élete* (A man's life), vols. 7–8 covering 1918–19); several studies of József Lengyel's autobiographical notes in his two-volume *Mérni a mérhetetlent* (Measuring the unmeasurable), Budapest, Szépirodalmi, 1966; Béla Illés, *Ég a Tisza* (The Tisza is burning) (novel), Budapest, Szépirodalmi, 1966.

See also two works by Ervin Sinkó, a Hungarian writer resident in Yugoslavia. His novel *The Optimists* is based on the events of 1919, as are the above-mentioned writings of Böhm, Lengyel, Kassák and Illés. His journal, *Egy regény regénye* (The novel of a novel), 2 vols, Novi Sad, Forum, 1961, records Sinkó's stay in Moscow from 1935 to 1937 and his search for a publisher. Sinkó also includes his correspondence with Romain Rolland and an account of his meetings with the latter and with Béla Kun. See also Chapters 2 and 3 above.

9 Borsányi, *Kun Béla*, pp. 360–3; B. M. Leibzon and K. K. Sirinya, *Povorot v politike kominterna* (The turning-point in the policy of the Comintern), Moscow, Izdatelstvo Mysl, 1975; Hungarian translation, pp. 87f.

10 Borsányi, *Kun Béla*, p. 368.

11 Sinkó, *Egy regény regénye*, entry for March 1936. Sinkó also reports that, when he accompanied Malraux to the House of Soviet Writers, Malraux looked at the large hall full of people and then asked: 'And all that lot write?'

12 See Chapter 4 above.

13 Arvo Tuominen, *The Bells of the Kremlin*, Hanover and London, University Press of New England, 1983, pp. 221–4.

14 Sinkó, *Egy regény regénye*, pp. 329–31. Sinkó reproduces this personal communication from Romain Rolland in Hungarian translation.

15 Dimitrov is said to have explained Szántó's dismissal in resigned terms: 'What can you do? After all, a dozen or so of your near relatives have been placed under arrest.' True or false, this anecdote is a good illustration of the climate in Moscow in 1938 and also of the criteria used for promotion and demotion.

16 According to Philippe Robrieux, *Histoire intérieure du Parti communiste*, vol. 1, p. 382, Eugène Fried, Thorez's future *éminence grise*, arrived in Paris accompanied by Anna Pauker and Ernö Gerö.

17 See Zoltán Vas, 'Nem a tejes csenget', pp. 40–6, 64–6, 301, 444ff.

18 Several writers have mentioned his arrogant attitude to his comrades prior to his arrest, and also his carelessness in choosing collaborators, one of whom, Lajos Sámuel, was in fact an agent of Horthy's police. See *inter alia* Nándor Szekér, *Föld alatt és föld felett*, pp. 264–88. Several of his co-detainees in Szeged gaol also objected to his selfish and haughty behaviour (personal communications).

   According to Vas, though Rákosi's behaviour at the trial was criticized, no one ever accused him of betraying his comrades. Cf. Vas, 'Nem a tejes csenget', p. 43.

19 István Pintér, *A Magyar Front és az ellenállás* (The Hungarian Front and the Resistance), Budapest, Kossuth, 1970; Mihály Korom, *Magyarország ideiglenes nemzeti kormánya és a fegyverszünet (1944–1945)* (The Hungarian provisional government and the armistice (1944–1945)), Budapest, Akadémiai Kiadó, 1981, pp. 78–86, 117–18; *Dokumentumok a magyar forradalmi munkásmozgalom történetéböl, 1935–1945* (Documents from the history of the Hungarian revolutionary workers' movement, 1935–1945), Budapest, Kossuth, 1964. Cf. Chapter 5 above.

20 Korom, *Magyarország ideiglenes nemzeti kormánya*, pp. 237–43.

21 Among the many general works on the armistice negotiations, see particularly Károly Vigh, *Ugrás a sötétbe* (A leap in the dark), Budapest, Magvetö, 1984. See also György Ránki, *A második világháboru története* (History of the Second World War), Budapest, Gondolat, 1976, pp. 442–63; Gyula Juhász, *Magyarország külpolitikája (1919–1945)* (Hungary's foreign policy, 1919–1945), Budapest, 1968; Mihály Korom, *Magyarország ideiglenes nemzeti kormánya*; Miklós Horthy, *Emlékirataim* (Memoirs), Buenos Aires, 1953; Péter Gosztonyi, 'A magyar-szovjet fegyverszüneti tárgyalások' (The Soviet–Hungarian armistice negotiations), in *Uj Látóhatár*, vol. 5, 1969; and the many sources acknowledged in that article. See also some of the memoirs mentioned in the bibliography. Finally, for a fictionalized but very well-documented version of the events, see András Simonffy, *Kompország katonái* (The ferry soldiers), Budapest, Magvetö, 1981.

22 For the negotiations, see Ross, *The Foreign Office and the Kremlin*.

23 See particularly Korom, *Magyarország ideiglenes nemzeti kormánya*.

24 Ibid., p. 209.

25 The Soviets were, of course, anxious to choose people who had crossed the line literally as well as figuratively rather than men in the regent's personal circle. *Inter alia*, they started negotiations with such leading political personalities as Count István Bethlen, the former prime minister. See Zoltán Vas, *Viszontagságos életem* (My chequered life), Budapest, Magvetö, 1980. Vas met Count Bethlen while the latter was still under surveillance by the Soviet military authorities. The idea of the count's possible participation in the political life of his country was eventually abandoned, probably by both parties. The former prime minister, who had held no government office for almost fifteen years and who was known to have pro-Western sympathies, was then taken to the Soviet Union and kept there under close guard until his death.

26 In his *Viszontagságos*, Zoltán Vas even claims that 'Rákosi and Gerö knew nothing about it [the negotiations]. Molotov kept it secret even from them that the [Horthy's] generals were in Moscow.' Though Vas's testimony must be treated with some reservation, it does reflect the utter bafflement of Hungarian émigrés when, after a quarter of a century of struggle against the Horthy regime, the Kremlin asked them to come to terms with the regent's representatives. Cf. Zoltán Vas, 'Nem a tejes csenget', pp. 300f.

Notes

27 Korom, *Magyarország ideiglenes nemzeti kormánya*, pp. 243ff.
28 Ibid., p. 263.
29 See Chapter 7.
30 My authority is Korom, *Magyarország ideiglenes nemzeti kormánya*, pp. 323–50. In the absence of minutes, Korom has had to rely on what personal testimony he was able to collect.
31 In 1943 differences also arose between the Soviet leaders and the Hungarian Communists about the use of Hungarian military units in the war against Nazi Germany. After Stalingrad, the Hungarian émigrés wanted to set up a Hungarian Legion recruited from Hungarian prisoners of war, but the Soviet authorities demurred. The same thing happened again after the start of the armistice negotiations in the autumn of 1944. Thus, neither did the First Hungarian Army under the command of General Béla Miklós de Dálnok receive orders to attack the Germans until after the general had gone over to the Russians, nor did the Russian leaders agree to the recruitment of Hungarian prisoners of war. The Rumanians were treated much more handsomely, and not only because they had returned to the fray earlier and more effectively, but also because the Soviet Union was anxious to compensate Bucharest for the annexation of Bessarabia and northern Bukovina. This also explains why Rumania was awarded northern Transylvania by the 1947 treaty.
32 Korom, *Magyarország ideiglenes nemzeti kormánya*, pp. 264–6.
33 Bálint Szabó, *Népi demokrácia és forradalomelmélet* (People's democracy and revolutionary theory), Budapest, Kossuth, 1979, p. 94.
34 Zoltán Vas was the only one among the émigrés back from Moscow to speak very frankly about the party's so-called democratic programme. In connection with the friction between the 'Muscovites' and Communist veterans at home dumbfounded by the new programme, he mentions that one of the latter asked him: 'Tell me, Comrade Vas, what is the truth about that Hungarian Independence Front of yours? How much longer are we to tell the masses that we don't want the dictatorship of the proletariat?' And Zoltán Vas goes on to explain that all these programmes were no more than tactical moves to reach the party's true objective, namely, the dictatorship of the proletariat. 'We, the Hungarian émigrés back form Moscow, had all been taught at the time of the Hungarian Soviet Republic to look forward to the dictatorship of the proletariat. We had continued to nourish that hope in Moscow. And five years later, in 1948, ditching all our other programmes, we made it at long last.' Vas, 'Nem a tejes csenget', pp. 307f.

Chapter 7: The Totalitarian Road

1 Berend and Ránki, *Hungary. A Century of Economic Development*, pp. 180–2.
2 According to official Hungarian statistics, the figure was 9,317,000 in 1941. See *Statisztikai Évkönyv 1981* (1981 Statistical Yearbook), Budapest, Központi Statisztikai Hivatal, 1982, p. 1.
3 Mihály Korom, 'A magyar népi demokrácia elsö évei, 1944–1948' (The first years of the Hungarian Peoples' Democracy, 1944–1948), in *Valóság*, vol. 27, no. 3, 1984, pp. 1–9.
4 Here we shall disregard the Gypsy question, which did not cause concern until about ten years after the war, when the high birth rate of this group was widely discussed.
5 Paul Lendvai, *L'antisémitisme sans Juifs*, Paris, Fayard, 1971, pp. 34, 321, 347.
6 Ferenc Donáth, *Demokratikus földreform Magyarországon 1945–1947* (Democratic land reform in Hungary 1945–1947), Budapest, Akadémiai Kiadó, 1969; *A népi*

Magyarország negyed százada (A quarter of a century of People's Hungary), Budapest, Akadémiai Kiadó, 1972.

7 *The Peace Treaty with Hungary, 1947* (from official French text).

8 For a year and a half, Hungary suffered unprecedented inflation. Prices and wages reached astronomic levels: a chunk of bread cost millions of milliards pengös. Paper money became useless currency within hours of peace being declared; Hungarians worked for practically nothing until the currency was stabilized in 1946, when the pengö was replaced with the new forint. Until then, the economy was based on barter, on the black market and on wild speculation; the government was reduced to trading in foreign currency and to engaging in other more or less illegal transactions so as to build up the foreign currency reserves. The new forint was equivalent to 400,000 quadrillion (4×10^{27}) pengös.

9 For instance György Marosán, who also tells us in his memoirs which bear the significant title *Az úton végig kell menni* (One must go to the end of the road), Budapest, Magvetö, 1972, pp. 65, 66, 79 and *passim*, that he was acting under the orders of Mátyás Rákosi, the then leader of the Communist Party.

The other parties also included several secret Communists. Thus, among the Smallholders' ministers and secretaries of state, János Gyöngyösi, minister of foreign affairs, István Dobi, minister and later prime minister, Ferenc Z. Nagy (not to be confused with Ferenc Nagy, the prime minister until 1947), and Gyula Ortutay, were all said to have been secret members of the Communist Party – according to Zoltán Vas at least. See 'Nem a tejes csenget', (It isn't the milkman ringing), pp. 325, 483 and *passim*.

10 These adjectives do little more than define attitudes to the CP. The pro-Communist wing was led by József Darvas and Ferenc Erdei.

11 In fact, the (Catholic) People's Democratic Party was eventually given leave to participate in the elections, but by then it was too late. Its members accordingly decided to present themselves on the Smallholders' list.

12 See 'The Hungarian Communist Party's Path to Power, 1944–1948' by the Israeli historian Yehuda Lahav; PhD thesis, Hebrew University, Jerusalem, 1976, pp. 198–206. Yehuda Lahav quotes numerous witnesses and also the Foreign Office archives.

13 As in Bulgaria and in Rumania, the British and American members of the commission took a back seat in Hungary, unlike what happened in Italy where the Soviet representative played second fiddle after the 1943 armistice. For the Italian case, see Bruno Arcidiacono, *Le 'précédent italien' et les origines de la guerre froide. Les Alliés et l'occupation de l'Italie, 1943–1944*, Brussels, Bruylant, 1984.

14 There were isolated attacks on Communist officials, but no concerted campaign against the CP.

15 The reputation of the CP probably suffered more from these thefts, robberies and rapes than it gained from Red Army aid to a number of popular causes. It is impossible to arrive at any definitive conclusion in this area.

16 See François Fejtö, *Histoire des démocraties populaires*, Paris, Le Seuil, 1969; and also *Le coup de Prague 1948*, Paris, Le Seuil, 1976.

17 Cf. the writings of François Fejtö, Hugh Seton-Watson and Stephen D. Kertesz listed in the bibliography below.

18 Mátyás Rákosi, *Válogatott beszédek és cikkek* (Selected speeches and articles), Budapest, Szikra, 1952, quoted by Lahav in 'Hungarian CP's Path to Power', p. 226. The quoted passage has been omitted from the 1955 Hungarian edition of Rákosi's book.

19 During the events of 1956, Kovács resumed leadership of his old party and adopted an exceptionally moderate line.

20 *Legyözhetetlen erö.*

21 See *inter alia* Lukács, *Schriften zur Literatursoziologie*; József Révai, *Literarische Studien*, Berlin, Dietz, 1956. Cf. Tamás Aczél and Tibor Méray, *La révolte de l'esprit*, Paris, Gallimard, 1968, and Miklós Molnár, *Budapest 1956. A History of the Hungarian Revolution*, London, George Allen & Unwin, 1971. It is impossible to go fully into this complex subject here, except to remark that the party, while exploiting public attachment to the literary tradition, was careful to exclude classical writers known to be conservative or 'lukewarm'. The party's new slogan 'Our banner is Petöfi's' emphasized the revolutionary tradition at the expense of a less flamboyant but equally important heritage.

22 Little known in the Western world, István Bibó is the most original thinker of that generation. In his essays, he examines the heavy burden of Hungarian conservatism and also discusses the Jewish question, the definition and essence of the new democracy, the role of the Communist Party and the problem of local administration. See István Bibó, *Összegyüjtött munkái* (Collected works), ed. István Kemény and Mátyás Sárközi, 4 vols, Berne, Protestáns Magyar Szabadegyetem, 1981–3.

23 See László Kardos (ed.), *Sej, a mi lobogónkat . . .*, on people's colleges.

24 Cf. *inter alia* Dominique Gros's unpublished thesis, 'Les conseils ouvriers, espérances et défaites de la révolution en Autriche-Hongrie. 1917–1920', University of Dijon, n.d.

25 The reality was more confused still: in many places, the former town clerks, magistrates or police chiefs also interfered with the workings of the committees.

26 *A Budapesti Nemzeti Bizottság jegyzökönyvei 1945–1946* (Minutes of the Budapest National Committee, 1945–1946), Budapest, Source Publications, City of Budapest Archives, 1975. For the whole question, see Béla Balázs, *Népmozgalom és nemzeti bizottságok 1945–1946* (The people's movement and the national committees 1945–1946), Budapest, Kossuth, 1961.

27 *A Budapesti Nemzeti Bizottság.* See also Ágnes Ságvári, *Népfront és koalició Magyarországon 1936–1948* (Popular Front and coalition in Hungary 1936–1948), Budapest, Kossuth, 1967, pp. 113–18.

28 Szabó, *Népi démokrácia és forradalomelmélet*, pp. 84–5.

29 Ferenc Erdei, its general secretary who was close to the CP, considered these territorial committees the basis of a new form of state, of a system of popular self-government. See his 'On the road to popular self-government' published in *Néplap* (People's Daily) on 31 Dec. 1944. Quoted by Ságvári in *Népfront és koalició*, p. 118.

30 See particularly William O. McCagg, *Communism and Hungary, 1944–1955*, New York, Columbia University Press, 1964. Cf. the various theses examined in Yehuda Lahav, 'The Hungarian CP's Path to Power'.

31 See *Dictionary*, under 'Demény, Pál'.

32 The clandestine *Szabad Nép*, in its Dec. 1944 issue (vol. 4), launched a vigorous attack on the leftists who were organizing a (new) Party of Hungarian Communists, and whose politics and tactics were 'opposed in several respects to the policies and tactics of the Communist Party' (i.e. the Moscow-based party). The article describes the negotiations, at the end of which the dissident party was said to have dissolved itself.

33 *Demény Pál visszaemlékezése* (Memoirs of Pál Demény) recorded on magnetic tape.

34 Cf. Zoltán Vas's memoirs, *Akkori önmagunkról* (What we were then), Budapest, Magvetö, 1981, pp. 124–6.

35 Rákosi, Apró, Bandúr, Donáth, Farkas, Gerö, Horváth, Kállai, Kádár, Kiss, Kossa, Kovács, Mme Kovács, Nagy, Oszip, Papp, Péter, Rajk, Révai, Mme J. Szabó, Mme P. Szabó, Szobek, Vas and Zgyerka. See *A Magyar Kommunista Párt I. Országos értekezlete. Gyorsirói jegyzökönyv 1945 május 20–21* (First National

Conference of the Hungarian Communist Party. Stenographic minutes 20–1 May 1945), PTI, Section, 274f.

36 *A Magyar Kommunista Párt és a Szociáldemokrata Párt határozatai 1944–1948*, p. 84.

37 Several historians have mistakenly included István Kossa among the 'Muscovites'. In fact, Kossa, who was taken prisoner on the Russian front in 1942, was not a member of the émigré establishment.

38 In his unpublished memoirs, Zoltán Vas also describes the dissensions and rivalries between the 'Muscovites' themselves. According to him, as we mentioned earlier, Gerö was Moscow's creature even more than Rákosi. He had even set his sights on taking first place in the party hierarchy though he did not openly intrigue against Rákosi. Farkas, too, is said to have been in a strong position thanks largely to his close links with Beria. That would have made Révai No. Four in the hierarchy, despite the fact that he was intellectually superior to the rest. (Farkas, who came from the Hungarian part of Czechoslovakia, knew even less about conditions in Hungary than the others.) As for Vas himself, he is said to have come lower down on the list of leaders despite the fact that he had been Rákosi's prison comrade. This was because of his Jewish origins – there were apparently too many Jews as it was. See Zoltán Vas, 'Nem a tejes csenget', pp. 40–4, 301, 444–6.

39 All these documents corroborate the presence of Kádár in the leading party organizations. Kádár was personally blamed for the dissolution of the party in 1943 and for the subsequent formation of the Peace Party. The charges were communicated to him by Ernö Gerö in a peremptory manner that brooked no argument. Apparently it was Rákosi's return that helped Kádár to climb back on to the party ladder with the relatively humble appointment as police vice-captain in Budapest. See Kádár's confidences in László Gyurkó, *Arcképvázlat történelmi háttérrel*, pp. 140–42. Cf. Zoltán Vas, *Akkori önmagunkról*, pp. 37f., 43f., 109–12 and 125f. Vas confirms that Gëro took a hard line with his Hungarian comrades, whereas Rákosi adopted a friendly and trusting attitude. As for Kádár's appointment as assistant police chief of Budapest, Vas claims that he himself proposed Kádár as chief of police but that Kádár preferred to take second place to László Sólyom for reasons of personal modesty. The latter, a former army officer and courageous resistance fighter, later became a victim of the trial Rákosi unleashed against Rajk and many other members of the 'home-based' party. Not much later, their fate was shared by Kádár and another group of veteran Communists. The conflict between the 'Muscovites' and their 'home-based' comrades was not therefore closed with the appointment of the latter to various political posts in 1945.

40 I refer to personal conversations in 1975 and 1983 with two former members of the Central Committee and also to my own experiences in the party from 1947 to 1956.

41 Sándor Nógrádi, *Avant 56. Chronique Hongroise*, Paris, Éditions du Pavillon, 1969, pp. 192f.

42 See the recapitulation of these discussions in Lahav, 'Hungarian CP's Path to Power', chap. 7.

43 The two previous congresses were those of the Party of Hungarian Communists held respectively in Vienna in 1925 and near Moscow in 1930.

44 Quoted in Lahav, 'Hungarian CP's Path to Power', pp. 270–89 of the Hungarian translation of the MS.

45 Ibid. for the relevant quotations.

46 In a 'Manifesto to the Working People of Hungary', distributed at the end of Jan. 1945, the provisional executive of the SDP nevertheless declared its intention to work for future union with the CP in 'a revolutionary workers' party'. *Resolutions*, document 13.

Notes

47 *Népszava*, 13 Aug. 1947, quoted in Lahav, 'Hungarian CP's Path to Power', p. 320.

48 György Marosán, Imre Vajda, Pál Justus, Ferencz Révész, Pál Schiffer and Zoltán Horváth made up this group. Antal Bán, by contrast, kept aloof and accepted the post of assistant general secretary of the party, the better to defend it against Communist attacks.

49 Cf. François Fejtö, 'Un itinéraire d'historien', *Contrepoint*, vol. 13, Feb. 1974.

50 Rákosi declared, most prominently in an article in *Szabad Nép* on 16 Jan. 1949, that 'the People's Democracy . . . is the dictatorship of the proletariat without the Soviet form'. He went on to confess that 'we Hungarian Communists, failed to examine in full the question of the nature, role and development of our people's democracy . . . Some comrades, while pointing out what we have in common with the Soviet form of the dictatorship, have laid too much emphasis on what separates [us] from it.' Rákosi, *Válogatott beszédek és cikkek*, pp. 263 and 268.

51 *A magyar forradalmi munkásmozgalom története*, vol. 3, pp. 197f.

52 Joseph Révai, *La littérature et la démocratie populaire. A propos de G. Lukács*, Paris, Nouvelle Critique, 1950, pp. 8–11.

53 See particularly Ágnes Ságvári, 'A magyar kül- és belpolitika néhány összefüggéséröl a népi demokratikus forradalom idöszakában' (Some questions of Hungarian foreign and home policy during the period of the people's democratic revolution), in *Századok* 6, 1972, pp. 1336f. and 1361–5; and also her article 'Népfront és proletárdiktatura', in *Történelmi Szelme* (History Review), vol. 9, no. 2, pp. 204–26.

54 Among others, Ágnes Ságvári, the Hungarian historian quoted above. See also Lilly Marcou, *Le Kominform*, Paris, Presses de la Fondation nationale des sciences politiques, 1977, p. 42, alleging that the future policy of the parties was laid down at the founders' meeting at Szklarska Poreba in Sept. 1947. Lilly Marcou bases her view, *inter alia*, on a document quoted by Ágnes Ságvári and by Bálint Szabó, another Hungarian historian. That document is said to be the minutes of the Szklarska Poreba meeting or the Hungarian report of that meeting intended for the internal use of the HCP.

55 Quoted in Ágnes Ságvári, 'A Magyar kül- és belpolitika', p. 1351.

56 Ibid., p. 1365. Á. Ságvári refers to a document in the PTI archives, viz. 247f. 1/13/191.

57 Ibid. The reference to the leaders of the MDP is explained by the fact that Ágnes Ságvári gives a general appreciation of the party including the period when it was part of the unified Magyar Dolgozók Pártja (MDP), the Hungarian Workers' Party.

58 Ibid., p. 1363.

59 Szabó, *Népi demokrácia és forradalomelmélet*, pp. 171–90ff.

60 Ibid., pp. 192f.

61 Ibid., pp. 232–5.

62 Ibid., pp. 245–50. In the preceding pages, Bálint Szabó also analyses the report by József Révai, which takes more or less the same line. It was presented to the Sept. 1948 Party Conference devoted to educational problems.

63 Szabó, *Népi demokrácia és forradalomelmélet*, pp. 246f.

Chapter 8: Stalinism in Action

1 The nationalization of enterprises employing more than 100 persons was decreed on 25 Mar. 1948. At the end of 1949, the decree was extended to enterprises with more than 10 employees.

2 According to the official Statistical Yearbook, a total of 1,593,851 Hungarian

citizens were prosecuted between 1948 and 1955, 862,797 being found guilty. Most of these cases were 'offences involving state property'. The number of sentences for political offences is not recorded, nor is that of administrative detentions by the secret police. See *Statisztikai évkönyv 1949–1955* (Statistical Yearbook), Budapest, Központi Statisztikai Hivatal, pp. 355–8.

3 *L'affaire Rajk*. Shorthand minutes of the proceedings of the People's Court, Budapest, 16–24 Sept. 1949, with a Preface by Pierre Courtade, Paris, Éditeurs français réunis, 1949.

4 Released from detention in 1954, Noel Field never returned to the United States. Until his death he worked in a Budapest publishing house. In 1961, he published his reminiscences in the US review, *Mainstream*, and also in the Hungarian literary review *Kortárs*, without mentioning his part in the trial. He does, however, describe his first meeting with his wife on his release. '"Is Stalin still alive?" I asked her. – "No, he has been dead for a year." – We again burst into sobs.'

5 For the workings, significance and function of the trials, see Annie Kriegel, *Les grands procès dans les systèmes communistes: un monde en expansion*, Paris, Gallimard, 1972; cf. Stephen Fischer-Galati (ed.), *The Communist Parties of Eastern Europe*, New York, Columbia University Press, 1979. For the links between the Gomulka, Dzodze, Patrascanu, Rajk, Kostov, Slansky, Pauker– Luca–Georgescu and Marty–Tillon affairs, see Lilly Marcou, *Le Kominform*, pp. 244–8.

6 See especially François Fejtö's articles on the Rajk trial and also his *Histoire des démocraties populaires*, 1972.

7 *L'affaire Rajk*, pp. 373, 392.

8 For a staggering eyewitness account of the trial, see Vincent Savarius (the pseudonym of Béla Szász), *Volontaires pour l'échafaud*, Paris, Lettres Nouvelles/ Juilliard, 1963.

9 Ibid., pp. 198f.

10 State intervention was reflected even more clearly in the fact that the whole of economic life was subjected to control by the Supreme Economic Council, a government agency. In particular, industry derived 75 per cent of its revenues from state orders. Its dependence on the state was thus very strong even before the nationalization of private enterprise. Cf. Sándor Szakács, 'A népi demokrácia gazdaságpolitikája Magyarországon 1945–1948' (The economic policy of the Hungarian people's democracy, 1945–1948), in *A népi Magyarország negyedszázada*, pp. 225–43.

11 *Statisztikai évkönyv 1981* (Statistical Yearbook), Budapest, Központi Statisztikai Hivatal, 1982, p. 3.

12 It should be recalled that the HCP adopted the name of Hungarian Workers' Party (Magyar Dolgozók Pártja – MDP) on merging with the SDP in 1948. The congress at which this merger was ratified was therefore the Second Congress of the united party. After 1956, the party, under its new name of Hungarian Socialist Workers' Party (Magyar Szocialista Munkáspárt – MSzMP), numbered its congresses beginning with the First HCP Congress held in 1925.

13 István Barta, 'A szocialista iparosítás eredményei és problémái az elsö ötéves terv idöszakában' (The results and problems of socialist industrialization during the First Five-Year Plan), in *A népi Magyarország negyedszázada*, pp. 273–87.

14 Sándor Orbán, *Két agrárforradalom Magyaroszágon (Demokratikus és szocialista agrárátalakulás 1945–1961)* (Two agrarian revolutions in Hungary: the democratic and socialist transformations of agriculture, 1945–1961), Budapest, Akadémiai Kiadó, 1972, pp. 91–113.

15 Here we need merely recall the writings of François Fejtö (see Bibliography below), the journals *Esprit* and *Les Temps modernes* and the testimony of Tamás Aczél and Tibor Méray in *La révolte de l'esprit*.

16 József Révai, *Kulturális forradalmunk kérdései* (The problems of our cultural revolution), Budapest, Szikra, 1952. See also Miklós Molnár, *Budapest 1956. A History of the Hungarian Revolution.*

17 The stage, the cinema, the arts, music and architecture were also purged of 'bourgeois', 'decadent' and 'cosmopolitan' elements, just as literature was. Here we cannot list all the victims of these purges. The method and spirit of this 'rectification' campaign were based on those used by Zhdanov in the Soviet Union.

18 Pierre Hassner, 'Le totalitarisme vu de l'Ouest', in Guy Hermet, Pierre Hassner and Jacques Rupnik (eds), *Totalitarismes*, Paris, Economica, 1988.

Chapter 9: Imre Nagy and the 1956 Revolution

1 The delegation was in Moscow on 13 and 14 June 1953 and included Rákosi, Gerö, Imre Nagy, András Hegedüs, István Hidas, Rudolf Földvári, Béla Szalai and István Dobi. After the delegation's return home, the Central Committee was summoned to an extraordinary meeting, which was held on 27 and 28 June. The reports, discussions and resolutions of that meeting have never been published in full. In 1984 (10th issue) the *samizdat* publication *Beszélö* was the first to publish the report presented by Imre Nagy on 27 June; another *samizdat* publication, *A Hirmondó*, published the resolution in 1985 (2nd issue).

2 Zoltán Vas, 'Nem a tejes csenget', pp. 577f.

3 Imre Nagy, *Un communisme qui n'oublie pas l'homme* with a preface by François Fejtö entitled 'Un communiste qui a choisi le peuple', Paris, Plon, 1957. This publication is an abridged version of the memoirs Imre Nagy wrote in 1955–6 while he was excluded from the party and from political life. See Imre Nagy, *A magyar nép védelmében* (In defence of the Hungarian people), n.p., n.d.; new edition: *A magyar nép védelmében, Vitairatok és beszédek 1955–1956*, Paris, A Magyar Füzetek kiadása, 1984.

4 Nagy, *Un communisme qui n'oublie pas l'homme*, p. 216.

5 Thanks largely to a cut of the compulsory delivery quota, which had often meant the total requisition of the entire harvest and livestock, including the part reserved for peasant families.

6 The Péter affair has never been fully clarified. It seems that he was arrested and closely questioned in February 1953 on the orders of Rákosi – who was keen to see the back of a man who had been his right hand in all the political trials held since 1945. Péter was accused of being a spy and a Zionist agent, like the 'terrorists in white coats', the Jewish doctors who were being tried in the Soviet Union at the time, and like Rudolf Slansky, who had just been executed (in December 1952). It appears that Rákosi had a hand in all these trials. After Stalin's death and the rehabilitation of the alleged 'Zionist terrorists' in April 1953, Péter was investigated for alleged Titoist activities. Not long afterwards, in July, he was alleged to have been Beria's Hungarian agent and, according to Rákosi who alluded to the affair in several of his later speeches, sentenced as such. Rákosi, moreover, refused to accept any responsibility for his right-hand man's actions in the Rajk affair. Péter, who had also been in charge of the Kádár inquiry in 1951, was released from prison in 1959.

7 *Szabad Nép*, 20 Oct. 1954.

8 On 23 Oct. 1954 the Paris agreement opened the way for West Germany's entry into NATO.

9 Imre Nagy, *Un communisme qui n'oublie pas l'homme*.

10 See András Hegedüs, *Élet egy eszme árnyékában. Életrajzi interju Készitette: Zsille Zoltán* (A life in the shadow of an ideal. Biography in interview form by Zoltán

Zsille), Vienna, Zoltán Zsille, 1985, p. 242.

11 François Fejtö, *1956 Budapest, l'insurrection: La première révolution antitotalitaire,* Brussels, Complexe, 1981.

12 For the events of 1956 see particularly United Nations Organization, *Report of the Special Committee on the Hungarian question, General Assembly of UNO. Official Documents: 11th Session,* New York, UNO, 1957; *The counter-revolutionary forces in the October events in Hungary* (White Book, vols 1–4), Information Office of the Council of Ministers of the Hungarian People's Republic, Budapest, n.d.; *Nagy Imre és büntársai ellenforradalmi összeesküvése* (The counter-revolutionary conspiracy of Imre Nagy and his accomplices) (White Book, vol. 5), Information Office of the Council of Ministers of the Hungarian People's Republic, Budapest, n.d.; Melvin Laski and François Bondi (eds), *La révolution hongroise,* Paris, Plon, 1957; Balázs Nagy, J.-J. Marie and Pierre Broue (eds), *Pologne–Hongrie,* Paris, Études et documentations internationales, 1966; *La vérité sur l'affaire Nagy,* Paris, Plon, 1958; Hungaricus, *Full text of a study by 'Hungaricus', written, published and distributed clandestinely among progressive circles in Hungary,* Brussels, Institut Imre Nagy de sciences politiques, 1959; 'Second part of the text by Hungaricus', Budapest, February 1957 (Hungarian manuscript in the author's possession); Imre Nagy, *Un communisme qui n'oublie pas l'homme*; János Kádár, *Szilárd népi hatalom: független Magyarország* (Solid people's power: independent Hungary, collected addresses), Budapest, Kossuth, 1959; *A forradalom sajtója* (The press of the revolution), reproduction of 1956 newspapers, collected and published by Ernö Nagy, Giromagny, 1983. See also the Bibliography at the end of this book.

13 *A magyar forradalom és szabadságharc a hazai rádióadások tükrében, 1956 október 23–november 9* (The revolution and the struggle for freedom as reflected in Hungarian radio transmissions), New York, Free Europe Press, n.d.

14 Meeting during the night of 23 October, the Central Committee co-opted, apart from Nagy, the philosopher Georg Lukács, Ferenc Donáth and Géza Losonczy, all close to Nagy, together with Ferenc Münnich. Among the old members of the committee, Nagy could count on the support of a very small group only. Donáth and Losonczy, for their part, refused to accept the nomination for four days, holding out for more radical changes.

15 See particularly László Földes, *A második vonalban* (In the second line), Budapest, Kossuth, 1984; *A magyar forradalmi munkásmozgalom története,* vol. 3, p. 238.

16 Several Hungarian historians allege that it was only Imre Nagy's 'sabotage' that prevented the party and the armed forces loyal to him from suppressing the 'counter-revolution'. See, for instance, János Molnár, *Ellenforradalom Magyarországon 1956-ban. A polgári magyarázatok birálata* (Counter-revolution in Hungary in 1956: a critique of bourgeois interpretations), Budapest, Akadémiai Kiadó, 1967; J. Sólyom and F. Zele, *Harcban az ellenforradalommal* (Fighting the counter-revolution), Budapest, Móra, 1957. We lack the space to go into this controversial question. The present author's own view is based on the fact that, apart from isolated skirmishes, the insurgents were opposed by Soviet forces alone. It is implausible that 'sabotage' or opposition by the prime minister would have been capable of stopping determined Communists from making common cause with the Red Army.

17 In particular, the two newly co-opted members of the Central Committee, namely Géza Losonczy and Ferenc Donáth, who had held back because they disagreed with its policies, and the journalists Miklós Gimes, József Szilágyi and Miklós Vásárhelyi.

18 There were three ministerial reshuffles – on 27 and 30 Oct. and on 3 Nov. The first introduced several persons less compromised than the old ministers. The cabinet appointed on 30 Oct. consisted of three Communists (Nagy, Kádár and

Losonczy), two members of the Smallholder's Party (Zoltán Tildy, a former President of the Republic, and Béla Kovács, a former secretary of his party), one representative of the Peasant Party (Ferenc Erdei) and one post kept vacant for the Social Democrats, who refused to accept it on the grounds that the measures taken by the government were inadequate. On 3 Nov. the cabinet assumed the form of a four-party coalition, modelled on the 1945–8 coalition, with four Communists and eight ministers drawn from the other parties.

19 Claude Lefort, *L'invention démocratique. Les limites de la domination totalitaire*, Paris, Fayard, 1981.

20 Jacques Levesque, 'Les effets du conflit sino-soviétique sur les relations entre l'URSS et les démocraties populaires de Pologne et Roumanie', thesis, Paris, Fondation nationale des sciences politiques, 1968.

21 Veljko Mićunović, *Journées de Moscou 1956–1958*, Paris, Laffont, 1979.

22 N. Khrushchev, *Khrushchev Remembers*, New York, Littlejohn, 1971. Quoted from p. 401 of the French edition.

23 See pp. 163–5 above.

24 *A magyar forradalom és szabadságharc a hazai rádióadások*, radio transmissions on 1 Nov. 1956, p. 277.

25 Ibid., p. 278.

Chapter 10: The Kádár Régime

1 Other members took refuge elsewhere. István Bibó, a minister belonging to the Petöfi Party (the former National Peasant Party), remained in the parliament building and issued a protest note from there.

2 *Legyözhetetlen erö*, p. 236.

3 According to official figures, 17 persons were expelled from the party for 'illegal conduct' and 6 more for having plotted with Rákosi and Gerö. See *A Magyar Szocialista Munkáspárt Központi Bizottságának határozata a személyi kultusz éveiben a munkásmozgalmi emberek ellen inditott törvénysértö perek lezárásáról* (Resolution of the Hungarian Socialist Workers' Party on winding up the illegal trials staged during the years of the personality cult against members of the workers' movement), Budapest, Kossuth, 1962.

4 The minutes are included in the Bibliography below.

5 Iván Szenes, *A kommunista párt ujjászervezése Magyarországon 1956–1957* (The reorganization of the Hungarian Communist Party, 1956–1957), Budapest, Kossuth, 1976.

6 See particularly the first collection of articles by János Kádár, *Szilárd népi hatalom*, which begins with an address delivered by János Kádár on 16 Jan. 1957, on the occasion of a visit by a Chinese delegation.

7 Party publications also omit the first two texts issued by the new party government, namely 'Felhivás a magyar néphez' (Appeal to the Hungarian people) by the revolutionary workers' and peasants' government, and 'Magyar kommunisták: A Magyar Dolgozók Partjának tagjai: Elvtársak' (Hungarian Communists: Members of the Hungarian Workers' Party: Comrades), a manifesto showing sympathy with the revolution (indicated in the very name of 'revolutionary government') and also with former comrades in the MDP who were anxious to break with the Rákosi past. These appeals are missing from the *A Magyar Szocialista Munkáspárt határozatai és dokumentumai 1956–1962* (Resolutions and documents of the Hungarian Socialist Workers' Party 1956–1962), 3rd edn, Budapest, Kossuth, 1979. They do, however, appear in facsimile in Iván Szenes, *A kommunistapárt ujjászervezése.*

8 Many of the negotiations between the Nagy group and Kádár's representatives

Notes

were conducted through intermediaries, Nagy and his friends rejecting all compromises. Finally, on 21 Nov., in a letter addressed to the Yugoslav embassy, János Kádár promised that Nagy and his friends would be allowed to go to their respective homes without let or hindrance. Upon leaving the embassy building, Nagy, his friends and their families were nevertheless seized by the Soviet authorities, taken to an airport and then flown into forced exile in Rumania. See *La vérité sur l'affaire Nagy.*

9 Iván Szenes, *A kommunista párt ujjászervezése*, p. 113. Szenes mentions a meeting in Feb. 1957 at which the provisional Central Committee formed on 11 Nov. 1956 was enlarged to 37 members.

10 See p. 177 above.

11 Iván Szenes, *A kommunista párt ujjászervezése*, p. 113. In the note to that page, Szenes gives the names of the 37 members of the Central Committee.

12 See particularly Iván T. Berend, *Gazdasági útkeresés 1956–1965. A szocialista gazdaság magyarországi modelljének történetéhez* (The search for the economic path, 1956–1965. Contribution to the history of the Hungarian socialist economic model), Budapest, Magvetö, 1983, pp. 51f.

13 'Interjú Rácz Sándorral, a Nagy-Budapesti Központi Munkástanács elnökével', (Interview with Sandor Rácz, President of the Greater Budapest Central Workers' Council), *Beszélö*, Budapest, vol. 7, 1983.

14 At the same time, the authorities also closed the offices in the Kossuth Club, Budapest, and banned the *Information Bulletin* of the Revolutionary Committee of Intellectuals.

15 *Az MSzMP Országos értekezletének jegyzökönyve, 1957 június 27–29* (Minutes of the national conference of the MSzMP, 27–9 June 1957), quoted in Berend, *Gazdasági útkeresés*, p. 54.

16 Berend, *Gazdasági útkeresés*, pp. 58–61.

17 According to Bill Lomax, 'The Hungarian Revolution of 1956 and the Origins of the Kádár regime' (MS), Kádár wanted to pursue a policy of reconciliation from the very outset, but was not strong enough to do so. Supported by only a small group in the party leadership, he had to bow to Ferenc Münnich who represented the 'Moscow line'.

18 *La vérité sur l'affaire Nagy.*

19 *A Magyar Szocialista Munkáspárt Központi Bizottságának kongresszusi irányelvei* (Directives to the Congress by the Central Committee of the Hungarian Socialist Workers' Party), Budapest, Kossuth, 1962, pp. 39–49.

20 Address published exclusively in *New Hungarian Quarterly*, vol. 13, no. 48, 1972.

21 György Aczél did, however, regain his place in the Politburo and remained in charge of cultural affairs until 1985. Nyers, by contrast, while remaining a member of the Central Committee, lost his place in the Politburo.

22 *A Magyar Szocialista Munkáspárt XI. kongresszusának jegyzökönyve 1975 március 17–22* (Minutes of the 11th Congress of the Hungarian Socialist Workers' Party 17–22 Mar. 1975), Budapest, Kossuth, 1975.

23 *Magyar statisztikai zsebkönyv 1983* (Statistical Pocketbook 1983), Budapest, Statisztikai Kiadó, 1984, II: economic indicators.

24 *Statisztikai évkönyv 1981* (Statistical Yearbook 1981), Budapest, Statisztikai Kiadó, 1982, I: long-term indicators.

25 *Magyar statisztikai zsebkönyv*, p. 97.

26 It should, however, be noted that during the war there was a marked increase in consumption which continued until the final phase of the conflict when destruction and penury became rife.

27 *Népszabadság*, 25, 26, 29 and 30 Mar. 1985; *A Magyar Szocialista Munkáspárt XIII. kongresszusa 1985 március 25–28* (The 13th Congress of the Hungarian Socialist Workers' Party, 25–8 Mar. 1985), Budapest, Kossuth, 1985, pp. 60f.

Notes

28 Berend, *Gazdasági útkeresés*, p. 193.

29 Ibid., p. 39.

30 This was the main argument of Kornai's first and very important book. He has subsequently published other books, including particularly *A hiány* (Penury), Budapest, Közgazdasági és Jogi Könyvkiadó, 1980 (also published in English and in French translation).

31 These were probably communities set up by employees of state enterprises who were allowed to use company-owned machinery or tools after their normal hours of work. On the different forms taken by small enterprises, see Teréz Laky, 'Mitoszok és valóság' (Myths and reality) in *Valóság*, vol. 27, no. 1, Jan. 1984.

32 *Magyar statisztikai zsebkönyv; Statisztikai évkönyv 1981, passim; Statisztikai évkönyv 1983*, Budapest, Statisztikai Kiadó, 1984.

33 Works councils began to spring up at the beginning of 1985. They comprised workers' representatives together with representatives from the trade unions, from the party and from the Young Communist League. In smaller enterprises, the workers elected the head of the company by direct vote.

34 For an excellent analysis of these difficulties, see Wlodzimierz Brus, 'Le bloc soviétique après Brejnev: la perspective économique', and also Pierre Kende, 'De la capacité d'évolution interne des régimes est-européens', in W. Brus, P. Kende and Z. Mlynar, *Les systèmes soviétiques après Brejnev. Project de recherche: les crises des systèmes de type soviétique*, Study 5, Munich, 1984.

35 In addition to *samizdat* publications produced in Hungary, see the periodical *Magyar füzetek* (Hungarian notebooks) published by Pierre Kende in Paris. This periodical has for many years been reproducing the most important writings by members of the opposition.

36 For all that, the vast network of associations whose number rose to 14,000 in 1932 was practically destroyed. Apart from sports and stock-breeding associations under state supervision, only 225 general associations survived. See Elemér Hankiss, 'Második társadalom?' (A second society?), *Valóság*, vol. 27, no. 11, Nov. 1984, pp. 25–44, n. 5.

37 István Huszár, 'A társadalom szerkezetének átalakulásáról' (On the structural transformation of society), *Valóság*, vol. 28, no. 2, Feb. 1985, p. 7.

38 *Magyar statisztikai zsebkönyv, 1983*, p. 33.

39 *A Magyar Szocialista Munkáspárt XII. kongresszusának jegyzökönyve 1980 március 24–27* (Minutes of the 12th Congress of the Hungarian Socialist Workers' Party, 24–27 Mar. 1980), Budapest, Kossuth, 1980, pp. 9–11.

40 *A Magyar Szocialista Munkáspárt XII. kongresszusa*, pp. 7–9.

41 Ibid., pp. 134–44; and *A Magyar Szocialista Munkáspárt XIII. kongresszusa*, pp. 150–9.

42 *A Magyar Szocialista Munkáspárt VII. kongresszusának jegyzökönyve, 1959 november 30–december 5* (Minutes of the 7th Congress of the Hungarian Socialist Workers' Party, 30 Nov.–5 Dec. 1959), Budapest, Kossuth, 1960, pp. 545–50. *A Magyar Szocialista Munkáspárt IX. kongresszusának jegyzökönyve, 1966 november 28–december 3* (Minutes of the 9th Congress of the Hungarian Socialist Workers' Party, 28 Nov.–3 Dec. 1966), Budapest, Kossuth, 1967.

43 *Népszabadság*, 29 Mar. 1985.

44 The Central Committee regularly publishes its resolutions and all important documents deemed suitable for free circulation. It is impossible to list and analyse all of these in a short book. See the last volumes of *A Magyar Szocialista Munkáspárt határozatai és dokumentumai* (Resolutions and documents of the Hungarian Socialist Workers' Party), Budapest, Kossuth. The volume published in 1974 and covering 1967–70 runs to 750 pages, the next volume covering 1971–5 runs to 1045 pages, and the last volume covering the years up to 1980 runs to no fewer than 1241 pages.

45 See Miklós Molnár, *Pouvoir et société civile dans le système communiste* (forthcoming, 1990).
46 See Preface to the English Edition.

Conclusion

1 Földes, *A második vonalban* (In the second line), p. 159. Földes, who was responsible for the cadre section, puts the number of militants who returned from Western countries at 600 to 700.
2 See Chapter 10, p. 205.
3 Gyurkó, *Arcképvázlat*, pp. 78–82, 176–80.
4 Révai, *La littérature et la démocratie populaire: Lukács*, pp. 9–11.
5 In the light of the Hungarian experience, the concept of the dictatorship of the proletariat becomes a purely terminological problem. All it means is party power.
6 'After the insurrection of 17 June [in Berlin in 1953], the secretary of the Writers' Union ordered the distribution of pamphlets in Stalin Allee, declaring that the people had lost the confidence of the government and that the only way to regain it was to work twice as hard as before. Would it not be simpler for the government to dissolve the people and choose another?' *Die Lösung* (The solution), in Bertolt Brecht, *Gesammelte Werke*, vol. 10, Frankfurt/Main, Suhrkamp, 1967, pp. 1000–10.
7 The party in power, by contrast, had quite a few characteristics of a 'gubernatorial society' with its own ideology and its own structure *vis-à-vis* society at large.
8 These privileges nevertheless exist not only when it comes to social advancement but also in respect of access to such coveted items as apartments, second homes, motor cars, foreign currency and so forth. The obscure criteria and procedures presiding over their allocation have shocked public opinion no less than did the existence of 'special shops', formerly reserved for party officials.
9 See particularly *Pouvoirs*, Spring 1982, special issue on international Communism; Annie Kriegel 'Le système mondial. Les dimensions de l'expansionisme soviétique' in *Les systèmes communistes*; and Annie Kriegel's study in *Revue européenne des sciences sociales et Cahiers Vilfredo Pareto*, vol. 19, no. 57, 1981.
10 We now know that two powerful pressure groups joined forces in this 'workers' opposition', namely the bureaucratic apparatus, afraid of losing its decision-making power, and the '50 barons', heads of the biggest factory conglomerates whose losses were periodically made good by the state. On this subject, see various articles published in the Budapest journal *Valóság* (Reality), and particularly the contribution by Erzsébet Szalai in no. 5, 1982.

Select Bibliography

Documents and Memoirs

L'affaire Rajk: compte rendu sténographique complet des séances du Tribunal du Peuple, à Budapest du 16 au 24 septembre 1949, with a Preface by Pierre Courtade. Paris, Éditeurs français réunis, 1949

Archives of the French Ministry of Foreign Affairs. 'Europe 1918–1929' (Paris)

Archives of the French Armed Forces Ministry (Château de Vincennes)

Balogh, Edgár, *Szolgálatban. Egy nemzedék története 1935–1944* (On active service: history of a generation, 1935–1944). Budapest, Magvetö Könyvkiadó, 1981

Bernachot, General Jean, *Les armées françaises en Orient après l'armistice de 1918*, vol. 1: *L'Armée française d'Orient. L'armée de Hongrie (11 novembre 1918–10 septembre 1919)*. Paris, Historical Service of the French Armed Forces Ministry, Imprimerie nationale, 1970

Bibliothèque de documentation internationale contemporaine (Contemporary International Document Library). Dossiers Klotz

[*Blum tésisek. Blum's Theses*], *Tézisterveset a magyar politikai és gazdasági helyzetröl és a KMP feladatairól* (Project for a thesis on the political and economic situation of Hungary and on the tasks of the HCP). *Párttörténeti Intézet Archivuma* (Archives of the Institute of Party History), Section 677, 1/220e

Böhm, Vilmos, *Két forradalom tüzében* (In the fire of two revolutions), 2nd edn. Budapest, Népszava Kiadó, 1946

——, 'Könyvtervezetének kézirata' (Manuscript of a projected book). Stockholm, 1948–9 (unpublished).

A Budapesti Nemzeti Bizottság jegyzökönyvei 1945–1946 (Minutes of the Budapest National Committee, 1945–1946). Budapest, Source Publications, City of Budapest Archives, 1975

The Counter-revolutionary Forces in the October Events in Hungary, vols 1–4 (White Book). Budapest, Information Office of the Council of Ministers of the Hungarian People's Republic, n.d.

Demény, Pál Magvetö (Memoirs of Pál Demény). Budapest, 1989

Déry, Tibor, *Befejezetlen mondat* (The unfinished sentence). Budapest, Szépirodalmi Könyvkiadó, 1947

Bibliography

Dokumentumok a magyar forradalmi munkásmozgalom történetéböl 1939–1945 (Documents on the history of the Hungarian Revolutionary Workers' Movement, vol. V, 1939–1945). Budapest, Kossuth Könyvkiadó, 1964

Dokumentumok a magyar párttörténet tanulmányozásához. 4. köt: 1929 októberétöl–1939 szeptemberéig (Documents for the study of party history, vol. 4: October 1929–September 1939). Budapest, Szikra Könyvkiadó, 1955

Dokumentumok a magyar párttörténet tanulmányozásához. 5. köt: 1939 szeptemberétöl–1945 áprilisáig (Documents for the study of party history, vol. 5: September 1939–April 1945). Budapest, Szikra Könyvkiadó, 1955

Fehér, Lajos, *Igy történt* (It happened thus). Budapest, Magvetö Könyvkiadó, 1979

Les forces contre-révolutionnaires dans les événements d'octobre en Hongrie, vols 1–4 (White Book), Budapest, Information Office of Council of Ministers of the Hungarian People's Republic, n.d.

A Forradalmi Kormányzótanács jegyzökönyve (Proceedings of the Revolutionary Governing Council). Archives of the Institute for Party History, Section 601 f.1–35

Földes, László, *A második vonalban* (In the second line). Budapest, Kossuth Könyvkiadó, 1984

Hegedüs, András, *Élet egy eszme árnyékában. Életrajzi interju. Készitette Zsille Zoltán* (A life in the shadow of an ideal. Biographic interview by Zoltán Zsille), Vienna, Zsille, 1985

Horthy, Miklós, *Emlékirataim* (Memoirs), Buenos Aires, 1953

Illés, Béla, *Ég a Tisza* (The Tisza is burning). Budapest, Szépirodalmi Könyvkiadó, 1966

Imre, Magda, and Szerényi, Imre (eds), *Budapest–Moszkva: Szovjet–Ororszország és a Magyarországi Tanácsköztársaság kapcsolatai táviratok tükrében* (Budapest–Moscow: relations between Soviet Russia and the Hungarian Soviet Republic reflected in telegrams). Budapest, Kossuth Könyvkiadó, 1979

Irodalom és demokrácia, Az irodalmi (u.n. Lukács) vita dokumentumai (1949–1951) (Literature and democracy. Documents on the (so-called Lukács) literary debate, 1949–1951). Budapest, A Filozófiai Figyelö évkönyve, 1982

József, Attila, *Öszes müvei*, 3–4. köt (Complete Works, vols 3–4). Budapest, Akadémiai Kiadó, 1958–67

——, *Poèmes choisis*. Paris, Éditeurs français réunis, and Budapest, Corvina Kiadó, 1961

Juhász, Gyula (ed.), *Magyar–Brit titkos tárgyalások 1943-ban* (Secret Hungarian–British negotiations in 1943: documents). Budapest, Kossuth Könyvkiadó, 1978

Kádár, János, *Szilárd népi hatalom: független Magyarország* (Solid people's power: independent Hungary. Collected speeches). Budapest, Kossuth Könyvkiadó, 1959

Bibliography

——, *A szocialista Magyarországért: Beszédek és cikkek 1968–1972* (For a socialist Hungary: speeches and articles 1968–1972). Budapest, Kossuth Könyvkiadó, 1972

Kállai, Gyula, *Életem törvénye* (My life's law). Budapest, Kossuth Könyvkiadó, 1972

——, [pseud. of Révai, József], *Népiség, demokrácia, szocialismus* (Populism, democracy, socialism). Budapest, Társadalmi Könyvtár, 1943

Kardos, László (ed.), *Sej, a mi lobogónkat fényes szelek fujják . . . Népi kollégiumok 1939–1949: Dokumentumgyüjtemény* (Those luminous winds in our banner . . . People's Colleges 1939–1949: collected documents). Budapest, Akadémiai Kiadó, 1977

Károlyi, Michael, *Faith without Illusions*. London, Cape, 1956

Károlyi, Mihályné, *Együtt a forradalomban* (Together in the revolution). The Memoirs of Mme Károlyi. Budapest, Europa Könyvkiadó, 1967

Kassák, Lajos, *Egy ember élete* (A man's life). Budapest, Magvetö Könyvkiadó, 1966

Kertesz, Stephen D., *Between Russia and the West: Hungary and the Illusions of Peacemaking 1945–1947*. Notre Dame and London, University of Notre Dame Press, 1984

Khrushchev, Nikita, *Khrushchev Remembers*. New York, Littlejohn, 1971

Kiss, Károly, *Nincs megállás* (No stopping). Budapest, Kossuth Könyvkiadó, 1974

A KMP elsö kongresszusa (The First Congress of the HCP). Budapest, Kossuth Könyvkiadó, 1975

A KMP KB 1932 májusi teljes ülésének határozatai (Resolutions of the Plenary Session of the Central Committee of the HCP in May 1932). Vienna, Arbeiterbuchhandlung, n.d.

A KMP KB 1933 szeptemberi határozata a magyarországi helyzetröl és a KMP alapvetö feladatairol (Resolution of September 1933 by the Central Committee of the HCP on the situation in Hungary and the fundamental tasks of the HCP). N.p., n.d.

A kommunista pártok határozataiból, amelyeket a Kommunista Internacionále VB elnökségének a Komintern feloszlatásáról szóló 1943 május 15-i, határozatával kapcsolatban hoztak (Extracts from the resolutions passed by Communist parties concerning the 15 May 1943 Comintern Executive Council resolution on the dissolution of the Comintern). Pamphlet, n.p., n.d.

A Kommunisták Magyarországi Pártja II. kongresszusának irányelvei (Resolutions of the Second Congress of the Party of Hungarian Communists). Vienna, Vermey, 1930. Cover: *Irányelvek. Elfogadta a Kommunistak Magyarországi Pártja II. kongresszusa 1930 májusában* (Directives. Approved by the Second Congress of the Party of Hungarian Communists in May 1930). Vienna, Vermy, 1930

Kun, Béla, *A Magyar Tanácsköztársaságról: Válogatott tanulmányok és irások* (On the Hungarian Soviet Republic: selected speeches and writings).

Budapest, Kossuth Könyvkiadó, 1958

——, *Válogatott irások és beszédek* (Writings and selected speeches), 2 vols. Budapest, Kossuth Könyvkiadó, 1966

Kun, Bélané, *Kun Béla: Emlékezések* (Recollections of Mme Béla Kun on Béla Kun). Budapest, Magvetö Könyvkiadó, 1966

Landler, Jenö, *Válogatott beszédek és irások* (Selected speeches and writings). Budapest, Kossuth Könyvkiadó, 1960

Laski, Melvin, and Bondy, François (eds), *La révolution hongroise*. Paris, Plon, 1957

Lengyel, József, *Elévült tartozás* (Remitted debt). Budapest, Szépirodalmi Könyvkiadó, 1960

——, *Mérni a mérhetetlent* (Measuring the unmeasurable), 2 vols. Budapest, Szépirodalmi Könyvkiadó, 1966

Litván, György, *Documents des relations Franco-Hongroises des années 1917–1919*. Budapest, Akadémiai Kiadó, 1975. Published separately in *Acta Historica Academiae Scientiarum Hungaricae*, vol. 21, 1975

——, (ed.), *Károlyi Mihály levelezése. 1. köt: 1905–1920* (Correspondence of Michael Károlyi, vol. 1: 1905–1920). Budapest, Akadémiai Kiadó, 1978

Lukács, Georg, *History and Class Consciousness*. London, Merlin Press, 1971

——, *Schriften zur Ideologie und Politik*. Neuwied and Berlin, Luchterhand, 1967

——, *Schriften zur Literatursoziologie*. Neuwied and Berlin, Luchterhand, 1970

Az MKP I. országos értekezlete. Gyorsiröi jegyzökönyv 1945 május 20–21. (First national conference of the Hungarian Communist Party. Stenographic minutes, 20–21 May 1945). Archives of the Institute for Party History, Section 274: Documents of the Central Committee of the HCP. See also *Szabad Nép* (Free People), 23 May 1945

A Magyar Dolgozók Pártja II. kongresszusának határozata (Resolution of the Second Congress of the Hungarian Workers' Party). Edited by the Central Committee of the HWP, n.p., n.d.

A magyar forradalom és szabadságharc a hazai rádióadások tükrében. 1956 oktober 23–november 9 (The revolution and the fight for freedom as reflected in Hungarian radio transmissions). New York, Free Europe Press, n.d.

A magyar internacionalisták a Nagy Októberi Szocialista Forradalomban és a polgárháboruban: Dokumentumgyüjtemény. 2. köt (Hungarian internationalists in the Great Socialist October Revolution and in the civil war: collected documents), 2 vols. Budapest, Kossuth Könyvkiadó, 1968

A Magyar Kommunista Párt és a Szociáldemokrata Párt határozatai 1944–1948 (Resolutions of the HCP and the SDP 1944–1948). Budapest, Kossuth Könyvkiadó, 1967

A Magyar Kommunista Párt IV. Kongresszusa: 1948 junius 12. – A Szociál-

Bibliography

demokrata Párt XXXVII. Kongresszusa: 1948 junius 12. – *A Magyar Kommunista Párt és a Szociáldemokrata Párt Egyesülési Kongresszusa jegyzökönyve: 1948 junius 12, 13, 14* (Proceedings of Fourth Congress of the Communist Party: 12 June 1948. – Proceedings of the Thirty-seventh Congress of the Social Democratic Party: 12 June 1948. – Proceedings of the Congress for the Merger of the HCP and the SDP: 12, 13 and 14 June 1948). Budapest, Szikra Könyvkiadó, 1948

A magyar munkásmozgalom történetének válogatott dokumentumai. 5. köt (Selected documents on the history of the Hungarian Workers' Movement, vol. 5: 7 November 1917–21 March 1919). Budapest, Szikra Könyvkiadó, 1956

Ibid. *6. köt. 1–2 rész* (ibid., vol. 6, Parts 1 and 2: March 1919–1 August 1919). Budapest, Kossuth Könyvkiadó, 1959–60

A Magyar Szocialista Munkáspárt határozatai és dokumentumai 1956–1962, 3. kiad (Resolution and documents of the Hungarian Socialist Workers' Party, 1956–1962, 3rd edn). Budapest, Kossuth Könyvkiadó, 1979

Ibid., *1963–1966.* Kossuth Könyvkiadó, 1978

Ibid., *1967–1970.* Kossuth Könyvkiadó, 1974

Ibid., *1971–1975.* Kossuth Könyvkiadó, 1979

Ibid., *1976–1980.* Kossuth Könyvkiadó, 1983

A Magyar Szocialista Munkáspárt VII. kongresszusának jegyzökönyve, 1959 november 30–december 5 (Minutes of the Seventh Congress of the Hungarian Socialist Workers' Party, 30 Nov.–5 Dec. 1959). Budapest, Kossuth Könyvkiadó, 1960

Ibid., Ninth Congress, 28 Nov.–3 Dec. 1966. Kossuth Könyvkiadó, 1967

Ibid., Tenth Congress, Kossuth Könyvkiadó, 1971

Ibid., Eleventh Congress, 17–22 Mar. 1975. Kossuth Könyvkiadó, 1975

Ibid., Twelfth Congress, 24–27 Mar. 1980. Kossuth Könyvkiadó, 1980

Ibid., Thirteenth Congress, 25–8 Mar. 1985. Kossuth Könyvkiadó, 1985

A Magyar Szocialista Munkáspárt Központi Bizottságának határozata a személyi kultusz éveiben a munkásmozgalmi emberek ellen inditott törvénysértö perek lezárásáról (Resolution of the Central Committee of the Hungarian Socialist Workers' Party on winding up the illegal trials of members of the workers' movement). Budapest, Kossuth Könyvkiadó, 1962

A Magyar Szocialista Munkáspárt Központi Bizottságának kongresszusi irányelvei (Directives of the Central Committee of the Hungarian Socialist Workers' Party to the congress). Budapest, Kossuth Könyvkiadó, 1962

Mantoux, Paul, *Les délibérations du Conseil des Quatre: 24 mars–12 juin 1919,* 2 vols. Paris, Éditions du CNRS, 1955

Marosán, György, *Ember és kenyér* (Man and bread). Budapest, Táncsics Könyvkiadó, 1979

——, *Az uton végig kell menni* (One must go to the end of the road). Budapest, Magvetö Könyvkiadó, 1972

Az MSzMP Országos értekezletének jegyzökönyve: 1957 junius 27–29 (Proceedings of the National Conference of the MSzMP: 27–29 June 1957).

Bibliography

Budapest, Kossuth Könyvkiadó, 1972

Nagy, Balázs, Marie, Jean-Jacques, and Broue, Pierre (eds), *Pologne-Hongrie*. Paris, Études et documentations internationales, 1966

Nagy, Ferenc, *The Struggle behind the Iron Curtain*. New York, Macmillan, 1948

Nagy, Imre, *Egy évtized: Válogatott beszédek és irasók* (Ten years: Selected speeches and writings). Budapest, Szikra Könyvkiadó, 1954

——, *A magyar nép védelmében: Vitairatok és beszédek 1955–1956, átd. jav. kiad* (In defence of the Hungarian people: debates and speeches; augmented and revised edn). Paris, Magyar Füzetek kiadása, 1984

——, *Un communisme qui n'oublie pas l'homme*. Recollections with an Introduction by François Fejto. Paris, Plon, 1957

Nagy Imre és büntársai ellenforradalmi összeesküvése (The counter-revolutionary plot of Imre Nagy and his accomplices), vol. 5 (White Book). Budapest, Information office of Council of Ministers of the Hungarian People's Republic, n.d.

Nagy, Vince, *Októbertöl–októberig: Emlékiratok – önéletrajz* (From October to October: Recollections and autobiography). New York, Pro Arte, 1962

Nemes, Dezsö (ed.), *Iratok az ellenforradalom történetéhez 1919–1945. 1. köt: Az ellenforradalom hatalomrajutása és rémuralma Magyarországon 1919–1921* (Documents for the study of the counter-revolution 1919–1945, vol. 1: The accession to power and the terror of the counter-revolution in Hungary 1919–1921). Budapest, Szikra Könyvkiadó, 1956

Nógrádi, Sándor, *Avant 56: Chronique hongroise*. Paris, Éditions du Pavillon, 1969

——, *Történelmi lecke* (History lesson). Budapest, Kossuth Könyvkiadó, 1970

——, *Uj történet kezdödött* (A new history has begun). Budapest, Kossuth Könyvkiadó, 1966

Normai, Ernö, 'Memoirs'. Unpublished manuscript entrusted to François Fejtö.

Ormos, Mária, *Pádovától Trianonig, 1918–1920* (From Padua to Trianon, 1918–1920). Budapest, Kossuth Könyvkiadó, 1984

Országos Levéltár. Magyar Népköztársaság. Külügyminisztérium. K 66: Sajtó és kulturosztály. K 84: Berni Követség (National Archives. Hungarian People's Republic. Ministry of Foreign Affairs. K 66: Press and Culture Dept. K 84: Berne Legation). Budapest, n.d.

Papers Relating to the Foreign Relations of the United States: The Paris Peace Conference, 1919, vols 12–13. Washington, DC, 1942–57

Papp, Lajos, *Törvényen kivül: Emlékiratok* (Outlawed: recollections). Budapest, Kossuth Könyvkiadó, 1973

A pártélet és a pártmunka idöszerü kérdései (Topical questions and problems of party work). Budapest, Kossuth Könyvkiadó, 1973

Párttörténeti Intézet Archivuma (Archives of the Institute for Party History), Budapest

Bibliography

The Peace Treaty with Hungary. Official Text in Russian, English, French and Hungarian. Paris, 10 February 1947. Printed in USA, n.p., n.d.

Rákosi, Mátyás, *Válogatott beszédek és cikkek* (Selected speeches and articles). Budapest, Szikra Könyvkiadó, 1952; 4th augmented edn, Budapest, Szikra Könyvkiadó, 1955

Révai, József, *Kulturális forradalmunk kérdései* (The problems of our cultural revolution). Budapest, Szikra Könyvkiadó, 1952

——, *La littérature et la démocratie populaire. A propos de G. Lukács.* Paris, La Nouvelle Critique, 1950

——, *Marxismus, népiesség, magyarság* (Marxism, populism and Hungarianism). Budapest, 1947

Romanelli, Guido, *Nell'Ungheria di Bela Kun e durante l'occupazione romena: La mia missione, maggio–novembre 1919.* Udine, Doretti, 1964

Ross, Graham (ed.), *The Foreign Office and the Kremlin: British Documents on Anglo-Soviet Relations 1941–1945.* Cambridge, Cambridge University Press, 1984

Rudas, László, *Abenteurer und Liquidatoren: Die Politik Béla Kuns und die Krise der KPU.* Vienna, 1922

Savarius, Vincent [pseudonym of Béla Szász], *Volontaires pour l'échafaud.* Paris, Lettres nouvelles/Juillard, 1963

Sik, Endre, *Vihar a levelet.* (The Storm Drives the Leaf). Budapest, Zrinyi Katonai Kiadó, 1970

Sinkó, Ervin, *Egy regény regénye* (Novel of a novel), 2 vols. Novi Sad, Forum, 1961

——, *Optimisták: Történelmi regény 1918–1919 böl* (The optimists: a historical novel of 1918–1919). Novi Sad, Forum, 1965

Sulyok, Desiderius, *Zwei Nächte ohne Tag.* Zurich, Thomas, 1948

Szántó, Zoltán, *Visszaemlékezések* (Memoirs). Unpublished manuscript.

Szárszó 1943. Elözményei, jegyzökönyve és utóélete. Dokumentumok (Szárszó 1943: antecedents, minutes and sequels. Documents). Budapest, Kossuth Könyvkiadó, 1983

Szekér, Nándor, *Föld alatt és föld felett* (Underground and in the open). Budapest, Kossuth Könyvkiadó, 1968

A Tanácsok országos gyülésének naplója, 1919 junius 14–1919 junius 23 (Proceedings of the National Assembly of Councils, 14 June 1919–23 June 1919). Budapest, Athenaeum, 1919

Tanuságtevök: Visszaemlékezések a magyarországi munkásmozgalom történetéböl 1905–1918 október (Witnesses: recollections from the history of the Hungarian workers' movement, 1905–October 1918). Budapest, Kossuth Könyvkiadó, 1976

Tanuságtevök: Visszaemlékezések a magyarországi munkásmozgalom történetéböl, 1941–44 (Witnesses: recollections from the history of the Hungarian workers' movement, 1941–44). Budapest, Kossuth Könyvkiadó, 1985

Tanuságtevök: Visszaemlékezések a magyarországi munkásmozgalom történe-

téből, 1944–48 (Witnesses: recollections from the history of the Hungarian workers' movement, 1944–48). Budapest, Kossuth Könyvkiadó, 1975

United Nations Organization, *Report by Special Committee on the Hungarian Question. General Assembly of UNO. Official Documents: 11th Session.* New York, UNO, 1957

Vadász, Ferenc, *Tenyérnyi ég* (A patch of sky). Budapest, Kossuth Könyvkiadó, 1970

Vas, Zoltán, *Akkori önmagunkról: Önéletirás* (What we used to be: Autobiography), vol. 2. Budapest, Magvető Könyvkiadó, 1982

——, *Hazatérés, 1944* (Homecoming, 1944). Budapest, Szépirodalmi Könyvkiadó, 1980

——, 'Nem a tejes csenget' (It isn't the milkman ringing). Unpublished recollections of Zoltán Vas deposited in Paris

——, *Viszontagságos életem* (My chequered life). Budapest, Magvető Könyvkiadó, 1980

La vérité sur l'affaire Nagy, with a Preface by Albert Camus. Paris, Plon, 1958

Z. Nagy, Ferenc, *Ahogy én láttam . . .* (As I saw it . . .). Budapest, Gondolat, 1965

Zamertsev, I. T., *Emlékek, arcok, Budapest . . .: Egy szovjet városparancsnok visszaemlékezései* (Recollections, faces, Budapest . . .: recollections of a local Soviet military governor). Budapest, Zrinyi Katonai Kiadó, 1969

General Studies

Aczél, Tamás and Méray, Tibor, *La révolte de l'esprit*. Paris, Gallimard, 1962

Anthologie de la poésie hongroise. Paris, Le Seuil, 1962

Arvon, Henri, *Georges Lukács ou le Front populaire en littérature*. Paris, Seghers, 1968

Bahr, Ehrhardt, *La pensée de Georg Lukács*. Toulouse, Privat, 1972

Balázs, Béla, *Népmozgalom és nemzeti bizottságok 1945–1946* (The People's movement and national committees 1945–1946). Budapest, Kossuth Könyvkiadó, 1961

Berecz, János, *Ellenforradalom tollal és fegyverel: 1956*, 2. böv. és jav. kiad. (Counter-revolution with pen and gun: 1956), 2nd augmented and revised edn. Budapest, Kossuth Könyvkiadó, 1981

Berend, Iván T., *Gazdasági útkeresés 1956–1965. A szocialista gazdaság magyarországi modelljének történetéhez* (The search for the economic path 1956–1965: contribution to the history of the Hungarian socialist economic model). Budapest, Magvető Könyvkiadó, 1983

——, Ivan and Ránki, György, *Hungary: A Century of Economic Development*. Newton Abbot, David & Charles/New York, Barnes & Noble, 1974

Bibliography

——, *Underdevelopment and Economic Growth: Studies in Hungarian Social and Economic History*. Budapest, Akadémiai Kiadó, 1979

Bibó, István, *Összegyüjtött munkái*, 1–4. köt (Collected works of István Bibó, 4 vols), ed. István Kemény and Mátyás Sárközi. Berne, Protestáns Magyar Szabadegyetem, 1981–4

Borbándi, Gyula, *A magyar népi mozgalom* (The Hungarian populist movement). New York, Püski, 1983

Borsányi, György, *Kun Béla: Politikai életrajz* (Béla Kun: political biography). Budapest, Kossuth Könyvkiadó, 1979

——, and Kende, János, *Magyarországi munkásmozgalom 1867–1980* (The Hungarian Workers' Movement, 1867–1980). Budapest, Kossuth Könyvkiadó, 1982

Bourdet, Yvon, *Figures de Lukács*. Paris, Anthropos, 1972

Brus, W., Kende, P., and Mlynar, Z., *Les systèmes soviétiques après Brejnev. Projet de recherche: les crises des systèmes de type soviétique*. Study 5, Munich, 1984

Brutyó, János, *Munkás-évek* (Working years). Budapest, Kossuth Könyvkiadó, 1980

Csatári, Dániel, *Forgószélben: Magyar-román viszony 1940–1945* (In the Whirlwind: Hungarian–Rumanian relations 1940–1945). Budapest, Akadémiai Kiadó, 1968

Donáth, Ferenc, *Demokratikus földreform Magyarországon 1945–1947* (Democratic land reform in Hungary 1945–1947). Budapest, Akadémiai Kiadó, 1969

Fejtö, François, *Le coup de Prague 1948*. Paris, Le Seuil, 1976

——, *L'héritage de Lénine*. Paris, Castermann, 1973

——, *Histoire des démocraties populaires*, 2 vols. Paris, Le Seuil, 1969 and 1972

——, 'Un itinéraire d'historien', *Contrepoint*, vol. 13, Feb. 1974, pp. 123–40; and vol. 14, pp. 109–28

——, *1956 Budapest, l'insurrection: La première révolution antitotalitaire*. Brussels, Complexe, 1981

Fischer-Galati, Stephen (ed.), *The Communist Parties of Eastern Europe*. New York, Columbia University Press, 1979

Fukász, György, *A magyarországi polgári radikalizmus történetéhez, 1900–1918* (On the history of Hungarian bourgeois radicalism, 1900–1918). Budapest, Gondolat, 1960

Gábor, Sándorné, *Ausztria és a Magyarországi Tanácsköztársaság* (Austria and the Hungarian Soviet Republic). Budapest, Akadémiai Kiadó, 1969

Gati, Charles, 'Two Secret Meetings in Moscow in October 1944 and the Communist Quest for Power in Hungary'. Prepared for delivery at the annual meeting of the American Association for the Advancement of Slavic Studies in Columbus, Ohio, n.d.

Gosztonyi, Péter, *Magyarország a második világháboruban, I–II* (Hungary in the Second World War, I–II). Munich, HERP, 1984

——, *Die ungarische antifaschistische Bewegung in der Sowjetunion während des zweiten Weltkrieges.* Karlsruhe, Braun, 1972. Special reprint from *Militär-geschichtliche Mitteilungen,* vol. 1, 1972

Gros, Dominique, 'Les conseils ouvriers. Espérances et défaites de la révolution en Autriche-Hongrie 1917–1920.' PhD thesis, 3 vols. University of Dijon, n.d.

Gyurkó, László, *Arcképvázlat történelmi háttérrel* (Portrait sketch with a historical background). Budapest, Magvetö Könyvkiadó, 1982

Hadifogoly magyarok története. 2. köt: Az oroszországi hadifogság es a magyar hadifoglyok hazaszállitásának története (History of Hungarian prisoners of war, vol. 2: History of Hungarian prisoners of war in Russia and their repatriation). Budapest, Atheneaum

Hajdu, Tibor, *Az 1918-as magyarországi polgári demokratikus forradalom* (The Hungarian bourgeois-democratic revolution of 1918). Budapest, Kossuth Könyvkiadó, 1968

——, *Károlyi Mihály: Politikai életrajz* (Michael Károlyi: a political biography). Budapest, Kossuth Könyvkiadó, 1978

——, *A magyarországi Tanácsköztársaság* (The Hungarian Soviet Republic). Budapest, Kossuth Könyvkiadó, 1969

Hanák, Péter, *Magyarország a Monarchiában* (Hungary in the Monarchy). Budapest, Gondolat, 1975

Hanák, Tibor, *Az elmaradt reneszánsz* (The abortive renaissance). Munich, Protestáns Magyar Szabadegyetem, 1979

Horváth, Zoltán, *Magyar századforduló* (Hungary at the turn of the century). Budapest, Gondolat, 1961

Horváth, Zoltánné, *A KMP második kongresszusa* (The Second Congress of the HCP). Budapest, Kossuth Könyvkiadó, 1964

Huber, Maria, *Die ungarische sozialistische Arbeiterpartei: Binnenstruktur und Funktionsprobleme.* Cologne, Berichte des Bundesinstituts für ostwissenschaftliche Studien, 1984

Hungaricus, texte intégrale d'une étude de 'Hungaricus' écrit, publié et distribué clandestinement en Hongrie dans les milieux progressistes. Brussels, Institut Imre Nagy de sciences politiques, 1959

[Hungaricus], 'Second part of Hungaricus's clandestinely distributed study' (Hungarian manuscript in the possession of Miklós Molnár). Budapest, 1957

Jászi, Oszkár, *Magyar kálvária, magyar feltámadás* (Hungarian Calvary and Resurrection) Vienna, 1920

Józsa, Antal and Milei, György, *A rendithetetlen százezer: Magyarok a nagy oktoberi szocialista forradalomban és a polgárháboruban* (The hundred thousand intransigents: Hungarians in the Great Socialist October Revolution and during the civil war). Budapest, Kossuth Könyvkiadó, 1968

Juhász, Gyula, *Magyarország külpolitikája: 1919–1945* (Hungary's foreign policy: 1919–1945). Budapest, Kossuth Könyvkiadó, 1968

Kállai, Gyula, *A magyar függetlenségi mozgalom: 1936–1945* (The Hungarian independence movement: 1936–1945). Budapest, Kossuth Könyvkiadó, 1965

Bibliography

Kende, Pierre, Moïsi, Dominique, and Yannakakis, Illios (eds), *Le système communiste: un monde en expansion*. Paris, Institut français des relations internationales, 1982

——, Strmiska, Zdenek et al., *Égalité et inégalités en Europe de l'Est*. Paris, Presses de la Fondation nationale des sciences politiques, 1984

Kende, Zsigmond, *A Galilei Kör megalakulása* (The foundation of the Galilei Circle). Budapest, Akadémiai Kiadó, 1974

Kertész, Stephen D., *The Fate of East Central Europe*. Notre Dame, Ind., University of Notre Dame Press, 1956

——, *Between Russia and the West. Hungary and the Illusions of Peacemaking, 1945–1947*. Notre Dame, Ind., University of Notre Dame Press, 1984

Kirschner, Béla, *A KMP stratégiai vonalának alakulása 1919. augusztus–1925. augusztus* (The development of the strategic line of the HCP, August 1919–August 1925). Budapest, Akadémiai Kiadó, 1985

A Kommunista Párt szövetségi politikája 1936–1962 (The alliance policy of the Communist Party 1936–1962: collected studies). Budapest, Kossuth Könyvkiadó, 1966

Kommunisticheskii Internatsional' (The Communist International). Moscow, Izdatel'stvo Politicheskoi Literatury, 1969. Translated as: *A Kommunista Internacionále és a Kommunisták Magyarországi Pártja* (The Communist International and the Hungarian Communist Party: historical survey). Budapest, 1971

Kornai, János, *A hiány* (Penury). Budapest, Közgazdasági és Jogi Könyvkiadó, 1980. (Also published in English translation.)

Korom, Mihály, *Magyarország ideiglenes nemzeti kormánya és a fegyverszünet: 1944–1945* (The provisional national government of Hungary and the armistice: 1944–1945). Budapest, Akadémiai Kiadó, 1981

Kovács, Imre, *Im Schatten der Sowjets*. Zurich, Thomas Verlag, 1948

——, *A Márciusi Front* (The March Front). New Brunswick, 1980

Kovrig, Bennett, *Communism in Hungary: From Kun to Kadar*. Stanford, Hoover Institution Press, 1979

Kriegel, Annie, *Communismes au miroir français*. Paris, Gallimard, 1974

——, *Les grands procès dans les systèmes communistes: un monde en expansion*. Paris, Gallimard, 1972

Lackó, Miklós, *Szerep és mü* (Role and oeuvre: studies in cultural history). Budapest, Gondolat, 1981

—— (ed.), *Tanulmányok a magyar népi demokrácia történetéböl* (Studies in the History of the Hungarian People's Democracy). Budapest, Akadémiai Kiadó, 1955

——, *Válságok – választások* (Crises – choices: collected papers). Budapest, Gondolat, 1975

Lahav, Yehuda, 'The Hungarian Communist Party's path to power: 1944–1948'. PhD thesis, Hebrew University, Jerusalem, 1976

Lazitch, Branko, and Drachkovitch, Milorad M., *Biographical Dictionary of the Comintern*. Stanford, Hoover Institution Press and Stanford University, 1972

——, ——, *Lenin and the Comintern*, vol. 1. Stanford, Hoover Institution Press and Stanford University, 1972

Lefort, Claude, *L'invention démocratique: les limites de la domination totalitaire*. Paris, Fayard, 1981

Legyözhetetlen erö: A magyar kommunista mozgalom szervezeti fejlödésének 50 éve (Invincible force: fifty years of evolution of the organization of the Hungarian Communist Movement). Budapest, Kossuth Könyvkiadó, 1968

Leibzon, B. M., and Sirinya, K. K., *Povorot v politike kominterna* (The turning-point in the policy of the Comintern). Moscow, Izdatel'stvo Mysl, 1975

Lendvai, Paul, *L'antisémitisme sans juifs*. Paris, Fayard, 1971

A lenini úton: Cikksorozat az MSzMP politikájáról 1956–1981 (In Lenin's path: series of articles on the political approach of the MSzMP, 1956–1981). Budapest, Népszabadság/Kossuth Könyvkiadó, 1981

Levesque, Jacques, 'Les effets du conflit sino-soviétique sur les relations entre l'URSS et les démocraties populaires de Pologne et Roumanie'. Thesis. Paris, Fondation nationale des sciences politiques, 1968

Liptai, Ervinné, *A Magyarországi Szocialista Munkáspárt: 1925–1928* (The Hungarian Socialist Workers' Party: 1925–1928). Budapest, Kossuth Könyvkiadó, 1971

Lomax, Bill, 'The Hungarian Revolution of 1956 and the Origins of the Kadar Regime'. Manuscript.

——, *Hungary 1956*. London, Allison & Busby, 1976

Low, Alfred D., 'The Soviet Hungarian Republic and the Paris Peace Conference', *Transactions of the American Philosophical Society*, Philadelphia, vol. 53, no. 10, 1963

Löwy, Michel, *Pour une sociologie des intellectuels révolutionnaires: l'évolution politique de Lukács 1909–1929*. Paris, Presses Universitaires de France, 1976

McCagg, William O., *The Struggle for Leadership in the Hungarian Communist Party 1944–1948*. New York, Columbia University Press, 1964

A magyar forradalmi munkásmozgalom története (History of the Hungarian Revolutionary Workers' Movement), 2nd edn; 3 parts in 2 vols. Budapest, Kossuth Könyvkiadó, 1970

A magyar népi demokrácia története 1944–1962 (History of the Hungarian People's Democracy 1944–1962). Budapest, Kossuth Könyvkiadó, 1978

Magyar önkéntesek a spanyol nép szabadságharcában (Hungarian volunteers in the Spanish people's fight for freedom). Budapest, Kossuth Könyvkiadó, 1959

A Magyar Tanácsköztársaság: A Kommunisták Magyarországi Pártjának harca a Horthy fasizmus ellen (The Hungarian Soviet Republic: the struggle of the Hungarian Communist Party against Horthy's fascism). Budapest, Szikra Könyvkiadó, 1952

Bibliography

Magyarország története. 7. köt 1–2. rész.: 1890–1918 (History of Hungary, vol. 7, parts 1 and 2: 1890–1918). Budapest, Akadémiai Kiadó, 1978

Magyarország története. 8. köt: 1918–1919, 1919–1945 (History of Hungary, vol. 8: 1918–1919, 1919–1945). Budapest, Akadémiai Kiadó, 1976

A Magyarországi Tanácsköztársaság 50. évfordulója: Nemzetközi tudományos ülésszak (The 50th anniversary of the Hungarian Soviet Republic: international symposium) Budapest, Akadémiai Kiadó, 1970

Marcou, Lilly, *Le Kominform*. Paris, Presses de la Fondation nationale des sciences politiques, 1977

Mátyás Rákosi face au tribunal fasciste. Paris, Éditions sociales, 1952

Mayer, Arno J., *Politics and Diplomacy of Peacemaking: Containment and Counter-revolution at Versailles 1918–1919*. New York, Knopf, 1967

Méray, Tibor, *Thirteen Days that Shook the Kremlin*. New York, Praeger, 1959

Mérei, Gyula, *A magyar októberi forradalom és a polgári pártok* (The Hungarian October revolution and the bourgeois parties). Budapest, Akadémiai Kiadó, 1969

Mićunović, Veljko, *Journées de Moscou 1956–1958*. Paris, Laffont, 1979

Milei, György, *A Kommunisták Magyarországi Pártjának megalakitásáról* (On the foundation of the Hungarian Communist Party). Budapest, Kossuth Könyvkiadó, 1962

Molnár, János, *Ellenforradalom Magyarországon 1956-ban: A polgári magyarázatok birálata* (Counter-revolution in Hungary in 1956: a critique of bourgeois interpretations). Budapest, Akadémiai Kiadó, 1967

Molnár, Miklós, 'Un poète entre Freud et Lénine: Attila József', *Cadmos*, vol. 3, no. 12, 1980, pp. 86–106

——, *Victoire d'une défaite: Budapest 1956*. Paris, Fayard, 1968 (in English: *Budapest 1956. A History of the Hungarian Revolution*, London, George Allen & Unwin, 1971)

—— and Nagy, László, *Imre Nagy, réformateur ou révolutionnaire?* Geneva, Droz, 1959

Munkásmozgalomtörténeti Lexikon (Historical dictionary of the Workers' Movement). Budapest, Kossuth Könyvkiadó, 1972; 2nd edn, 1976

Nagy, Zsuzsa L., *A Párizsi békekonferencia és Magyarország 1918–1919* (The Paris Peace Conference and Hungary 1918–1919). Budapest, Kossuth Könyvkiadó, 1965

Nemes, Dezsö, *Az ellenforradalom története Magyarországon 1919–1921* (The history of the counter-revolution in Hungary 1919–1921). Budapest, Kossuth Könyvkiadó, 1962

——, *Magyarország felszabadulása* (The liberation of Hungary), 2nd edn. Budapest, Kossuth Könyvkiadó, 1960

Német, Andor, 'József Attila és kora' (Attila József and his epoch), republished in: Német, Andor, *Szélén behajtva: Válogatott müvek* (The dogeared page: selected writings). Budapest, Magvetö Könyvkiadó, 1973

'Nemzet és demokrácia Kelet-Europában' (Nation and democracy in Eastern Europe), *Magyar Füzetek* (Hungarian Notebooks), vol. 13, 1984

Bibliography

A népi Magyarország negyedszázada (A quarter century of People's Hungary: Transactions of the international symposium held on the occasion of the twenty-fifth anniversary of the liberation of Hungary). Budapest, Akadémiai Kiadó, 1972

Orbán, Sándor, *Két agrárforradalom Magyarországon: Demokratikus és szocialista agrárátalakulás 1945–1961* (Two agrarian revolutions in Hungary: the democratic and socialist transformations of agriculture 1945–1961). Budapest, Akadémiai Kiadó, 1972

Pintér, István, *A Magyar Front és az ellenállás: 1944. március 19–1945. április 4* (The Hungarian Front and the Resistance: 19 March 1944–4 April 1945). Budapest, Kossuth Könyvkiadó, 1970

——, *A Magyar kommunisták a Hitler-ellenes nemzeti egységért: 1941 junius– 1944 március* (Hungarian Communists for anti-Hitlerian national unity: June 1941–March 1944). Budapest, Kossuth Könyvkiadó, 1968

——, *Rózsa Ferenc: Életrajz és dokumentumok* (Ferenc Rózsa: biography and documents). Budapest, Kossuth Könyvkiadó, 1983

——, *A Szociáldemokrata Párt története: 1933–1944* (History of the Social Democratic Party: 1933–1944). Budapest, Kossuth Könyvkiadó, 1980

Puskás, A. I. *Magyarország a II. világháboruban* (Hungary in the Second World War), abridged and revised edn, translated from the Russian. Budapest, Kossuth Könyvkiadó, 1971

Ránki, György, *1944 március 19: Magyarország német megszállása* (19 March 1944: the German occupation of Hungary). Budapest, Kossuth Könyvkiadó, 1968

——, *A második világháboru története* (History of the Second World War). Budapest, Gondolat, 1976

Révai Nagy Lexikona (Révai Great Encyclopaedia), vols 1, 19, 20, Suppl. Budapest, Révai Kiado, 1911–27

Robrieux, Philippe, *Histoire intérieure du Parti communiste*, vol. 1: *1920– 1945*. Paris, Fayard, 1980

Romsics, Ignác, *Ellenforradalom és konszolidáció: A Horthy rendszer elsö tiz éve* (Counter-revolution and consolidation: the first ten years of the Horthy régime). Budapest, Gondolat, 1982

Rupnik, Jacques, *Histoire du Parti communiste tchécoslovaque: des origines à la prise du pouvoir*. Paris, Presses de la Fondation nationale des sciences politiques, 1981

Ságvári, Ágnes, *Népfront és koalició Magyarországon 1936–1948* (Popular Front and coalition in Hungary 1936–1948). Budapest, Kossuth Könyvkiadó, 1967

Salamon, Konrád, *A Márciusi Front* (The March Front). Budapest, Akadémiai Kiadó, 1980

——, *Utak a Márciusi Front felé* (Paths towards the March Front). Budapest, Magvetö Könyvkiadó, 1982

Schöpflin, George (ed.), *The Soviet Union and Eastern Europe: A Handbook*. London, Anthony Blond, 1970

Bibliography

Schöpflin, Gyula, *Szélkiáltó: Emlékezések* (Curlew: Recollections). Paris, IUS, 1983

Schreiber, Thomas, 'L'Europe de l'Est en 1970: Étude', *Notes et études documentaires*, 1971, pp. 3781–2.

—— (ed.), 'L'URSS et l'Europe de l'Est en 1979', *Notes et études documentaires. 4587–4588*, 1980

Seton-Watson, Hugh, *The East European Revolution*. New York, Praeger, 1951.

Simonffy, András, *Kompország katonái* (The ferry soldiers). Budapest, Magvetö Könyvkiadó, 1981

Sólyom, J. and Zele, F., *Harcban az ellenforradalommal* (Fighting the counter-revolution). Budapest, Móra Könyvkiadó, 1957

Statisztikai évkönyv 1983 (Statistical Yearbook 1983). Budapest, Központi Statisztikai Hivatal, 1984

Szabó, Ágnes, *A Kommunisták Magyarországi Pártjának ujjászervezése: 1919–1925* (The reorganization of the Party of Hungarian Communists: 1919–1925). Budapest, Kossuth Könyvkiadó, 1970

——, Borsányi, György and Pintér, István, 'A Kommunista Internacionálé és a Kommunisták Magyarországi Pártja: történelmi vázlat, kézirat' (The Communist International and the Party of Hungarian Communists: historical survey). Manuscript, Archives of the Institute for Party History.

Szabó, Bálint, *Népi demokrácia és forradalomelmélet: A marxista forradalomelmélet néhány kérdése Magyarországon 1935–1949* (People's democracy and the theory of revolution: some problems of Marxist theory of revolution in Hungary 1935–1949). Budapest, Kossuth Könyvkiadó, 1970

Szabolcsi, Miklós, *Érik a fény: József Attila élete és pályája 1923–1927* (The light matures: the life and work of Attila József 1923–1927). Budapest, Akadémiai Kiadó, 1977

——, *Fiatal életek indulója: József Attila pályakezdése* (The march of young lives: the beginning of Attila József's career). Budapest, Akadémiai Kiadó, 1963

Szélpál, Árpád, *Les 133 jours de Béla Kun*. Paris, Fayard, 1959

Szenes, Iván, *A kommunista párt ujjászervezése Magyarországon 1956–1957* (The reorganization of the Hungarian Communist Party 1956–1957). Budapest, Kossuth Könyvkiadó, 1976

Szerémi, T. Borbála, *szabadság vértanui. Életrajzok MSzMP KB Párttörténeti Intézete* (The martyrs of freedom. Biographies by B. T. Szerémi, Institute for Party History of the Central Committee of the Hungarian Socialist Workers' Party). Budapest, Kossuth Könyvkiadó, 1960

Társadalmi rétegzödés Magyarországon (Social stratification in Hungary). Study published under the direction of Mme Aladár Mód. Budapest, Központi Statisztikai Hivatal, 1966

Tökés, Rudolf L., *Béla Kun and the Hungarian Soviet Republic: The Origins* and *Role of the Communist Party of Hungary in the Revolutions of 1918–1919.* New York, Praeger, 1967

Vágó, Márta, *József Attila* (Attila József). Budapest, Szépirodalmi Könyvkiadó, 1975

Valiani, Leo, 'La politica estera dei governi revoluzionari ungheresi di 1918–1919', *Rivista storica italiana*, vol. 78, no. 4, 1966, pp. 850–911

Válság és megújulás: Gazsdaság, társadalom és politika Magyarországon. Az MSzMP 25 éve. Tudományos ülésszak 1981 szeptember 29–oktober 1 (Crisis and renewal: economics, society and politics in Hungary. The Hungarian Socialist Workers' Party over twenty-five years. Scientific session 29 September–1 October 1981). Budapest, Kossuth Könyvkiadó, 1982

Vértes, György, *József Attila és az illegális kommunista párt* (Attila József and the clandestine Communist Party). Budapest, Magvető Könyvkiadó, 1964

Vigh, Károly, *Ugrás a sötétbe* (A leap in the dark). Budapest, Magvető Könyvkiadó, 1984

Völgyes, Iván (ed.), *Hungary in Revolution 1918–1919: Nine Essays*, Lincoln, University of Nebraska Press, 1971

Index

Index

Index

Index